FOUNDATIONS OF EVIDENCE LAW

Foundations of Evidence Law

ALEX STEIN

OXFORD
UNIVERSITY PRESS

*This book has been printed digitally and produced in a standard specification
in order to ensure its continuing availability*

OXFORD
UNIVERSITY PRESS

Great Clarendon Street, Oxford OX2 6DP

Oxford University Press is a department of the University of Oxford.
It furthers the University's objective of excellence in research, scholarship,
and education by publishing worldwide in

Oxford New York

Auckland   Cape Town Dar es Salaam   Hong Kong   Karachi
Kuala Lumpur Madrid Melbourne Mexico City   Nairobi
New Delhi Shanghai   Taipei Toronto
With offices in
Argentina Austria Brazil Chile Czech Republic France Greece
Guatemala Hungary Italy Japan South Korea Poland Portugal
Singapore Switzerland Thailand Turkey Ukraine Vietnam

Oxford is a registered trade mark of Oxford University Press
in the UK and in certain other countries

Published in the United States
by Oxford University Press Inc., New York

ISBN 978-0-19-825736-3

For Shirley

Acknowledgements

First things first. I am lucky to have friends whose unconditional friendship matches their quality as scholars. Eyal Benvenisti read my entire manuscript and made a number of important suggestions. Zohar Goshen read and commented on Chapter 5. Ariel Porat, with whom I have co-authored several publications in the area of torts, has been a partner to discussions that validated and invalidated many of my ideas. Alon Harel has engaged me in a decade-long conversation about legal theory that extended to many issues discussed in this book. Alon also facilitated the book's completion by persistently asking me whether I really *want* to finish it.

My first acquaintance with evidence law took place in Eliahu Harnon's Evidence class, which I took as a student at the Hebrew University of Jerusalem. Several years later, Eliahu became my friend and colleague when I joined the Hebrew University Faculty of Law. I hope that this book lives up to his expectations.

This book expounds a general perspective under which evidence rules allocate the risk of error under uncertainty, rather than facilitate the discovery of the truth. The initial development of this idea took place in my doctoral dissertation at University College London. I am profoundly grateful to William Twining for supervising this dissertation and for being an exemplary mentor. I wrote this book at the Benjamin N. Cardozo School of Law of Yeshiva University, where I have found a wonderful academic environment, thoroughly conducive to scholarly research and writing. For this I thank Dean David Rudenstine and the entire Cardozo community. I also thank my colleagues who participated in a faculty workshop in which I presented Chapter 3. Special thanks go to Paul Shupack, Stewart Sterk and Martin Stone for their individual comments and suggestions.

Last but not least, I am grateful to Dr Peninah Petruck for superb editorial assistance that much improved the book's style and substance.

Preface

A prestigious publishing house advises that a book proposal 'should give an answer to what might be called the Passover question: How is this book different from all other books?'[1] My publisher does not profess such a crude instrumentalism. Nonetheless, this Preface attempts to answer the Passover question.

Foundations of Evidence Law is not a doctrinal treatise. Unlike many excellent treatises, it does not offer a descriptive account of a jurisdictional set of rules and principles that describe a particular law of evidence. This book tells readers about evidence laws generally. The account begins with identifying the core features of the Anglo-American systems of evidence. These features are the systems' objectives and the mechanisms for attaining these objectives. The emerging big picture exhibits the foundations of evidence law. This picture also marks the point at which my account ceases to be descriptive and becomes normative.

This picture constitutes the book's general framework for developing a normative theory of evidence law.[2] The book develops this theory within this framework. As an alternative to this endogenous theory, one may consider developing evidence law from scratch ('exogenically'). Why hang the normative on the descriptive and risk the accusation that an 'ought' is derived from an 'is'? Unlike other questions discussed in this book, the answer to this question is relatively uncontroversial. A set of incontrovertible foundational factors is a prerequisite for a meaningful normative discussion about evidence law. These factors include the legal system's objectives and institutional set-up. Disagreement about these factors precludes any workable consensus about evidence law mechanisms.

In Anglo-American legal systems, impartial adjudication is foundational. Other foundational factors are rationality and the justification requirement

---

[1] See http://www.hup.harvard.edu/editors_page/author_resources/manu_submit.html.

[2] This normative inquiry does not consider the history of evidence rules and their projected future. Readers interested in these subjects should consult James Bradley Thayer, *A Preliminary Treatise on Evidence at the Common Law* (1898); John H. Wigmore, *Evidence in Trials at Common Law* Vol. 1 (Tillers edn, 1983), § 8a; Edmund M. Morgan, The Jury and the Exclusionary Rules of Evidence (1937) 4 U. Chi. L. Rev. 247; Stephan Landsman, The Rise of the Contentious Spirit: Adversary Procedure in Eighteenth Century England (1990) 75 Cornell L. Rev. 497 (these writings describe the development of the rules of evidence by the institution of jury trial, by the adversarial format of litigation, or by both); Mirjan R. Damaška, *Evidence Law Adrift* (1997) (predicting that disappearance of adversarial jury trials and the shift to a multistage litigation format will prompt abolition of existing evidence rules).

for adjudicative decisions. Foundational factors also include the problem of uncertainty and the risk of error in fact-finding. These factors identify the uncertainty problem as unavoidable and the risk of error as omnipresent. Allocation of the risk of error in adjudicative fact-finding is therefore a foundational factor as well. Fact-finders must apportion this risk between the parties in a rational, impartial, and justified way. In doing so, they need to consider what is at stake. Fact-finders need to account for the rights, duties, and liabilities that might be determined erroneously. Substantive laws that evidence law helps to administer turn into a foundational factor for any normative discussion about evidence law. These and other foundational factors determine the direction a normative analysis of evidence law must take. They also identify the limits for what such an analysis may offer.

This book offers a normative analysis of evidence law that is both new and comprehensive. My analysis focuses on fact-finding procedures and decisions in American and English courts. The analysis develops an innovative interdisciplinary theory of evidence law that uses epistemology, probability, economics, and political morality. Under this theory, the key function of evidence law is to apportion the risk of error in conditions of uncertainty, rather than facilitate the discovery of the truth. The book develops this theory in seven chapters. To properly understand this theory, readers need to read Chapters 1 through 5 in that order. Chapters 6 and 7 apply this theory to criminal and civil adjudication, respectively. These chapters can be read in any order.

Chapter 1 delineates the domain of evidence law by identifying rules and doctrines that are genuinely evidential, as opposed to evidence-related rules and doctrines that promote objectives extraneous to fact-finding. This discussion singles out three categories of genuinely evidential rules and doctrines: (1) rules and doctrines that minimize the risk of error by enhancing the accuracy of fact-finding; (2) rules and doctrines that reduce the costs that fact-finding procedures and decisions incur; and (3) rules and doctrines that apportion the risk of error between litigants. Chapter 1 also analyses the means-end relationship between evidence rules and the controlling substantive law.

Chapter 2 defines the characteristics of adjudicative fact-finding (labelled above as foundational factors). This discussion identifies and analyses two fundamental problems—uncertainty and justification. It underscores the importance of the best-evidence principle as an epistemic device for controlling evidence-selection. The discussion also identifies the epistemic criteria for determining the probabilities of the relevant factual scenarios on the evidence previously selected. These criteria are empirical. They include common sense, logic, and general experience.

Subsequently, Chapter 2 analyses the sceptical challenges to these criteria. Stemming from diverse disciplines—analytical philosophy and cognitive science or behavioural law and economics—these challenges point to the impossibility of rational and justified fact-finding. Chapter 2 underscores the methodological and operational inadequacy of these challenges. Philosophical scepticism is not an option for practical reasoning, to which adjudicative fact-finding belongs. This theory is also methodologically inferior to the common sense view of the world. Cognitive science has succeeded in establishing that lay reasoners systematically miscalculate probabilities. Such findings, however, identify failures in cognitive performance, not in cognitive competence.

Chapter 3 analyses and resolves two epistemological paradoxes, *Lottery* and *Preface*, together with their legal derivatives, *Gatecrasher*, *Blue Bus*, *Two Witnesses*, and *Prisoners in the Yard*. This analysis identifies the fundamental function of evidence law as apportioning the risk of error under uncertainty. The traditional perception of evidence law as facilitating the discovery of the truth is set aside. Specifically, Chapter 3 develops the principle of maximal individualization that eliminates the paradoxes. This principle has a number of features that have different applications in civil and criminal adjudication. Chapter 3 identifies these features as distributed across two dimensions, epistemological and moral. Within the epistemological dimension, the maximal individualization principle contributes to fact-finding. Within the moral and political dimension, this principle apportions the risk of error. The principle assumes this second role after completing the first: morality takes up what the epistemology leaves off. Within this dimension, the maximal individualization principle competes with utilitarian allocations of the risk of error. The results of this competition, reported in Chapters 5, 6, and 7, are variable.

Chapter 4 considers the question 'What is evidence law for?' This chapter analyses the conventional evidence doctrine and criticizes it for insufficiently regulating adjudicative fact-finding. This discussion levels a general opposition to free evaluation of evidence or free proof. This idea is flawed, but, nonetheless, influential amongst practitioners, law reformers, and legal scholars. Its endorsement by law reformers is responsible for the ongoing abolition of evidentiary rules and for the flowering of discretion in fact-finding matters. The *Criminal Justice Act 2003* is the most radical manifestation of this development in Great Britain. Chapter 4 argues that evidence law should develop in exactly the opposite direction. Legal regulation of adjudicative fact-finding needs to be tightened up, not scaled down. Evidence law should regulate the risk of error in adjudicative fact-finding. This regulation ought to apply to two categories of decision: apportionment of the risk of error between the parties and the various trade-offs between the cost of fact-finding errors and the cost of fact-finding procedures that aim at avoiding those errors. There is no moral, political, or economic justification for authorizing individual adjudicators (such as trial judges) to allocate the risk of error as they deem fit.

The principal question of this book is 'What evidence rules are desirable?' I do not discuss the institutional question 'Who should produce those rules: the legislator or common law judges?'. The common law model, within which judges make rules that the legislator can repeal and modify, has several advantages. The federal rules system, under which the judicial branch promulgates evidence rules subject to Congress's overriding legislative authority, is probably the best common law model of evidence rules. But direct democratic legislation also has merits. The issue is beyond the book's scope. The theory that Chapter 4 develops makes only one institutional point. Apportionment of the risk of error in fact-finding is a task that must not be left to individual adjudicators, such as trial judges.

Chapter 5 entertains an economic analysis of evidence law. This analysis makes an unqualified utilitarian assumption (subsequently softened in Chapters 6 and 7) that evidential rules and doctrines are geared towards cost-efficiency. Cost-efficiency requires adjudicators to minimize the aggregate cost of accuracy-enhancing procedures and fact-finding errors. Chapter 5 examines the evidential mechanisms to attain this goal. These mechanisms enhance cost-efficiency by eliminating the problem of private information and the misalignment between the private litigants' incentives and the social good. These mechanisms include decision rules that determine the burdens and the standards of proof, as well as different process rules that determine what evidence is admissible and what fact-finding methodologies are allowed. Decision rules minimize the aggregate cost of accuracy and errors by skewing the risk of error in the desirable direction (by preferring false positives over false negatives, or vice versa). Process rules minimize the aggregate cost of accuracy and errors by applying a different technique. These rules attach fact-finding methodologies that are more meticulous and more expensive to adjudication in which the cost of error is relatively high. Adjudication in which the cost of error is relatively low is equipped with more rudimentary and correspondingly inexpensive fact-finding methodologies. Mechanisms geared towards cost-efficiency also include credibility rules. These special rules elicit credible signalling from litigants with private information through adjustment of penalties and rewards.

Chapters 6 and 7 shift from utility to fairness and, correspondingly, from economics to morality. They examine the apportionment of the risk of fact-finding error in criminal and civil adjudication, respectively. These chapters identify and analyse two fundamental precepts: the equality principle that controls the apportionment of the risk of error in civil litigation; and the 'equal best' standard that needs to be satisfied in every criminal case in order to convict the accused. These precepts derive from political morality. They also attach to the maximal individualization principle, developed in Chapter 3.

These precepts justify and explain many evidential rules and doctrines in the Anglo-American legal systems. Chapters 6 and 7 provide a principled exposition of these rules and doctrines. This exposition is more attractive than the conventional portrayal of evidence rules as scattered and isolated exceptions to free proof. This exposition offers new rationales to the hearsay doctrine, to the rule against character evidence, to the rules regulating the admission of expert testimony, and to the existing burdens and standards of proof.

Contents

1

Groundwork

A. Preliminaries

This chapter identifies the domains of evidence law discussed throughout the book. The chapter draws a fundamental distinction between the fact-finding objectives of the law and objectives extraneous to fact-finding that the law promotes through rulings on evidence. This distinction calls for a differentiation between the various legal rules that regulate evidential matters: rules that promote objectives intrinsic to fact-finding are the only ones that classify as genuinely evidential; rules furthering other objectives and values are evidence-related, but situated outside the domains of evidence law.

Under this framework, rules classifying as evidential are those that promote the following objectives: (1) enhancement of accuracy in fact-finding or, in other words, minimization of the risk of error; (2) minimization of the expenses that fact-finding procedures and decisions incur; and (3) apportionment of the risk of error with the consequent risk of misdecision between the parties to litigation. A robustly utilitarian approach, for example, diagnoses in adjudicative fact-finding two types of social cost: the cost of error, the 'substantive cost', and the cost of error-minimizing procedures, the 'procedural cost'. This approach keys all its evidential rules to the minimization of the aggregate sum of both substantive and procedural costs.[1] This fundamental utilitarian precept relates to the first two of the three evidential objectives. Furthermore, a robust utilitarian approach also allocates the risk of error in a way that minimizes the total cost of error and error-avoidance. Under this approach, none of the litigants has a right to demand the reduction, let alone elimination, of private costs—substantive and procedural alike—irrespective of the social good. Such claims are only respected in a legal system that either abandons or qualifies its utilitarian urge. In such a system, evidence law may produce a different trade-off between fact-finding accuracy and its costs. This trade-off depends on the system's non-utilitarian objectives and values and on

---

[1] See Chapter 5 below.

their relative significance. The system allocates the risk of error in accordance with these objectives and values.

A non-utilitarian risk-allocating scheme may well crystallize into individual rights that override social welfare. Under the utilitarian approach, allocation of the risk of error is always instrumental to the trade-off that reduces the aggregate sum of error costs and error-avoidance expenses (the total sum of substantive and procedural costs). The rights-based legal systems overturn this relationship of means and ends. Under these systems, fact-finding expenditures are instrumental to the right apportionment of the risk of error, rather than vice versa. These systems rely on a non-utilitarian political morality that transforms into individual rights. These rights do not merely escape from utilitarian calculus. They actually trump utility.[2] Consequently, rights that litigants have with respect to risk-allocation are not measured against the substantive and procedural costs that they incur. Because the prevalent political morality favours these rights, it deems the costs that these rights incur money well-spent.

This tension between the individual and the social is one of the book's principal themes. At this introductory stage, the reader need only note that this tension attaches to each of the three evidential objectives. The reader also need not accept my depiction of these objectives (although my ultimate project is to prove that it is correct). At this juncture, it is enough to acknowledge that these objectives are plausible. Accuracy in fact-finding is a logical prerequisite to proper administration of the controlling substantive law. Accuracy, however, is costly: it consumes the efforts of litigants and their attorneys, as well as those of judges and juries. The extent to which risk of error can be reduced depends on both private and social investments in the fact-finding procedures. This observation derives from experience and is virtually undisputed. Consequently, fact-finding efforts and investments should be used with wisdom: regardless of what one thinks about utilitarianism in general, one ought to be reluctant to expend £100 on a dispute over £90. Because absolute certainties are presently unavailable—a proposition that both experience and philosophy of induction confirm—adjudicative fact-finding, as, indeed, any fact-finding, is bound to be conducted in conditions of uncertainty. It is bound to rest upon probabilities, not certainties, and therefore involves risk of error. The legal system must choose how to allocate this risk.

This risk may be imposed in its entirety upon one of the parties, say, upon the prosecution in criminal cases or upon claimants in civil litigation. Alternatively, the legal system may devise risk-sharing formulae that divide the

---

[2] See Ronald Dworkin, Rights as Trumps, in Jeremy Waldron (ed.), *Theories of Rights* (1984), p. 153.

risk of error between the adversaries. Finally, the system may allow this risk to fall where it happens to fall—a normatively questionable, but still possible, approach. There is no escape from deciding how to allocate the risk of error in adjudicative fact-finding.[3]

These fact-finding objectives are not the only objectives that *evidence-related* rules may promote. Evidence-related rules may also promote objectives altogether alien and even antithetical to fact-finding. Such rules do not really belong to evidence law. Their most recurrent feature is a motivation to set aside accuracy of fact-finding for the sake of other goals and values. For example, a legal rule that suppresses evidence in order to protect a person's privacy or to remedy its violation is a rule that belongs to the law of privacy rather than to evidence law. Evidential remedy supplementing a person's right to privacy is functionally equivalent to compensatory remedy that attaches to the same right. Both remedies rectify the same wrong and therefore belong to the same branch of the law: that of privacy. Affiliating the privacy's evidential remedy to the law of evidence is as appropriate as associating the compensatory remedy with the 'law of money'. Evidential sanctions and remedies that attach to non-evidential rights or promote goals unrelated to fact-finding are outliers. This chapter eliminates these outliers from my subsequent discussion.[4] Separating intrinsically evidential rules from evidence-related outliers helps setting the focus for the entire book. *This book focuses on the rules, principles, and doctrines that forge the instrumental relationship between evidence and fact-finding.*

This instrumental-relationship criterion does not only have exclusionary implications, but also functions as a basis for expanding the body of rules, principles, and doctrines that integrate into the law of evidence. Under this criterion, any rule that facilitates fact-finding objectives qualifies as evidential. The rule's formal affiliation to another branch of the law (such as procedure, criminal law, contract law, torts, and so forth) is immaterial. My analysis determines the identity of a legal rule by its functioning and consequences, rather than by its formal placement on the doctrinal map. For example, criminal law often mitigates a murderer's liability and punishment by reducing the crime to manslaughter if the murderer acted under provocation. The typical

---

[3] See Alex Stein, The Refoundation of Evidence Law (1996) 9 *Can. J. Law & Jurisp.* 279.

[4] This definition of the book's agenda does not suggest that such outliers are unimportant. As demonstrated by Chris Sanchirico, primary activities taking place outside of courtrooms—accidents, for example—can be efficiently regulated by directly conditioning the relevant legal sanctions on the presence or absence of particular types of evidence. See Chris Sanchirico, Games, Information and Evidence Production: With Application to English Legal History (2000) 2 *Am. L. & Econ. Rev.* 342; Chris Sanchirico, Relying on the Information of Interested—and Potentially Dishonest—Parties (2001) 3 *Am. L. & Econ. Rev.* 320; Chris Sanchirico, Evidence Tampering (2004) 53 *Duke L. J.* 1215. Such direct-incentive mechanisms belong to the relevant branches of the substantive law: torts, contracts, criminal law, and so forth.

provocation doctrine has an objective limitation: it demands that the action or the event that provoked the homicide be capable of destabilizing a person of ordinary temper and mental make-up. From the substantive criminal law perspective that determines the perpetrator's culpability by his or her subjective mens rea, this requirement is problematic. If it is the perpetrator's state of mind that separates murder from manslaughter, then the law should be interested in whether the provocative act (or event) had destabilized the perpetrator subjectively, not in whether it also could have destabilized an average person. However, a purely subjective standard for provocation both involves substantial fact-finding expenditures and increases the risk of error. Because evidence about a person's subjective state of mind is easy to concoct and difficult to refute, many killers—justifiably or not—would seek refuge in the defence of provocation. This prediction is especially troubling in a system that allows criminal defendants to benefit from any reasonable doubt arising in connection with their guilt. To counterbalance this problem, the police and the prosecution must invest more efforts into their fact-finding missions. Because information about the defendant's state of mind is largely controlled by criminal suspects and defendants, these efforts might be more expensive than productive. The aggregate sum of error costs and error-avoidance expenses would, consequently, rise. The legal system, therefore, understandably avoids this deleterious consequence by setting an objective limitation to the provocation defence. This choice is situated in the domain of evidence law, not in the criminal law domain. It advances evidential objectives rather than the goals of substantive criminal law, such as deterrence, desert, and retribution.

A second example is the 'parol evidence' rule. Despite its evidential self-identification, this rule is commonly affiliated to contract law. Under this rule, testimony contrary to a written agreement is generally inadmissible: a party can only tender such testimony in conjunction with a document written or signed by his or her opponent. Similar to many other legal rules, this rule serves more than one purpose. It promotes certainty and the consequent reliability of contracts and shields contracting parties from the adverse testimony of false witnesses. The evidential purpose of this rule is puzzling. Is there empirical evidence to the effect that most (or many) witnesses testifying against written agreements commit perjury? Apparently, there is no such evidence. The contractual purpose of this rule is puzzling too. If there is no good reason to suspect most witnesses of lying, and if an oral exchange of promises (subject to the consideration requirement) can yield a binding contract, why not allow witnesses to contradict documented agreements? The most persuasive answer to these questions rests on conventions and customs. Arguably, because the parol evidence rule operated at common law for many years, people got used to it and predominantly follow its precepts in forming their agreements. A proposition stating that a particular agreement deviating from these precepts and from the corresponding habituation was nonetheless formed becomes suspicious. If people customarily followed the rule's precepts, then most such propositions would likely be false, which—in civil trials—gives a good reason to dismiss them *ab initio*. But is there such a customary practice? Apparently, there is none, for if such a practice were prevalent, then, presumably, we would not have witnessed so many court-authorized departures from the parol evidence rule as we presently do.[5]

There is, however, a more straightforward rationale for the rule. The parol evidence rule has no ambition to reduce the incidence of fact-finding errors. Rather, it aims to reduce the procedural costs of error-avoidance. It achieves this by inducing contracting parties to document their undertakings comprehensively. The witness-disqualification penalty, a mechanism that markedly differs from the custom theory, effects this inducement.[6] Under the custom theory, the parol evidence rule functions as a contractual default provision that emulates the typical contractual stipulation and thereby reduces the transaction costs that contracting parties would otherwise incur. Under my rationale, the rule functions as a penalty-default provision[7] that induces contracting parties not to externalize the cost of their anticipated litigation.[8] By using witness-disqualification as a sanction, the rule induces contracting parties to reduce the social cost of error-avoidance.[9]

A third example quarters in the area of torts. Under the 'nationwide practice' standard, adopted by a growing number of jurisdictions across the United States, compliance with the 'local medical practice' is generally not a defence against medical malpractice allegations.[10] This doctrine requires

---

[5] See Alan Schwartz and Joel Watson, The Law and Economics of Costly Contracting (2004) 20 *J. L. Econ. & Org.* 2, 23–4 (identifying the courts' tendency to broaden the scope of 'interpretive' contract disputes to permit extensive recourse to prior negotiations and other oral evidence—a phenomenon that increases the cost of enforcing contracts).

[6] See Alex Stein, An Essay on Uncertainty and Fact-Finding in Civil Litigation, with Special Reference to Contract Cases (1998) 48 *U. Toronto L.J.* 299, 341–4.

[7] This rationale derives from Ian Ayres and Robert Gertner, Filling Gaps in Incomplete Contracts: An Economic Theory of Default Rules (1989) 99 *Yale L.J.* 87.

[8] See Stein, above note 6.   [9] Ibid.

[10] See, e.g., *Shilkret v Annapolis Emergency Hospital Ass'n* 349 A.2d 245, 252 (Md. 1975) ('the traditional locality rules no longer fit the present-day medical malpractice case'); *District of Columbia v Wilson*, 721 A.2d 591 (D.C.,1998) (medical malpractice defendant's conduct measured by a national standard, rather than by a local one); *Sheeley v Memorial Hospital*, 710 A.2d 161 (R.I. 1998); *Gallucci v Humbryd*, 709 A.2d 1059, 1065 (R.I. 1998) (both rejecting the 'locality rule'); *Pemberton v Tallahassee Memorial Regional Medical Center, Inc.*, 66 F.Supp.2d 1247 (N.D. Fla., 1999) (rejecting the 'locality rule' while restricting the nationwide standard to board-certified physicians). See, however, *Fowler v Springer*, 2003 WL 1984771, Ark.App., Apr 30, 2003; *Perry v Magic Valley Reg. Med. Ctr.*, 995 P.2d 816, 821 (2000); *Shane v Blair*, 2003 WL 21467829 (Idaho 2003) (all recognizing and applying the 'locality rule'). Consider also *Estate of Braford ex rel. Braford v O'Connor Chiropractic Clinic*, 624 N.W.2d 245 (2000) (holding that, ordinarily, in the medical malpractice

physicians to align with the general nationwide standards that apply in their fields of medicine. No physician can claim in his or her defence that, being a member of some particular locale that practices different standards of medical care, he or she was entitled to deviate from the general nationwide standard. As one of the courts explained:

The modern physician bears little resemblance to his predecessors. As we have indicated at length, the medical schools of yesterday could not possibly compare with the accredited institutions of today, many of which are associated with teaching hospitals. But the contrast merely begins at that point in the medical career: vastly superior postgraduate training, the dynamic impact of modern communications and transportation, the proliferation of medical literature, frequent seminars and conferences on a variety of professional subjects, and the growing availability of modern clinical facilities are but some of the developments in the medical profession which combine to produce contemporary standards that are not only much higher than they were just a few short years ago, but also are national in scope.[11]

By setting this standard of care, the doctrinal rejection of the local-practice defence ostensibly belongs to where it quarters, namely, to the law of torts.

This explanation is not altogether satisfactory. After all, the nationwide standard approach has failed to attract the courts and legislators of other jurisdictions. These jurisdictions prefer to use local medical practice as a decisive criterion for negligence, with the local standards being affected, but not dominated, by the general national standards.[12] 'Local' is not synonymous

context, the standard of care for *general practitioners* derives from practice standards in the local community, while the standard of care *for specialists* derives from the standards practised across the nation), as well as *Magee v Pittman*, 761 So.2d 731 (2000) (holding that, in a medical malpractice action, the 'locality rule' applies solely to non-specialists and requires that the degree of care to which the physician is to be held be based upon the standard of practice in a similar community or locale and under similar circumstances, whereas specialists are held to a national standard requiring the degree of care ordinarily practised by physicians within the involved medical specialty).

[11] *Shilkret v Annapolis Emergency Hospital Ass'n* 349 A.2d 245, 252 (Md. 1975).

[12] See *Fowler, Perry* and *Shane*, note 10 above, as well as *Hollis v United States*, 2003 WL 689261 (2003) (reaffirming that, under Texas law, a physician's duty is to align with the degree of prudence and skill exercised by physicians of similar training and experience in the same or similar community under the same or similar circumstances); *Sommer v Davis*, 317 F.3d 686 (2003) (under Tennessee law, the controlling medical care standard refers to the locality of the alleged malpractice); *Nestorowich v Ricotta*, 740 N.Y.S.2d 668, 671 (2002) ('The prevailing standard of care governing the conduct of medical professionals has been a fixed part of our common law for more than a century (see generally *Pike v Honsinger*, 155 N.Y. 201, 49 N.E. 760 [1898]). The *Pike* standard demands that a doctor exercise "that reasonable degree of learning and skill that is ordinarily possessed by physicians and surgeons in the locality where [the doctor] practices". Although malpractice jurisprudence has evolved to accommodate advances in medicine, the *Pike* standard remains the touchstone by which a doctor's conduct is measured and serves as the beginning point of any medical malpractice analysis'); *Mercado v Leong*, 50 Cal.Rptr.2d 569, 574 (1996) (a physician's duty is to possess the degree of learning and skill ordinarily possessed by physicians of good standing practising in the same locality); *Kernke v Menninger Clinic, Inc.*, 172 F.Supp.2d 1347 (D. Kan. 2001) (under Kansas law, a physician

of 'parochial'. Unlike the past, when judges and juries had 'to equitably account for real disparities in medical knowledge, as well as access to the latest technology, with the touchstone being the physician's geographic location of practice',[13] the contemporary local-practice standard no longer exempts physicians from the duty to stay current.[14] At the same time, it is perfectly appropriate (nowadays, also fashionable) for a court to take a pluralistic view of medical science under which two different treatments of a patient may both be legitimate. Framed as the 'respectable minority' defence or as the 'schools of thought' limitation of liability, this pluralistic approach is part and parcel of the contemporary medical malpractice doctrine.[15]

The American shift to the nationwide medical practice standard can, however, be justified on evidential grounds. The local-practice standard generates an anti-competitive environment for medical experts, the key witnesses in virtually every medical malpractice case. Under this standard, medical experts not sufficiently familiar with the local medical practice do not qualify as expert witnesses. The expert witness status thus exclusively attaches to the local professional insiders. Courts have shifted from the local to the nationwide standards in an attempt to address this problem. They held that the local-practice standard facilitates the 'silence conspiracy' amongst doctors. Typically, this conspiracy assumes the form of an implicit agreement that stipulates 'You won't testify against me, and I won't testify against you'.[16]

To this plausible scenario one should add other monopolistic repercussions. Even if the limited circle of experts does not form an impenetrable 'silence conspiracy', it may still limit its output and raise prices. The anti-competitive environment that the local-practice standard creates enables experts to extract high fees for a low amount of work. Local physicians may also be tempted to form coalitions in order to subject rival physicians to predatory measures. Such measures may include 'testimonial conspiracy' that would expose rival physicians to false accusations of malpractice. These sombre scenarios gain plausibility from the physicians' opportunity to conspire and to monitor the implementation of their conspiracies at a relatively low cost. The nationwide standard eliminates this opportunity by magnifying the pool of qualified

---

has a duty to use reasonable and ordinary care and diligence in the diagnosis and treatment of his or her patients, to use his or her best judgment, and to exercise that reasonable degree of learning, skill, and experience which is ordinarily possessed by other physicians in the same or similar locations under like circumstances).

[13] Amy Jurevic Sokol and Christopher J. Molzen, The Changing Standard of Care in Medicine (2002) 23 *J. Legal Med.* 449, 474.   [14] Ibid, at 475–7.

[15] See Tim Cramm, Arthur J. Hartz, and Michael D. Green, Ascertaining Customary Care in Malpractice Cases: Asking Those Who Know (2002) 37 *Wake Forest L. Rev.* 699, 704–6 (relating the 'respectable minority' defence to the local-practice standard).

[16] See, e.g., *Sheeley v Memorial Hospital,* 710 A.2d 161 (R.I. 1998).

medical experts. Because the number of qualified medical experts becomes very large, and because these experts are dispersed, any form of expert conspiracy becomes prohibitively expensive (in terms of both transaction costs and the costs of monitoring holdouts). This competitive environment also impels medical experts to trade their services for competitive prices.

To sum up, the nationwide standard is preferable not because it has a clear substantive merit that elevates it over the local-practice standard in the domain of torts. Evidential reasons dictate the adoption of the nationwide practice standard. Both the need to minimize fact-finding errors and to reduce the error-avoidance expenses necessitate the adoption of this standard.

These examples are paradigmatic.[17] It would be bizarre if any substantive law that requires enforcement through adjudication were crafted in isolation from fact-finding costs and other adjudicative expenses. A substantive law policy would never be sound if it were to ignore anticipated enforcement expenses that include the costs of both fact-finding errors and their avoidance. Mechanisms reducing these costs can therefore often be found in the substantive law. Failure to account for these evidential mechanisms due to their formal affiliation to specialized branches of the substantive law would produce a disintegrated and distorted understanding of the law of evidence.

Many rules formally affiliated to civil procedure are, in fact, evidential in nature. The rules that control pre-trial disclosure of evidential materials make this clear. These rules and their underlying principle of full disclosure promote accuracy of fact-finding.[18] Similarly, a criminal procedure rule that exempts witness-rebuttal evidence from pre-trial disclosure[19] is evidential, rather than procedural, in character. By preferring unanticipated rebuttal of one's testimony over advance disclosure of rebuttal materials, this rule functions both as an epistemologically driven truth-revealing device and as an economic inducement that reduces the witnesses' opportunity to lie and deters potential liars. Such rules promote cost-efficient pursuit of the truth.

Together with the prohibition of adverse inferences from silence, the right to silence (or the privilege against self-incrimination) is also best understood as

---

[17] See, e.g., James A. Henderson Jr., Process Constraints in Tort (1982) 67 Cornell L. Rev. 901 (advancing the process-cost factor as a general limit to liability in torts); Fred C. Zacharias, The Politics of Torts (1986) 95 Yale L.J. 698 (exemplifying non-liability rules motivated by the need to reduce the costs of legal proceedings); and Dauglas Lichtman, Copyright as a Rule of Evidence (2003) 52 Duke L.J. 683 (fixation and creativity criteria that determine works' eligibility for copyright protection are, in essence, evidential cost-savers).

[18] See Adrian Zuckerman (2003) *Civil Procedure* pp. 462–6.

[19] See, e.g., Federal Rule of Criminal Procedure 16(e) (2004) that limits disclosure of prosecution materials to evidence to be presented in-chief and to information material to the preparation of the defence; *United States v Windham*, 489 F.2d 1389, 1392 (5th Cir. 1974); *United States v Dicarlantonio*, 870 F.2d 1058, 1063 (6th Cir. 1989); *United States v Delia*, 944 F.2d 1010, 1018 (2nd Cir. 1991) (exempting rebuttal evidence from pre-trial disclosure requirements).

an evidential, rather than substantive or procedural, device. The law confers this right upon criminal defendants and suspects on grounds commonly perceived as extraneous to fact-finding. However, this understanding of the right is inadequate. The right to silence is best understood as allocating the risk of error in criminal trials in a way that reduces the number of erroneous convictions at the price of increasing the number of erroneous acquittals. The right to silence helps fact-finders to differentiate between factually innocent and factually guilty defendants.[20] This differentiation is achieved by an important anti-pooling effect of the right to silence. Absent a right, a criminal's self-interested response to questioning would impose externalities (in the form of wrongful convictions) upon innocent suspects and defendants who tell the truth but cannot corroborate their responses.[21] Absent a right, criminals would make false exculpatory statements as long as they believe that their lies are unlikely to be exposed. Knowing criminals' incentives, fact-finders would rationally discount the probative value of uncorroborated exculpatory statements, at the expense of some unfortunate innocents who cannot corroborate their true exculpatory stories. By contrast, neither pooling nor the ensuing wrongful convictions would occur were a right available. As Bentham famously noted, innocents would still tell the truth,[22] whereas criminals would separate from the innocents by rationally exercising the right to silence. Note that the right to silence would only operate in this way in legal systems that observe the 'proof beyond all reasonable doubt' requirement. In such systems, criminals would opt for silence because lies either in court or during police interrogation are amenable to refutation that might secure the defendant's conviction. Silence, on the other hand, can help a guilty defendant to obtain an acquittal based on a reasonable doubt. The right to silence, therefore, allocates the risk of error in criminal adjudication in a way that benefits *both* guilty and innocent defendants.

By referring to the fact-finding objectives in plural, I have already emphasized that adjudicative fact-finding has more than one intrinsic (as opposed to extraneous) objective. This underscoring is not a prelude to radical pluralism. As stated at the outset, the number of objectives that I have in mind is only three. To repeat: one of these objectives is accuracy in fact-finding or error-avoidance. Another objective is minimization of the costs that error-avoidance—as compared with the possible non-avoidance of errors—would involve. Thirdly, there is adequate or equitable apportionment of the risk of error, yet another intrinsic objective of evidence law. Adjudicators are not only required to determine the facts of the case as accurately and as cost-efficiently

[20] See Daniel J. Seidmann and Alex Stein, The Right to Silence Helps the Innocent: A Game-Theoretic Analysis of the Fifth Amendment Privilege (2000) 114 Harv. L. Rev. 430.   [21] Ibid.

[22] Jeremy Bentham, *A Treatise on Judicial Evidence* (Etienne Dumont, ed. 1825), p. 241.

as possible. They also need to consider the possibility of committing errors in fact-finding, which would require them to allocate the risk of error in a proper way.

Accuracy in fact-finding (also identified as error-avoidance, or 'rectitude of decision', in Bentham's terms) is a straightforward understandable objective of the law. Getting the facts right is a prerequisite to proper determination of the litigated entitlements and liabilities. This objective even appears tautological. In ordinary language, fact-finding is 'fact-finding' only when it is accurate. If adjudicators determine the facts inaccurately, then what they determine is not 'facts'. In adjudication, any factual determination that adjudicators make— erroneous and accurate alike—counts as a 'fact' for the purposes of their decision. Any such 'fact' shapes the determination of the litigated liability or entitlement. Because adjudicators may err in their factual findings, the law-maker may decide to evaluate the different risks of error by their nature and skew those risks in the desirable direction. Materialization of the risk of error in adjudicative fact-finding may have different consequences that vary in their gravity. The gravity of these consequences depends on the nature of the justice denied. In particular, it depends on the value of the entitlement erroneously annihilated and on the cost of the liability erroneously imposed. Aware of these consequences, the lawmaker may decide to formulate preferences with respect to the allocation of the risk of error. Adjudicators would then have to implement these particular preferences.

As demonstrated in Chapters 4–7, this lawmaking strategy is ingrained in the Anglo-American systems of evidence. These chapters expound the origins of the risk of error in adjudicative fact-finding, demonstrate the inevitability and pervasiveness of this risk, and set forth different political morality reasons that determine its apportionment. The present chapter merely charts a map for the evidence law domains; it does not investigate the domains. Also this chapter does not go beyond common knowledge that certifies the presence of the risk of error in adjudicative fact-finding. Because adjudicative fact-finding involves risk of error (a diagnosis explained in Chapter 2), allocation of this risk is fact-finders' intrinsic task.

The fashion in which fact-finders discharge this task may be discretionary or regulated. The law (common law or a statute) may allow fact-finders to allo-cate the risk of error as they deem fit. Alternatively, it may exercise control over risk-allocation by setting up rules that fact-finders would have to obey. My present discussion assumes that the regulatory strategy is a plausible course of lawmaking. This assumption is common knowledge amongst legal profession-als and academics. Later in this book, I advance a stronger claim that justifies the regulatory strategy on its merits. I also make a number of more specific normative claims that identify the scope, the form, and the substance of this strategy. As stated, this chapter aims to categorize evidence-related rules as either intrinsic or extraneous to fact-finding and as belonging or not belonging to evidence law. This categorization is analytic in character. It does not depend on the validity of the normative arguments that I subsequently invoke to justify the regulatory strategy.

My categorization of evidence-related rules as either intrinsic or extraneous to fact-finding makes no claims with regard to the rules' form. In pursuing its regulatory objectives, both intrinsic and extraneous to fact-finding, the lawmaker may lay down a detailed list of specific prescriptions that narrow the adjudicators' discretion. The existing jurisprudential vocabulary brands such particularized prescriptions as 'rules', to differentiate them from the general 'standards' and 'principles' that structure the adjudicators' discretion, but have no ambition to dictate individual decisions.[23] The lawmaker also may promote its objectives by formulating just a few general principles that merely identify the chosen objectives. Adjudicators would then be left free to decide about the means for attaining these objectives. Alternatively, the lawmaker may devise a more nuanced set of provisions that accommodates both principles and rules. The lawmaker's choice between these different forms of regulation may have far-reaching consequences.[24] Evidence law is no exception to this observation. In this chapter, however, all forms of legal regulation are often labelled generically as 'rules'. I distinguish between 'rules' on the one hand, and 'principles' or 'standards' on the other, only when necessary.

This chapter divides the realm of evidence law into two distinct domains, epistemological and moral. The epistemological domain of evidence law is governed by the broad 'best evidence' principle, explained in Chapter 2. Rules and principles allocating the risk of error belong to the moral domain of evidence law. Based upon moral and economic grounds, these rules and principles are analysed in Chapters 5, 6, and 7. The economic grounds for these rules and principles are utilitarian. Utilitarianism, of course, is a variant of political morality. This chapter therefore categorizes these rules and principles as situated in the domain of political morality.

Unlike other moral domains, the moral domain of evidence law has no deontological rules. As emphasized (and famously claimed by Bentham more than two hundred years ago[25]), evidence law is invariably adjectival in nature. This instrumentalist explanation has no exceptions. There is no such thing as a

---

[23] For this distinction in general see Ronald Dworkin, *Taking Rights Seriously* (1977), pp. 22–31; Louis Kaplow, Rules Versus Standards: An Economic Analysis (1992) 42 Duke L.J. 557.

[24] See Duncan Kennedy, Form and Substance in Private Law Adjudication (1976) 89 Harv. L. Rev. 1685.

[25] See Jeremy Bentham, *The Principles of Judicial Procedure, 2 Works of Jeremy Bentham* (John Bowring ed., 1838–43), p. 6 ('of the adjective branch of law, the only defensible object . . . is the maximization of the execution and effect given to the substantive branch of the law'). For an illuminating discussion of Bentham's theory of procedure see Gerald Postema, The Principle of Utility and the Law of Procedure: Bentham's Theory of Adjudication (1977) 11 Ga. L. Rev. 1393.

free-standing rule of evidence, unassociated with any of the law's three fact-finding objectives: minimization of fact-finding errors; reduction of the error-avoidance expenses; and, finally, apportionment of the risk of error. This chapter explains why.

This chapter also identifies the interplay between the rules and principles of the two evidence law domains. Rules and principles allocating the risk of error (on utilitarian or other moral grounds) supplement the workings of the best evidence principle. Adjudicators activate the risk-allocating rules and principles only after exhausting the application of the best evidence principle. Generally, when the epistemological reasons for fact-finding no longer apply, adjudicators allocate the risk of error by applying the rules and the principles from the moral domain of evidence law. *Morality picks up what the epistemology leaves off.* This motto summarizes the principal thesis of this entire book.

B. Between the Moral and the Epistemological

Amid the many complexities that pervade adjudicative fact-finding, one proposition stands out as clear. Fact-finding rules and procedures are crucial to the protection of substantive rights. Two factors explain substantive rights' dependence upon fact-finding rules and procedures. First, the accuracy of the court's decision is crucial to the vindication of any substantive right. Getting the facts right is a basic condition for accuracy. Second, because adjudicators carry out their fact-finding tasks in conditions of uncertainty, determination of facts always entails risk of error. Any decision that relates to fact-finding, including any ruling that admits or excludes evidence, allocates this risk. Vindication of substantive rights becomes crucially dependent on the allocation of the risk of error. A court's decision allocating this risk affirms the prospect of divesting the bearer of the risk of his or her substantive right. This prospect becomes real when the risk of error materializes and the court actually makes a wrong decision.

The first of these factors—the need that adjudicative findings of fact coincide, to the extent feasible, with the actual events that give rise to the relevant substantive entitlements and liabilities—is situated in the epistemological domain. The best-evidence principle[26] regulates this domain. Under this principle, adjudicators must seek reconstruction of the relevant events by forcing the production of the best evidence available, relying on that evidence alone, and following the epistemologically most effective truth-certifying procedures. Epistemological in character, the best evidence principle

---

[26] See generally Dale A. Nance, The Best Evidence Principle (1988) 73 Iowa L. Rev. 227.

promotes the accuracy of adjudicative findings of fact by demanding that adjudicators ground such findings on the most reliable sources of information and follow the most effective procedures for testing information for veracity. The truth-certifying criteria that this principle applies across the board are empirical validation, logic, and general experience.

The second factor—the effect that allocation of the risk of error exerts on fact-finding and on the underlying substantive rights—is situated in the moral and political domain. Reasons identifying the bearer of the risk of error and determining the extent to which she or he will carry this risk are moral and political in character. These reasons supplement the reconstruction of the litigated event. They apply in the moral domain, in which the question 'Good or bad?' replaces the epistemological inquiry into 'What happened?'. This shift occurs when any question that arises in connection with the epistemological 'What happened?' becomes unanswerable. Adjudicators turn from the best evidence principle to the apportionment of the risk of error after exhausting their epistemic reasons for resolving the relevant evidential or factual issue. The unresolvable evidential or factual issue transforms into the question 'Who should carry the risk of a potentially erroneous finding?'. Any criterion for identifying the bearer of this risk—or, alternatively, for dividing the risk between the parties—can acquire normative validity only on moral and political grounds (egalitarian, utilitarian, or other). The traditional grounds for devising such criteria are fairness and equality, on the one side, and utility, on the other. I expound these criteria in the pages ahead. Here, I identify the interplay between the epistemological and the moral in adjudicative fact-finding. Allocation of the risk of error is a moral decision that adjudicators have to make in order to settle factual issues that the epistemological best-evidence principle fails to resolve. Once again, morality picks up what the epistemology leaves off.

Moral considerations that inform risk-allocating decisions belong to the domain of politics. Risk-allocating decisions that adjudicators make determine the application of state power against individuals. Any such decision forms part of the court's final verdict that directs the coercive law-enforcement mechanism, sponsored by the state, to operate against one of the parties. By delivering a verdict against the defendant, the court licenses the state to apply its law-enforcement power against the defendant. By delivering a verdict against the claimant, the court effectively orders the state not to use its law-enforcement power against the defendant and to protect the status quo, should that become necessary. Allocation of the risk of error, therefore, is a matter of political morality rather than morality in general.

There is, therefore, a special category of claims, moral and political in nature, with respect to evidential rights. Arguably, litigants ought to be given rights against risks or, more precisely, rights against various impositions of the risk of error in adjudicative fact-finding.[27] This book broadly identifies such claims as 'arguments from fairness' to distinguish them from the different utilitarian theories that oppose the idea of rights against risks. Under these theories, risk of error is allocated in a way that augments social welfare. These theories seek augmentation of social welfare by mediating between two types of the risk of error that exist in adjudication: 'false positive', the risk of holding a non-liable defendant liable; and 'false negative', the risk of holding a liable defendant not liable. Because these two risks are both mutually exclusive and jointly exhaustive, they are amenable to interactive trade-offs. The lawmaker can devise rules that reduce one of these risks by increasing the other.

Theoretically, false positives can be totally eliminated by a rule prescribing that any factual uncertainty is resolved in favour of the defendant. Conversely, turning any factual uncertainty into a conclusive reason for rendering a finding in favour of the claimant, or the prosecution in a criminal case, completely eliminates false negatives. Both rules, of course, are unrealistic. Because some degree of uncertainty is present in every single case, an adoption of any of these rules would predetermine the outcomes of all trials, making adjudication unnecessary. Under any of these rules, the error rate in the legal system would also be unbearably high. The utilitarian theories therefore attempt to determine the extent to which a reduction of one of the two risks and the corresponding increase of the other are socially optimal. The optimality criterion that these theories commonly employ is social welfare. This criterion alludes to a comprehensive utilitarian calculus that accounts for the cost of fact-finding errors and error-avoidance expenses. Under this criterion, the legal system ought to minimize the total sum of these costs.[28] This criterion originates from Jeremy Bentham.[29]

The utilitarian approach holds that, generally, the risk of fact-finding error and of the corresponding misdecision must be allocated in a way that maximizes the number of correct decisions in the long run of cases.[30] This allocation of

---

[27] See Stein above note 3; Larry Alexander, Are Procedural Rights Derivative Substantive Rights? (1998) 17 Law & Phil. 19.

[28] See Richard A. Posner, *Economic Analysis of Law* (6th edn., 2003), p. 599 (stating that the objective of a procedural system, viewed economically, is to minimize the sum of two types of cost: the cost of erroneous judicial decisions and the cost of operating the procedural system that reduces the incidence of errors); Steven Shavell, *Foundations of Economic Analysis of Law* (2004), pp. 387–418 (identifying procedural mechanisms that reduce this sum).

[29] See Gerald J. Postema, *Bentham and the Common Law Tradition* (1986), pp. 344–7 (explaining Bentham's utilitarian system of procedure as based upon provisions 'for minimizing evil in each individual case'—with 'evil' representing the cost of decisional error and the cost of avoiding it).

[30] See A. Mitchell Polinsky and Steven Shavell, The Economic Theory of Public Enforcement of Law (2000) 38 J. Econ. Lit. 45, 60–2.

the risk generates the greatest possible space for the controlling substantive law. Under this approach, the largest possible number of factually liable defendants assume liability, while the largest possible number of factually non-liable defendants are found not liable.[31] This approach consequently holds that preponderance-of-the-evidence generally functions as a decisive criterion for settling factual issues. This criterion demands that adjudicators base their decisions on factual scenarios that are more probable than not. By focusing on the amount rather than on substantive consequences of adjudicative errors, this criterion treats false positives and false negatives alike. Every error is treated as a fixed disutility unit (u). A party whose factual scenario has probability P should win the case whenever $Pu > (1-P)u$, that is, whenever $P > 0.5$.[32] When the competing scenarios are equally probable (that is, when $P = 0.5$), adjudicators should normally decide against the claimant. This rule of decision reduces both the enforcement costs and (by deterring unmeritorious lawsuits) the costs of litigation.[33]

Under the accuracy-maximizing criterion, any evidence that pertains to a trial issue is generally admissible. This criterion recognizes only two distinct grounds for suppressing evidence. First, evidence may be suppressed on the grounds intrinsic to fact-finding when the best evidence principle so requires. Second, evidence may be suppressed on the grounds extraneous to fact-finding, with respect to which the accuracy-maximizing criterion has no say. Equitable apportionment of the risk of error, however, is not one of the grounds that can justify suppression of evidence under this criterion. This criterion deems false positives and false negatives equally harmful and leaves no room for skewing the risk of error in either direction. The legal system randomizes this risk by allowing it to eventuate in any individual case. Together with the $P > 0.5$ rule, this principle of broad evidential admissibility minimizes the general incidence of fact-finding errors.

Both Bentham and the contemporary utilitarian theory have accounted for the possible asymmetry between false positives and false negatives. Formally, when the average harms associated with false positives and false negatives equal, respectively, p and n, claimants are entitled to prevail upon any probability that surpasses the $p/(n + p)$ threshold. Conversely, when the probability of the defendant's case exceeds $n/(n + p)$, the defendant prevails.[34] If a

---

[31] Ibid.

[32] See Alex Stein, Of Two Wrongs that Make a Right: Two Paradoxes of the Evidence Law and their Combined Economic Justification (2001) 79 Texas L. Rev. 1199, 1205–6.

[33] See ibid, at 1206 n. 13 and sources cited therein.

[34] See John Kaplan, Decision Theory and the Fact-Finding Process (1968) 20 Stan. L. Rev. 1065, 1071–5. Both here and throughout this book I assume that standards of proof determine the expected and, ultimately, the actual ratio of false positives vs. false negatives. This claim may appear straightforward, but it is not. See Michael L. DeKay, The Difference Between Blackstone-like Error

particular type of error—say, conviction of an innocent person—is considered to be more harmful than the opposite type of error (acquittal of the guilty), utilitarianism would then demand that adjudicators (together with the entire legal system) decrease the incidence of the more harmful error (p) at the price of increasing the incidence of the less harmful error (n). For example, if convicting an innocent defendant is considered to be one hundred times more harmful than acquitting a guilty criminal, the probability threshold for convictions would be 0.99(100/101). Accordingly, the minimal probability of innocence (a reasonable doubt) guaranteeing the defendant's acquittal would be 0.01(1/101).

Any such framework may also utilize evidence-suppressing rules that skew the risk of error in the chosen direction. For example, broad admission of prior-conviction evidence might excessively intensify the fact-finders' distrust of criminal defendants as witnesses. Suppression of such evidence, however, can also produce fact-finding errors. Unaware of the defendant's criminal past, the fact-finders may credit his or her testimony with greater credibility than it deserves. Both types of error would distort the ultimate probabilities of guilt and innocence. Because false positives and false negatives do not inflict similar harms, the distortions that are likely to occur do not cancel each other out. There is, therefore, a sound utilitarian reason for excluding evidence that reveals the defendant's criminal record. Similar rationales can be mounted against the admission of hearsay and some other evidence against criminal defendants. I discuss those rationales in Chapter 5. My point here is to underscore *the utilitarian linkage between evidence-suppressing rules and the asymmetry between false positives and false negatives as producers of harm.*

Fact-finding errors are not slanted by nature. Adjudicative decisions lower the risk of error on one side of the scales of justice by increasing the risk on the other side. The power to determine the criteria for apportioning the risk of error is legislative in character. In a democracy, this power should be vested in the elected, accountable, and removable legislator (subject to the legislator's approval, judge-made common law may also develop criteria for apportioning the risk of error). Apportionment of the risk of error is a moral and political decision with far-reaching consequences. Leaving it to individual judges and juries would therefore create a serious institutional problem (discussed in detail in Chapter 4). Why should unelected adjudicators be in charge of such decisions?

Ratios and Probabilistic Standards of Proof (1996) 21 Law & Soc. Inquiry 95 (arguing that, in criminal cases, this ratio also depends on the accuracy of the fact-finding system and on the number of guilty criminals brought to trial). As argued throughout this book, proper allocation of the risk of error is an objective set for the entire system of fact-finding, not just for the standards and burdens of proof. As for the selection of cases for trial, I assume it to be unbiased. My discussion postulates that lawsuits and criminal charges are filed on the basis of prima facie evidence that only guarantees a reasonable prospect (rather than virtual certainty) of success.

The domain of the best-evidence principle is markedly different. Logic and experience set the appropriate epistemic standards for resolving case-specific factual issues that arise in this domain. Democratic procedures and institutions that operate in the domain of politics cannot adequately resolve such issues.[35] At their very best, democratic mechanisms can only produce decisions classifying as politically correct, not findings that are factually accurate. This book claims that adjudicators should only be in charge of case-management (a task particularly appropriate for judges) and of whatever genuinely classifies as fact-finding (a task that both judges and juries can perform). Moral and political controversies over the apportionment of the risk of error ought to be resolved by the law (if not legislatively, then by common law). Resolution of some of these controversies merits constitutional protection.[36]

Fairness arguments counter the utilitarian theories, offering a different ideology for allocating the risk of fact-finding error. This ideology embraces an ironclad conception of entitlements—one that treats a person's right as valuable in itself, rather than as an instrument that the person can use strictly for attainment of some general social goal. Branded 'rights as trumps',[37] this ideology rejects the vision of rights as regulatory devices that induce alignment of individual actions with social good. Under this non-instrumentalist conception of rights, a person's right serves both as an essential component of his or her well-being and as a manifestation of the person's intrinsic value, altogether immune from utilitarian calculus.[38] Based on this conception, fairness arguments hold that individuals deserve rights against impositions of the risk of error in adjudicative fact-finding and that social welfare must not override any such right. This theory provides for risks of error from which a person should be protected as an individual pursuer of his or her own well-being, irrespective of the social consequences of this protection. This theory thus exhibits a clash between utilitarianism and Kantian morality. Analysis of this clash is a job for ethical theories, and its normative resolution is an objective for meta-ethics. For obvious reasons, these issues are not part of this book's agenda. To the extent relevant to the allocation of the risk of error in adjudicative fact-finding, I take up these issues in Chapters 7 and 8.

Fairness arguments make an additional anti-utilitarian point, called 'a rule against recalculation'. Traditionally, this point is associated with the rule against retroactive lawmaking. But in my discussion the 'rule against recalculation' is conceptually a more accurate description. The rule against recalculation is a legal

---

[35] The claim that they can is adventive. I therefore acknowledge it without discussion.

[36] See Alex Stein, Evidential Rules for Criminal Trials: Who Should be in Charge?, in Sean Doran and John Jackson (eds.), *The Judicial Role in Criminal Proceedings* (2000), p. 127.

[37] See Dworkin, above note 2.

[38] See Joseph Raz, *Value, Respect, and Attachment* (2001), pp. 145–58.

prohibition that does not allow adjudicators to redo a legal trade-off that already worked to the individual's detriment. If an individual sustains the deprivation that the relevant legal trade-off originally imposed, the individual should then also recover the trade-off's original benefits. These benefits are to be left unmodified in the case of this particular individual. From the constitutional law perspective, the rule against recalculation constrains not only judges, but also the legislator.

The United States Supreme Court's decision *Carmell v Texas*[39] exemplifies this point in the area of evidential rights. In that case, the court examined the constitutionality of a Texas statute that repealed a corroboration arrangement for cases of rape and sexual assault. Under the old arrangement, a rape defendant could not be convicted upon his complainant's testimony if the latter was not corroborated by the complainant's prompt outcry or by evidence extraneous to the complainant.[40] The old statute exempted from this arrangement complainants below fourteen years of age. The new statute broadened this exemption by extending it to complainants below eighteen years of age. The statute provided that the jury can convict the defendant on the uncorroborated testimony of such a young complainant if it finds it credible beyond all reasonable doubt.[41] Carmell's complainant belonged to this new category of corroboration-exempted complainants.

According to the indictment, however, Carmell raped this complainant on numerous occasions that predated the new statute. Carmell therefore claimed with regard to these crimes that the court was not authorized to treat his complainant as a corroboration-exempted witness. He further contended that the jury could not properly convict him of any of these crimes on the uncorroborated testimony of his complainant. According to Carmell, the new statute can only be applied prospectively and thus cannot extend to any alleged offence that predates it. Carmell grounded this argument on his constitutional immunity from retroactive legislation (the Ex Post Facto clause).[42]

In response, the state of Texas contended that the application of its new statute to Carmell's old offences did not violate the retroactivity clause because the latter only protects substantive, as opposed to procedural, entitlements.[43] Because the new statute did not modify the offences with which Carmell was charged, there was no detraction from Carmell's substantive entitlements. The repealed corroboration requirement qualified as an evidential, rather than substantive, entitlement. This requirement and the ensuing right to acquittal in the absence of corroboration could only be activated at trial. Before trial, a person holds no evidential entitlements whatsoever. At trial, he or she captures

---

[39] *Carmell v Texas*, 529 U.S. 513 (2000) (hereinafter: '*Carmell*').
[40] See Tex. Code Crim. Proc. Ann., Art. 38.07 (Vernon 1983).
[41] See *Carmell*, above note 39, at 518–19.
[42] See U.S. Const., Art. I, § 10; *Carmell*, above note 39, at 521–2.
[43] See *Carmell*, above note 39, at 520–1; 537–9.

only those evidential entitlements that the law recognizes at that time. Changes in the law of evidence that preceded the defendant's trial therefore cannot be invalidated on retroactivity grounds.

The state's arguments have only attracted the dissenting Justices.[44] The *Carmell* court held that the repealed corroboration requirement qualified as a substantive entitlement because it determined the level of proof necessary for conviction.[45] In justifying this conclusion, the court distinguished between two types of evidential rules: rules that determine what evidence can be admitted, which the retroactivity clause does not protect, and the protected category of rules which fix the level of proof that incriminating evidence needs to reach in order to allow the jury to convict the defendant.[46] The dissenting Justices drew the same distinction, but reached the opposite conclusion. In their opinion, the corroboration requirement set a formal credibility condition for basing a defendant's conviction on the complainant's testimony.[47] The dissent explained that this requirement did not affect the criminal standard of proof, constitutionally protected by the Due Process clause.[48] As emphasized by the dissent, the fundamental demand that the prosecution proves its case against the accused beyond all reasonable doubt remained intact in Carmell's trial. As in other criminal cases, the jury were told that they can only convict Carmell if they believe the complainant beyond any reasonable doubt.[49]

Both the dissent and the court's opinions are flawed. The prosecution's license to utilize particular evidence (such as uncorroborated testimony of rape complainants) in order to satisfy a demanding proof requirement and obtain conviction by such evidence alone is similar in every respect to the prosecution's license to obtain conviction by satisfying a less demanding proof requirement (such as the jurors' license to convict the defendant on the basis of the complainant's testimony alone). There is no principled difference between the legislative power to reduce the measuring stone on one side of the scales of justice and the legislative power to add weight to evidence that the prosecution can throw on the other side of the scales. The dissent's concurrence with the court's proposition that rules regulating evidential sufficiency classify as 'substantive' therefore ought to have produced an identical categorization of the rules that control the admission of evidence.

There is, however, a more fundamental issue that all the Justices seem to have overlooked. What makes evidential sufficiency rules 'substantive'? The court provided only a partial answer to this question by intimating that evidential sufficiency rules *attach* to the system of legal arrangements that determine crimes and punishments.[50] If so, what is the exact nature of this

---

[44] See *Carmell*, above note 39, at 553–75.
[45] See *Carmell*, above note 39, at 529–53.
[46] See *Carmell*, above note 39, at 530.
[47] See *Carmell*, above note 39, at 553.
[48] See *Carmell*, above note 39, at 560–1.
[49] Ibid.
[50] See *Carmell*, above note 39, at 532–3.

attachment? How are we to identify the normative forces that create it? The court left this issue open, and I now attempt to resolve it.

The attachment of evidential mechanisms to the rules that determine criminal offences is engendered by legal trade-offs. The most typical of these trade-offs is the overenforcement paradigm.[51] To understand this paradigm, consider the special corroboration requirement that common law attaches to its overbroad prohibition of perjury.[52] This requirement bars conviction for perjury solely on the testimony of a single witness. Any such testimony must be corroborated by additional testimony or other evidence.[53] In the absence of corroboration, the jury must acquit the defendant.[54] This requirement is special because it constitutes an exception to the general law, under which 'the touchstone is always credibility; the ultimate measure of testimonial worth is quality and not quantity. Triers of fact . . . are, with rare exceptions, free in the exercise of their honest judgment, to prefer the testimony of a single witness to that of many.'[55] Despite this general rule, the corroboration requirement for perjury prosecutions 'is deeply rooted in past centuries'.[56] It applies in several jurisdictions across the United States[57] that follow English law.[58] In England, section 13 of the Perjury Act 1911 provided that[59]

A person shall not be liable to be convicted of any offence against this Act, or of any offence declared by any other Act to be perjury or subornation of perjury, or to be

---

[51] This discussion originates from Richard A. Bierschbach and Alex Stein, Overenforcement (2005) 93 Georgetown L.J. (forthcoming).
[52] See *Weiler v United States*, 323 U.S. 606 (1945) (upholding the common law corroboration requirement for cases in which a single prosecution witness accuses the defendant of perjury); section 13 of the Perjury Act, 1911.   [53] See *Weiler*, 323 U.S. at 608.
[54] See ibid.; *United States v Chaplin*, 25 F.3d 1373, 1378 (7th Cir. 1994) (holding that 'although criticized by some, the two-witness rule remains viable in perjury prosecutions, at least in those perjury prosecutions brought under a statute in which the rule has not been expressly abrogated').
[55] See *Weiler*, 323 U.S. at 608.   [56] See *Weiler*, 323 U.S. at 608–9.
[57] See, e.g., *Weiler*, 323 U.S. at 610–11; *United States v Chaplin*, 25 F.3d 1373, 1376 (7th Cir. 1994); *Hammett v State*, 797 So.2d 258 (Miss. App. 2001); *People v Ellsworth*, 15 P.3d 1111 (Colo. App. 2000); *Watson v State*, 509 S.E.2d 87 (Ga. App. 1998); *Murphy v U.S.*, 670 A.2d 1361 (D.C. 1996); *State v Barker*, 851 P.2d 394, 396 (Kan. App. 1993) (each jurisdiction requires corroboration for a single witness whose testimony accuses the defendant of perjury). See in particular *Hammer v United States*, 271 U.S. 620, 626 (1926) ('The general rule in prosecutions for perjury is that the uncorroborated oath of one witness is not enough to establish the falsity of the testimony of the accused set forth in the indictment as perjury. The application of that rule in federal and state courts is well nigh universal'). See also West's Ann. Cal. Penal Code § 123 ('No person shall be convicted of perjury where proof of falsity rests solely upon contradiction by testimony of a single person other than the defendant . . .'); McKinney's Penal Law (N.Y.) § 210.50 ('In any prosecution for perjury . . . or in any prosecution for making an apparently sworn false statement, or making a punishable false written statement, falsity of a statement may not be established by the uncorroborated testimony of a single witness').
[58] See, *Hammer v United States*, 271 U.S. 620 (1926); *Weiler v United States*, 323 U.S. 606, 610 n. 4 (1945). See also *Marvel v State*, 33 Del. 110, 113 (1925) (the corroboration rule represents a partial abandonment of the quantitative theory of evidence in favour of measures of evidentiary credibility).
[59] This section codified the common law. See *Weiler v United States*, 323 U.S. 606, 610 n. 4 (1945).

punishable as perjury or subornation of perjury solely upon the evidence of one witness as to the falsity of any statement alleged to be false.

Courts interpret this provision as a stringent corroboration requirement,[60] while legal scholars criticize it.[61]

Finding a rationale for this requirement in a system that generally allows adjudicators to convict the defendant on the testimony of a single witness cannot be easy. If one witness's testimony that adjudicators find credible beyond all reasonable doubt is good enough for convicting the defendant in a murder trial, why should it not be enough in trials for perjury? One commonly offered answer is that the corroboration requirement for perjury prosecutions is necessary to avoid chilling prospective witnesses with the prospect of easy prosecution for perjury.[62]

This rationale flows from the overenforcement paradigm. Under its common law definition, perjury is any false statement regarding a material matter that a witness makes knowingly and under oath in a judicial proceeding.[63] This definition contains three mutually related ambiguities. First, what counts as a 'statement'? Would it include, for example, a witness's demeanor when the witness uses it deliberately as a form of communication? Second, what classifies as 'false'? Would this description attach, for example, to untruthful testimony when the witness hesitantly—but still deliberately—signals the court that his testimony is not to be believed (along the lines of the famous 'Liar Paradox'[64])? Would reticent non-acknowledgement of the truth qualify as perjurious deceit?[65] Third, does any of these puzzles impact the determination of the defendant's mens rea?

---

[60] See, e.g., *Hamid and Hamid* (1979) 69 Crim. App. R. 324 (CA).

[61] See Ian H. Dennis, *The Law of Evidence* (1999), p. 488 (arguing that the corroboration requirement 'no longer has a plausible justification and could be scrapped without loss'); Paul Roberts and Adrian Zuckerman, *Criminal Evidence* (2004), p. 470 (writing that 'even if section 13 of the 1911 Act might originally have been justified as a bulwark against witness intimidation or manipulation, this rationalization no longer validates the continuing demand for corroboration').

[62] See *Weiler*, 323 U.S. at 609 ('The rule may originally have stemmed from quite different reasoning, but implicit in its evolution and continued vitality has been the fear that innocent witnesses might be unduly harassed or convicted in perjury prosecutions if a less stringent rule were adopted'); Roberts and Zuckerman, above note 61, at p. 470. Roberts and Zuckerman, however, favour other methods of reducing this chilling effect. Conditioning prosecutions for perjury upon the approval of the Director of Public Prosecutions is one such method.

[63] Under Section 1 of the Perjury Act of 1911, 'If any person lawfully sworn as a witness...in a judicial proceeding wilfully makes a statement material in that proceeding which he knows to be false or does not believe to be true, he shall be guilty of perjury, and shall, on conviction thereof on indictment, be liable to imprisonment for a term not exceeding seven years, or to a fine or to both such imprisonment and fine'. The federal definition of perjury in the United States, U.S.C.A. § 1621, is similarly broad.   [64] See R. M. Sainsbury, *Paradoxes* (2nd edn, 1995), pp. 111–17.

[65] Thomas Nagel argues that it would not because it flows from generally known conventions. See Thomas Nagel, Concealment and Exposure (1998) 27 Phil. & Pub. Aff. 3. See also Bernard A. O. Williams, *Truth and Truthfulness: An Essay in Genealogy* (2002), pp. 96–100 (acknowledging the validity of the distinction between lying and being reticent or even misleading).

These ambiguities in the definition of perjury are important because many witnesses testifying in courts would rather not be there. Testifying costs time and money and often generates considerable stress in the form of questions about vague, unsavoury, or personal events, circumstances and relationships. Witnesses facing these disincentives have much to lose and little to gain from telling the truth. Many of them nonetheless choose to testify because they fear punishment for contempt (and in some cases, moral reprobation as well). A witness thus often will deliver evasive testimony that obfuscates the truth without making any affirmative attempts to mislead the court. Indeed, his or her testimony might openly display reticence that does not induce the court to make a wrong factual finding. It says, in effect, 'I am forced to testify against my will, and am very uncomfortable doing so, so please don't place too much weight on what I'm saying'. Is this testimony perjury?

Courts generally interpret perjury broadly by resolving any ambiguities in the prosecution's favour. Any part of a witness's testimony amounts to perjury if it is untrue and material to the case. Falsity cannot be offset by the witness's self-acknowledged reticency or evasiveness or by any other signal that induces the court not to believe the witness.[66] The witness also need not harbour any specific intent to mislead the court. His or her awareness of the statement's untruthfulness would satisfy the mens rea requirement.[67] In short, witnesses must always tell 'the truth, the whole truth, and nothing but the truth', and any deliberate violation of this requirement qualifies as perjury.[68] The reason

---

[66] See, e.g., *Ostendorf v State*, 128 P. 143, 154 (Okla. Crim. App. 1912) (wilful suppression of part of the truth is equivalent to an affirmative statement of falsehood); *Flowers v State*, 163 P. 558 (Okla. Crim. App. 1917) (same); Alan Heinrich, Note: Clinton's Little White Lies: the Materiality Requirement for Perjury in Civil Discovery (1999) 32 Loy. L.A. L. Rev. 1303, 1311–16 (demonstrating that courts uniformly interpret the 'materiality' condition for perjury in very broad terms).

[67] *United States v Williams*, 874 F.2d 968, 980 (5th Cir. 1989) (explaining that for perjury purposes, absence of such a motive to deceive the court does not exonerate a witness who knowingly gives false testimony on one of the material issues); *United States v Lewis*, 876 F.Supp. 308, 312 (D. Mass. 1994) ('[P]erjury does not require proof that the defendant had the specific intent to impede justice'); cf. 18 U.S.C.S. § 1623(a) (2004) (in order to convict a defendant of making false statements to a grand jury or court, the prosecution only has to show knowledge by the defendant that the statement was false).

A few states reject this broad interpretation. See Tex. Penal Code Ann. § 37.02(a) (Vernon 2003) ('Perjury. A person commits an offense if, with intent to deceive and with knowledge of the statement's meaning, he makes a false statement under oath . . .'); Mo. Ann. Stat. § 575.040 (West 1995) ('A person commits the crime of perjury if, with the purpose to deceive, he knowingly testifies falsely to any material fact upon oath or affirmation legally administered, in any official proceeding before any court, public body, notary public or other officer authorized to administer oaths'); Tenn. Code. Ann. § 39–16–702 (2004) ('Perjury. A person commits an offense who, with intent to deceive . . . makes a false statement, under oath . . .').

[68] See, e.g., Model Penal Code § 241.1 ('A person is guilty of perjury . . . if in any official proceeding he makes a false statement under oath or equivalent affirmation . . . when the statement is material and he does not believe it to be true'); Jared S. Hosid (2002) Perjury, 39 Am. Crim. L. Rev. 895.

for this approach is simple. Broadly defining perjury in this way strengthens the incentives of all witnesses to tell the truth[69] and eases the prosecution's burden in cases in which witnesses have in fact lied.

But it also creates a problem: the definition of perjury becomes overbroad in that it condemns and punishes individuals who do not necessarily produce the mischief at which the criminal prohibition against perjury aims. This mischief is an erroneous verdict that false testimony actively induces.[70] Openly evasive testimony does not do this because everyone can see that the witness passively defies the request to assist the court in its pursuit of the truth. At its worst, such testimony amounts to contempt of court—conduct that is certainly reprehensible, but not as pernicious as perjury. Indeed, as many commentators have noted, evasive as opposed to affirmatively misleading testimony raises normatively difficult questions about the extent to which an individual's moral entitlement to privacy and non-exposure should limit his or her truth-telling obligations to society.[71] From a moral (as opposed to formal legal) point of view, it is one thing actively to bring about an injustice, and it is quite another thing to withdraw one's testimonial assistance from a justice-making proceeding. On this view, only outright liars can properly be identified and condemned as perjurers.[72]

Why not redefine perjury as demanded by this nuanced approach? The answer to this question points to the law's operational concerns. Narrowing down the prohibition to capture only outright liars but not evaders would make perjury prosecutions more difficult than they presently are. This would dilute the incentives for people who are contemplating lying in court not to do so. Adoption of the broad definition of perjury—one that pools liars with evaders—is the best that the lawmaker can do. The resulting overenforcement of the law is the law's operational necessity, and this evil can still be attenuated.

The common-law corroboration requirement attenuates this evil. By making perjury convictions more difficult to obtain and, consequently, less probable

---

[69] For economic analysis of these incentives see Robert Cooter and Winand Emons, Truth-Bonding and other Truth-Revealing Mechanisms for Courts (2004) 17 Eur. J. Law & Econ. 307.

[70] See, e.g., *Bronston v United States*, 409 U.S. 352, 362 (1973) (holding that literally true statements made under oath that are evasive or unresponsive must be resolved under further questioning by counsel, not by prosecution for perjury, and that such statements do not fall within the federal perjury statute, 28 U.S.C.S. § 1621 (2004)); see also *United States v Shotts*, 145 F.3d 1289, 1299 (11th Cir. 1998) ('[T]he prosecutor's purpose must be to obtain the truth. Perjury, of course, thwarts that proper purpose. It must not be the prosecutor's purpose, however, to *obtain* perjury, thus avoiding more precise questions which might rectify the apparent perjury').

[71] Cf. Williams, above note 65, at 96–100.

[72] See Stuart P. Green, Lying, Misleading, and Falsely Denying: How Moral Concepts Inform the Law of Perjury, Fraud, and False Statements (2001) 53 Hastings L.J. 157, 168–73, 179–80 (distinguishing on moral grounds between lying and misleading; defending the 'literal falsity' approach to perjury; and arguing that defensive deception is excusable on self-preservation grounds).

ex ante, the law reduces the chilling effect that the overbroad definition of the crime exerts. Due to the corroboration requirement, many evasive—but still not affirmatively lying—witnesses would escape criminal liability. The effect of this mechanism is to require the prosecution to identify a particular falsity in the defendant's testimony, to demonstrate that this falsity was material to the proceedings in which the defendant appeared as a witness, and to provide additional and independent proof to back up a witness who testifies about this falsity. It will be much harder for the prosecution to discharge this burden in criminal proceedings initiated against evasive as opposed to deliberately misleading witnesses.[73] This trade-off is imperfect, but it is better than the alternative.[74]

With these observations in mind, I return to *Carmell*. The definition of sexual assault—the crime with which Carmell was charged[75]—is not overbroad. Under this definition, the prosecution must prove beyond all reasonable doubt that the defendant made a sexual contact with the victim without her consent while he was aware of both the nature of his conduct and of the possibility that the victim may not be consenting to it. There was no trade-off relationship whatsoever between the corroboration requirement that Carmell wished to retain and the definition of the crime with which he was charged. The repealed corroboration requirement therefore did not attach to the Texas definitions of rape and sexual assault. Rather, it was attached to the alleged victims of those crimes on the questionable theory that doubted their trustworthiness. This requirement belonged to the era of indiscriminate group-based disbelief that the Anglo-American systems of criminal justice exhibited towards women complaining about rape and

---

[73] Some scholars claim that the prosecution's burden is already too heavy, to the detriment of society. See, e.g., Glanville Williams, *The Proof of Guilt* (3rd edn., 1963), p. 68 (noting the difficulty of proving the guilty mind as affecting all prosecutions for perjury); Michael Stokes Paulsen, Review: Dirty Harry and the Real Constitution (1997) 64 U. Chi. L. Rev. 1457, 1488–9 ('Oaths are taken less seriously today ... fewer people believe in hell, and an oath is no longer thought to be effective because of extratemporal consequences for false swearing. The only real bite behind an oath is the specter of a perjury prosecution, and perjury is notoriously difficult to prove ... Indeed, the ethos of today is that perjury is commonplace . . .').

[74] For another similar example, consider Article III, Section 3(1) of the United States Constitution, which provides , 'No person shall be convicted of Treason unless on the Testimony of two Witnesses to the same overt Act, or on Confession in Open Court.' U.S. Const. art. I, § 3, cl. 1. This corroboration requirement offsets a definition of treason that is both overbroad and ambiguous: as stated by the same constitutional provision, 'Treason against the United States shall consist . . . [inter alia] in adhering to their Enemies, giving them Aid and Comfort'. U.S. Const. art. I, § 3, cl. 1. See also 18 U.S.C.A. § 2381 (2004) ('Whoever, owing allegiance to the United States, levies war against them or adheres to their enemies, giving them aid and comfort within the United States or elsewhere, is guilty of treason and shall suffer death, or shall be imprisoned not less than five years and fined under this title but not less than $10,000; and shall be incapable of holding any office under the United States'). [75] See § 22.011 of the Texas Penal Code.

sexual assault.[76] This era ended, and hence the abolition of the corroboration requirement. Carmell had no vested interest in the continuation of this era because it did not subject him to any trade-off (such as overenforcement). *Carmell v Texas* was a wrong decision.

C. What Does and Does not Belong to Evidence Law?

Arguably, execution of the best evidence principle and allocation of the risk of error do not fully define evidence law. Evidence law operates in yet another domain that accommodates rules and doctrines unrelated to the best evidence principle and allocation of the risk of error. These rules and doctrines are driven by concerns altogether extraneous to fact-finding. They determine the outcomes of the clashes between fact-finding and other goals and values that the law upholds and promotes. Resolution of such clashes often results in suppressing fact-finding for the sake of other goals and values. Anglo-American legal systems prefer ignorance to fact-finding when the latter: entails revelation of state secrets or other confidential information;[77] infringes privacy;[78] disrupts marital harmony;[79] forces criminal defendants and suspects into the choice between contempt, perjury, and self-incrimination;[80] discourages potential producers of accidents from taking precautions that might signal an admission of fault;[81] chills peer review and other critical evaluation of professionals;[82] creates a disincentive for benevolent actions interpretable as acknowledgement of responsibility;[83] destabilizes contractual relationships by

---

[76] This unflattering portrayal derives from simple facts. Traditionally, the jury's power to convict the accused on the testimony of a single witness extended to virtually all crimes, except rape and sexual assault; the corroboration requirement never applied universally. See Roberts and Zuckerman. above note 61, at p. 479 (explaining that 'with the benefit of hindsight, it seems more likely that the complainant corroboration warning reflected sexist stereotyping of—predominantly, female—sexual assault complainants, rather than well-founded assessments of complainants' testimonial unreliability); Michelle J. Anderson, The Legacy of the Prompt Complaint Requirement, Corroboration Requirement, and Cautionary Instructions on Campus Sexual Assault (2004) 84 B. U. L. Rev. 945, 977–86 (prompt-complaint, corroboration, and caution requirements in rape trials are predominantly misogynistic and do not deter shrewd liars).

[77] See McCormick, *On Evidence* Vol. 1 (4th edn., 1992), pp. 268–72.

[78] Ibid, at p. 269.   [79] Ibid.   [80] Ibid, at pp. 430–5.

[81] See Federal Rule of Evidence 407; *Flaminio v Honda Motor Co.*, 733 F.2d 463 (7th Cir. 1984) (Posner, J.).

[82] See, e.g., Alissa M. Bassler, Federal Law Should Keep Pace with States and Recognize a Medical Peer Review Privilege (2003) 39 Idaho L. Rev. 689.

[83] Consider Federal Rule of Evidence 409: 'Evidence of furnishing or offering or promising to pay medical, hospital, or similar expenses occasioned by an injury is not admissible to prove liability for the injury.'

allowing testimony to substitute or undermine documented agreements;[84] inhibits settlement negotiations and plea-bargain discussions;[85] and these are just representative examples.

The exclusionary rule is another familiar example of such preferences. This rule suppresses confessions and other probative evidence that incriminates the defendant when the police obtain such evidence through violation of one of the defendant's fundamental rights.[86] These rights typically include a person's entitlements to physical integrity and to privacy, the right to remain silent, the right to counsel, and the more general entitlement against coercive interrogation. The exclusionary rule aims at promoting a number of socially important objectives, all extraneous to fact-finding. First and foremost, these objectives include provision of meaningful legal remedies to the persons wronged by the police,[87] as well as prevention of police misconduct through incentives that discourage the police from breaking the law.[88] Other objectives that the exclusionary rule promotes are the integrity of the criminal justice system and the acceptability of criminal verdicts. The exclusionary rule promotes these objectives by not allowing criminal convictions to rest upon illegally obtained evidence. The ideology animating this approach justifies the workings of the criminal justice machinery in so far as it enforces criminal law within the bounds of the legal. Legality cannot be reinstated through illegality.[89]

Another mechanism that promotes objectives extraneous to fact-finding is mandatory inferences. This mechanism typically assumes the form of legal presumptions. An example is a legal rule that conclusively presumes any child below the age of seven to be incapable of committing felonies.[90] Phrased in evidential terms, this presumption is not truly evidential. It establishes a principle of substantive criminal law that exempts minors below the age of seven from criminal liability for felonies.[91] This presumption relates to fact-finding only as a trumping device. It does not allow the prosecution to introduce evidence demonstrating that a particular child—who was below the age of seven at the time that he or she committed the alleged felony—perpetrated that offence. Another example is the 'birth within wedlock' presumption that

---

[84] See E. Allan Farnsworth, *Contracts* (3rd edn., 1999), pp. 363–7, 427–30 (discussing statutes of frauds, the parol evidence rule and their underlying rationales).

[85] See Federal Rules of Evidence 408 and 410 (evidence about settlement and plea-bargain negotiations generally inadmissible). [86] See McCormick Vol. 1, above note 77, at pp. 673–8.

[87] Ibid, at pp. 677–8. See also Andrew Ashworth, Excluding Evidence as Protecting Rights [1977] Crim. L. Rev. 723. [88] See McCormick Vol. 1, above note 77, at pp. 674–5.

[89] Ibid, at pp. 676–7. For a broader layout of the legitimacy rationale, as controlling criminal evidence in general, see Ian Dennis, Reconstructing the Law of Criminal Evidence [1989] Current Legal Problems 21. [90] See McCormick, *On Evidence* Vol. 2 (4th edn., 1992), p. 451.

[91] Ibid.

extends to a child born to a mother living with her husband. This presumption deems any such child to be the child of the marriage unless the husband or the wife comes forward with counter-proof.[92] As Justice Scalia explained, this presumption is a substantive rule of family law that protects the stability of the family—and, more contestably, the well-being of the child—at the expense of accuracy in fact-finding.[93] Finally, consider the employment discrimination presumption that applies in the United States in Title VII 'mixed-motive' cases. In such cases, both legitimate and discriminatory motives explain the employer's decision against the employee. Because the resulting indeterminacy makes it practically impossible for the employee to establish her or his employer's discriminatory animus, the discrimination presumption tilts the scales in her or his favour in order to fulfil the egalitarian promise of Title VII.[94] Accuracy in adjudicative fact-finding is not an objective of this presumption. Indeed, when the discrimination and the non-discrimination scenarios are equally likely, there is no *evidential reason* for preferring the former scenario over the latter. There is, however, a non-evidential reason for according preference to the discrimination scenario. Deciding indeterminate cases in this way effectively promotes the egalitarian objectives of Title VII.

Such rules and doctrines do not belong to the law of evidence. Their design and operation are evidence-related, but their essence is not evidential. Their affiliation to evidence law exhibits contingent instrumentality, rather than immutable bond. Underlying any such rule and doctrine is the treatment of its evidence-related mechanism as (arguably) the best means for attaining the ends that are chosen to prevail over accuracy in fact-finding. As the foregoing examples reveal, these ends include protection of civil and other individual rights, sustainment of moral values and political virtues, and a general pursuit of social welfare. The strength of the instrumental linkage between any such end and the underlying evidence-related mechanism is always contingent upon the comparative advantage of that mechanism over other means for attaining the end. Thus, in settings in which suppression of evidence functions as an inducement of some socially beneficial conduct, say, safety improvement, the evidence-suppressing mechanism can be substituted with direct payoffs, both positive and negative.

This competition is inevitable. Virtually any objective that the legal system can accomplish through suppression of evidence can also be attained by introducing the appropriate downward or upward adjustment into the relevant penalty or remuneration. A stick and a carrot are two equally functional sides of the same economic coin. For example, a manufacturer's decision not to

---

[92] *Michael H. v Gerald D.*, 491 U.S. 110 (1989).   [93] Ibid, at 119–21; 124–32.
[94] *Price Waterhouse v Hopkins*, 490 U.S. 228 (1989).

improve the safety of its products may constitute a ground for raising the level of its compensation duty above and beyond the actual damages. A substantive law provision to this effect would create an incentive for manufacturers to improve the safety of their products. Under this regime, evidence demonstrating that the defendant-manufacturer introduced new safety measures after the occurrence of the litigated accident would not just be admissible. Manufacturers would be eager to generate and present it in courts.[95] There would no longer be a need to exclude such evidence—as the law presently does[96]—in order not to discourage manufacturers from introducing safety improvements.

The existing evidential privilege that functions as a carrot can be replaced with a liability enhancement that would function as a stick. To be sure, such a replacement does not always work to the benefit of society. The heightened liability regime would force manufacturers to demand higher prices for their products. Consumers may ultimately succumb to this demand. In some cases, the new legal regime would drive manufacturers out of business, yet another effect that might ultimately prove detrimental to society. Furthermore, heightened liability induces more claimants to file lawsuits, which increases both the litigation expenses and the number of unmeritorious lawsuits. The issue consequently reduces to the choice between two types of legal mechanisms, of which one is evidence-related and the other (that of direct pay-offs) is not. Such choices often derive from utilitarianism. In other cases, a rights-based morality takes the lead. In the remaining cases, the lawmaker opts for pragmatic solutions accommodating both utility and individual rights.

The exclusionary rule qualifies my observation about the plausibility of both evidence-suppressing and direct-pay-off mechanisms. This rule suppresses evidence obtained by the police through violation of constitutional or other rights that belong to criminal defendants and suspects. In the domain over which this rule exercises control, liability enhancements (specifically, criminal and disciplinary penalties, as well as compensatory and punitive payments under the law of torts) can hardly compete with the suppression of evidence as an instrument for deterring the police (and other law-enforcement agencies). A liability enhancement that places police officers under the right level of deterrence should, *ex hypothesi*, dissuade them from breaking the law in furthering their investigations. In this scenario, police officers never obtain evidence using unconstitutional and other illegal means. The exclusionary rule, therefore, is instrumentally superior to the alternative methods of deterrence. This point is quite straightforward. In the right course of things—that is, under the scenario in which police officers are adequately deterred and do

---

[95] This mechanism aligns with Chris Sanchirico's direct-incentive approach. See note 4 above.
[96] See Federal Rule of Evidence 407.

not break the law—evidence that the exclusionary rule currently suppresses does not come into existence.[97] The loss of such evidence under the exclusionary rule is, therefore, illusory rather than real. This loss cannot properly be counted as the rule's social cost—a point that underscores the advantage of the exclusionary rule over its disciplinary, criminal, and tort alternatives. Because each of these alternatives requires a separate proceeding mechanism, its administration would also be costlier than that of the exclusionary rule.

This feature is not present in other rules that suppress probative evidence in order to attain objectives extraneous to fact-finding. The exclusionary rule and other evidence-suppressing rules to which my present discussion refers are, however, still similar in one crucial respect. None of those rules facilitates fact-finding or allocates the risk of error. None of them consequently qualifies as evidential.

Sometimes, the forces of supply and demand that set remuneration for a socially desirable activity can secure its endurance even in the absence of the evidence-suppressing rule. Candid peer review, for example, is not likely to shrink in the absence of peer-review privileges. Instead, professional reviewers whose opinions are essential will both demand and recover larger payments for their work. Their remuneration will compensate them not only for their professional efforts, but also for the potentially unpleasant revelation of their identities and opinions. The issue transforms into a comparison between two types of social cost: the cost that society bears by paying reviewers greater remuneration and the cost incurred by suppressing peer-review evidence and by reducing the accuracy of court verdicts. The same argument applies to the settlement negotiations privilege. To the extent that both parties to such negotiations are interested in the privilege, they can create it in a separate agreement. The general contract law, under which such agreements are enforceable,[98] needs only one fortification. The law should protect such 'off-the-record' agreements against the demands for disclosure that come from third parties.[99] Apart from this provision, there is no need for a special evidential privilege that extends to settlement negotiations. In this domain, unregulated market forces perform at least as well as the privilege.

A plausible response to this argument comes from the standard default-rule theory of contracts.[100] Under this theory, default rules by which the law

---

[97] See Richard A. Posner, An Economic Approach to the Law of Evidence (1999) 51 Stan. L. Rev. 1477, 1533.

[98] See John W. Strong, Consensual Modifications of the Rules of Evidence: The Limits of Party Autonomy in an Adversary System (2001) 80 Neb. L. Rev. 159.

[99] As judicially provided in *Rush & Tompkins Ltd v GLC* [1988] 3 All ER 737 (HL).

[100] See Alan Schwartz, Incomplete Contracts, in *The New Palgrave Dictionary of Economics and the Law* Vol. 2 (Peter Newman ed., 1998), pp. 277, 279–80.

supplements private transactions reduce transaction costs. Because settlement negotiators are typically willing to enter into an 'off-the-record' agreement, the law eliminates the transaction costs that such agreements incur by introducing a general default rule in the form of a settlement negotiation privilege. This strategy, however, imposes transaction costs upon parties willing to negotiate their settlement without the privilege. The unprivileged-negotiations possibility might attract negotiators willing to base their negotiations upon credible signalling. The issue once again boils down to the choice between two social expenditures. The existing privilege would only be justified if settlement negotiators were typically to prefer an 'off-the-record' environment to that of credible signalling. However, if an unprivileged negotiation environment reflects the negotiators' typical preference, the law should then opt for a default rule that denies the privilege. This point underscores both the instrumental contingency of the settlement negotiations privilege and its affiliation to contract law. The privilege's domicile in the evidence law domain is merely formal. This formality must not obscure the understanding of the privilege.

Arguably, many evidential privileges escape this instrumental analysis. Among these privileges are the privilege against self-incrimination and several other privileges that protect secrecy and secure confidential communications between clients and professionals. The relationship between these privileges and fact-finding is that of a head-on collision. Under any such privilege, forced revelation of the information that the privilege protects is generally perceived as a harm in itself. This vision of direct as opposed to consequential harm leaves no room for incentive-based alternatives to the suppression of evidence. If forced revelation of some privileged information were just to distort the individuals' incentives for acting in some socially beneficial way, these alternatives would then have been firmly on the agenda. However, because revelation of such information constitutes a harm in itself, these alternatives have no scope for application.

For methodological reasons that will become apparent, I assume that such privileges are grounded in sound rationales. If so, the intrinsic nature of the revelational harm that such privileges avert expels them from the evidence law domain. To the extent that a revelational harm is intrinsic, its occurrence cannot plausibly depend on the setting within which it was inflicted. Such harm can be inflicted both with and without connection to adjudicative fact-finding. The rule averting this harm within the framework of adjudicative fact-finding (typically labelled as 'privilege') must, therefore, be understood as instantiating a more general set of rules that avert the same harm in other settings. This understanding would affiliate the rule to the privacy law, the attorney services law, the state secrets law, and so forth. This understanding would also help evidence law to function as *law of evidence*.

I conclude this section by registering my reservations about the normative validity of the intrinsic-revelational-harm rationale for the privileges. Consider a criminal case in which keeping evidence secret—say, on state security grounds—exposes the defendant to a serious risk of wrongful conviction. Why not consider wrongful conviction and its consequences as intrinsically harmful as well? Consider yet another criminal case in which honouring the defendant's self-incrimination privilege and setting him or her free would seriously dilute deterrence. More innocent victims than previously would consequently become exposed to and, inevitably, suffer from crime. Why not consider their entitlement to protection from crime as intrinsic, too? My point is simple. In law, balancing and trade-offs are unavoidable. This anti-deontological point brings me to the final section of this chapter.

D. Free-Standing Evidential Rights?

According to Tribe,

Both the right to be heard from, and the right to be told why, are analytically distinct from the right to secure a different outcome; these rights to interchange express the elementary idea that to be a *person*, rather than a *thing*, is at least to be *consulted* about what is done with one.... For when the government acts in a way that singles out identifiable individuals—in a way that is likely to be premised on suppositions about specific persons—it activates the special concern about being personally *talked to* about the decision rather than simply being *dealt with*.[101]

This view is held by other scholars, who apply it to additional procedural and evidential domains.[102] Arguably, a criminal defendant's right to cross-examine prosecution witnesses and the consequent exclusion of hearsay statements should also be perceived as belonging to the family of participation rights that are valuable per se. Hearsay evidence is not inadmissible because of the risk of error that its admission would produce. It is inadmissible because forcing a person into a criminal trial without providing her or him a fair opportunity to confront adverse witnesses is devoid of political warrant. Findings made upon testimonial accounts untested by cross-examination may well be accurate. Their accuracy is not the issue. The issue is whether the community in which criminal trials are conducted without full participation of the accused is attractive in moral and political terms.[103]

---

[101] Laurence Tribe, *American Constitutional Law* (2nd edn., 1988), pp. 666–7.

[102] Robert Summers, Evaluating and Improving Legal Process—A Plea for 'Process Values' (1974) 60 Cornell L. Rev. 1; Michael D. Bayles, Principles for Legal Procedure (1986) 5 Law & Phil. 33.

[103] See Stein, above note 3, at 292–3.

Based on this deontological theory, one may also justify the law's ban on incriminating inferences that emanate from the defendant's past crimes. By treating personality and action as causally interrelated, such inferences undermine the anti-deterministic postulate of free agency, epitomized by the famous precept 'Judge the act, not the actor'. Free agency indeed serves as a pillar of the liberal theory of criminal liability.[104] From this perspective, using the defendant's personality as incriminating evidence undermines his or her autonomy and degrades his or her individuality.[105]

The idea of free-standing rights with respect to evidence and procedures is quite compelling. I am, however, sceptical about this idea for a number of reasons.[106] My first reason focuses on the costs of fact-finding procedures. These costs are far from negligible. In many cases, they might also be expended without producing any offsetting benefits. The resulting disutility might impel the lawmaker to consider a replacement for the costly procedure. To properly examine this possibility, the lawmaker has to conduct a cost–benefit analysis that compares the new procedure with the existing procedure. This analysis compares the new amount aggregating the cost of errors and error-avoidance expenses with the old amount. Based on this analysis, the lawmaker opts for the lowest possible amount. This analysis requires the lawmaker to evaluate the litigants' substantive entitlements.

The theory of free-standing procedural rights rejects such calculations on deontological grounds. This rejection, however, creates an insurmountable problem. Resources that society can expend on adjudication are always limited. There are not enough resources for employing the best fact-finding procedures in every legal dispute. Any procedural theory therefore needs to devise its criteria for allocating these resources one way or another. To coin a phrase: *there can be no free-standing procedural rights because procedural rights cannot stand for free.*

My second reason analogizes litigation to a zero-sum game. Court hearings and other procedures postpone the enforcement of the litigated substantive rights. Such postponements are obviously detrimental to the right-holders. Justice delayed is justice denied. A party's right to be heard ought to be understood as including the right to subject the opponent to a temporary deprivation of her or his substantive right.[107] This temporary deprivation is inevitable. This deprivation, however, could hardly be justified if the right to be heard were to be perceived as deontological. Assume, for the sake of

---

[104] See H. L. A. Hart, *Punishment and Responsibility* (1968), pp. 46–9.

[105] See Stein, above note 3, at 293.   [106] See Stein, above note 36, at 133–5.

[107] For an illuminating discussion of this problem see Adrian A. S. Zuckerman, Quality and Economy in Civil Procedure—The Case for Commuting Correct Judgments for Timely Judgments (1994) 14 Oxford J.L. Stud. 353.

argument, that the right to be heard is unrelated to the risk of error in fact-finding and is also completely divorced from the underlying substantive right. If so, why prefer the hearing interest of one party over the non-delayed-justice interest of his or her opponent? If a person whose rights are adjudicated without a hearing is treated, in Tribe's words, *as a thing* rather than as a person, then what about a person temporarily deprived of his or her rights by a hearing provided to his or her adversary?[108] Would that person be treated as a thing as well?

There is also a logical reason for being sceptical about free-standing procedural and evidential rights. Assume, counterfactually, that the epistemic fallibility problem does not exist and that fact-finders are infallible. Would there be a room in such a world for procedural and evidential rights that are valuable intrinsically, rather than instrumentally? This question merits a negative answer, unless, of course, one alludes to rituals or to an exotic recourse to procedural and evidential rights as an indispensable source of psychological satisfactions.[109] If so, the theory of free-standing rights in the domain of evidence and procedure would fail completely. The right to be heard, and, indeed, the entire package of trial participation rights, are rights that ultimately derive from epistemic fallibility, not from moral virtuousness.

---

[108] As suggested by Alexander, above note 27, the justification for procedures temporarily depriving a person of his or her substantive right can be found only in treating the substantive rights as *ab initio* qualified by procedurally necessitated delays. Together with other procedural requirements that derive from the societal preferences with regard to risks and resources, delays that society deems procedurally necessary would attach to many substantive rights, but certainly not to all of them.

[109] See, e.g., David P. Leonard, The Use of Character to Prove Conduct (1986–7) 58 U. Colorado L. Rev. 1 (offering a catharsis-based explanation for the right to adduce evidence highlighting one's character).

2

Epistemological Corollary

A. Fundamentals

Adjudicative fact-finding instantiates practical reasoning. This goal-oriented reasoning aims at producing the best decision available, not at finding the truth for its own sake. What qualifies as a best fact-finding decision is a major issue that defines the agenda for this entire book. This chapter begins the exploration of this issue by identifying the principal characteristics of adjudicative fact-finding and its epistemological background.

Any provision of substantive law, as addressed to decision-makers, prescribes '*if F, decide X*'; '*if not-F, decide Y*'; or '*if neither F nor not-F, decide Z*'.[1] Adjudicators have to make decisions that modify the existing state of affairs or immunize it from attempted modifications. Adjudication is about applying the coercive power, monopolized by the state, against individuals.[2] At the end of any trial, application of this power is prescribed or not. Adjudication can never be halted in indecision. A decision not to decide the case is actually a decision to reaffirm the status quo. Adjudicators have to resolve the disputed issues of fact one way or another and are not authorized to withhold their decision in the presence of uncertainty. This is what practical—as opposed to theoretical—reasoning is about.

Adjudicative fact-finding reconstructs past events not susceptible to direct observation. Adjudicators must provide authoritative answers to backward-looking questions of fact that reduce to 'What happened?'. Questions such as 'What is happening now?' and 'What might happen in the future?' are not alien to adjudication. Yet, cases hinging solely on such questions are rare. Such questions arise almost invariably in combination with past events that have legal consequences.[3] This dependency flows from the inherently reactive

---

[1] Z usually means either X or Y, as prescribed by the burden of proof.

[2] See Dale Nance, Legal Theory and the Pivotal Role of the Concept of Coercion (1985) 57 U. Colo. L. Rev. 1.

[3] For example, determination of present and future facts—such as present employment and earnings and future employment prospects—is often required for assessing the victim's losses in personal injury cases.

function of the substantive laws that operate in liberal legal regimes.[4] Such regimes resort to coercion in a strictly remedial mode. They apply it against an individual in order to restore the legally protected equilibrium that the individual has upset. Further, liberal regimes provide citizens with a fair opportunity to avoid state-sponsored coercion by announcing in advance the conditions for its application. If a given legal regime is to remain liberal, it cannot execute its substantive laws retroactively.[5]

The event-reconstructive nature of adjudicative fact-finding underscores the uncertainty problem that attaches to every case. Evidence, by its very definition, is an item of information that evidences additional information. When witness W testifies about event H the information that this testimony immediately provides is 'W says H'. This information, however, does not evidence H by itself. The only proposition that transforms W's testimony into evidence is 'W says H; *therefore* H'. This transforming proposition goes beyond the assertive content of W's testimony. Chapter 3 identifies such propositions as fact-generating arguments that depend on generalizations. These generalizations are inherently uncertain in their application to individual cases. Only the inferential analogy links a generalization to a new case not encompassed by past experience. Any such analogy can only make it probable, but not certain, that the reconstructed event is actually identical to the past experience to which the applicable generalization attests. Fact-generating arguments, to which adjudicators have to resort, are therefore intrinsically uncertain, too. Adjudicative fact-finding is about probabilities, not about certainties.

The uncertainty problem is further exacerbated by the time-constraints that apply in adjudication. Adjudicators have to decide cases within reasonable time-limits. Justice delayed is justice denied. This requirement forces adjudicators to curtail their fact-finding inquiries and decide cases based on limited informational resources. Facts contested in adjudication have to be reconstructed on the basis of deficient evidence. Adjudicators have to determine those facts by relying on accounts of fallible and biased witnesses; by not considering all evidence that they possibly could consider; by invoking generalizations and inferences that are nothing but rough approximations; and, finally, by subjecting the existing evidence to credibility tests that are never carried through to perfection.[6] These constraints, as Wigmore once put it,

---

4 See Mirjan R. Damaška, *The Faces of Justice and State Authority* (1986), pp. 73–80.

5 See John Rawls, *A Theory of Justice* (1971), pp. 238–41.

6 For a particularly insightful discussion of this constraint and its implications see Henry M. Hart and John T. McNaughton, Evidence and Inference in the Law, in D. Lerner et al., *Evidence and Inference* (1959), p. 48 ff. See also Chaim Perelman, *The Idea of Justice and the Problem of Argument* (1963), pp. 98–108.

'may lead to special rules of the art, as distinguished from the science,—just as an architect who cannot find limestone available in his region and must use granite ... will find his construction-style modified thereby'.[7]

The following excerpt from Judge Weinstein's classic article on evidence law provides an account of the uncertainty problem and its origins almost identical to mine. Judge Weinstein observes:

Even were it theoretically possible to ascertain truth with a fair degree of certainty, it is doubtful whether the judicial system and rules of evidence would be designed to do so. Trials in our judicial system are intended to do more than merely determine what happened. Adjudication is a practical enterprise serving a variety of functions. Among the goals—in addition to truth finding— ... are economizing of resources, inspiring confidence, supporting independent social policies, permitting ease in prediction and application, adding to the efficiency of the entire legal system, and tranquilizing disputants.[8]

Adjudicative decisions on matters of both law and fact also need to be justified.[9] Adjudicators, both judges and juries, make these decisions about other people's rights, duties, and liabilities. These decisions are concerned with the application of state-sponsored coercion against individuals. To be legitimate, any such decision needs to derive from the accepted authority (common law or statute) and must rest on reasons that qualify as authoritative.[10] Xavier can only be forced to pay Yvonne compensation for a breach of contract if there are authoritative reasons—legal and factual—for holding that the two exchanged promises, which generated a valid contract, and that Xavier failed to deliver on his promise. Yvonne can only be denied that compensation if there are authoritative reasons—legal and factual—for holding that she either did not enter into a valid contract with Xavier or that Xavier actually performed his contractual obligations. Xavier, Yvonne, and any other individual are entitled to know the reasons—legal and factual—for the adjudicators' decision about his or her duties, liabilities, and entitlements. An individual is also entitled to dispute these reasons. To be authoritative, these reasons need to align with the appropriate legal rules and standards. To secure this alignment, an individual should be also able to subject these reasons to examination by an appellate court. The demand for justification placed on judges and juries derives from the combination of these factors.

  [7] John H. Wigmore, *The Principles of Judicial Proof* (2nd edn., 1931), pp. 955–6.
  [8] Jack Weinstein, Some Difficulties in Devising Rules for Determining Truth in Judicial Trials (1966) 66 Colum. L. Rev. 223, 241.
  [9] See, e.g., Christopher H. Schroeder, Liberalism and the Objective Point of View (1986) XXVIII NOMOS 100, 106–9.
  [10] Chapter 4 explores the relationship between this demand and the individual's right to autonomy.

These factors also enable me to remove a somewhat tempting objection that can be raised against the idea of extending the justification requirement to adjudicative determination of facts. According to this objection, fact-finders heavily rely upon 'tacit knowledge.'[11] Formed by complex experiences and intuitions—never translatable into linguistic forms—this knowledge has established its creditworthiness. Discarding this knowledge with all its epistemic richness would be wrong. Although adjudicators, like other people, are not infallible decision-makers, they ought to be allowed to invoke their 'tacit knowledge' in deciding on matters of fact. On the strength of these arguments, the 'tacit knowledge' theory paved its way into both case-law[12] and academic writings.[13]

Assume that unarticulated 'tacit knowledge' is rational from an epistemological point of view. Who would exercise control over the intuitions that adjudicators apply? Presumably, no one. Under the 'tacit knowledge' theory, such control is unnecessary because adjudicators are trustworthy. Adjudicative fact-finding consequently never unfolds itself to scrutiny. Erroneous decisions that fact-finders deliver pool with correct decisions. A neutral observer of this system is scarcely able to tell rationality from whim and bias. The line separating the justified from the arbitrary becomes blurred. Ultimately, it fades away completely. This scenario can only be averted by not allowing the 'tacit knowledge' theory to wear away the justification requirement.

---

[11] See Michael Polanyi, *The Tacit Dimension* (1966), pp. 1–25.

[12] Under the 'rational fact-finder rule' that controls the appellate review of criminal convictions in the United States, 'the relevant question is whether, after viewing the evidence in the light most favorable to the prosecution, *any* rational trier of fact could have found the essential elements of the crime beyond a reasonable doubt'. *Jackson v Virginia*, 433 U.S. 307, 319 (1979). As explained by the Supreme Court (ibid), this standard of review 'gives full play to the responsibility of the trier of fact fairly to resolve conflicts in the testimony, to weigh the evidence, and to draw reasonable inferences from basic facts to ultimate facts'. See also *Lewis v Jeffers*, 497 U.S. 764, 779–83 (1990) (same); *Herrera v Collins*, 113 S. Ct. 853, 861 (1993) (same); *Nixon v Hargett*, 194 F.Supp.2d 501 (2002) (same); *Jentges v Milwaukee County Circuit Court*, 733 F. 2d 1238, 1241 (7th Cir. 1984), a decision that followed *State v Berby*, 81 Wis. 2d 677, 686 (1978) ('motive is an evidentiary circumstance which may be given as much weight as the fact-finder deems it entitled to'); *Delk v Atkinson*, 665 F. 2d 90, 98–100 (6th Cir. 1981) (no room for scrutinizing the actual reasoning process used by the fact-finder); *Bose Corporation v Consumers Union of United States Inc.*, 466 U.S. 485, 501n.17 (1984) (distinguishing between 'ordinary principles of logic and common experience which are ordinarily entrusted to the finder of fact' and 'the realm of a legal rule upon which the reviewing court must exercise its own independent judgment').

[13] See Peter Tillers, Modern Theories of Relevancy, in *Wigmore On Evidence*, Vol. 1A (Tillers Revision, 1983), p. 1082; Peter Tillers, Mapping Inferential Domains (1986) 66 B. U. L. Rev. 883, 936; Richard W. Wright, Causation, Responsibility, Risk, Probability, Naked Statistics, and Proof: Pruning the Bramble Bush by Clarifying the Concepts (1988) 73 Iowa L. Rev. 1001, 1018; Steven L. Winter, *A Clearing in the Forest: Law, Life, and Mind* (2001), p. 3 ('Much of what we know is at the level of tacit knowledge. We can ride bicycles, compose new sentences, and make complex judgments about all sorts of everyday things without conscious effort or thought').

Fact-finding by jury does not escape the justification requirement, under the 'tacit knowledge' or other theory. Fortunately, jurors' interactive deliberation in the jury room is not the only means of securing their alignment with the appropriate fact-finding standards. This alignment can and should be secured by the arsenal of monitoring and structuring devices which include *voir dire*, judgments as a matter of law, evidential admissibility rules, judicial instructions, mistrial, and, finally, the appellate review. The prevalent legal doctrine employs these devices in order to secure this alignment.[14]

This point instantiates a more general observation that belongs to the philosophy of action. In his contributions to philosophy and jurisprudence, Jonathan Cohen underscored the requirement that adjudicators determine facts through mechanisms of 'acceptance' rather than 'belief'. Belief, in his terms, is a passive state of mind, a product of some psychological causality. Beliefs simply dawn upon people, come over them, and grow on them. They may be held independently of their reflective endorsement by the believer. Acceptance, in contrast, is a standard-based categorization of propositions of fact as true, false, or probable. This categorization proceeds upon standards extraneous to the fact-finder's belief system. It involves the fact-finder's reflective encounter with the evidence, as well as construction and critical examination of fact-generating arguments. Factual propositions that become accepted at the end of this process are deemed true, false, or probable, irrespective of whether they are actually believed or not. In developing their explanatory and predictive theories, scientists ground their inquiries upon acceptance rather than beliefs. Adjudicators, according to Cohen, ought to do the same. Their decisions ought to be justified. Fact-finding founded upon belief, instead of acceptance, would never satisfy this demand. Acceptance is a prerequisite for a justified decision.[15] It demands that fact-finders articulate the reasons upon which their decision is intended to rest and juxtapose those reasons against the controlling standards. Acceptance also demands that fact-finders substitute their reasons and decision by different reasons and decision, if the controlling standards so require. Under the acceptance framework, fact-finders are allowed to apply their 'tacit knowledge' only when it is not open to a reasonable dispute, that is, if the knowledge is generally acceptable.[16]

---

[14] See Ronald J. Allen, Structuring Jury Decision-Making in Criminal Cases: A Unified Constitutional Approach to Evidentiary Devices (1980) 94 Harv. L. Rev. 321.

[15] See L. Jonathan Cohen, Belief and Acceptance (1989) 98 *Mind* 367; L. Jonathan Cohen, Should a Jury Say What it Believes or What it Accepts? (1991) 13 Cardozo L. Rev. 465; L. Jonathan Cohen, *An Essay on Belief and Acceptance* (1992), pp. 1–39, 117–25.

[16] This requirement parallels the judicial notice standard. See Federal Rule of Evidence 201(b) ('A judicially noticed fact must be one not subject to reasonable dispute in that it is either (1) generally known within the territorial jurisdiction of the trial court or (2) capable of accurate and ready determination by resort to sources whose accuracy cannot reasonably be questioned').

Fact-finders' recourse to unarticulated intuitions and reasons should be reduced to a minimum. Correspondingly, the scope of the justification requirement would expand.[17]

To sum up, adjudicative fact-finding is bound to be conducted in conditions of uncertainty. In order to be legitimate, it must be conducted in accordance with the appropriate justification standards. The remainder of this chapter examines the epistemological components of these standards. These components include the best evidence principle that controls evidence-selection and a number of criteria for determining the probabilities of the relevant factual scenarios on the evidence previously selected. These criteria articulate the epistemic meaning of the controlling standards of proof, 'preponderance of the evidence' for civil litigation and 'beyond all reasonable doubt' for criminal trials. My entire discussion falls within the rationalist tradition, which I briefly discuss at the end of this chapter along with some sceptical challenges that attempt to shatter its foundations.

B. The Best Evidence Principle[18]

The best evidence principle requires each party to a civil or criminal litigation to produce the best evidence available. This obligation is restricted to evidence logically relevant to the facts in issue and is qualified by rules and principles that suppress probative evidence on non-epistemic grounds.[19] The criterion for classifying a piece of evidence as 'best' is epistemological. The mobilization of this criterion, explains Dale Nance, 'tends to concentrate the tribunal's energies on the rational dimensions of the problem of proof'.[20] This criterion should be free from non-epistemological pragmatics, such as cost-efficient balancing of probative value against the risk of misdecision. It also postulates that fact-finders are rational decision-makers that generally follow its precepts.[21] The best evidence principle is global.[22] The traditional 'best evidence rule' that prefers original documents over their duplicates[23] is one of the many manifestations of the best evidence principle.

Failure to produce available evidence classifying as epistemically best constitutes a violation of the best evidence principle. To secure compliance with this principle any violation triggers a number of sanctions, both evidential and non-evidential.[24] The evidential sanctions include adverse inferences as well as

---

[17] See Alex Stein, The Refoundation of Evidence Law (1996) 9 Can. J. Law & Jurisp. 279, 310–12.

[18] This section draws on Dale A. Nance, The Best Evidence Principle (1988) 73 Iowa L. Rev. 227.

[19] Ibid, at 239–43.   [20] Ibid, at 240.   [21] Ibid, at 240–1.   [22] Ibid, at 229–30.

[23] Ibid.   [24] Ibid, at 244–7.

suppression of the epistemically inferior evidence that the violator offers. A party's failure to produce a witness whose testimony could be important to the trial normally leads to adverse inferences against that party. Fact-finders generally assume that the witness, if subpoenaed, would have testified unfavourably to that party. Adverse inferences are also due against a party who withholds documentary or physical evidence relevant to the trial.[25] Furthermore, when a party adduces epistemically inferior evidence—such as a copy instead of the original document; an out-of-court statement instead of witness testimony; an in-court, as opposed to line-up identification of the suspect; and a lay instead of expert witness—the court excludes the evidence if the party could produce different evidence that classifies as best. Similarly, if a witness testifies in-chief and subsequently refuses to answer questions at his or her cross-examination by the party-opponent, his or her testimony becomes inadmissible. Such testimony can only be admitted under the forfeiture principle if the party-opponent commits a wrongdoing that silences the witness. In such circumstances, the witness's testimony in-chief also turns into the best available evidence.[26]

By its very definition, the best evidence principle does not overstep the epistemological domain. This principle is one step behind the maximal individualization principle, developed in the subsequent chapters of this book.[27] The principle of maximal individualization performs two functions. Like the best evidence principle, it aims at securing that fact-finders base their decisions on the best *individualized* evidence that the parties can reasonably be expected to produce. This function of the maximal individualization principle is epistemic. This principle, however, also allocates the risk of error—an altogether separate and markedly non-epistemic function that the best evidence principle does not perform.

C. Probability and Weight of Evidence

The concept of probability represents the degree of confirmation that evidence E lends to hypothesis H.[28] This confirmation derives from an argument ascribing a particular feature (F), common to a set of previously experienced events (S), to an entirely new S-like case. Such arguments can be

---

[25] See Nance, above note 18, at 224–7.   [26] Ibid.

[27] See below, Chapters 3, 4, 6, and 7.

[28] See Georg H. Von Wright, *A Treatise on Induction and Probability* (1951), pp. 167–222; William Kneale, *Probability and Induction* (1949), pp. 114–73; Rudolf Carnap, *Logical Foundations of Probability* (1950), pp. 19–51; L. Jonathan Cohen, *An Introduction to the Philosophy of Induction and Probability* (1989), pp. 1–39.

constructed in several ways, roughly divided into frequentist, personalist, and inductivist.[29]

Frequentist probability assessments flow from the empirically enumerated incidence of Fs (#F) in a given set of S cases (#S). Under this framework, probability amounting to #F/#S—that captures the frequency of the examined occurrences or, alternatively, the investigated causal propensity[30]—represents the extent to which a new S-like case confirms the presence of F. Decision-makers calculate such probabilities by employing two fundamental principles: the complementation principle for negation and the multiplication principle (or the 'product rule') for conjunction. Both principles operate on a scale of cardinal numbers, ranging from 0 (factual impossibility) to 1 (absolute certainty). The complementation principle holds that $P(F) + P(\text{not-}F) = 1$; hence, $P(F) = 1 - P(\text{not-}F)$. The multiplication principle applies to any conjunction of two (or more) events (say, F_1 and F_2). Under this principle, $P(F_1 \& F_2) = P(F_1) \cdot P(F_2)$; and if F_1 and F_2 are mutually dependent in their occurrence, then $P(F_1 \& F_2) = P(F_1|F_2) \cdot P(F_2)$. These two principles are supplemented by the disjunction rule that applies in calculating the probability of alternate possibilities: $P(\textit{either } F_1 \textit{ or } F_2) = P(F_1) + P(F_2) - P(F_1 \& F_2)$.[31]

Personalist probability assessments originate from the degrees of belief stated by the decision-maker in numerical terms in relation to all #F/#S ratios pertaining to his or her decision. The decision-maker's degrees of belief need to be internally consistent. Usually, such beliefs derive from the decision-maker's personal experience.[32] Any such belief also may derive from the experienced frequency of the relevant occurrence (although unenumerated). Deviation from the consistency requirement entails that illogic taints the decision-maker's reasoning.[33] The decision-maker must combine the relevant degrees of belief into the overall probability assessment—a procedure ordinarily performed with the help of Bayes' theorem. Under this theorem, the probability of hypothesis H on evidence E_1—denoted as $P(H|E_1)$—equals $P(H) \cdot P(E_1|H)/P(E_1)$. When the decision-maker knows the prior probability of H and the probability of coming across evidence E_1 in a both long and random series of cases, then—if he or she also knows the probability of coming

---

[29] These are the principal categories into which such arguments fall. See Cohen, above note 28, at pp. 4–39; Tillers (1983), above note 13, at pp. 1046–95. For a more recent and more refined account, see Mike Redmayne, Objective Probability and the Assessment of Evidence (2003) 2 Law, Probability and Risk 275.   [30] Cohen, above note 28, at pp. 53–8.

[31] The probability of the conjunctive event featuring both F_1 and F_2 needs to be subtracted from the right side of this equation in order to avoid double-counting. See Kneale, above note 28, at pp. 125–6.

[32] See, e.g., Michael D. Resnik, *Choices: An Introduction to Decision Theory* (1987), pp. 68–74.

[33] Ibid. See also Bernard Robertson and G. A. Vignaux, Probability—The Logic of the Law (1993) 13 Oxford J. Leg. Stud. 457.

across E_1 in the occurrence of H—he or she would be able to determine the probability of H on E_1. Subsequently, the decision-maker uses this probability as prior in processing a further item of evidence (E_2)—a calculation that has to be repeated time and time again, until all the items of evidence (E_3, E_4, ... E_n) are taken into account.[34] Bayes' theorem expresses the logical relationship between any chosen propositions of fact. For example, if the decision-maker were to determine the probability of coming across feature F in event S— P(F|S)—his or her Bayesian formula would then be P(F)·P(S|F)/P(S). Alternatively, if he or she were to determine in probabilistic terms the extent to which feature F evidences event S, then S would become the decision-maker's hypothesis, while F would function as evidence. P(S|F) = P(S)·P(F|S)/P(F).[35]

These frameworks for probability assessment are known as aleatory or Pascalian.[36] Their foundational principles markedly differ from those of the inductivist or Baconian probability.[37] The two basic modes of probabilistic reasoning—aleatory-Pascalian and inductivist-Baconian—are logically distinct from each other. As Jonathan Cohen explains:

> Baconian probability-functions ... deserve a place alongside Pascalian ones in any comprehensive theory of non-demonstrative inference, since Pascalian functions grade probabilification *on the assumption that* all relevant facts are specified in the evidence, while Baconian ones grade it *by the extent to which* all relevant facts are specified in the evidence.[38]

Pascalian probability estimates capture chances, either in objective frequentist terms or subjectively. Baconian probability estimates capture an altogether different dimension of uncertain reasoning. They determine how informative the decision-maker's evidence is by relating that evidence to the facts in issue. Baconian estimates thus determine the extent to which the existing evidence

---

[34] Application of Bayes' theorem would face severe computational difficulties in cases involving numerous items of evidence. See Craig R. Callen, Notes on a Grand Illusion: Some Limits on the Use of Bayesian Theory in Evidence Law (1982) 57 Ind. L. J. 1, 15.

[35] Proof of Bayes' theorem is straightforward: P(F&S) = P(F|S)·P(S) = P(S|F)·P(F); hence, P(F|S) = P(F)·P(S|F)/P(S). This proof also establishes that Bayes' theorem can generate no inferential progress whatsoever. Under this theorem, in order to determine P(F|S), the decision-maker needs to know (amongst other things) P(S|F). Under the same theorem, P(S|F) = P(S)·P(F|S)/P(F), which entails that the decision-maker cannot know P(S|F) unless he or she already knows P(F|S). Bayes' theorem, therefore, can only help decision-makers to examine the inner logic of their personalist probability determinations. See Alex Stein, Judicial Fact-Finding and the Bayesian Method: The Case for Deeper Scepticism About their Combination (1996) 1 Int. J. Evidence & Proof 25; Alex Stein, Bayesioskepticism Justified (1997) 1 Int. J. Evidence & Proof 339.

[36] L. Jonathan Cohen, *The Probable and the Provable* (1977), pp. 39–43, 48–57.

[37] Ibid, at pp. 121–66.

[38] L. Jonathan Cohen, On the Psychology of Prediction: Whose is the Fallacy? (1979) 7 *Cognition* 385, 389. For detailed accounts of Baconian probability see Cohen, above note 36, at pp. 121–216; Cohen, above note 28, at pp. 4–13, 145–75.

covers the hypothesis under examination.[39] The Baconian approach favours case-specific or individualized proof over naked statistics. By 'naked statistics' I mean any information about a category of people or events not evidencing anything relevant in relation to any person or event individually. A piece of evidence is nakedly statistical when it applies to an individual case by affiliating that case to a general category of cases. Under the Baconian approach, unlike that of naked statistics, evidential support for factual propositions is determined comparatively. Decision-makers determine its relative strength—or informativeness—by measuring the gap between the existing composition of evidence and its ideal composition. The evidential support gains strength as the gap narrows and vice versa.

Under the Baconian approach, instead of calculating the favourable and the unfavourable odds under ignorance, the decision-maker evaluates the scope of the existing body of information. The decision-maker cannot perform this evaluation mathematically because it is too complex to be translated into a set of commensurable cardinal numbers. Common sense reasoning that people use in everyday life (and in adjudicative fact-finding as well) is the most prominent example of Baconianism.[40] The decision-maker's Baconian probability estimates must always rest upon experience and logic. To the extent that logic and experience warrant, the decision-maker may determine such estimates by decomposing the existing evidence into granular inferences,[41] by conducting holistic comparisons between undivided accounts of events or 'stories'[42] or by both.[43]

Under the Pascalian (aleatory) framework, the probability of the proposition 'event A either occurred or did not occur' amounts to 1 when 1 stands for certainty and 0 for impossibility. Hence, $P(A) = 1 - P(not-A)$—a canon already identified as the complementation principle for negation. Under the

---

[39] See Cohen, above note 28, at pp. 4–13, 94–109, 145–75.

[40] See L. Jonathan Cohen, Freedom of Proof, in William Twining, ed., *Facts in Law* (1983) 16 A.R.S.P. 1, 21.

[41] See John H. Wigmore, *The Principles of Judicial Proof* (2nd edn., 1931); John H. Wigmore, *The Science of Judicial Proof* (3rd edn., 1937); William Twining, *Rethinking Evidence* (1990), pp. 238–42; Peter Tillers and David Schum, Charting New Territory in Judicial Proof: Beyond Wigmore (1988) 9 Cardozo L. Rev. 907.

[42] Twining, above note 41, at pp. 219–61; Jerome Frank, *Courts on Trial* (1949), pp. 165–85; D. Neil MacCormick, *Legal Reasoning and Legal Theory* (1978), pp. 87–93; D. Neil MacCormick, The Coherence of a Case and the Reasonableness of Doubt (1980) 2 Liverpool L. Rev. 45; D. Neil MacCormick, Coherence in Legal Justification, in W. Krawietz et al. (eds.), *Theorie Der Normen* (1984), p. 37; M. A. Abu-Hareira, An Early Holistic Conception of Judicial Fact-Finding (1986) Juridical Rev. 79; Richard K. Sherwin, Law Frames: Historical Truth and Narrative Necessity in a Criminal Case (1994) 47 Stan. L. Rev. 39; Ronald J. Allen, Factual Ambiguity and a Theory of Evidence (1994) 88 NW. U. L. Rev. 604.

[43] See Twining, above note 41, at pp. 308–31; Lewis H. LaRue, Stories Versus Theories at the Cardozo Evidence Conference: It's Just Another Metaphor to Me (1992) 14 Cardozo L. Rev. 121.

Baconian (inductivist) framework of reasoning, meagre evidential support for proposition A does not entail, *ipso facto*, massive support for not-A, and vice versa. Evidential support is an empirical matter, also describable as a positive knowledge-indicator. This indicator derives from the informativeness of the existing evidence: it reflects the information that the decision-maker actually possesses, not the information that he or she does not have. Under the Pascalian framework, probability of the scenario in which two events (A and B) occur jointly is not as high as the individual probability of A or B. Indeed, succeeding in a simple one-event gamble (with regard to A only) is generally much easier than succeeding in a compound gamble (with regard to both A and B). Consequently, $P(A\&B) = P(A|B) \cdot P(B)$—a canon already identified as the multiplication principle for conjunction. Under the Baconian framework of probabilistic reasoning, evidential support for proposition A&B is equal either to the support for A or for B, whichever is weaker. Assessment of the known and gambling on the unknown are two logically distinct intellectual endeavours. Both are rational, but each is governed by its own, different type of probabilistic logic.

Pascalian probabilities can be extracted from any information, however thin it may be. Thus, if I were to toss a coin without knowing whether or not the coin is rigged, it would be warranted for me to place 1:1 odds on either heads or tails. If I later were to discover that the coin is fair, I could justifiably make an identical bet. Under the aleatory framework, my first assessment of the odds is no less warranted than my second. If I happen not to know something, it is warranted for me to assume that the unknown possibilities, some favourable and some unfavourable to my hypothesis, are equally probable.[44] Pascalian probability theories call this assumption the 'principle of indifference' or the 'principle of insufficient reason'.[45] This principle eliminates informational open-endedness that frustrates mathematical attempts at determining probability. The principle of indifference replaces this open-endedness with informational closure, easily governed by mathematical logic. Consequently, probability is calculated on the assumption that facts relevant to the calculation are fully specified in the existing evidence. Artificial as it may appear, this assumption may be justified in the long run of cases. Because the existing evidence furnishes no reasons for holding the unknown information as slanted in some particular direction, the decision-maker can rationally deem the unknown possibilities to be distributed evenly across cases. These possibilities—some favourable and some unfavourable to the examined hypothesis—can be expected to cancel each other out as the gambling proceeds. By systematically

---

[44] See Cohen, above note 28, at pp. 43–7; John M. Keynes, *A Treatise on Probability* (1921), p. 44.
[45] See Keynes, ibid.

ignoring these possibilities, the decision-maker can exercise control over the expected ratio of right versus wrong decisions.

The Baconian framework of probabilistic reasoning is founded on the 'principle of difference'. Under this framework, a proposition supported by a large amount of informative evidence qualitatively differs from a proposition resting on a slim evidential base. The decision-maker treats the former proposition as more evidenced and therefore more probable than the latter. Under the Baconian framework, knowledge is not allowed to be created from ignorance.

Consider reasoner R, reasonably familiar with English football, who was asked to estimate the outcome of an unreported match between Manchester United and Unknown Amateurs that took place in 2003. R's familiarity with English football allows him to estimate that it is highly probable, although not absolutely certain, that Manchester United won the match. If so, what probability should be attributed by R to the proposition that Manchester United did *not* win the match? Under the Pascalian framework, R's state of knowledge versus ignorance would logically compel him to ascribe some probability to this proposition. If R were rationally to translate his estimation of Manchester United's victory into betting odds, he would have to assign some numerical value to the possibility that United had not won the match. To say that R is almost, but not absolutely, certain about his estimation entails an acknowledgement of the chance that this estimation failed to capture the reality. Therefore, if R's betting odds on United's victory are, say, 500 to 1, this would logically entail that R estimates the probability of the proposition 'Manchester United won the match' as amounting to 500/501. This probability is very high indeed, but it still falls short of certainty. If R wants to be a coherent bettor, his betting odds on 'Manchester United did *not* win the match' would therefore have to be 1 to 500 which would imply the probability of 1/501. In this way, R's probability estimates will be forced to obey the complementation principle for negation according to which probabilities of any proposition and its negation always add up to 1.

Now assume that R was asked, under similar conditions, to estimate the outcome of another unreported match played by Manchester United in 2003. R was informed that this match had been played against Uncredited Amateurs (and was totally independent of the match against Unknown Amateurs[46]). Once again R estimated that the probability of United's victory is 500/501. The probability that Manchester United had won twice would thus have to be estimated by R as 250,000/251,001. This conclusion is logically inevitable

---

[46] I make this assumption in order to avoid unnecessary complications in the subsequent probability calculation.

because R's chances of not capturing the reality by *one* of his estimations have been doubled. The probability of the proposition 'Manchester United had not won at least one of the two matches' would consequently have to be estimated by R as 0.004. In this and similar examples, absence of evidence functions—rather anomalously—as a reason for increasing the relevant probability. This feature of the Pascalian calculus exhibits creation of knowledge from ignorance.

I now turn to Baconian reasoning. Assume that R—the very same person, situated under similar conditions—was asked to estimate the *degree of evidential support* for the following propositions:

(1) Manchester United had won the match against Unknown Amateurs;
(2) Manchester United had won the match against Uncredited Amateurs.

In making his estimations, R was requested to use, instead of words, the scale of cardinal numbers ranging from 0 to 100. R's familiarity with English football allows him to generalize that teams staffed by skilled professional players virtually always defeat amateur teams. This generalization has a strong evidential support, but still falls short of certainty. This is so because the informational base of this generalization is incomplete, which is true of any generalization that may be used in practical matters.[47] Aware of this obvious limitation (that attaches to any inductive reasoning[48]), R grades the evidential support for both proposition (1) and proposition (2) as amounting to 98. This grading does not imply that in 2 out of 100 similar instances one of the amateur teams avoids the defeat. Rather, it indicates the presence of a very strong—although not complete—evidential support for propositions (1) and (2).

Subsequently, R was asked to estimate the degree of evidential support for propositions:

(3) Manchester United had not won the match against Unknown Amateurs; and
(4) Manchester United had not won the match against Uncredited Amateurs.

Upon reflection, R finds out that his knowledge about English football lends no support to any of these propositions. He is not aware of any match in which an amateur team played against professionals and did not lose. At the

---

[47] See below pp. 92–9.
[48] Provided, of course, that the fact-finder's induction is intended to amplify the existing knowledge, rather than merely restate it in one form or another. See Cohen, above note 28, at pp. 1–4.

same time, R well recognizes that his information is incomplete. R then embarks upon the following reasoning:

(i) Evidential support for propositions (1) and (2) is very strong, but not entirely comprehensive. Ascribing full evidential support to these propositions, without accounting for this incompleteness, would be unwarranted.

(ii) Propositions (3) and (4) have no evidential support whatsoever, since I am aware of not a single game in which amateurs have surprised professionals. Ascribing *any* epistemic credential to these altogether unevidenced propositions would therefore amount to creating knowledge from ignorance. Consequently, evidential support for propositions (3) and (4) is 0.

There is still *a chance* that either proposition (1) or proposition (2) is false. Correspondingly, there is still a chance that either proposition (3) or proposition (4) is true. However, calculus of chances and evaluation of evidential support are two different frameworks of reasoning in conditions of uncertainty. Each of these frameworks applies its own distinct criteria for determining probability. The Pascalian framework commits itself *a priori* to the complementation principle because any chance—both evidenced and unevidenced—counts as a chance.[49] This, however, is not the case with the Baconian framework of reasoning. Under the Baconian framework, informational voids do not evidence anything. Scanty evidential support for proposition A does not entail, *eo ipso*, the existence of massive support for not-A (or vice versa).

Therefore, if R were to evaluate the evidential support for the proposition 'Manchester United had won twice', his assessment would stand unmodified. He would be bound to estimate this support as *not* falling below 98. In evaluating evidential support, as distinguished from calculating chances, the multiplication principle for conjunction is, therefore, also inapplicable. To be sure, by committing himself to both proposition (1) and proposition (2), R increases his chances of not capturing the reality. This, however, does not detract anything from the evidential base supporting each of those propositions and, correspondingly, their conjunction.

The two modes of probabilistic reasoning may be brought closer to each other. Pascalian probability assessments may be accompanied by judgements regarding their resiliency or evidential weight. This criterion may also be

---

[49] Under the Pascalian framework, for example, the reasoner would have to ascribe some probability to the proposition 'Manchester United may not have won one of the games because Ryan Giggs may have decided to upset Tim Howard by scoring own goals'.

called invariance.[50] Under this criterion, the weight (that is, the resiliency) of a given probability assessment will depend on its survival (or the extent of its survival) in the event of change in its underlying informational base that might be effected by the flow of new evidence. Because evidence is always lacking, the potential for arrival of new evidence makes any probability assessment open to revision. An assessment's susceptibility to such revision—that is, the degree of its variance and invariance—will determine its resiliency and corresponding weight. Some probability assessments are less open to revision and, consequently, more invariant than others; and hence the need to account for this factor. The greater the ability of a probability assessment to withstand potential changes in its informational base, the more resilient, more invariant, and, correspondingly, more reliable a probability assessment it is.[51]

In practical reasoning, to which adjudicative fact-finding belongs, the resiliency criterion cannot be too demanding. If carried to its logical extreme, this criterion would not take fact-finders very far. Because each factual occurrence is unique—so that two separate occurrences are never identical in every individual respect—the most resilient, but plainly unhelpful, proposition would be one that denies validity to all probability assessments. A non-absolute, but still stringent, resiliency criterion would disqualify less, but still too many, probability assessments. In practical affairs, this disqualification would block the entire fact-finding enterprise and must, therefore, be rejected for this reason alone. From a theoretical viewpoint, too, this disqualification is profoundly problematic. Holding a probability assessment insufficiently evidenced and holding it unhelpful are two analytically separate decisions. A non-resilient probability assessment might still be helpful to bookmakers and, in some contexts, to adjudicators as well. As demonstrated in Chapters 3 and 4, the right adjudicative combination of probability and weight (or probability and resiliency) depends on how the legal system wants to apportion the risk of error.[52] Adjudicative apportionment of the risk of error is not an epistemological problem. This problem is situated in the domain of political morality.

Application of the Pascalian probability calculus in adjudicative fact-finding can be rejected when it yields probability assessments that are not sufficiently resilient. Any such rejection, however, would be motivated by moral and political reasons that determine the right apportionment of the risk of

[50] As a general criterion that defines objectivity as invariance under a range of possible transformations, this concept was coined by Robert Nozick, *Invariances: The Structure of the Objective World* (2001), pp. 75–90, 99.

[51] See, e.g., R. A. Fisher, Statistical Methods for Research Workers (7th edn., 1938), p. 120; ff., James Logue, *Projective Probability* (1995), pp. 78–95; Neil B. Cohen, Confidence in Probability: Burdens of Persuasion in a World of Imperfect Knowledge (1985) 60 N. Y. U. L. Rev. 385.

[52] I first made this point in my doctorate dissertation 'The Law of Evidence and the Problem of Risk-Distribution' (University of London, 1990).

error. There are no cogent epistemological reasons for rejecting adjudicative Pascalianism. Jonathan Cohen, however, famously claimed that such reasons actually exist.[53] According to Cohen, introduction of Pascalianism into adjudicative fact-finding would generate paradoxes and anomalies—a controversial claim that led to the famous 'Probability Debate'.[54] Most of Cohen's paradoxes, along with several others, are analysed and explained away in Chapter 3. Here, I only discuss and explain away Cohen's 'conjunction paradox'. Relative to other paradoxes and anomalies pointed to by Cohen, this paradox has received the greatest scholarly attention.

Consider a civil lawsuit filed by claimant C. In order to succeed in that lawsuit, C needs to preponderantly establish two mutually independent propositions, p1 and p2. Apparently, it would not suffice for C to establish that the probability of p1 and that of p2 both equal 0.7. Under the product rule for conjunctive probabilities (the multiplication principle), the overall probability of C's case would only amount to 0.49. This probability fails to satisfy the preponderance-of-the-evidence standard, under which (in numerical terms) a claimant will only prevail if the probability of his or her case exceeds 0.5. According to Cohen, this counterintuitive outcome demonstrates that grounding adjudicative fact-finding on Pascalian probabilities is anomalous.[55]

This paradox is unreal. A distinction needs to be drawn between *elemental propositions* (such as formation of a contract, its breach by the defendant, and the ensuing damage) and *intermediary propositions* (such as those that specify the terms of the transaction offered by the claimant and the defendant's acceptance of this offer). Elemental propositions refer to the lawsuit's constitutive elements as determined by the controlling substantive law. Hohfeld termed them 'operative facts'.[56] Intermediary propositions are ones that establish elemental propositions. Normally, in order to establish an elemental proposition, one needs more than one intermediary proposition. This distinction needs to be maintained at its clearest because the law requires each elemental proposition to be established separately by the party upon whom the burden of proof lies.[57] There is no requirement in the law that the entire conjunction of the elemental propositions be established as more probable than not.[58]

Assume now that C is seeking a declaratory judgment to the effect that there is a binding contract between her and the defendant. The probability of

---

[53] See Cohen, above note 36, at pp. 58–120.
[54] For summary of this debate see William L. Twining and Alex Stein (eds.), *Evidence and Proof* (1992), pp. xxi–xxiv.   [55] See Cohen, above note 36, at pp. 58–62.
[56] Wesley N. Hohfeld, *Fundamental Legal Conceptions as Applied in Judicial Reasoning* (1923), pp. 32–5.
[57] See Alex Stein, Of Two Wrongs that Make a Right: Two Paradoxes of the Evidence Law and their Combined Economic Justification (2001) 79 Texas L. Rev. 1199, 1204–5.   [58] Ibid.

this allegation is established as equalling 0.7, and the judgment is rendered as requested. At some later stage, C comes to court complaining that the contract was breached by the same defendant and requests another declaratory judgment that confirms this new allegation. The judge finds that the probability of this allegation equals 0.7 and awards C the requested judgment. Finally, C sues the same defendant for damages, and the probability of her allegations in this lawsuit is also found by the judge to equal 0.7. Under the controlling proof doctrine, C should be allowed recovery.

C would have been equally entitled to recovery if the three issues were tried together. The compensatory remedy sought by C would have rested upon two interim declaratory judgments, as described above. Analytically, there would be three judgments here, which combine into one for expediency reasons alone. Because each judgment stands on its own proof as successfully provided by C, C is entitled to the requested series of judgments.[59] This outcome aligns with any plausible fairness standard because C's evidence prevailed over that of her opponent.[60]

This approach also has an economic justification, particularly suitable for tort cases.[61] The civil proof doctrine focuses on accuracy *ex post* by requiring adjudicators to reconstruct the relevant events, as they unfolded in reality, including the actual damage to the claimant, based on the information available at the trial. This accuracy *ex post* is both expensive and does not contribute to optimal deterrence. The average person contemplating a potentially damaging action is unaware of the information that might become available at his or her subsequent trial. He or she can only take into account the information reasonably available before the action (*ex ante*). The average person is also unaware of the actual damage that his or her contemplated action might produce. He or she can only take into account the average damage associated with similar activities. Ideally, therefore, a tort defendant should only pay for the expected damage, that is, for the average damage associated with his or her action multiplied by the action's *ex ante* probability of inflicting that damage. The state should collect this amount – a Pigouvian tax[62] – from every person creating risk of damage. This regime would set optimal incentives for individuals contemplating hazardous actions. Such actions would only take place when the actor's expected benefit exceeds the Pigouvian tax. Consequently, such actions would only be taken when they increase the aggregate social welfare.

---

[59] See Alex Stein, An Essay on Uncertainty and Fact-Finding in Civil Litigation, with Special Reference to Contract Cases (1998) 48 U. Toronto L.J. 299, 311–12, n. 27.

[60] For more details see below pp. 220–2.

[61] This justification was initially developed in Stein, above note 57.

[62] See generally William J. Baumol, On Taxation and the Control of Externalities (1972) 62 *Am. Econ. Rev.* 307 (delineating Pigou's tax criteria and identifying their operational limitations).

The state prosecution mechanism, however, is inefficient for remedying torts. Because many risks are invisible until they materialize into damages, the state cannot exercise efficient control over impositions of risk. The state is also unable to police many, if not most, damaging occurrences on the ground because doing it is too expensive. The state prosecution mechanism therefore only applies in special regulatory areas, such as criminal law, that involve particularly harmful (and therefore regulated) activities. As a result of this enforcement constraint, torts are prosecuted by self-interested individuals— the tort victims—upon whom the state confers a license to sue.[63]

This system would be doomed to failure if these individuals had no private incentive to sue, that is, if their litigation expenditures were to exceed their expected return from the litigation. The state therefore provides the required incentive by taking two measures. First, it subsidizes adjudication. More importantly, it allows a tort victim to recover compensation for his or her entire damage, as opposed to the expected average damage (the total average damage reduced by its *ex ante* probability of not being inflicted). The winner-takes-all principle thus substitutes the ideal-world formula for optimal awards. Under this principle, when the claimant's case against the defendant is more probable than not, the claimant is awarded full recovery. When the claimant's case falls below that probability threshold, the claimant recovers nothing.

Under the ideal-world formula, the number of underusers of the adjudication facility (meritorious claimants who decide not to sue) would be greater than under the winner-takes-all regime. Awards awaiting successful claimants under the ideal-world formula are less attractive than under the winner-takes-all principle. For the average claimant, proving the expected average damage figure (a general social fact) is also more expensive than demonstrating his or her personal damage. The ideal-world formula therefore drives away many deserving claimants and thereby dilutes deterrence.

Under this formula, the number of overusers of the adjudication facility (unmeritorious claimants) would also be greater than under the winner-takes-all regime. Because any meaningful probability that attaches to a lawsuit would be good for recovery, more unmeritorious lawsuits would be filed and adjudicated than under the winner-takes-all principle. The overuse problem would be further exacerbated by the externalized adjudication expenses. The ideal-world formula invites too many claimants to impose litigation expenses upon defendants and to eat away the adjudication subsidy. This problem is more acute in the United States than in England. The American system of civil procedure generally rejects the English 'costs follow the event' approach.[64]

---

[63] See Richard A. Posner, *Economic Analysis of Law* (6th edn., 2003), p. 209.
[64] See Adrian A. S. Zuckerman, *Civil Procedure* (2003), pp. 872–4.

Under that system, a litigant does not participate in the payment of the opponent's expenditures when the opponent wins the case.[65] This system enables a party to impose part of the litigation expenses upon his or her adversary.[66]

Overusers of the adjudication facility would also fail to produce the deterrence benefits that the ideal-world formula strives to attain. Because their only interest is to secure for themselves a profitable outcome of the venture, such claimants would settle for any award that *they*—not the social welfare perspective—would consider agreeable.[67] They would generally accept cheap settlement offers made by defendants. Cheap settlements that leave wrong-doers undeterred can consequently be expected to mushroom.[68] Frivolous lawsuits initiated by the overusers would also generate adverse selection or, alternatively, an additional social cost. Aware of their lawsuits' frivolous nature and cognizant of the ensuing institutional mistrust of *all* lawsuits, the overusers would attempt to pool with the owners of good lawsuits. The owners of good lawsuits would consequently have to invest more resources and efforts in litigation (by gathering more evidence, for example) in order to separate their lawsuits from the bad ones. Because the ideal-world formula already reduces the expected return for the average lawsuit, this additional investment would turn some good lawsuits into non-profitable. Holders of those lawsuits would prefer not to initiate them. The market-for-lemons scenario[69] would,

---

[65] See *Alyeska Pipeline Co. v Wilderness Soc'y*, 421 U.S. 240 (1975) (holding that a court may not award attorneys' fees to a prevailing party unless expressly authorized by statute).

[66] See Steven Shavell, The Fundamental Divergence Between the Private and the Social Motive to Use the Legal System (1997) 26 J. Leg. Stud. 575, 584. Under the ideal-world formula, a low-probability lawsuit would not be considered 'frivolous'. The cost-shifting measure provided by Rule 11 of the Federal Rules of Civil Procedure would consequently not apply.

[67] See Shavell, ibid, at 581–97.

[68] Such claimants would usually be represented by attorneys acting on a contingent-fee basis and running portfolios of cases. Those attorneys would initiate settlements at a point at which their expected earnings from the litigation equalize with their opportunity costs (calculated on the hourly-fee basis). This point is well-developed with regard to class action attorneys. See John C. Coffee, Jr., The Unfaithful Champion: The Plaintiff as Monitor in Shareholder Litigation (1985) 48 (3) Law & Contemp. Probs. 5; John C. Coffee, Jr., Understanding the Plaintiff's Attorney: The Implications of Economic Theory for Private Enforcement of Law Through Class and Derivative Actions (1986) 86 Colum. L. Rev. 669. For defence of frivolous lawsuits see Charles M. Yablon, The Good, the Bad, and the Frivolous Case: An Essay on Probability and Rule 11 (1996) 44 UCLA L. Rev. 65.

[69] As famously set by George Akerlof, The Market for Lemons: Quality Uncertainty and the Market Mechanism (1970) 84 *Quart. J. Econ.* 488. This scenario unfolds when honest people are imitated by liars and consequently cannot credibly transmit their private information to others. Sellers of used cars, both honest and dishonest, are typically unable to credibly inform potential buyers about the quality of their cars. Consequently, consumers cannot discriminate between cars and would pay no more than the average price for any car that is offered for sale. Owners of the best used cars therefore decide not to sell them, thereby reducing the average quality and price of second-hand cars. Faced with this situation, owners of the second-best used cars also decide not to sell their cars, thus dragging the average car quality and price further down. This process is repeated until the market is turned into a 'market for lemons', where only the poorest quality cars are traded.

perhaps, be too morbid for the present context. The additional separating
investment that the owner of a good lawsuit would have to make in the average case does not appear to be large enough to wipe out his or her expected
returns (this point is more intuitive than analytical). But even in this scenario,
meritorious claimants and society in general incur unnecessary expenses. The
winner-takes-all principle is therefore preferable to the ideal-world formula.
This principle increases the number of meritorious lawsuits and decreases the
number of unmeritorious lawsuits in the real world. This real-world rationale
turns trial awards into a discrete component of tort litigation and removes
the probability of the claimant's damage from the multiplication formula.

The remaining elements of that formula—the probability of the allegation
that the claimant is entitled to the defendant's precautions and the probability
of the allegation that the defendant breached this entitlement—still require
discussion.[70] The product rule for conjunctive probabilities does not apply to
these elements as well, and I now explain why.[71] The probability of the allegation that the defendant breached the claimant's entitlement needs to be greater
than 0.5 to identify the claimant as the victim of the defendant's transgression
(for reasons stated above, only victims can sue). This *ex post* probability of
transgression is problematic from the deterrence perspective because it does

[70] Ronald J. Allen and Sarah A. Jehl, Burdens of Persuasion in Civil Cases: Algorithms
v. Explanations (2003) Mich. St. L. Rev. 893, 922–9, dispute my three-element depiction of a
paradigmatic lawsuit. They claim that the number of elements is an empirical matter and point to different examples that allegedly contradict my model. Based on these examples, Allen and Jehl contend
that I have mismodelled the legal system. One of these examples is a hostile-environment harassment
claim, filed under the California law. Allen and Jehl argue (ibid, at 928, n. 140) that any such lawsuit
involves no less than eight elements, namely: (1) the employment relationship between the claimant
and the defendant employer; (2) the employment relationship between the defendant employer and
the person engaging in a harassing conduct at the workplace; (3) the claimant must either witness or
be directly victimized by that harassment; (4) the claimant's protected status (say, as a female
employee) must be a motivating factor for that harassment; (5) the harassment must be unwelcome
and sufficiently severe or pervasive that it had the purpose or effect of worsening the claimant's
employment conditions and creating an intimidating, hostile, abusive, or offensive working environment; (6) a reasonable person in the same position as the claimant would perceive that environment
as intimidating, hostile, abusive, or offensive; (7) the claimant, too, must perceive the environment as
intimidating, hostile, abusive, or offensive; (8) the environment must cause the claimant injury,
damage, loss, or harm. I think it is easy to see that elements (1), (2), (4), and (5) combine into the
claimant's entitlement, that element (3) constitutes the entitlement's breach and that elements (6),
(7), and (8) combine into the claimant's damage. Under my theory, the product rule should apply in
calculating the conjunctive probabilities of (1), (2), (4), and (5) and of (6), (7), and (8), respectively.
The same reasoning applies to all other examples brought by Allen and Jehl, and it is easy to see
why. Every action for money damages needs to rely on the claimant's entitlement, its breach by the
defendant and the ensuing damage. The way in which these elements are worded should not matter.
Adjudicators basing their decisions on such linguistic contingencies are wrong. My thesis does not
purport to model such errors (they are uninteresting from the normative point of view). Instead, it
develops a normative model for making economically correct decisions under the real-world
constraints (the 'second-best'). See Stein, above note 57, at 1201–3, 1221–34.

[71] See also Stein, above note 57, at 1221–34.

not align with the *ex ante* probability of transgression relied upon by prospective transgressors. The law therefore uses the probability of the entitlement to attain the desired alignment. The visibility element, uniformly featured by legal entitlements, facilitates this alignment. Under the definition of any entitlement, the entitlement needs to be reasonably ascertainable at the time and in the circumstances of its breach (*ex ante*). Information about the entitlement's existence is reasonably available to potential violators. This feature permeates the entire body of private law. The publicity requirements that attach to property rights,[72] the mutual disclosure that defines contractual entitlements,[73] and the duty of care requirement in torts exhibit this feature.[74] By establishing the entitlement's existence as more probable than not, the claimant therefore would also establish that the entitlement was reasonably ascertainable *ex ante*. Failure to establish this condition would result in the claimant's defeat.

This condition aligns the information available at the defendant's trial with what the defendant knew or ought to have known about the claimant's entitlement at the time of the action. From the defendant's perspective, the *ex ante* probability of breach only attaches to the hypothetical scenario in which the action contemplated by the defendant falls under the relevant liability rule after causing damage to the claimant. This hypothetical scenario depends on one factor alone: the probability of the claimant's entitlement to the defendant's precautions against the claimant's damage. An individual contemplating a potentially damaging action considers this scenario by asking the following question: Would I be liable in torts if I take the action and it causes damage to someone? The probability of this hypothetical scenario therefore overlaps the probability of the claimant's entitlement. This factor explains the combined, rather than conjunctive, functioning of the entitlement's probability and the *ex post* probability of the entitlement's breach. The probability of the claimant's entitlement to the defendant's precautions—the *ex ante* probability of the breach in the hypothetical scenario in which the defendant fails to take the necessary precautions and causes damage to the claimant—functions as a misalignment-corrector for the *ex post* probability of the breach, and not as its conjunctive companion. The two probabilities, therefore, must not be multiplied in

---

[72] See, e.g., Jason S. Johnston, Legal Formalities, in Peter Newman, ed., *The New Palgrave Dictionary of Economics and the Law* Vol. 2 (1998), pp. 524–30.

[73] See, e.g., Avery W. Katz, Contract Formation and Interpretation, in Peter Newman, ed., *The New Palgrave Dictionary of Economics and the Law* Vol. 1 (1998), pp. 425, 429–30.

[74] Strict liability is not an exception to this observation, as there are virtually no cases in which a reasonably unascertainable entitlement has received a strict liability protection. See W. Page Keeton, *Prosser & Keeton On Torts* (5th edn., 1984), pp. 537, 545–59.

determining the probability of the claimant's entire case. This point is analytical[75] and normative.[76]

In this model, the concept of 'entitlement' refers to the claimant's case-specific entitlement. In the domain of torts, this concept encapsulates the claimant's entitlement to the defendant's precautions against the claimant's possible damage. The probability of this entitlement depends on the case-specific factual background that may or may not give rise to the entitlement under the controlling substantive law. The concept of 'entitlement' does not refer to the entitlement's general existence in the book of laws.[77]

Ronald Allen explains away the conjunction paradox in a different way which I find persuasive. According to him, the product rule ought to be suppressed because in adjudication, disjunctive arguments that rely upon merely statistical cumulation of doubts are generally not allowed. Both the claimant and the defendant must present before the court their competing accounts of events *as coherent stories*. Disjunctive arguments uniformly fail to satisfy this criterion. For example, a defendant ought not to be allowed to benefit from the combined probability of the proposition 'I did not do what the claimant says I did; and even if I did it, the claimant did not sustain any damage; and if she did sustain it, then what I did is causally unrelated to the damage'.[78]

Allen's criterion for fact-finding, however, is not an epistemological must. From a purely epistemological viewpoint, insisting on the application of the product rule is perfectly reasonable. To justify his rationale for suppressing the product rule, Allen needs to delineate its advantages outside the epistemological domain. These advantages are yet to be articulated. My theory does not offer an epistemological must either. It only points out that under the proper

[75] Allen and Jehl (above note 70, at 922) describe this point as a theory in which 'the formalities of the microeconomic argument are held hostage to an unjustified and ad hoc vision of the empirical world'. For reasons stated in the text, I beg to disagree.

[76] Allen and Jehl (above note 70, at 921) correctly categorize my theory as economic modelling. They also intimate that such modelling is methodologically inferior to 'empirical accuracy' (ibid, n. 119). This critique is misdirected. Empirical data need to be perceived through theoretical lenses (models) in order to make sense. See Milton Friedman, The Methodology of Positive Economics, in Daniel M. Hausman, ed., *The Philosophy of Economics: An Anthology* (2nd edn., 1994), pp. 180–213. Allen and Jehl also do not articulate the methodological objectives and limitations of their 'empirical accuracy' approach. Consider the following empirical observation. One judge determines facts by tossing a coin and another by reference to what he had for breakfast. Although empirically accurate, this observation lacks normative significance and therefore does not advance the understanding of the law. It provides potentially useful information about two idiosyncratic judges, but tells nothing about the law's normative demands.

[77] As wrongly understood by Allen and Jehl, above note 70, at 921. Allen and Jehl misconstrue my model by stating that, under the model's conditions, the entitlement's probability would virtually always be either 1 or 0 (because, as a matter of law, the entitlement is either present or not). See ibid, at 921, 923–4. For obvious reasons, factual propositions underlying legal entitlements always have probabilities ranging between 0 and 1. Factual scenarios are never absolutely certain or absolutely impossible.

[78] See Ronald J. Allen, The Nature of Juridical Proof (1991) 13 Cardozo L. Rev. 373.

understanding of positive law suppression of the product rule is not counter-intuitive at all when it comes to elemental propositions. To propositions classifying as intermediary the product rule should apply with full force.[79]

The legal system's choice between suppressing and applying the product rule is not epistemological in character. This choice is about the apportion-ment of the risk of error which once again is a moral and political, rather than epistemological, issue. This and related issues are taken up in the subsequent chapters of this book. Allocation of the risk of error generated by the doctrinal suppression of the product rule can, indeed, be justified on the grounds of both fairness[80] and utility.[81]

D. Scepticism vs. Rationalism

Adjudicative fact-finding rests on a number of foundational assumptions, properly described as rationalist.[82] These assumptions identify accuracy or, in Bentham's terms, rectitude of decision as the fact-finding's principal objective. Attainment of this objective is a prerequisite for implementing the substantive law in accordance with its demands. Accuracy of decision refers to the correspondence between the adjudicative findings of fact and the empirical truth. This correspondence can virtually never be certain, but can be probable. Fact-finders can rationally determine this probability relationship by analysing evidence and by relying on experience-based generalizations. To facilitate this task, the legal system can utilize trial procedures that include adversarial presentation of evidence and cross-examination of witnesses.

These rationalist assumptions face sceptical challenges. These challenges come from two distinct domains. One of these domains is philosophical. The other is cognitive psychology, also tagged as 'behavioural economics' (or as 'behavioural law & economics', when it targets law and legal decisions). Philosophical challenges to rationalism in adjudicative fact-finding go along two different routes.[83] One of these routes is metaphysical. Arguments taking this route go all the way back to Descartes. They deny the very possibility of knowing or probabilistically approximating the truth. The other route is epistemological. Arguments taking this route hold that adjudicative (and,

---

[79] See above, note 70 and accompanying text.

[80] See Richard Lempert, The New Evidence Scholarship: Analyzing the Process of Proof (1986) 66 B. U. L. Rev. 439, 450–4; Alex Stein, The Refoundation of Evidence Law (1996) 9 Can. J. L. & Juris. 279, 336–8.

[81] Richard A. Posner, An Economic Approach to the Law of Evidence (1999) 51 Stan. L. Rev. 1477, 1512–14; Stein, above note 57; Saul Levmore, Conjunction and Aggregation (2001) 99 Mich. L. Rev. 723.   [82] See Twining, above note 41, at pp. 71–82.

[83] I brush subtleties aside.

indeed, any other) fact-finding can never have adequate epistemological justification. This predicament—say the sceptics—makes the facts that fact-finders determine 'socially constructed' at best.[84] In the worst scenario, adjudicative fact-finding becomes imbued with arbitrariness (in a disguise of 'pragmatism') and politics.[85]

The metaphysical route is unpromising. Those who take it begin with the unfalsifiable 'brains in a vat' scenario. In this scenario, all of us are brains in a vat wired to some computer operated by an evil demon. This computer feeds us—the brains—with the sensations that we happen to experience.[86] The common-sense view of the world, as situated outside us, dismisses this scenario, but cannot refute it. Arguably, there are no such things as miscarriage of justice, capital punishment, race discrimination, and sexual harassment. These are just our mental representations that will all go away when the demon decides to replace the current computer program with more pleasant stuff.

Looking forward to the demon's benevolence is not our most rational course of action, though. We can *rationally* reject the 'brains in a vat' scenario without refuting it. This scenario explains our experiences in a very peculiar way that, admittedly, cannot be refuted. Yet, its explanation of our experiences does not survive the methodological competition with the common-sense view of the world. First, the sceptical scenario is a patchwork of untestable ad-hoc stories. If I ask the sceptic to explain to me the demon's desire to foist on me the 'snow in New York' sensation, he or she may well tell me that there is a second demon that manipulates the first one.[87] Such stories are methodologically inferior to the common-sense view of the world that does not merely point to the 'snow sensation', but also gives us a well-integrated reasoning apparatus that explains where the snow comes from and how.[88] Second, the common-sense view of the world is uncomplicated. It provides a straightforward causal explanation for our beliefs as induced by the objects in our surroundings.[89] The sceptical scenario, by contrast, offers us a highly complicated mechanism featuring demons, computers, and brains in a vat, but no causal theory at all. Other things being equal, the common-sense view of the

---

[84] For summary and discussion of this claim see Twining, above note 41, at pp. 112–17.

[85] See Kenneth Graham Jr., There'll Always be an England: The Instrumental Ideology of Evidence (1987) 85 Mich. L. Rev. 1204; Michael L. Seigel, A Pragmatic Critique of Modern Evidence Scholarship (1994) 88 Nw. U. L. Rev. 995; Donald Nicolson, Truth, Reason and Justice: Epistemology and Politics in Evidence Discourse (1994) 57 M.L.R. 726.

[86] For a particularly useful account see Jonathan Vogel, Cartesian Skepticism and Inference to the Best Explanation (1990) 87 *J. Phil.* 658.   [87] Ibid.

[88] Ibid.

[89] Cf. Hilary Putnam, *Reason, Truth and History* (1981), pp. 5–21 (offering such causal explanation).

world should therefore be accorded preference on the grounds of methodological simplicity.[90]

The common-sense view of the world systematically employs higher-level regularities to explain the lower-level explanations and phenomena. For example, in explaining snow in New York, it has physics, chemistry, and geography to rely upon. This pivotal feature is not present in the sceptical scenario. This scenario has only one level of explanations, which makes it methodologically inferior to the common-sense view of the world.[91] Amongst the reasons participating in the Cartesian investigation, reasons supporting the common-sense view of the world therefore classify as strongest. The common-sense view of the world may not be proven beyond all reasonable doubt. Yet, any philosopher would have to adopt this view if he or she were to select 'clear and convincing evidence' as the controlling proof standard.

The epistemological challenge to fact-finding rationalism fails on more or less similar grounds. If best reasons available were to classify as satisfying the epistemological justification requirement for fact-finding, the burden of proof that epistemological sceptics would have to discharge would be onerous. The sceptics, however, refuse to consider the balance-of-reasons as good enough a justification. By making this move they alleviate their own burden of proof. They adopt a position akin to that of a criminal defendant who only needs to raise a doubt in order to be acquitted. Amongst the stringent criteria for epistemological justification that help the sceptics develop their challenge, 'justified true belief'[92] is probably the most popular. Typically, this criterion (or one of its variants) supports the sceptical claim that fact-finding in general and adjudicative fact-finding in particular are a social construct that sustains itself by fiat rather than reason. Under this criterion, a fact-finder's belief in a hypothesis would only qualify as 'knowledge' if it is both 'justified' and 'true'. The fact-finder must have good evidence for believing in the hypothesis. Holding such evidence would make the fact-finder's belief 'justified', although not yet true. To qualify as true, a properly evidenced hypothesis needs to correspond to reality—a criterion never satisfied in such practical reasoning as adjudication that resorts to non-verifiable findings of fact. Apart from that, evidential reasons justifying the fact-finder's belief in a particular hypothesis need to have a both instrumental and non-accidental connection to the truth of that hypothesis. The justification for the fact-finder's belief needs to track the belief's truth which is yet another stringent criterion that can scarcely, if ever, be satisfied.[93] Under this criterion, when a fact-finder believes that

[90] See Vogel, above note 86.   [91] Ibid.

[92] See Edmund L. Gettier, Is Justified True Belief Knowledge? (1963) 23 *Analysis* 121.

[93] See Robert Nozick, *The Nature of Rationality* (1993), pp. 64–100 (analysing and criticizing this requirement).

witness W testified truthfully and W's testimony turns out to be actually true, the fact-finder would only classify as *knowing* that W testified truthfully if his or her reasons for believing W are amongst the reasons that make W's testimony true. For example, the fact-finder believes W because W served as a lieutenant-colonel in the Air Force where he earned an impeccable reputation for integrity and developed a unique ability to perceive and memorize events. In reality, however, W's testimony is true because it happened to be successful guesswork. The fact-finder's belief would then fail to qualify as knowledge, even though it would be both justified and true.

Adjudicators do not even purport to satisfy the 'justified true belief' standard or similar criteria for knowledge. Instead, they identify the most plausible factual scenario and evaluate the evidential supporting reasons. In a civil case such reasons generally warrant a verdict when they are preponderantly strong. To convict a criminal defendant, such reasons need to be overwhelmingly strong. Failure to meet these standards results in a factual finding against the party upon whom the burden of proof lies. These relaxed criteria make adjudicative fact-finding an easy target for epistemological sceptics. Treating verdicts, both civil and criminal, as social—and, consequently, politicized—constructions of reality becomes not only intellectually engaging, but also plausible.

Under the 'best reasons' approach, however, the sceptical challenge will not do. This challenge posits a philosophically seductive dilemma, a grand Either/Or. Epistemological sceptics tell us that we must either subscribe to and satisfy the most stringent foundationalist criteria for knowledge or accept the forces of subjectivism and relativism that envelop us with epistemological chaos.[94] Richard Bernstein identifies this dilemma as 'Cartesian Anxiety'[95] that originates from a false dichotomy.[96] Absence of proven foundations upon which fact-finders' knowledge can safely rest does not entail the relativist 'everything goes' as a consequence. This inference is unwarranted. Before taking one of the relativist positions, we should consider the 'best evidential reasons' approach. Specifically, we should compare the methodological credentials of this approach with those of epistemological scepticism. Epistemological scepticism is self-refuting. By marking all knowledge-claims as unjustifiable, this form of scepticism excludes itself from the category of knowledge. Epistemological scepticism also offers no higher-level and lower-level standards by which its theory can be judged. It clashes with the common-sense view of the world.[97]

---

[94] Richard Bernstein, *Beyond Objectivism and Relativism* (1983), pp. 1–25.

[95] Ibid, at pp. 16–20.   [96] Ibid.

[97] Sceptical philosophers sometimes develop justified true beliefs in aircraft boarding passes. They behave as if they *know* that those passes allow them to embark on the aircraft that will take them to the next sceptical conference.

The 'best evidential reasons' approach does not suffer from any of these methodological predicaments. This approach embodies a set of empirical and probabilistic criteria for fact-determination. It generates principled distinctions between good and bad reasons for fact-finding. It accords with the common-sense view of the world.[98] Admittedly, application of this approach involves risk of error (indeed, the principal message of this book is that evidence law should engage systematically in the apportionment of this risk). Epistemological sceptics are to be credited for rebuking complacent endorsements of official 'truths' and for intensifying our sensitivity to the risk of fact-finding error. This acknowledgement, however, need not be accompanied by epistemological despair or with a wholesale substitution of epistemology by politics. This response to the sceptical message, in Joan Williams's words, 'has at once reassuring and frightening implications, for it highlights our responsibilities for the certainties we choose'.[99]

Cognitive psychologists tell us that people systematically commit errors in determining probabilities. The alleged cognitive quirks include 'availability', 'representativeness', 'adjustment and anchorings', and inadequate integration of prior probabilities or base rates.[100] If correct, these findings would have far-reaching implications for adjudicative fact-finding.[101]

Availability is a judgmental heuristic that causes people to estimate the frequency of a particular occurrence by the ease with which it can be retrieved

[98] Arguably, therefore, the entire epistemological project ought to naturalize itself by substituting its demand for an *a priori* justification with *a posteriori* inquiries into the existing fact-finding practices and methodologies. See W. V. O. Quine, Epistemology Naturalized, in *Ontological Relativity and Other Essays* (1969), pp. 69–90. For implications of this powerful argument on evidence law see Brian Leiter, Prospects and Problems for the Social Epistemology of Evidence Law (2001) 29 *Philosophical Topics* 319; Ronald J. Allen and Brian Leiter, Naturalized Epistemology and the Law of Evidence (2001) 87 Va. L. Rev. 1491.

[99] Joan Williams, Critical Legal Studies: The Death of Transcendence and the Rise of the New Langdells (1987) 62 N. Y. U. L. Rev. 429, 496.

[100] See Amos Tversky and Daniel Kahneman, Judgment under Uncertainty: Heuristics and Biases (1974) 185 *Science* 1124 and the collection of essays reproduced in Daniel Kahneman, Paul Slovic, and Amos Tversky (eds.), *Judgment under Uncertainty: Heuristics and Biases* (1982).

[101] These and related findings form the foundations of the Behavioural Law and Economics movement that bases its legal policy recommendations upon people's cognitive limitations. See, e.g., Christine Jolls, Cass R. Sunstein, and Richard Thaler, A Behavioral Approach to Law and Economics (1998) 50 Stan. L. Rev. 1471; Russell B. Korobkin and Thomas S. Ulen, Law and Behavioral Science: Removing the Rationality Assumption From Law and Economics (2000) 88 Cal. L. Rev. 1051; Russell Korobkin, Bounded Rationality, Standard Form Contracts, and Unconscionability (2003) 70 U. Chi. L. Rev. 1203. For criticism see Richard A. Posner, Rational Choice, Behavioral Economics and the Law (1998) 50 Stan. L. Rev. 1551. As recently demonstrated by Chris William Sanchirico, Evidence, Procedure, and the Upside of Cognitive Error (2004) 57 Stan. L. Rev. 291, people's cognitive limitations also produce social utility (because memorization capacity is limited, it is generally harder for a person to keep a false story straight than to account for actually remembered events: cross-examination that requires witnesses to give prompt responses to questions makes it difficult for them to hold to their lies for very long).

and brought to mind. Arguably, fact-pattern P, well-familiar to the fact-finder, induces him or her to increase P's probability irrespective of its actual frequency.[102] Representativeness is a different heuristic that causes people to determine probabilities through resemblance and stereotyping. If event B resembles event A, B's occurrence would cause the fact-finder to increase the probability of A, irrespective of A's actual frequency.[103] Adjustment and anchoring are heuristics that block people's revision of their initial estimates of probability. Processing of information by people with high starting probabilities systematically produces higher probability estimates; processing of the same information by people with lower starting probabilities ends up with lower estimates.[104] People also tend not to integrate the existing base rates (or prior probabilities) in forming their probability judgements.[105]

This discouraging finding is supported by numerous experiments[106] that include the famous Blue Cab setting.[107] There, fact-finders faced a car accident case taking place in a city in which 85 per cent of the cabs were Green and the remaining 15 per cent were Blue. The fact-finders also heard a witness testifying that the cab involved in the accident was Blue and were given an uncontested generalization that the witness gives correct cab-identification in 80 out of 100 cases. Fact-finders participating in that experiment systematically failed to determine the probability of the victim's case against the Blue Cab Company.[108] Their typical estimation—80 per cent—coincided with the given credibility of the witness,[109] but not with the basic rules of probabilistic calculus. Under these rules, the prior odds attaching to the scenario in which the cab involved in the accident was Blue rather than Green—$P(B)/P(G)$—equalled $0.15/0.85$. To calculate the posterior odds—$P(B|W)/P(G|W)$, with W denoting the witness's testimony—these prior odds had to be multiplied by the likelihood ratio. This ratio had to be determined by the odds attaching to the scenario in which the witness identified the cab's colour correctly, rather than incorrectly: $P(W|B)/P(W|G)$. The posterior odds consequently amounted to $(0.15 \cdot 0.8)/(0.85 \cdot 0.2)$, that is, to $12/17$. The probability of the victim's allegation against Blue Cab thus equalled $12/(17+12)$, that is, 0.41—an outcome that fails to satisfy the preponderance-of-the-evidence standard that generally applies in civil litigation. This outcome also sharply differed from the fact-finders' decision to allow the victim to prevail.[110]

---

[102] See Kahneman, Slovic, and Tversky, above note 100, at pp. 11–14, 163–208.

[103] Ibid, at pp. 4–11, 23–98.

[104] Ibid, at pp. 14–18. See also Ehud Guttel, Overcorrection (2005) 93 Georgetown L.J. 241 (arguing that individuals overcorrect their beliefs in processing new information that substracts from the individuals' prior beliefs).

[105] See Kahneman, Slovic, and Tversky, above note 100, at pp. 153–60.   [106] Ibid.

[107] Ibid, at pp. 156–7.   [108] Ibid, at pp. 156–9.   [109] Ibid, at p. 157.   [110] Ibid.

These and related experiments do not really establish that fact-finders drawn from the ordinary population pool are irrational. The experiments themselves are faulty.[111] Consider again the Blue Cab experiment. The critical datum that the fact-finders had to process was unclear: 'The court tested the reliability of the witness under the same circumstances that existed on the night of the accident and concluded that the witness correctly identified each one of the two colours 80% of the time and failed 20% of the time.'[112] Did the court consider the prior odds in reaching its conclusion about the witness? If it did, the fact-finders' ascription of a 0.8 probability to the victim's case would then be absolutely correct. If the court did not consider these odds—as most certainly was the case—what exactly was the reason for *not* telling the fact-finders about it? The fact-finders processed the witness's 0.8 credibility as invariant. They thought that the distribution of Blue and Green cabs in the city did not affect the witness's ability to identify colours correctly.[113] In formal terms, they must have assumed that $P(B|W) = 0.8$. The fact that the prior probability—$P(B)$—was relatively low (0.15) does not make this assumption irrational, as the likelihood ratio—$P(W|B)/[P(W|B) + P(W|G)]$—may have been estimated as sufficiently high. Be that as it may, irrationality was not the fact-finders' problem. Furthermore, the fact-finders may have been focusing on the Baconian case-specific probability. That is, they may have been focusing on the strength of the evidential support for the victim's allegation that the witness identified the cab's colour correctly. After all, ordinary reasoners resort to Baconian probabilities more often than to Pascalian ones, which is yet another factor that required the researchers to formulate the fact-finders' task as accurately and as comprehensively as possible.[114]

The 'availability', 'representativeness', and 'anchoring' heuristics also do not qualify as irrationality or bounded rationality. Experiments identifying these heuristics can only prove that fact-finders err—perhaps even systematically err—in formulating their evidential base.[115] This problem is fixable, and I now state this crucial point.

Behavioural researchers systematically misconstrue cognitive *performance* as cognitive *competence*.[116] Fact-finders remain cognitively competent even

---

[111] See L. Jonathan Cohen, Can Human Irrationality be Experimentally Demonstrated? (1981) 4 *Behavioral & Brain Sciences* 317.

[112] Kahneman, Slovic, and Tversky, above note 100, at p. 156.

[113] Cohen, above note 111, at pp. 328–9.   [114] Ibid, at p. 330.

[115] Ibid, at p. 325. Fact-finders' recourse to Baconian probabilities often explains their decision more accurately. See ibid, at p. 330. See also Charles M. Yablon, The Meaning of Probability Judgments: An Essay on the Use and Misuse of Behavioral Economics (2004) U. Ill. L. Rev. 899 (demonstrating that the existence of different probability concepts often frustrates the theories of cognitive psychologists that attribute probabilistic irrationality to lay reasoners).

[116] Cohen, above note 111, at 321, 325–30.

when they fail to perform. They can avoid errors in probability computations if properly alerted to those errors. Admittedly, fact-finders also fall into traps set by behavioural researchers in order to test their rationality. These traps, however, can only function as the conjurer's sleight of hand. Each trick can be played only once. The play reveals and thereby destroys the trick.[117]

---

[117] This observation parallels the 'teleological paradox' that looms in the area of ethics. Sometimes, targeting a particular goal (such as the occurrence of friendship) directly is counterproductive to its attainment—a predicament that places the goal out of reach. See T. M. Scanlon, *What We Owe to Each Other* (1998), p. 383, n. 15.

3

Understanding the Law of Evidence through Paradoxes of Rational Belief

A. Overview

This chapter analyses and resolves two epistemological paradoxes, *Lottery* and *Preface*, with their legal derivatives, *Gatecrasher, Blue Bus, Two Witnesses*, and *Prisoners in the Yard*. This analysis identifies the defining characteristics of adjudicative fact-finding. It also identifies the fundamental function of evidence law: apportionment of the risk of error under uncertainty. This analysis sets aside the traditional vision of evidence law as facilitating the discovery of the truth.

Specifically, this chapter demonstrates that evidential adequacy—a fundamental criterion for rational fact-finding—has two distinct dimensions: qualitative and quantitative. Ideally, evidence upon which fact-finders make their findings needs to qualify as adequate both quantitatively and qualitatively. To be quantitatively adequate, it needs to cover every segment of the relevant factual allegations. To be qualitatively adequate, it needs to eliminate any dependency upon extrinsic information that determines its credibility (identified below as the 'second-order evidence'). In real life, evidence is constantly missing, and so these criteria can never be met. Fact-finders have to settle for less. Their evidential adequacy criteria, both quantitative and qualitative, substitute the ideal by the feasible. This trade-off forces fact-finders into making probability estimates based on evidence that suffers from some degree of inadequacy: quantitative, qualitative, or, as usually is the case, both. Fact-finding consequently involves risk of error in all its stages. Adjudicators allocate this risk not only in their ultimate findings—as they ought to do under the applicable burdens and standards of proof—but also in selecting evidence (through admission and exclusion mechanisms) and in relying upon particular evidence as a basis for their findings. Allocation of the risk of error is a pervasive phenomenon. This phenomenon is one of the defining characteristics of adjudicative fact-finding. Evidence law needs to apportion the risk of error and its potential consequences between the litigants. The criteria for apportioning this risk cannot be epistemological. Allocation of such risks is not an epistemological issue. Criteria for apportioning the risk of error in adjudicative fact-finding are situated in the domain of political morality. Evidence law, therefore, should be both understood and designed as a domain that combines both moral and epistemological reasons. In this domain, morality picks up what the epistemology leaves off.

B. Generalizations and Paradoxes

Adjudicative fact-finding rests on probabilistic reasoning that derives from experience.[1] When fact-finders decide to base their verdict on a testimony of a disinterested witness, they invoke a generalization that, by and large, witnesses uninterested in the outcome of the trial testify truthfully. Fact-finders generalize from experience, too, when they use against the defendant evidence demonstrating that he or she had a motive for committing a crime. In such cases, fact-finders rely on the generalization that, in most cases involving intentional crime, a person who had a motive perpetrates the crime. Similarly, fact-finders allude to a generalization when they decide to disbelieve a houseowner's testimony that, in the past nine years, four of his residential houses were burnt down by accidental fire. The generalization in this example holds that four accidental fires in a nine-year period are extremely unlikely to have occurred in four different houses owned by the same person. This proposition enables the fact-finders to adopt an altogether different scenario, namely, that the houseowner set fire to his or her own houses in order to fraudulently collect insurance payments from the insurer.[2] These and all other generalizations that fact-finders invoke[3] originate from general experience. Such generalizations are indispensable. If they were unavailable, adjudicative fact-finding would have been altogether impossible. Such generalizations can be described as glue

---

[1] See generally William Twining, *Rethinking Evidence: Exploratory Essays* (1990), pp. 32–91 (identifying empiricist methodology as prevalent in adjudicative fact-finding).

[2] See *United States v Veysey*, 334 F.3d 600 (7th Cir. 2003). According to an actuary who testified in this case as a prosecution witness, the chances of this actually happening are one in 1.773 trillion.

[3] The list of these generalizations is practically unlimited. To give just a few examples: 'Witnesses not interested in the outcome of the trial generally testify truthfully'; 'Eyewitness identification of suspects is often inaccurate'; 'Experts basing their testimony on peer-review publications are generally trustworthy'; 'Out-of-court statements are generally not as credible as in-court testimony'. Consider also *United States v Hitt*, 981 F.2d 422 (9th Cir. 1992) (invoking three generalizations: 'firearms are designed so the internal parts suffer most of the strain from the discharge'; 'many people view weapons, especially guns, with fear and distrust'; and 'someone . . . interested in guns would naturally keep them clean and in good working order').

that joins unconnected pieces of evidence together, enabling the fact-finders to do their job.[4]

This reasoning features two fundamental components: probability and deduction. Any finding that fact-finders make can only be probable, rather than certain. In my two examples, things would be no different if both the ill-motivated defendant and the greedy houseowner were to admit the commission of their alleged wrongs to judges. If this were to happen, the judges in both cases would have deployed yet another generalization: one that attaches general veracity to voluntary admissions of guilt. According to this generalization, such admissions are generally true because rational people do not speak against their interests, unless they are compelled to do so by facts that cannot be denied or by pressures that cannot be resisted. Voluntary admissions of guilt are generally elicited by true facts. For obvious reasons, this generalization, too, is inherently probabilistic. Similarly to all other generalizations, it speaks about general, rather than universal, occurrences—ones that take place in most, but not all, cases.

The fashion in which fact-finders relate generalizations to individual events is deductive. Fact-finders turn generalizations into 'covering uniformities'[5] by treating individual events not exhibiting any special traits as falling under these regularities. An individual event not involving atypical facts would classify as typical and would consequently be covered by the applicable generalization. By covering the normal, generalizations also transform themselves into norms that require no special reasons for application. Fact-finders only require special reasons for treating an event as exceptional, that is, as falling outside the norm.[6] This reasoning from general to particular could be impeccable if the controlling generalization were factually certain, rather than merely probable. By recalling probably the most famous and, sadly, certain generalization 'All men are mortal' one can safely conclude that since Socrates qualified as a man, then he was mortal, too.[7] However, more practical generalizations, such as 'Disinterested witnesses normally tell the truth', are far from possessing the same degree of trustworthiness. Such generalizations are inherently probabilistic and dangerous to rely upon. Recall Bertrand Russell's (in)famous chicken, uniformly fed and nurtured until it was butchered and turned into meat.[8] A generalization may adequately capture the normal course

    [4] See David Schum, *Evidential Foundations of Probabilistic Reasoning* (1994), p. 82 ('Generalizations and ancillary evidence help us to defend the strength of links in chains of reasoning we construct; generalizations and ancillary evidence represent the "glue" that holds our arguments together. Naturally, there will be argument about whether we have used either the correct or strong enough "glue" to hold our arguments together').

    [5] See Carl G. Hempel, Deductive-Nomological vs. Statistical Explanation (1962) 3 *Minn. Stud. Phil. Sci.* 98.   [6] Twining, above note 1, at pp. 290–3.

    [7] See Richard A. Posner, *The Problems of Jurisprudence* (1990), pp. 38–42.

    [8] See Bertrand Russell, *The Problems of Philosophy* (1967), p. 35.

of events. Yet, there is no guarantee, nor even good reason to believe, that any such typicality reproduces itself in all cases that do not appear atypical. If so, why perceive any particular set of facts through generalizations? Cutting a generalization from experience may well be epistemologically appropriate, but pasting it into an individual case is an altogether different decision. Such decisions can only be justified on separate epistemological (or other) grounds. More often than not, however, these grounds are unavailable.

Because generalizations are both indispensable and abundant, probabilistic deduction creates a fundamental problem for adjudicative fact-finding. Two epistemological paradoxes sharpen the understanding of this problem. One of these paradoxes is called *Lottery*,[9] and the other, *Preface*.[10] The *Lottery Paradox* is about an agent facing a box that contains one thousand lottery tickets, randomly arranged. These tickets are drawn from the box one by one by the participants in the lottery. There is only one ticket in this box that wins the lottery, which is the only information available to the agent. Throughout the lottery, the agent is uninformed about both the number and the outcomes of the previous ticket-drawings. The agent, therefore, has an epistemologically sound reason to believe that the first ticket-drawing will not win the lottery. Any other belief would be epistemologically unsound and irrational (the agent's possibility of forming and acting upon partial beliefs is discussed later in this chapter). The same proposition, however, equally applies to any other drawing of the lottery ticket, including the winner. This outcome is paradoxical. Our agent knows that one of the tickets in the box actually wins the lottery. The *Lottery Paradox* unveils an important aspect of the probabilistic deduction problem: creation of knowledge from ignorance. This aspect of the problem manifests itself in the extension of the generalization 'These tickets are losers' to every single lottery ticket. Contrary to the agent's positive knowledge that one of these tickets is actually the winner, this generalization forces the agent to treat all the tickets alike. This epistemological disorder is ingrained in any insertion of a known general uniformity into a decision about an individually unknown event.[11]

---

[9] See Henry E. Kyburg, Jr., *Probability and the Logic of Rational Belief* (1961), p. 197 (presenting and analysing the *Lottery Paradox*).

[10] See David C. Makinson, The Paradox of the Preface (1965) 25 *Analysis* 205 (presenting and analysing the *Preface Paradox*).

[11] See L. Jonathan Cohen, *An Introduction to the Philosophy of Induction and Probability* (1989), pp. 47–53 (identifying the intrinsic limitations of such generalized arguments). Based on Jonathan Cohen's other writings, Chapter 2 underscored the requirement that adjudicators determine facts through mechanisms of 'acceptance' rather than by 'beliefs'. See above, at pp. 37–9. This requirement prefers objectively justified ('accepted') beliefs over beliefs that fact-finders develop and hold subjectively. Here, I only focus on objectively justified beliefs, identifiable as 'knowledge'. For that reason, the concepts of 'knowledge' and 'belief' are used interchangeably and do not follow the epistemologists' technical taxonomy.

The *Preface Paradox*[12] is about a book accommodating a well-researched empirical project. The book's author nonetheless warns in the *Preface* that although he or she made every effort to eliminate mistakes, he or she makes no guarantee that the book is error-free. This general caveat tells the readers that errors are bound to spoil the book here and there. The author is only human. An educated agent reads the book page by page. The agent's task is to consider every single page and decide whether there is an epistemologically sound reason to believe that the page contains an error. The agent has no page-specific reasons to believe in the existence of an error on any particular page. The agent, therefore, is epistemologically driven to treat every page of the text as error-free. This decision, in turn, forces the agent to conclude that the entire book is error-free, too. This conclusion, however, contradicts the author's caveat in the Preface, hence the paradox. This paradox unveils another troubling aspect of the probabilistic deduction problem: perpetuation of the doubt. To account for the author's caveat, the agent has to ascribe some positive probability to the proposition that any chosen page in the book is tainted with an error.

The emergence of these problems demonstrates that some fundamental—and individually incontrovertible—principles upon which fact-finders proceed are logically inconsistent. Specifically, this tension arises between the following principles of rational fact-finding:

(1) If it is highly probable that a factual proposition is true, then it is rational to accept it as a basis for decision.

(2) If it is rational to accept as a basis for decision that p is the case and that q is the case, then it is rational to base the decision on the premise that both p and q are the case.

(3) Basing a decision on factual propositions that are logically inconsistent is always irrational.[13]

In both the *Lottery* and the *Preface* examples, the fact-finders properly applied principles (1) and (2). Nonetheless, they violated principle (3). Accepting that one of the tickets actually wins the lottery and that at least one page in the book has a flaw, entails an epistemic commitment. The fact-finders cannot identify all tickets as losers and the entire book as error-free. Adoption of a

---

[12] As developed by Makinson, above note 10.

[13] See Kyburg, above note 9; Makinson, above note 10. For a recent philosophical discussion of the two paradoxes see Igor Douven, A New Solution to the Paradoxes of Rational Acceptability (2002) 53 *Brit. J. Phil. Sci.* 391 (summarizing the existing literature and offering a new approach to both paradoxes, under which high probability per se is not a sufficient condition for the decision-maker's acceptance of the relevant factual proposition). See also Igor Douven and Jos Uffink, The Preface Paradox Revisited (2003) 59 *Erkenntnis* 389.

probability-based partial-belief standard appears to be the only way of escaping the paradoxes.[14] This solution, however, merely replaces one set of problems with another. I discuss this solution later in this chapter.

C. The Skeleton of the Argument

Both paradoxes have profound implications for adjudicative fact-finding. I analyse these implications in Section D. Every finding of fact involves generalizations. Any such finding creates knowledge from ignorance, as in the *Lottery Paradox*. Such findings, present in every litigated case, undermine the entire fact-finding enterprise. Furthermore, the doubt identified in the *Preface Paradox* is present in any factual setting that falls short of certainty. In adjudication, unavailability of certainty is a defining characteristic of all factual settings. To the extent that this perpetual doubt is epistemologically licit, it erects a wall that adjudicative fact-finding needs to surpass. It is no coincidence that *Lottery* and *Preface* paradoxes set the stage for more specific paradoxes—*Gatecrasher*,[15] *Blue Bus*,[16] *Prisoners in the Yard*,[17] and *Two Witnesses*[18]—that philosophers and legal scholars have invented to highlight the functioning of statistical evidence in law. The problem of probabilistic deduction that the *Lottery* and *Preface* paradoxes exhibit parallels in many respects the problem of naked statistics. The probabilistic deduction problem, however, is deeper than that of naked statistics. Any generalization deriving from experience is nakedly statistical. Yet, not any piece of naked statistical evidence qualifies as a generalization.

Section E resolves both aspects of the probabilistic deduction problem and relates this solution to adjudicative fact-finding. Specifically, it demonstrates that adjudicative fact-finding accommodates two distinct parameters, probability and weight. The probabilistic deduction problem attaches to a fact-finding system that resorts to probabilities alone. Probability generally represents the degree of confirmation that the available evidence supplies to the relevant factual hypothesis.[19] This confirmation degree rests on an argument that provides an extension to some particular trait (T), common to a set of particular data (D), by associating this trait with a new—and, therefore, previously

---

[14] See James Hawthorne and Luc Bovens, The Preface, the Lottery, and the Logic of Belief (1999) 108 *Mind* 241.   [15] L. Jonathan Cohen, *The Probable and the Provable* (1977), pp. 74–5.

[16] *Smith v Rapid Transit*, 58 N.E. 2d 754 (1945).

[17] Charles Nesson, Reasonable Doubt and Permissive Inferences: The Value of Complexity (1979) 92 Harv. L. Rev. 1187, 1192–3.   [18] Cohen, above note 15, at pp. 95–7.

[19] See William Kneale, *Probability and Induction* (1949), pp. 114–222; Rudolf Carnap, *Logical Foundations of Probability* (1950), pp. 19–51; Georg H. von Wright, *A Treatise on Induction and Probability* (1951), pp. 167–222; Cohen, above note 11, at pp. 1–39.

unexamined—setting that features D. The probability of finding T in any new case of D equals the fraction of cases featuring both T and D in all cases of D.[20] Both functionally and conceptually, this reasoning is aleatory in nature. Its objective is calculus of the chances that pertain to the case at hand. This reasoning has no ambition to support any factual proposition as attaching specifically to that case.

The notion of weight captures an altogether different dimension of fact-finding. This parameter measures the extent to which the existing evidence covers the specific factual allegations in the case. By insisting upon this case-specific evidential coverage, the weight parameter individualizes adjudicative findings of fact that attach to an individual event. This parameter blocks any probabilistic deduction unaccompanied by case-specific evidence. As such, it explains away the *Lottery Paradox*. There, the evidence enables the agent to form an epistemologically sound judgement about the assembly of lottery tickets, but not about any individual ticket. In the same fashion, the weight parameter explains away the paradoxes previously identified as derivatives of *Lottery* (*Gatecrasher, Blue Bus,* and *Prisoners in the Yard*). The *Preface Paradox* also disappears from the scene because the perpetual doubt it gives rise to is lacking case-specific evidential credentials. This purely statistical doubt is not weighty enough to impact the agent's evaluation of the book's pages. The prevalent legal taxonomy classifies such abstract and imperceptible doubts as not 'reasonable' enough to warrant acquittals of criminal defendants.[21] Similar reasons eliminate the *Two Witnesses Paradox*.

Section F continues this analysis by critically examining the weight parameter and its standards for individualization. Seemingly, 'case-specific' or 'individualized' evidence is a misnomer.[22] By its very definition, evidence entails inferential progress. Evidence refers to information from which fact-finders can derive some additional information. A piece of information qualifies as evidence only when it evidences something. This probative capacity, however, does not exist in a piece of information itself. To function as evidence for a yet unproven factual proposition (say, 'the claimant was hit by a car'), any piece of information (say, 'disinterested witness W tells that the claimant was hit by a car') needs to be combined with the relevant generalization (say, 'disinterested witnesses generally tell the truth'). W's case-specific testimony embodies no reason for making a case-specific finding that the claimant was actually hit by a

---

[20] Formally, $P(T|D) = P(T) \cdot P(D|T)/P(D)$. This is Bayes' theorem. See, e.g., Cohen, above note 11, at pp. 23–4; Kneale, ibid., at pp. 127–32.

[21] See, e.g., Adrian A. S. Zuckerman, *The Principles of Criminal Evidence* (1989), pp. 134–40.

[22] See Laurence H. Tribe, Trial by Mathematics: Precision and Ritual in the Legal Process (1971) 84 Harv. L. Rev. 1329 (arguing that statistical and individualized evidence differ from each other only in degrees of specificity); Judith J. Thomson, Liability and Individualized Evidence (1986) 49(3) Law & Contemp. Probs. 199 (same).

car. The reason for making this finding can only be found in the generalization holding that disinterested witnesses (such as W) generally testify truthfully. From the epistemological viewpoint, this reason is as strong as its underlying experience-based generalization. As emphasized at the outset, such generalizations transform individual pieces of information into evidence, and fact-finding would have been altogether impossible if they did not exist. The probabilistic deduction problem reappears. This problem attaches to fact-generating arguments that turn case-specific information into evidence by combining it with generalizations.

This reappearance of the problem does not obviate the weight parameter and its insistence upon case-specificity. Case-specific evidence always acquires its probative significance from generalizations. Yet, this dependency does not annihilate the operational significance of this evidence. Section F demonstrates that case-specific evidence is operationally significant as an individualizing device. This evidence is operationally significant because it enables individual litigants to develop fact-generating arguments that can stand against fact-generating arguments of their adversaries. More precisely, case-specific evidence enables individual litigants to challenge the applicability of experience-based generalizations unfavourable to their cases. Such challenges require information that can only be obtained by utilizing case-specific evidence. For example, cross-examination of a witness privy to some case-specific information may elicit new case-specific information. Evidence not having a potential for such utilization does not classify as case-specific.

An individual litigant has no control over an unfavourable generalization that acquired the 'covering uniformity' status. Using case-specific evidence, however, he or she can challenge the existence of the background conditions under which this generalization becomes operative. When this challenge is successful, the litigant is able to move the case from the unfavourable generalization to a different covering uniformity that supports his or her allegations. The dependency relation that exists between generalizations and case-specific evidence is mutual, rather than one-sided. Case-specific evidence does not simply acquire its probative significance from generalizations. This evidence acquires its probative significance from a fact-generating argument that identifies the applicable generalization. This identification crucially depends on the case-pattern that categorizes the case at hand as falling under one covering uniformity rather than another. Fact-generating arguments always need to formulate this pattern, a formulation that crucially depends upon case-specific evidence. To follow my last example, an accession of case-specific evidence pointing to a friendship between W and the claimant can move the case from 'disinterested witnesses generally tell the truth' to a more fitting generalization, according to which witnesses with a friendly relationship with one of the parties often testify untruthfully. The more case-specific evidence, the better.

This observation unfolds a fundamental fact-finding precept: the *principle of maximal individualization* (or *PMI*, for short). I offer this principle for adjudicative fact-finding rather than as a general epistemological principle. For obvious reasons, general epistemology needs to be more inclusive than the account offered in this chapter.[23] *PMI*'s application is meant to be all-encompassing. This principle applies both in relation to individual items of evidence and in relation to the case as a whole. *PMI* demands that fact-finders consider all case-specific evidence pertaining to the case. This principle also demands that fact-finders do not make any finding against a litigant when the evidence supporting the finding is not susceptible to maximal individualized testing. This testing includes cross-examination of witnesses and all other practical means for testing evidence for credibility and for obtaining new information about the case. Under *PMI*, any evidence adduced against a litigant must be susceptible to adverse utilization by that litigant. More generally, any factual finding against a litigant must be open to individualized testing by that litigant.

Section F also executes the transition from the epistemological domain to that of political morality. Factual findings in practical affairs are always made under uncertainty. Adjudicative fact-finding is no exception to this observation: it always involves risk of error. It encompasses the need to allocate this risk to one of the parties to the controversy over the relevant factual issue. Allocation of the risk of error is a zero-sum game. The risk of error that fact-finders allocate to the claimant is a risk that the defendant would otherwise bear, and vice versa.[24] Application of *PMI* is a zero-sum game, too. Banning factual findings unsubstantiated by case-specific evidence, this principle allocates the risk of error to the proponent of those findings. The findings' opponent consequently obtains an immunity from the risk of error. By validating factual findings that evidence qualifying as case-specific supports this principle allocates the risk of error to the findings' opponent. The proponent of those findings consequently obtains an immunity from the risk of error. All these choices are moral, rather than epistemological.

Application of *PMI* is also not cost-free. The fact-finding system may well discontinue the application of this principle when it becomes more costly than

---

[23] General epistemology must be satisfied with a partial-belief solution of both *Preface* and *Lottery*. See Hawthorne and Bovens, above note 14. Adjudicators, however, can hardly adopt this solution in setting their qualitative standards for justified beliefs. In adjudication, stipulated confidence levels (ibid, at pp. 255–6) also apportion the risk of error between litigants. This risk-apportionment requires special justification.

[24] See Alex Stein, The Refoundation of Evidence Law (1996) 9 Canadian J. Law & Jurisp. 279, 312–22.

productive. A rational system of fact-finding should minimize two kinds of social cost at once: the cost of substantive errors that erroneous findings bring about and the cost of procedures that eliminate such errors. Fact-finders ought to reduce the aggregate sum of these costs.[25] This economic precept (discussed in Chapter 5) requires fact-finders to discriminate between different risks of error in making risk-allocating choices. Fact-finders ought to expend greater efforts on the reduction of more serious risks (for example, the risk of erroneously convicting an innocent defendant). *PMI* needs to undergo a series of risk-skewing adjustments. The extent to which this principle should apply in different categories of cases, civil and criminal, becomes an intrinsically moral issue. This transformation is unsurprising. In every adjudicative decision that involves uncertain facts, morality picks up whatever the controlling epistemology leaves off.[26] Because the ultimate subject-matter of adjudication is coercive application of state power against individuals, this issue is not just moral, but also political.[27] Section F specifies the moral and political virtues of *PMI*.

Framing the issue along these lines opens it to the possibility of relativism. Different people may form starkly different—and yet equally legitimate— opinions as to how to allocate the risk of error in adjudicative fact-finding. Different people may hold altogether different views about the extent to which *PMI* should benefit one party rather than his or her opponent. One needs an uncontroversial moral theory to justify both general adoption of *PMI* and its particular applications. Fortunately,[28] there is none. At best, one can only find a unifying accommodation of different moral outlooks, held by people willing to live together in a diverse, but orderly, society.[29] Along with all its internal tensions, this accommodation transforms into positive law (a separate issue taken up in Chapters 5, 6, and 7).

D. The *Lottery* and the *Preface* Paradoxes

The *Lottery* and *Preface* paradoxes abstract from reality and in this sense are thoroughly unrealistic. This feature is methodologically beneficial. Abstracting from reality eliminates circumstantial contingencies that attach to real-life situations and disturb the view of the situations' essential

---

[25] See generally Richard A. Posner, An Economic Approach to the Law of Evidence (1999) 51 Stan. L. Rev. 1477.   [26] Stein, above note 24, at 285–9.

[27] Ibid.

[28] Some might consider this predicament unfortunate, rather than fortunate. Based upon humans' experience with moral theories self-proclaimed as uniquely correct, I beg to disagree.

[29] See Joseph Raz, *The Morality of Freedom* (1986), p. 181.

patterns.[30] By filtering out the circumstantial contingencies that attach to determinations of facts in real life, the two paradoxes uncover the defining characteristics of the fact-finding phenomenon. These characteristics function both as lenses for looking at this phenomenon and as a matrix through which this phenomenon ought to be understood.

The *Lottery Paradox* easily transforms into a paradox of adjudicative fact-finding. Take the following situation that commonly arises in civil and criminal litigation. Triers of fact heard three witnesses: the claimant, the defendant, and a neutral observer who verified the claimant's account of the events. The triers of fact suspect that both the claimant and the defendant bent the truth in a self-serving fashion. The triers of fact know that the claimant and the defendant are insiders: the two are both privy to the litigated events and have a personal interest in the outcome of the trial. Each of them had both an opportunity and a motive to obfuscate an unfavourable truth. The neutral witness, however, may have had an opportunity to obfuscate the truth, but no motive for doing so, given the price of exposing himself or herself to the risk of perjury. On these grounds, the triers of fact believe the neutral witness and decide the case in the claimant's favour.

As a great many decisions made in the same way, this decision rests on the generalization holding that disinterested witnesses generally tell the truth. This generalization is grounded in experience, and the decision therefore appears impeccable. This generalization, however, is still general, not universal. It holds true in most cases featuring disinterested witnesses, but not in all such cases. The triers of fact nonetheless had an epistemologically sound reason for using this generalization as a covering regularity. Because the case at hand did not exhibit anything unusual, the triers of fact could only classify it as regular and apply the generalization.

This reasoning is wanting because the case also did not exhibit any feature that could classify it as regular for sure. Arguably, in order to be properly covered by an experience-based generalization, the examined case must genuinely fit in. The case needs to be similar to the cases forming the past experience in every respect. This similarity standard can never be satisfied because the facts of each individual case are individual and unique. In the *Lottery* example, the similarity between ticket-drawings that the agent observes is merely superficial. In fact, each ticket-drawing is a separate and unique event that differs from others, which also holds true about disinterested witnesses testifying in trials. Because fact-finders know—as we do—that some disinterested witnesses do not testify truthfully, any such witness could, arguably, classify as

---

[30] See Milton Friedman, The Methodology of Positive Economics, in Daniel M. Hausman, ed., *The Philosophy of Economics: An Anthology* (2nd edn., 1994), pp. 180–213.

possibly untruthful. As any single ticket in the *Lottery Paradox* that may be the winner, any such witness may turn out to be untruthful. Treating every such witness as truthful would create knowledge from ignorance.

Aided by the *Preface Paradox*, I now take this point further by analogizing each page of the book to a disinterested witness who testifies in a separate trial. I also analogize the author's caveat in the Preface to a generalization holding that 'although disinterested witnesses generally testify truthfully, few of them occasionally do not tell the truth'. This generalization also derives from experience, and so there is no reason to doubt its general epistemological validity. If fact-finders believe the witness in each consecutive trial, they would violate the generalization's caveat ('there is no assurance that all disinterested witnesses testify truthfully') in exactly the same way in which the book-reader in the *Preface Paradox* violated the author's caveat. Fact-finders, however, would not do any better if they decide to disbelieve some of the witnesses. Unable to discriminate among different witnesses, they would have to turn down every single testimony without being able to support their decisions by case-specific reasons. Fact-finders, therefore, are caught between Scylla and Charybdis. They must either commit themselves to creation of knowledge from ignorance (which would be epistemologically unwarranted) or to treat the doubt that arises in relation to each witness as forestalling any fact-finding decision. This outcome is truly paradoxical. Rational fact-finders have embarked upon apparently acceptable reasoning from apparently acceptable premises. Yet, they reach an altogether unacceptable conclusion.[31] Is there a way out?

Probability theory provides a way. Fact-finders need not actually believe or disbelieve any witness. They may act upon partial beliefs.[32] Fact-finders only need to attach a proper degree of credibility to each witness which they can do using the relative frequency of events experienced in the past. Note, the present example involves a civil case in which the claimant's allegations need only be more probable than not in order to enable him or her to prevail. Therefore, the probability of each witness being truthful is high enough to proceed. The same probabilistic appraisal applies to each ticket in the *Lottery Paradox* and to every page of the book in the *Preface Paradox*. Every single ticket in the *Lottery* case has an extremely low probability (1/1,000) of winning the lottery. In the *Preface* case, every single page of the book has a very low probability of containing an error. This move to probability becomes possible due to its de-individualizing treatment of individual cases unaccompanied by case-specific information. The move averages any such case by

---

[31] See R. M. Sainsbury, *Paradoxes* (2nd edn., 1995) 1 (paradox is established when an apparently unacceptable conclusion is derived by apparently acceptable reasoning from apparently acceptable premises).   [32] See Hawthorne and Bovens, above note 14.

assuming that the missing information is not slanted in any particular direction. This assumption holds that, within the long run of similar cases in which the missing information becomes available, the number of instances in which it verifies the relevant hypothesis and the number of instances in which it refutes it are roughly equal. These instances cancel each other out. Statistical theories name this move 'the principle of insufficient reason' or 'the principle of indifference'.[33] The latter name underscores the postulated indifference towards unknown individual factors. It appears to be more appropriate than the former. Indeed, for statistics there are no individuals.

For individuals there are no statistics either. Ascription of frequentist probability to an individual event always entails arbitrariness. This mode of reasoning abstracts an individual event (into, say, 'disinterested witness W testified in a trial between P and D') and affiliates it to a large category of similarly conceptualized events ('10,000 disinterested witnesses testified in 10,000 trials and told the truth in 9,900 cases'). This move enables the reasoner to ascribe a compelling 0.99 probability to the proposition 'W testified truthfully' without affirmatively identifying the specific factual features that warrant the affiliation of the case at hand to the general category of 'disinterested witness' cases. Along with the entire formation of the relevant statistical pool, this affiliation derives from the absence of case-specific information that could distinguish between the cases falling within the pool. My description of these cases as 'falling within the pool' is, of course, strictly metaphorical. The cases do not affiliate to the pool by themselves. Rather, they are placed within the pool by the reasoner.[34]

Oxford philosopher William Kneale had diagnosed this arbitrariness in his penetrating critique of the indifference principle. Kneale wrote:

[the indifference principle] is supposed to justify the assertion that the probability of a die's falling with the number one uppermost is 1/6, but it could be used equally well to justify an assertion that the probability is 1/2. For we may consider as our alternatives the two cases falling-with-the-number-one-uppermost and falling-with-some-other-number-uppermost; and, when our only information is that a die has been thrown, we may say that we know of no reason to assert either of these alternatives rather than the other. From this it should follow that their probabilities are each equal to 1/2. A precisely

---

[33] See Cohen, above note 11, at pp. 43–7. See also John Maynard Keynes, *A Treatise on Probability* (1921), p. 45 ('The principle of indifference asserts that if there is no *known* reason for predicating of our subject one rather than another of several alternatives, then relatively to such knowledge the assertions of each of these alternatives have an *equal* probability. Thus *equal* probabilities must be assigned to each of several arguments, if there is an absence of positive ground for assigning *unequal* ones.' (emphasis in original)).

[34] Hawthorne and Bovens, above note 14, explain away the *Lottery* and the *Preface* paradoxes by placing all lottery tickets and all book pages in the same pool. This is what statistically standardized partial beliefs do.

similar argument can, of course, be constructed to show that the probability of a die's falling with the number two uppermost is 1/2, and so on for each of the six possible results, which is absurd.[35]

Further, Kneale noted that in order to escape from this absurdity, the indifference principle must only apply to factual scenarios that possess equal degree of specificity.[36] This condition entails that abstract scenarios are more amenable to measurement by frequentist probabilities than are propositions containing case-specific details. The possibility of framing actual events as abstract scenarios (such as 'disinterested witnesses generally tell the truth') is both attractive and problematic. This possibility is attractive because the entire fact-finding enterprise depends on the fact-finders' ability to generalize. This possibility, however, is also problematic because conversion of actual events into abstract propositions is operationally malleable and epistemologically unreal. How do fact-finders know that W actually is one of those 'disinterested witnesses' who 'generally tell the truth'? And what are the actual facts that hide behind the qualifier 'generally'? To know all this, fact-finders need to compare the specific facts attaching to W and his testimony with the specifics of other witnesses in the pool and their testimonial accounts. The need to carry out this comparison would drive the fact-finders towards expanding their inquiry in order to obtain more case-specific information. However, such sequential expansions of the fact-finders' informational base would gradually substitute the indifference principle with the 'principle of difference'. This substitution resonates with the administration of the 'weight' standard, analysed in Sections E and F. Here, it is sufficient to notice that the frequentist probability framework does not accommodate an epistemologically satisfying solution to the probabilistic deduction problem.

Gatecrasher and other paradoxes mentioned above highlight the problem of naked statistical evidence in adjudicative fact-finding. The methodological objectives of these paradoxes did not explicitly encompass the problem of probabilistic deduction as attaching to all experience-based generalizations. Yet, these paradoxes are ramifications of this general problem. A satisfactory solution of this problem would resolve each of these paradoxes. As indicated, these paradoxes are *Gatecrasher, Blue Bus, Prisoners in the Yard*, and *Two Witnesses*. Each of the first three paradoxes involves a setting that apparently satisfies the controlling proof requirement, civil or criminal. Yet, imposition of liability in each setting would be strikingly counterintuitive. The *Two Witnesses Paradox* features two suspicious witnesses who testify independently and identically on the same issue. The witnesses corroborate each other, and this factor should bolster their credibility. However, application of the

---

[35] Kneale, above note 19, at p. 147.   [36] Ibid., at pp. 148–50.

frequentist probability calculus to this setting produces an altogether different and counterintuitive outcome. Instead of increasing the probability of the scenario evidenced by the witnesses, the addition of the second witness actually lowers this probability as the doubt accumulates.

In the *Gatecrasher Paradox*, 1,000 people entered a rodeo, but only 499 paid for their admission. No other evidence is available (as the inventor of this paradox, L. Jonathan Cohen, clarifies 'suppose no tickets were issued and there can be no testimony as to whether A paid for admission or climbed over the fence'[37]). Hence, a preponderant 0.501 probability supports the rodeo-organizers' allegation that A, a randomly picked spectator, is one of the gatecrashers. The proposition that A actually paid for his or her admission to the rodeo only has a 0.499 probability. Under the preponderance-of-the-evidence standard that generally applies in civil litigation, the organizers appear to be entitled to recover the admission money from A. Under the accepted wisdom, however, virtually every judge would rule in A's favour on a motion for direct dismissal.[38]

The *Blue Bus Paradox* features a colour-blind person injured by a bus in a hit-and-run accident. As there are only Blue-Bus and Red-Bus companies in town, this claimant can blame his or her injury on either a blue or a red bus. Blue-Bus operates 80 per cent of the buses in town, while Red-Bus operates the remaining 20 per cent. No other evidence is available. Should the claimant's personal injury lawsuit against the Blue-Bus Company succeed? Apparently, it should: the probability of the claimant's case equals 0.8 which is more than the preponderance-of-the-evidence standard requires. Such an outcome, however, is widely regarded as both counterintuitive and legally impermissible.[39]

The *Prisoners in the Yard Paradox* is about a corrections facility accommodating 1,000 inmates. There, 999 inmates conduct a riot during which they kill a number of corrections officers. The remaining inmate stood against the wall and did not participate in the riot. However, this inmate is unidentifiable, and so every inmate accused of participating in the riot will claim to be him. Subsequently, each of the one thousand inmates is accused of murdering the officers. The probability of the accusation in each case thus equals 0.999. Does this probability surpass the conviction threshold set by the beyond-all-reasonable-doubt standard?[40] Apparently, it does: probability that equals 0.999 is extremely high, and so it should satisfy the criminal proof standard.[41]

[37] See Cohen, above note 15, at p. 75.
[38] See *Smith v Rapid Transit*, 58 N.E. 2d 754 (1945).   [39] Ibid.
[40] See Nesson, above note 17.
[41] See, e.g., Alexander Volokh, n Guilty Men (1997) 146 U. Pa. L. Rev. 173 (examining different probability thresholds for conviction under which a 0.999 probability of guilt is generally sufficient for convicting the accused).

However, the fact-finders' inability to distinguish between the inmates and the affirmative knowledge that one of these inmates is innocent block the possibility of convicting any of the inmates.

These paradoxes aim at extracting a broad principle that disqualifies naked statistical evidence as a basis for factual findings in adjudication.[42] Arguably, such evidence is altogether unsuitable for adjudicative fact-finding because it creates knowledge from ignorance. Adjudicative findings of fact should rest upon case-specific evidence, a claim that engendered a both lasting and lively controversy in the legal literature, known as 'the probability debate'. This debate focuses upon many important issues, some relevant and some irrelevant to the present discussion.[43]

Arguments supporting the case-specific evidence requirement are central to this discussion. As indicated, these arguments have a bearing on the probabilistic deduction problem that accompanies all generalizations that fact-finders employ. Because of its far-reaching implications, this problem is more substantial than that of naked statistical evidence. Fact-finders unaided by naked statistical evidence (not qualifying as a generalization) can still make epistemologically defensible findings. Availability of naked statistical evidence is not a prerequisite for inferential progress in fact-finding. Without generalizations, however, fact-finding would become altogether impossible. To recall the metaphor previously alluded to: if generalizations were to be altogether unavailable, then the glue that connects different pieces of evidence into a web of factual propositions would be unavailable, too. These problems are discussed in Section E. Section F offers a uniform solution to the *Lottery Paradox* and to its three legal derivatives.

The *Two Witnesses Paradox* originates from Jacob Bernoulli's probabilistic analysis of corroborative testimony.[44] This analysis focuses upon two witnesses,

---

[42] Charles Nesson, the inventor of the *Prisoners in the Yard*, had an additional—and a more ambitious—purpose in mind. According to him (above note 17, at 1198–9):

[t]he process of criminal adjudication requires something more than a high probability of a defendant's guilt. A trial is intended to gather all available relevant information bearing on what happened. If, at the conclusion of the evidence, any uncertainty remains about whether the defendant committed the crime, it is unlikely ever to be resolved. It is the function of the jury to produce an acceptable, albeit artificial, resolution of just such conflicts, and by its verdict to put to rest any lingering doubts. If the jury is to discharge this function successfully, the jurors must not only express their beliefs in the defendant's guilt by their verdict, but also the evidence upon which the jurors deliberated must do more than establish a statistical probability of the defendant's guilt: it must be sufficiently complex to prevent probabilistic quantification of guilt. Some uncertainty will always be present in criminal cases, but so long as the evidence prevents specific quantification of the degree of that uncertainty, an outside observer has no choice but to defer to the jury's verdict.

[43] Some of these issues are discussed above in Chapter 2. See also William L. Twining and Alex Stein (eds.), *Evidence and Proof* (1992), pp. xxi–xxiv (summarizing the probability debate).

[44] Jacob Bernoulli, *Ars Conjectandi*, Part IV, §iii (1713).

A and B, who give identical testimonial accounts independently of each other. The probability that witness A tells the truth equals p; the probability that witness B tells the truth equals q; and the fact-finder's task is to determine the probability that A and B both tell the truth when they converge in a statement. This probability (denoted as w) equals a fraction of cases in which A and B converge in a statement when they testify truthfully (pq) in the general cluster of cases in which A and B converge in a statement both truthfully and untruthfully. This general cluster of cases is represented by the sum of probabilities encapsulating every possible scenario: $pq + (1-p)(1-q)$. Hence, $w = pq$: $[pq + (1-p)(1-q)]$, which mathematically entails that the corroboration will be ineffectual when either p or q falls below 0.5. Therefore, when both A and B appear suspicious—one because of a prior conviction for perjury, the other because of poor eyesight—their testimonies will not corroborate one another, even though both witnesses testify independently to the same facts. Thus, if both p and q equal 0.4, then w would equal 0.31. This reduction of the probative force of mutually corroborating witnesses is plainly anomalous.[45]

This anomaly closely relates to the perpetuation of the doubt that the *Preface Paradox* exhibits. For the sake of simplicity, assume that this paradox features a ten-page brochure with a 0.1 probability of error on each page. This brochure's probability of containing an error is nearly a certainty.[46] Chances attaching to scenarios indeed get higher as the number of alternative scenarios increases. Technically, probability of a disjunctive scenario featuring either event A or event B equals the sum of the probabilities attaching to A and B individually, minus the probability of A and B occurring together (detraction of the probability attaching to the combined A&B event prevents double-counting).

The doctrine of chances applies indiscriminately to affirmatively evidenced scenarios and abstract possibilities of error. Abstract possibilities of error consequently acquire aggregating capacity. In the *Two Witnesses Paradox*, the probability that either witness A or witness B testified falsely would equal 0.69. This anomalous aggregation of the doubt parallels creation of affirmative knowledge from ignorance. Sections E and F sequentially develop a fact-finding mechanism that eradicates these anomalies.

E. Evidential Weight and Case-Specificity

The absence of case-specific evidence is a common feature of all paradoxical settings discussed in Section D. Does this feature constitute an epistemic disease, or is it merely a symptom?

---

[45] See Cohen, above note 15, at pp. 95–6.
[46] Cf. Hawthorne and Bovens, above note 14, at pp. 248–9.

Determination of facts in conditions of uncertainty is probabilistic by its very definition. When a particular occurrence is neither absolutely certain nor altogether impossible, then it is probable.[47] This truism, however, is just the beginning of the story, for it does not reveal what 'probable' means. On one understanding, any scenario that has any theoretical chance of materializing counts as probable. Since neither evidence nor logic completely rules out the possibility that a celebrated soccer team like Real Madrid will recruit me as a striker, this understanding would ascribe an extremely low, but still positive, probability to this unlikely development. Any other law professor willing to attach a similar probability to himself would be equally entitled to do so without falling into irrationality. Moreover, the probability of the scenario in which Real Madrid recruits either of us as a striker would then go higher than each of the previous two. Hence, given the number of law professors across the globe (including adjuncts), I have seemingly established that it is only the collective action problem—not the professors' ability as soccer players—that prevents them from accumulating a substitution threat to Raúl. This claim is assuredly preposterous. Yet, it would stay incontrovertible so long as fact-finders attach positive probabilities to unevidenced scenarios.

Fortunately, fact-finders do not have to do it. The concept of 'probable' has two dimensions. This concept encapsulates not only the calculated chances that probability estimates express, but also the degrees of evidential support that probability estimates rest upon. Chances of a chosen factual hypothesis to fit the actual event can be deduced from virtually any set of information, however slim it may be. Moreover, fact-finders may also extract such chances from a total absence of information. When a number of different scenarios are completely unaccompanied by evidence, fact-finders may assume that the missing information is not slanted in any particular direction and may, consequently, treat those scenarios as equally probable. Any probability estimate, therefore, is conditioned upon its evidential base: the stronger the base, the stronger the estimate. Some probability estimates may thus have more evidential credentials than others, and some less. In other words, probability estimates differ in weight, depending on how rich their supporting evidence is.

Fact-finders' rational reliance on a probability estimate depends both on how high it is and on how strong its evidential credentials are. Disregarding any of these factors would be irrational. Basing a decision on a high probability estimate with a slim evidential footing is obviously risky. Yet, ignoring high probability that rests on an evidentially deficient base is risky, too. If applied systematically, both strategies might produce decisions that are systematically wrong.

The evidential credentials criterion therefore always ought to accompany calculus of chances. This criterion differentiates between evidenced and

---

[47] See, e.g., Kneale, above note 19, at pp. 1–21.

unevidenced probability estimates and, in turn, between different degrees of evidential support that accompany different estimates of probability. Under this criterion, the relative strength or cogency of a probability estimate depends on the size of the factual ground that its supporting evidence covers.[48] Fact-finders should determine this factor by measuring the extent to which the existing evidence confirms the specific facts that form the examined hypothesis. From this angle, as already indicated, some probability estimates both can and should be perceived as more evidenced and, correspondingly, as weightier than others. Following the terminology coined by John Maynard Keynes,[49] I tag this criterion as weight (and register a parenthetic acknowledgement that other concepts capturing the same factor—such as 'cogency', 'robustness', 'invariance', or 'resiliency'[50]—are just as good).[51]

This criterion introduces the demand for case-specificity in attaching probability estimates to individual events. For example, gamblers' experience allows them to attest—in the absence of any case-specific evidence—that a long series of throws of a randomly chosen unrigged coin will produce a roughly equal number of heads and tails. This experience-based attestation may consequently attach a 50 per cent probability of both heads and tails to each coin throw that belongs to the series. Plainly enough, this and similar attestations contain propositions about long series of cases. Probability estimates that such attestations express refer to general classes of events and are not case-specific. In the present example, granted that the gamblers' coin-tossing experience is genuine, the 50 per cent probability estimate would carry substantial weight so long as it speaks about a serial tossing of an unrigged coin and does not purport to say anything about any individual tossing.

---

[48] See Cohen, above note 11, at pp. 27–39.

[49] See Keynes, above note 33, at pp. 71–7. Keynes was first to systematically distinguish between probability and its weight. His most famous statement on the issue (ibid, at 77, 84) reads as follows:

As the relevant evidence at our disposal increases, the magnitude of the probability of the argument may either decrease or increase, according as the new knowledge strengthens the unfavourable or the favourable evidence; but something seems to have increased in either case,—we have a more substantial basis upon which to rest our conclusion. I express this by saying that an accession of new evidence increases the weight of an argument. New evidence will sometimes decrease the probability of an argument, but it will always increase its "weight". [W]eight, to speak metaphorically, measures the sum of the favourable and unfavourable evidence . . . probability measures the difference.'

For further analyses of this distinction see L. Jonathan Cohen, Twelve Questions About Keynes's Concept of Weight (1985) 37 *Brit. J. Phil. Sci.* 263; L. Jonathan Cohen, The Role of Evidential Weight in Criminal Proof (1986) 66 B. U. L. Rev. 635; Cohen, above note 11, at pp. 102–9.

[50] For analysis of these concepts see R. A. Fisher, Statistical Methods for Research Workers (7th edn., 1938), p. 120 ff; James Logue, *Projective Probability* (1995), pp. 78–95.

[51] Charles Peirce also endorsed this criterion when he wrote that 'to express the proper state of belief, not one number but two are requisite, the first depending on the inferred probability, the second on the amount of knowledge on which that probability is based'. Charles Hartshorne and Paul Weiss (eds.), *Collected Papers of Charles Sanders Peirce* Vol. 2 (1932), p. 421.

But what about an individual tossing of an unrigged coin, given that all other attributes of the coin, as well as the environmental conditions of its throw and the relevant laws of physics, are completely unknown? In this setting, too, fact-finders may rationally ascribe a 50 per cent probability to both heads and tails. This probability estimate, however, would not carry much weight because it does not rest upon evidence. Rather, it derives from the total absence of case-specific evidence, as well as from the indifference assumption that deems the missing evidence unslanted.[52] But the missing evidence is slanted, as much as it relates to any particular tossing of the coin. Any particular tossing will bring out either heads or tails—not 50 per cent of the each—and this outcome is predetermined.

This framework of fact-finding under uncertainty eliminates the *Lottery* and the *Preface* paradoxes along with their legal derivatives (*Gatecrasher, Blue Bus, Prisoners in the Yard,* and *Two Witnesses*). In the *Lottery* case, it is epistemologically proper for the fact-finder to attest about the entire series of ticket-drawings that it entails a slim prospect of victory for individual participants. The fact-finder has enough evidence for making this attestation. Yet the fact-finder has no evidence—and, consequently, no say—about any individual drawing of a ticket. As far as the basic principles of fact-finding rationality are concerned, because it is not highly probable that any particular lottery ticket is a loser (this proposition is simply unevidenced), the fact-finder cannot rationally accept this proposition as true.

In the *Preface* case, the book reader is epistemologically entitled to bear in mind that the book contains a few errors. The author's caveat provides the reader a sound evidential reason for perceiving the book in this way. The reader, however, has no epistemological warrant for ascribing any probability of error to any particular page of the book. Any such ascription of probability is unevidenced and, consequently, unwarranted. A fact-finding framework that employs weight as its epistemic criterion for validity treats such probability ascriptions as groundless. For exactly the same reason, the reader has no epistemological warrant for ascribing probability to the disjunctive proposition 'Either Page 1 or Page 2 contains an error'. Because the reader has no error-related evidence that specifically attaches to particular pages of the book, any statement about specific pages that he or she may decide to make would be epistemologically invalid. The reader can only speak about the possibility of error in the book in general—an important epistemological restriction that blocks proliferation of abstract statistical doubts.

This argument raises the following question: granted that weight is an epistemologically sound criterion for evaluating the cogency of probability

---

[52] See Keynes, above note 33, at pp. 44–69 (analysing and criticizing this assumption).

estimates, why allow it to veto unevidenced probabilities? There is no epistemological principle commanding that fact-finders should altogether refuse to make probability assessments in the absence of evidence. Assuming that fact-finders explicitly acknowledge the existing evidential void and introduce the appropriate caveats into their decisions, why accord preference to suspension of judgement over the best available probability assessment? There is nothing in epistemology that prescribes indecision as the best course of action for this type of cases. Epistemology is an evaluative theory of knowledge, not a prescriptive theory of action.[53] As such, it can only classify certain probability assessments as weaker or stronger than others. Epistemology cannot tell fact-finders that making an unevidenced probability assessment is worse than being halted in indecision.

This question does not present an objection to the weight criterion. Rather, it makes an argument that treats unevidenced probabilities as potentially suitable for certain types of decision, most notably, for gambling. Granted that unevidenced probabilities are not irrational (no one has ever suggested that they are), they still differ from probabilities resting on a solid evidential platform. If so, would fact-finders do better by relying upon high, but poorly evidenced, probabilities than by basing their decisions on probabilities that are not very high but have massive evidential support? This question is unanswerable because weighty and non-weighty probabilities are apples and oranges.[54] There is no common denominator to which these probabilities can be reduced in order to be compared against each other. Weighty and non-weighty probabilities are incommensurable.[55] Consequently, a fact-finding policy that (for whatever reason) accords preference to probabilities with a solid evidential support cannot integrate non-weighty probabilities. Any such policy disqualifies low-weight probabilities as a factor accounted for in fact-finding. Note that such policies can be suitable for practical reasoning as well. Contrary to what may appear at first glance, they do not necessarily produce impasse in cases in which evidenced probabilities are unavailable. Absence of evidenced probabilities need not engender decisional impasse in practical affairs. Decision-makers can always take the example of adjudicative fact-finding that employs burdens of proof to avoid impasse.

Based on the weight criterion, I now eliminate three legal paradoxes: *Gatecrasher, Blue Bus,* and *Prisoners in the Yard.* In the *Gatecrasher* case, the claimants' proposition that the defendant was a gatecrasher indeed has a 0.501 probability. Yet, this proposition—as directed individually against the

---

[53] See generally Alvin I. Goldman, *Epistemology and Cognition* (1988).

[54] Cf. David Kaye, Apples and Oranges: Confidence Coefficients and the Burden of Persuasion (1987) 73 Cornell L. Rev. 54.

[55] See Cohen, above note 49, in (1985) 37 *Brit. J. Phil. Sci.* 263.

defendant—has a slim evidential base, and its weight is correspondingly low. This proposition is not weighty because most of the evidence that could verify or refute it is missing. Thus, this proposition can be directed with equal force against any of the 1,000 spectators, of whom 499 are positively known to have paid for their admission to the rodeo. The rodeo-organizers' lawsuit against the defendant can, therefore, rationally be dismissed. In the *Blue Bus* example, too, the claimant has no case that survives the defendant's motion for direct dismissal. The mere fact that the defendant, Blue Bus, operates 80 per cent of the buses in town does not generate a weighty 0.8 probability for the claimant's case. The claimant's allegation that he or she was actually hit by a blue, rather than red, bus is completely unevidenced. Although it is logically possible to ascribe this allegation a 0.8 probability—in the sense that systematic rulings in favour of the claimants in similar cases would produce, in the long run, eighty correct decisions out of one hundred—this probability ascription would not carry much weight. Similarly, the prosecution's evidence in the *Prisoners in the Yard* case is not sufficient for convicting the accused. This evidence does not cover the factual grounds of the individual accusation, and its weight is correspondingly low. The weight of this evidence is equal for each of the 1,000 prisoners, while it is positively known that one of them did not commit the crime.[56]

The *Two Witnesses Paradox* is eradicated by slightly different reasons. As in any other trial, in this trial, too, the issue is whether the claimant's account of the events is correct. The claimant produced two witnesses, A and B, who gave identical testimonial accounts independently of each other that support the claimant's case. Both witnesses appear suspicious—one because of a prior conviction for perjury, the other because of poor eyesight—and so each testimony is assumed to have a 0.4 probability of being accurate. As explained, the probability of the proposition that both A and B testified truthfully equals 0.31, which appears paradoxical. Because the two witnesses independently corroborate each other, the probability of the claimant's case should go up, not down.

This paradox is unreal. The heart of the problem is the definition of the claimant's case. The *Two Witnesses Paradox* is engendered by a wrong definition of what the claimant needs to establish in order to prevail. The claimant needs to establish that his or her account of the events is more probable than not. The claimant therefore only needs to establish by a preponderance of the evidence that *either* of the two witnesses, as corroborated by the other witness, testified truthfully. Technically, the claimant needs to establish that

---

[56] I identified these solutions in my previous writings. See Stein, above note 24, at 304 n. 115; Alex Stein, An Essay on Uncertainty and Fact-Finding in Civil Litigation, with Special Reference to Contract Cases (1998) 48 U. Toronto L. J. 299, 324–5.

the probability of the disjunctive proposition that either A or B testified truthfully is greater than 0.5. As explained long ago by John Stuart Mill, the probability that should interest us is that of the disjunctive inference that either A or B is a truthful witness.[57] In the present case, this probability equals $(p + q) - (pq)$, that is, 0.64 (the co-occurrence probability pq was detracted to avoid double-counting). This conceptualization of the issue precludes proliferation of abstract statistical doubts that attach to hypothetical scenarios unsubstantiated by the evidence. The *Two Witnesses Paradox* disappears and the claimant justifiably wins the case.[58]

A more realistic example, *State v Skipper*,[59] develops my analysis of probability and weight further. Roy Skipper was convicted of sexually assaulting a young girl on the basis of paternity statistics that the prosecution obtained through DNA examination. This examination was performed with blood samples taken from Skipper, from the victim, allegedly impregnated by him, and from the aborted fetus. Linking Skipper with the fetus, the examination indicated that only one out of 3,497 randomly selected males could have the same genetic pattern as he and the fetus both had. This match probability[60]— not yet a probability of guilt—was converted by the prosecution's expert into the posterior probability of Skipper's guilt that equals 0.9997. The expert arrived at this outcome by postulating that the prior probability of an intercourse between Skipper and the victim is 'neutral' and thus amounts to 0.5. The expert testified that, since the prior odds of the allegations against Skipper are 1/1, and since the chances of finding the DNA fit between the perpetrator and the fetus are 3,496/3,497, then—under Bayes' theorem—the posterior probability of Skipper's guilt equals $1/1 \cdot 3,496/3,497$, that is, 0.9997.

---

[57] See John Stuart Mill, *A System of Logic Ratiocinative and Inductive* (1891), p. 391.

[58] See Stein, above note 56, at 312 n. 28. In his analysis of the paradox, originally discovered by Jacob Bernoulli (above note 44), Jonathan Cohen did not ignore this solution, although he attributed it, instead of to John Stuart Mill, to P. Olof Ekelöf, Free Evaluation of Evidence (1964) 8 Scand. Stud. L. 47, 58 (see Cohen, above note 15, at p. 99). In Cohen's view, by explaining away the paradox, this solution engenders another difficulty, describable as 'the opposite-direction convergence paradox'. In the present example, since both p and q equal 0.4, the probability of A not telling the truth amounts to 0.6, which is also the case with B. Because these probabilities are mutually corroborating, their combined force amounts to 0.84 (0.6 + 0.6 − 0.6²).

This critique, however, is misdirected, because it conflates the tasks faced by a proponent of mutually corroborating pieces of evidence and by the opponent of that evidence. For the proponent of A and B in my example, it would be sufficient to establish that either of those witnesses testified truthfully. For the opponent of this evidence, to establish that either A or B testified untruthfully would not be sufficient. If one of these witnesses testified truthfully, the opponent's case will be lost. The opponent's burden is conjunctive in its nature, not disjunctive, as in the proponent's case. The probability of the opponent's case therefore equals 0.36 (0.6 · 0.6), not 0.84.

[59] *State v Skipper*, 637 A.2d 1101 (1994).

[60] See Bernard Robertson and G. A. Vignaux, *Interpreting Evidence: Evaluating Forensic Science in the Courtroom* (1995), pp. 16–20.

The Supreme Court of Connecticut held this postulation to be inconsistent with the presumption of innocence and—because the jury may have followed the expert—remanded the case for a new trial.[61]

Analysis of this case can benefit from comparing the key items of the prosecution's evidence: the outcome of the DNA examination and the complainant's testimony against Skipper. The first item tends to significantly increase the probability of Skipper's guilt. Yet, since there are several people, in addition to Skipper, whose genetic pattern would fit the bill, this item does not sufficiently cover the individual grounds of the accusation. With all other things being equal, this item generates an extremely high probability of guilt, 0.9997. Yet, because Skipper and the aborted fetus are far from being the only carriers of this genetic pattern, the weight of this probability does not satisfy the 'beyond all reasonable doubt' standard. The prosecution's expert misled the jury by intimating that this probability satisfies the standard.

The complainant's testimony covers the factual grounds of the accusation in their entirety. The weight of this second item of the prosecution's evidence is correspondingly heavy. Yet, this evidential item does not by itself rule out a number of scenarios in which Skipper is a victim of mistaken or malicious accusations. For example, it is arguable that the complainant could have desired to find a person to blame for her unwanted pregnancy. If so, the probability of Skipper's guilt that derives from her testimony alone would be insufficient for conviction.

The two evidential items, however, are mutually independent. They complement each other in both weight and probability dimensions. The complainant identified Skipper as her assailant prior to the DNA examination, so she could not know its outcome.[62] The complainant was unlikely to falsely accuse Skipper and obtain an unanticipated corroboration to her testimony in the DNA results. The probability of Skipper's guilt that derives from these results therefore attaches to the complainant's testimony (technically, it exponentially increases the probability of truthfulness that would otherwise attach to the complainant's testimony). The complainant's testimony, corroborated by the outcome of the DNA examination, becomes sufficient for Skipper's conviction. Conversely, evidential weight generated by the complainant's

---

[61] Specifically, the Court held (above note 59, at 1107–8) that:

Whether a prior probability of 50 percent is automatically used or whether the jury is instructed to adopt its own prior probability... an assumption is required to be made by the jury before it has heard all of the evidence—that there is a quantifiable probability that the defendant committed the crime. In fact, if the presumption of innocence were factored into Bayes' Theorem, the probability of paternity statistic would be useless. If we assume that the presumption of innocence standard would require the prior probability of guilt to be zero, the probability of paternity in a criminal case would always be zero.... In other words, Bayes' Theorem can only work if the presumption of innocence disappears from consideration.

[62] This was beyond dispute.

testimony attaches to the high—but still non-weighty—probability of Skipper's guilt that the DNA examination produced. The resulting evidential combination is equally sufficient for finding Skipper guilty as charged. One way or another, assuming that the prosecution's proof burden splits into two demanding weight and probability requirements, the synergetic operation of the two evidential items satisfies both.

Evidential weight that attaches to probability estimates does more than determine their relative strengths. It also affects the contents of the factual proposition to which the probability estimate attaches. If the examined proposition is general in character—say, if it holds that disinterested witnesses usually testify truthfully—its weight would depend on both the nature and the number of instances featuring different kinds of truthful and untruthful witnesses. If the examined proposition is case-specific—say, if it accuses Jim Smith of falsely corroborating the defendant's alibi in a murder trial—its weight would then depend on the extent to which evidence specifically relating to Jim Smith's testimony covers the accusation. Ascription of probability to a single event would always require case-specific evidential support in order to classify as weighty.

This point appears trivial. Yet, it serves as a prelude to a non-trivial observation that entails significant implications for adjudicative fact-finding. In the domain of specific occurrences, making the weight standard more exacting excludes from consideration probability estimates far removed from both certainty (indexed as 1) and impossibility (indexed as 0). Only those estimates that come close to certainty (or to impossibility[63]) survive. An addition of relevant information does not only enable the fact-finder to make a weightier estimate of the probability than previously; it also refines and thereby modifies the content of the proposition in question. The fact-finder is forced to revise his or her original proposition by ascribing a probability weightier than previously to a more refined proposition. This refined proposition is an entirely new proposition, altogether different from the proposition initially considered. The fact-finder has to continue with this refinement process as the flow of information continues. In the end, he or she formulates the most elaborate proposition allowed by the information at his or her disposal. This proposition is considerably more detailed and case-specific than the proposition originally examined. It is more resilient (or more invariant[64]) and, therefore, less likely to be shaken by potential additions to its informational base. The continual addition of case-specific information and its concurrent

---

[63] Impossibility is a form of certainty. To say that event E is impossible is similar to saying that it is certain that E did not or will not occur.

[64] See Robert Nozick, *Invariances: The Structure of the Objective World* (2001), pp. 17–19, 79–87.

filtering for credibility also impact the probability estimate that attaches to the proposition in question. This estimate would come close to certainty.[65]

Take a decision-maker whose task is to estimate the probability of trust-worthiness in relation to witness W without seeing that witness and without hearing his testimony. Assuming that W is either trustworthy or not, this task is no different from estimating the probability of heads (or tails) in relation to a coin that is about to be tossed. In the absence of information about W and his testimony, the decision-maker can only register the following attestation: 'Since there is no reason to believe that the absent information is slanted in any particular direction, W is as likely as not to turn out a trustworthy witness. His probability of trustworthiness therefore equals 0.5.' It is hard to quarrel with this estimation: its only rational alternative is withholding of the judgement, but the decision-maker is not allowed to do it. Similarly to judges and jurors, he or she must decide the case one way or another.

At this point, the decision-maker receives an additional piece of credible information. Specifically, he or she is informed that W testified as a defence witness in a murder trial and told the court that, when he served time in prison together with one Green, Green confided to him that it is he, not the defend-ant, who actually killed the victim. The decision-maker is well aware of the fabrication problem that such third-party admissions involve. After learning that W is also a career criminal with many prior convictions, the decision-maker decides to reduce the probability of W's trustworthiness from 0.5 to 0.2. Note that this new probability estimate (0.2) attaches to an entirely new factual proposition. The decision-maker no longer speaks about an unknown testimony of anonymous W. Rather, he or she speaks about a defence witness with many prior convictions, who testified similarly to many criminals by claiming that one of his prison inmates confessed to him to the crime that the prosecution attributes to the defendant.

Upon arriving at this probability estimate, the decision-maker becomes privy to yet another piece of credible information. The decision-maker is told that W's name is Jim Smith and that he and John Smith, the defendant, are brothers. Aware, as we are, that people are often driven towards getting their loved ones out of trouble—a natural desire that impels people to lie under oath—the decision-maker further reduces the probability of W's trustworthi-ness. He or she holds that this probability now equals 0.05. Once again, the decision-maker's previous proposition transforms into a new proposition that covers more particularities of the case. The decision-maker no longer speaks about an anonymous defence witness (W) with many prior convictions, who testified in a way many criminals do by claiming that one of his prison inmates confessed before him to the crime for which the defendant faces trial. The decision-maker speaks about Jim Smith, the brother of the defendant, John Smith, who has an obvious motive to exonerate his brother through false testimony and whose testimony is suspicious for two additional reasons: he, Jim Smith, is a career criminal with many prior convictions; and, similarly to many criminals, he produced a story about his prison inmate (Green) who allegedly told him (for whatever reason): 'Your brother, John Smith, did not kill the victim. I did it.' The decision-maker consequently concludes that Jim Smith must have lied in his testimony. It is highly probable that this conclusion is factually correct. Adherence to a strict weight standard makes this adjustment process both inevitable and desirable. Under this standard, middle-range probability estimates that attach to propositions about individual events will never be weighty enough to rely upon.

As must already be apparent, this observation does not extend to propositions about general categories of events. Any probability estimate that attaches to such propositions may be weighty. Thus, in the *Lottery Paradox* setting, a proposition holding—across all cases at once—that 'it is highly probable that these ticket-drawings will not win the lottery' is weighty. Similarly, a proposition holding—across all cases at once—that 'these ticket-drawings have a very low probability of winning the lottery', is weighty, too. In the unrigged coin case, the middle-range 0.5 probability of getting tails (or heads) also carries sufficient weight, as long as it cuts across all individual throws of the coin and does not purport to say anything about any individual throw.

Adjudicators, however, do not cut across categories of cases. They decide individual cases and focus upon individual events. Because the ultimate issue of virtually every trial is individual, adjudicators are seemingly bound to adhere to rigid standards in relation to both weight and case-specificity. As we just have seen, this adherence excludes from consideration middle-range probabilities, far removed from both certainty (denoted as 1) and impossibility (denoted as 0). A fact-finder certifying that 'This testimony is as likely as it is not to be truthful' must be either lazy or uninformed. After setting the laziness scenario aside, I can certify with certainty that this fact-finder does not know a good deal about the witness and his or her testimony. A gambler certifying 'This coin is unrigged and its tossing, therefore, is equally likely to produce heads and tails' is, in contrast, neither lazy nor uninformed. Adjudicative disputes, however, cannot be resolved by coin-tossing or (more exotically) by allowing a monkey to choose between two equally looking bananas, of which one carries an inscription GUILTY and the other NOT-GUILTY.

This exclusion of middle-range probabilities presents a problem for civil trials, adjudicated under the preponderance-of-the-evidence standard. Apparently, this standard prescribes judges and jurors that they should rule for the claimant whenever the probability of his or her case exceeds 0.5. If so, a rigid demand for evidential weight and case-specificity disenfranchises deserving claimants with stories featuring probabilities in the range of 0.6–0.7. This outcome is unjustifiable and I do not intend to support it. I address this issue in the next section.

The *Lottery* and *Preface* paradoxes also have a non-epistemic dimension. The two paradoxes convolute this dimension in order to remain in the epistemic domain, a move much responsible for the difficulties that arise in resolving the paradoxes. The decision-makers in both *Lottery* and *Preface* cases were actually required to take on the risk of error, a perspective that sheds an altogether different light upon their decisions. In the *Lottery* case, there is no inconsistency in allocating the risk of error in a way that deems every lottery ticket a loser. In the *Preface* case, there is no inconsistency in allocating the risk of error in a way that deems every page of the book error-free. In each of these cases, allocation of the risk of error becomes a decisional component for a simple reason: the decision-makers have no epistemologically sufficient grounds for riskless fact-finding. Allocation of the risk of error fills up the epistemic void. This decisional supplement, however, is not epistemic, even though the void that it fills up is. As Section F explains, the nature of this supplement in adjudicative fact-finding is defined by political morality. In both *Lottery* and *Preface* cases, this supplement has no relationship with morality and politics, but its nature is not epistemic either. This supplement has no identifiable frame of reference. This crucial decisional component hangs in the air. The resulting indeterminacy facilitates its implicit (and unwarranted) affiliation to the epistemological domain.

F. The Principle of Maximal Individualization

My foregoing discussion set forth the two-criterial fact-finding model that applies both probability and evidential weight in determining facts in conditions of uncertainty. Under this model, probability estimates must be adequately evidenced in order to play a role in the final decision. Estimates that are inadequately evidenced (or completely unevidenced) will not do even when they pass the probability threshold that the controlling standard of proof sets. Whether a particular estimate of probability is adequately evidenced depends on the proposition to which it attaches. Evidence supporting probability estimates needs to be credible as well. Furthermore, this evidence needs to cover the factual grounds of the proposition in question. If this proposition is general in character (for example, if it maintains that, generally, witnesses uninterested in the outcome of the trial testify truthfully), then the required evidence both can and should relate to the plurality of the instances that combine into the general category of events that the proposition describes. For any such proposition, evidence highlighting some specific factual setting would be irrelevant. However, when the proposition in question points to an individual event (such as 'Jim Smith gave an untruthful testimony in a murder trial of his brother, John Smith'), the fact-finders would need individualized evidence that covers the specifics of the event. An estimate of probability (high or low) that attaches to a general category of arguably similar events will not do.

This fact-finding model drives away the paradoxes of rational belief that opened up the discussion. These paradoxes originate from an epistemologically questionable move. They derive from the unwarranted transformation of a properly evidenced estimate of probability that attaches to a general category of events into an altogether unevidenced probability estimate that attaches to an individual event. In the process of this transformation, the numerical probability estimate does not change, but its propositional content and evidential weight do. There are, therefore, two different probability estimates here, not one, and these estimates are also incommensurable. They refer to two different sets of facts (one general and the other specific) and carry different evidential weights (one of these estimates is weighty and the other is not). Transformation of one of these estimates into another consequently becomes unwarranted. This transformation engenders paradoxes because it breaks the internal commensurability of the fact-finding system. This transformation is analogous to a violation of the algebraic rule under which cardinal numbers cannot be divided by zero. If they are, the algebraic system would unravel because it would no longer have commensurable concepts to work with.

This two-criterial fact-finding model is not easily applicable in adjudication. Adjudicative fact-finding abundantly consumes generalizations that derive from general experience. In applying such generalizations, fact-finders often resort to probabilistic deduction that violates the weight criterion. More often than not, this violation is invisible because experience-based generalizations that fact-finders invoke in their reasoning—as opposed to arguments linking those generalizations to individual cases—usually carry enough weight. To the extent that a generalization (a 'covering uniformity') derives from experience, this experience counts as the generalization's evidential support. The problem of insufficient weight, however, systematically accompanies probabilistic deductions through which fact-finders link generalizations to individual cases. Any such linkage is argumentative in nature, for it can only be provided by arguments classifying the case at hand as falling under one generalization or another. These classificatory arguments are far from arbitrary. They have argumentative strength, logical or other. These arguments, however, have no evidential support, nor can they satisfy the case-specificity requirement.

As indicated, experience-based generalizations are the moving force of adjudicative fact-finding. Adjudicative fact-finding is, indeed, altogether impossible when these generalizations are unavailable. Fact-finding is an interplay of two distinct categories of evidence: rudimentary and inferential. The rudimentary category accommodates witnesses, documents, and physical evidence. Any item of rudimentary evidence (such as an eyewitness testimony, an invoice, or a bullet) contains some specific assertive content. Any such item classifies as relevant by making an assertion about the case at hand. This assertive content, however, does not by itself transform the item into evidence. Take witness W who testifies that event E had occurred. The assertive content of this rudimentary evidence is 'W tells E', rather than just 'E'. When taken alone, W's testimony can only evidence its own existence, rather than the alleged occurrence of E. Fact-finders need to consume an inferential argument in order to establish E on the basis of this testimony or any other rudimentary evidence. By its very definition, evidence is a piece of information from which fact-finders can infer some additional information. A piece of information lacking this feature does not qualify as evidence because it does not evidence anything except its immediate assertive content. To qualify as evidence, a piece of information must lead fact-finders to discovery of some new information.[66]

This inferential progress can only be possible with the help of an argument that generates new information (old information does not generate new information by itself). To be persuasive, any such argument needs to set forth reasons for inferring a new factual proposition from the information that already exists. These reasons can only find credentials in the inferential, rather than rudimentary, category of evidence. Evidence belonging to the rudimentary category can only verify its own existence;[67] it cannot prove any other fact by itself. The fact-finder's awareness of W's testimony about the occurrence of E, as well as of the fact (subsequently established) that W has no personal interest in the outcome of the trial, still does not warrant a conclusion that E actually occurred. To draw this conclusion, the fact-finder also needs a generalization holding that, by and large, disinterested witnesses testify

[66] See Nicholas Rescher and C. B. Joynt, Evidence in History and in the Law (1959) 56 *J. Phil.* 561, 562.

[67] Technically, of course, in order to verify the very existence of rudimentary evidence, fact-finders need generalizations for the initial affirmation of their sensorial experiences (and, ontologically speaking, for the initial affirmation of their own existence, too: cogito, ergo sum?). My discussion, however, focuses solely upon practical reasoning, to which adjudicative fact-finding belongs. This framework incontestably postulates that evidence perceived by fact-finders verifies its own existence.

truthfully and are, therefore, creditworthy.[68] Otherwise, this conclusion is unwarranted—an observation that holds true about every single inference drawn from rudimentary evidence.[69]

The generalization that disinterested witnesses are largely truthful belongs to the inferential category of evidence. This category encompasses general regularities that fact-finders extract from common knowledge and experience. These regularities become evidenced by common knowledge and experience. These regularities facilitate fact-finding in new cases (that, in turn, further contribute to the experiential buildup of common knowledge). They do so by translating themselves into generalizations and covering uniformities. To be covered by one such generalization, a new case needs to exhibit a factual pattern similar to the general case-pattern to which the generalization extends (say, 'a disinterested witness testifies in a trial'). Such generalizations belong to the inferential-evidence category because they move the inferential process forward. Absence of such generalizations forestalls the inferential progress completely. Fact-finders need experience-based generalizations not only in order to complete the inferential process that rudimentary evidence initiates, but also in order to begin it. Without such generalizations, fact-finders are unable not only to draw inferences from rudimentary evidence (an observation I already made on several occasions), but also to properly identify its assertive contents.[70]

Rudimentary and inferential categories of evidence differ from one another not only functionally. There is yet another important difference between the two categories of evidence, one that identifies their informational domains. Rudimentary evidence is always case-specific, while inferential evidence (also describable as second-order evidence) is invariably general in character. Rudimentary evidence reveals information about a single event, as opposed to a regular course of events. This evidence identifies the specific features of the case at hand. Inferential evidence, in contrast, reveals nothing about the specifics of any individual case. Evidence belonging to the inferential category identifies the recurrent regularities that transform into generalizations and

---

[68] Fact-finders would also use other generalizations pertaining to witness testimony. These generalizations relate to individuals' ability to observe events and subsequently memorize and report them. See Edmund Morgan, Hearsay Dangers and the Application of the Hearsay Concept (1948) 62 Harv. L. Rev. 177 (rigorously identifying perception, memory, narration, and sincerity as testimonial parameters that fact-finders need to evaluate in every case); Laurence H. Tribe, Triangulating Hearsay (1974) 87 Harv. L. Rev. 957 (formulating the same parameters within a methodologically useful framework that delineates the scope for exceptions to the hearsay rule).

[69] See John H. Wigmore, *The Principles of Judicial Proof* (2nd edn., 1931), pp. 17–26.

[70] As Wigmore (ibid., at p. 11) explains, 'Bringing a knife into court is in strictness not giving evidence of the knife's existence. It is a mode of enabling the Court to perceive the existence of the knife, and is in that sense a means of producing persuasion, yet it is not giving evidence in the sense that it is asking the Court to perform a process of inference.'

move the inferential process forward by turning rudimentary information into evidence. Fact-finders make this inferential progress by resorting to arguments linking the relevant generalization to the rudimentary evidence that fits the generalization's fact-pattern.[71] These arguments conjoin the rudimentary evidence and the generalization and, subsequently, transform them into a factual finding in the case at hand. These fact-generating arguments are fundamental to adjudicative fact-finding. They are the only means for extracting facts from rudimentary evidence, on one side, and from the applicable generalizations, on the other.

These fact-generating arguments are not only all-important, but also intrinsically controversial. Both fact-finders and litigants can easily reach an agreement about the contents of their rudimentary evidence. These contents are rarely in dispute (and when they are, the real controversy would be about the fact-generating arguments that go beyond the agreed-upon description of rudimentary evidence). To the extent that generalizations derive from common experience, their domain would also be ruled by consensus. The only disagreement that may genuinely arise with regard to such generalizations is a disagreement about the generalization's scope and boundaries. Any such disagreement ultimately transforms into an issue of definition. For example, a generalization 'Witnesses uninterested in the outcome of the trial do not lie' may appear too strong to many people. Because it also appears too strong to me, I use a different generalization, namely, 'Disinterested witnesses generally tell the truth'. For some people, the qualifier 'generally' may not be strong enough; some may consider it too vague; and yet another group of equally respectable individuals may dislike the word 'truth' for being too metaphysical. To establish an agreement with all these people, I am quite prepared to substitute my generalization with 'Subject to (such and such) exceptional cases, disinterested witnesses generally do not lie'. My point is simple: individuals with common experience always have ways of moulding it into generalizations (linguistically).[72] How to apply such generalizations to individual cases is an

---

[71] Arguably, this inferential process would be altogether unnecessary when a proposition that rudimentary evidence comes to prove is 'self-evident'; that is, when fact-finders can straightforwardly extract this proposition from rudimentary evidence by a 'single act of sensible apprehension' (for example, when a knife is adduced as evidence in order to prove its very existence; or when an allegedly dumb person makes an utterance in order to prove that he or she is not dumb). See Wigmore, ibid. This argument is inaccurate because the veracity of sensible apprehensions is not evident per se. Rather, it receives confirmation from experience as yet another regularity. In practical matters, invoking and re-examining this regularity in every single case is both onerous and wasteful. However, suppressing the fact that this regularity is at work is dangerously misleading. This suppression distorts the understanding of fact-finding and blocks re-evaluation of the regularity's scope and validity in individual cases.

[72] Arguably, people living in the same society may also have radically different experiences, as well as rationality that radically differs from that of others. See generally Kenneth Graham Jr., There'll Always be an England: The Instrumental Ideology of Evidence (1987) 85 Mich. L. Rev. 1204. For

altogether different—and, indeed, both crucial and intrinsically controversial—matter that depends on fact-generating arguments.

Fact-generating arguments are controversial because of the difficulties that surround their assessment. The weight of any such argument depends on three factors: the rudimentary evidence that the argument relies upon; the generalization that it invokes; and, most problematically, the inference to new facts that the argument produces by combining the rudimentary evidence with the generalization. Of these three factors, rudimentary evidence is least problematic. As intimated by the adjective 'rudimentary', such evidence has no weight: it either exists or does not exist. Weight attaches to a piece of information only when the information evidences something above and beyond itself. The concept of weight and its evaluation criteria can only attach to a fact-generating argument, that is, to an epistemic activity that generates new facts by combining the rudimentary evidence with the relevant generalization.

The generalization factor is not intrinsically problematic either. Weight of generalizations that fact-finders use derives from the empirical instances systematically exhibiting the factual pattern that purports to be a generalization. The word 'systematically' embraces two criteria: that of number and that of variety.[73] A recurrent factual pattern acquires the generalization status when both the number of its individual instances and their variety increase (instances not featuring this pattern introduce definitional changes in the emerging generalization).[74] Generalizations satisfying these criteria provide credible information about the frequency of events to which they refer. In most real-life situations, this frequentist information lacks mathematical precision. Life has many attributes of lottery, but these do not include a fixed number of winning tickets. In a typical case, fact-finders can only attest roughly that, for example, most disinterested witnesses testify truthfully. Fact-finders virtually never convert this and similar experiences into percentages. These rough generalizations, however, still reliably represent the fact-patterns that exhibit recurrence. Fact-finders can properly use such generalizations up

such a divided society, absence of common denominators may be politically disastrous: a dependable adjudication system would be amongst many institutions that this society would fail to develop. Professor Graham, however, remains optimistic. According to him, evidence theory might still play an important role in such a divided community by developing a fact-finding framework that would prevent cultural imperialism.

But how? Stuck with the zero-sum-game problem, Professor Graham does not even attempt to answer this question. For a more or less similar critique of Professor Graham's approach, see Peter Tillers, Prejudice, Politics, and Proof (1988) 86 Mich. L. Rev. 768; William L. Twining, Hot Air in the Redwoods, A Sequel to the Wind in the Willows (1988) 86 Mich. L. Rev. 1523.

[73] See Cohen, above note 15, at pp. 199–244.

[74] See, e.g., Alan H. Goldman, *Empirical Knowledge* (1988), pp. 289–306 (advocating and philosophically defending a similar inductivist approach); Marc Lange, Lawlikeness (1993) 27 *Nous* 1 (defining lawlike generalizations, as contrasted with accidental events).

to a point at which they begin to carry them into unchartered domains. At this point, deep epistemological problems begin to emerge.

New domains, unaccounted for by past experience, are the field in which fact-generating arguments are at work. Fact-generating arguments are separate from the generalizations that they deploy: it is the argument—not the generalization's internal epistemic force—that links the generalization to the new factual setting. The generalization itself claims no such linkage. The generalization 'All men are mortal' did not claim its applicability to Socrates before it was established by argument that Socrates was a man similar in every relevant respect to the men covered by the generalization. The relative weight of a generalization that a fact-generating argument deploys only affects—not determines—the argument's weight (or epistemic force). The weight of any such argument depends crucially on the similarity between the factual patterns that the generalization and the rudimentary evidence exhibit respectively. When it is absolutely clear that these patterns are similar in every relevant respect, the fact-generating argument is as weighty as the deployed generalization. However, such certainty can never be available because the two informational sources—rudimentary evidence and generalizations—suffer from perennial incompleteness. Every generalization available to fact-finders emerges from an incomplete stock of information. This is why generalizations are inherently probabilistic, rather than certain, and their definitions are tentative. Any assembly of rudimentary evidence is incomplete, too. Some of the case-specific evidence that fact-finders need for their decisions is always missing (indeed, it is this informational void that generalizations help to fill up). Whether the actual facts of the case at hand converge with the fact-pattern of the applicable generalization is unknowable.

The perennial incompleteness of rudimentary evidence and generalizations makes fact-generating arguments inherently speculative. It is always possible to argue against any fact-generating argument that, if the missing evidence were available, it could have moved the entire case from one covering uniformity to another. This objection is constantly present because every fact-generating argument contains a claim, implicit or explicit, about its own resiliency (or invariance). According to that claim, the missing evidence—even if it were available—could not change the fact-generating argument. To have a concrete example, consider again a witness who testified in a trial without giving any special reason for believing or disbelieving his or her testimony. The fact-finders want more information concerning the credibility of this testimony, but do not have this information. Can they decide that the testimony is true, or at least sincere, based on the generalization that 'Witnesses uninterested in the outcome of the trial testify truthfully in most cases'? Apparently, this is the best (if not the only) decision that the fact-finders can make. Yet, how should they consider a possible claim that this decision is unwarranted, given the incompleteness of both the rudimentary evidence and the generalization? Specifically, this objection maintains that, if more case-specific (rudimentary) evidence were available, the fact-finders would then find reasons for doubting the alleged neutrality of the witness. This objection further claims that, if more general information about witnesses were to be found, it could have divided the 'disinterested witness' category into more refined sub-categories, featuring witnesses with stronger and weaker inclinations to testify truthfully in different types of trial. The second problem, of course, is not as serious as the first, given that past experience supports the generalization at hand quite strongly. Attaching the appropriate probability to the proposition for which the generalization stands would adequately respond to this problem. The first problem, however, is not as susceptible to a probabilistic solution as the second problem is. To resolve the first problem probabilistically, the fact-finders need to know the probability of the altogether unfamiliar counterfactual scenario in which the missing case-specific evidence becomes available, but still does not require the fact-finders to modify their initial conclusion about the credibility of the witness. This probability is unknowable because it targets a non-experienced counterfactual setting. This void is the essence of the probabilistic deduction problem.

As indicated, probability that attaches to an experience-based generalization measures the confirmation of the generalization's fact-pattern. This confirmation constitutes the generalization's inductive support. This support is inductive because it is particular instances that combine into a generalization, rather than vice versa (the fact-finder's reasoning infers the general from the particular). Correspondingly, the probability estimate that attaches to this combination of instances is an estimate of the entire combination; and to the extent that the confirmations of the generalization are adequate, this estimate is good too. The adequacy of these confirmations is a predominantly empirical issue. Fact-finders can resolve it experientially by considering the confirmations' number and variety. Far from trivial, such empirical-probability solutions are both workable and defensible on rational grounds.[75] Fact-generating arguments, however, are predominantly deductive. By selecting a generalization and imposing it on the case at hand, these arguments move from top to bottom (from the domain of generalizations to that of individual events). Such inferential moves have no empirical backup that could allow them to rely upon empirical probabilities. To use a distinction that two Swedish philosophers, Gärdenfors and Sahlin have devised,[76] experience-based

---

[75] See generally Goldman, above note 74 (laying out a comprehensive empiricist account of fact-finding).

[76] See Peter Gärdenfors and Nils-Eric Sahlin, Unreliable Probabilities, Risk Taking and Decision Making (1982) 53 *Synthese* 361. See also Frank H. Knight, *Risk, Uncertainty and Profit* (1921),

generalizations only involve risk of error, whereas fact-generating arguments entail epistemic risk. Risk of error is both knowable and manageable, while epistemic risk is incalculable and unruly.[77] This is why fact-generating arguments are intrinsically problematic.

Fact-generating arguments are incalculable and unruly for a reason that should already be apparent. These arguments require that fact-finders conduct a counterfactual assessment of the impact that the missing case-specific evidence would have in an altogether hypothetical fact-finding scenario in which this evidence—unknown and unavailable in reality—is both known and available. Under this framework, fact-finders evaluate the implications of the unrealized evidential possibilities. To be justified, these evaluations must be kept within the bounds of rationality and never disintegrate into guess-work. In making these evaluations, therefore, fact-finders can only use their past experience. Indeed, it is only through this experience that the numerous 'What if . . . ?' questions, arising in connection with unrealized evidential possibilities, can receive plausible (albeit still counterfactual) answers. These answers merge the relevant hypothetical possibilities (the 'possible worlds'[78]) with the evidence available to fact-finders. Combining both rejection and retention of the different hypotheses that fact-finders tentatively construct upon the existing evidence, this intellectual procedure follows three basic steps. First, the fact-finder has to add each available hypothesis ('the antecedent') to the existing evidence and generalizations. Second, he or she has to make whatever adjustments are necessary for maintaining logical consistency in fact-finding (without modifying the hypothetical belief in the antecedent). Finally, the fact-finder has to formulate the consequent factual propositions and determine their probability.[79]

---

pp. 19–20; 197–232 (distinguishing between randomness with knowable probabilities, conceptualized as 'risk', and randomness with unknowable probabilities, conceptualized as 'uncertainty').

[77] As Ronald J. Allen, Richard B. Kuhns, and Eleanor Swift, *Evidence: Text, Problems, and Cases* (3rd edn., 2002), pp. 159–60, point out:

The judge's rough estimate of the probability expressed in this generalization ['inmates who watch acts of violence against other inmates usually become afraid of the aggressor']—here, the frequency with which such people do become afraid, estimated as 'usually'—is the major component of the judge's estimate of the probative value of [the witness's] testimony. There is no single 'correct' way to articulate this generalization, and there is no precise or accurate way to estimate its degree of frequency. Human behavior rarely can be reliably predicted. *Indeed, the details of the offered evidence would affect how the generalization is framed.* How violent was the beating? Additional evidentiary facts may also increase or decrease the probative value of the offered item (emphasis added).

[78] See, e.g., Nicholas Rescher, *Hypothetical Reasoning* (1964) p. 21 ff; Richard Otte, Indeterminism, Counterfactuals, and Causation (1987) 54 *Phil. Sci.* 45. For a useful collection of essays on counterfactual reasoning see Frank Jackson (ed.), *Conditionals* (1991).

[79] See Robert Stalnaker, A Theory of Conditionals, in Jackson, ibid., at pp. 28, 33.

The first of these three steps is particularly problematic because it entails an inherently indeterminate epistemic risk (rather than a risk of error translatable into an empirically verifiable probability). This risk blemishes any factual finding that involves deductive superimposition of hypothetical scenarios upon actual facts. Unrealized evidential possibilities typically point to more than one such scenario (when they identify only one possible scenario, this scenario becomes real, rather than hypothetical, and so no evidence is really missing). Every available scenario is provable, but when anything is provable, nothing is. Because the missing case-specific evidence can take the fact-finder in different directions, its unavailability creates informational open-endedness for each individual case. This open-endedness allows numerous generalizations to lay mutually inconsistent claims for the covering uniformity status in the case at hand. The number of such generalizations is not as high as that of birds in the sky, but is high enough to create indeterminacy (especially since two clashing generalizations bring about factual impasse). Because this open-endedness results from the absence of evidence, hypothetical scenarios that fact-finders may invoke to remedy it would be lacking empirical credentials. Such scenarios have no ascertainable probabilities. As indicated, fact-finders can only superimpose such scenarios deductively on a set of inductively proven facts. Both the *Lottery* and the *Preface* paradoxes convolute this fundamental problem and exploit it by pushing the reasoners into the trap of probabilistic deduction.

Fact-generating arguments therefore need to overcome the open-endedness problem and to somehow install informational closure. To this end, fact-finders need and ought to apply the principle of maximal individualization, abbreviated as *PMI*. This principle unfolds into two specific requirements. *First, fact-finders must receive and consider all case-specific evidence pertaining to the case. Second, fact-finders must not make any finding against a litigant, unless the argument generating this finding and the evidence upon which this argument rests were exposed to and survived maximal individualized examination.* Under this framework, 'maximal individualized examination' is a rigid, but still practical standard. This standard requires that a fact-generating argument and its underlying evidence and generalizations unfold themselves to every practical testing for both relevancy and veracity, so that the opponent of the argument is able to examine its applicability to the case at hand. This standard coincides with many existing court procedures and practices. Thus, in my 'disinterested witness' example, the fact-finders need to have all available evidence that pertains to the witness's credibility, and the opponent of the witness's testimony must have an adequate opportunity to cross-examine the witness. These fundamental requirements are part and parcel of positive law.[80] To continue with the same example, if all available evidence and the cross-examination do not reveal anything special about the witness's credibility, it would then be epistemologically warranted for the fact-finders to conclude that there is really nothing special about that witness. The fact-finders would consequently be able to apply the generalization that disinterested witnesses testify truthfully in most cases. Based on this generalization, the fact-finders may conclude that the witness gave them a truthful testimony. This conclusion is proper. The same holds true about millions of similar decisions actually delivered by fact-finders in Anglo-American legal systems. Under these systems, evidential preponderance in a civil trial allows the claimant to prevail if his or her evidence unfolded itself to the appropriate examination under *PMI*. The claimant wins any such case even when the probability of his or her allegations is only slightly greater than 0.5.

PMI seems to have provided the remedy that fact-generating arguments required so badly. Under this principle, adjudicators ought to distinguish between two categories of factual issues: issues that fact-finders can examine using the *PMI* procedures, and issues not open to examination by these procedures. Fact-finders can only adjudicate issues falling into the former category and have no epistemic authority over the latter category of issues. The only decision that fact-finders can make about an issue not open to the *PMI* procedures is a decision that classifies the issue as unproven (so that in a trial, the party upon whom the burden of proof lies would suffer a defeat on that issue). In the *Lottery Paradox* setting, 'unproven' is the only decision that the fact-finder can make in relation to every individual drawing of a ticket. In the *Preface* case, after successfully applying *PMI* to every single page of the book, the fact-finder can justifiably conclude that the probability of correctness that attaches to each page is very high. This finding can rest on the evidence about the correctness of every single page in the book that the author and, presumably, his or her reputation have supplied. At the same time, since no evidence whatsoever points to any specific page of the book as possibly containing an error, the error hypothesis—that the fact-finder also considers—is

---

[80] See, e.g., *Crawford v Washington*, 541 U.S. 36 (2004) (holding that cross-examination is a constitutional prerequisite for admitting a testimonial statement as evidence against the accused); *Pointer v Texas*, 380 U.S. 400, 405 (1965) (reasoning that 'there are few subjects, perhaps, upon which this Court and other courts have been more nearly unanimous than in their expressions of belief that the right of confrontation and cross-examination is an essential and fundamental requirement for the kind of fair trial which is this country's constitutional goal'); John H. Wigmore, *Evidence* Vol. 5 (3rd edn. 1942), § 1367 (underscoring the significance of cross-examination as 'the greatest legal engine ever invented for the discovery of truth'); Federal Rules of Evidence 602 (only witnesses with personal knowledge of the matter can testify) and 802 (hearsay statements, untestable by cross-examination, are generally inadmissible in both civil and criminal trials).

not open to the *PMI* procedure. Consequently, the fact-finder must discard this hypothesis as unproven.

The settings that the *Lottery* and *Preface* paradoxes exhibit only appear similar. Both paradoxes attempt to exploit this superficial similarity. In fact, these settings are not similar at all. The *Lottery Paradox* exhibits a fully symmetric inapplicability of *PMI*: this principle is equally inapplicable to both the 'winning ticket' and the 'losing ticket' hypotheses that attach to each individual ticket-drawing. The *Preface Paradox* features an asymmetric applicability of *PMI*. In this setting, it is only the 'correct page' hypothesis that opens itself to scrutiny under *PMI* (this scrutiny would examine the author's testimony about his or her efforts to avoid errors in the book). The 'erroneous page' scenario is an unevidenced hypothesis that the *PMI* procedure cannot test (because the author only testified about the abstract possibility of error). The epistemological problems that the two paradoxes identify—creation of knowledge from ignorance and proliferation of the doubt—both originate from the ascription of positive probabilities to unevidenced scenarios that escape the examination under *PMI*. Hypotheses that fact-finders can examine using the *PMI* procedure would not involve these problems.

From an epistemological viewpoint, a factual proposition that underwent full examination under *PMI* is neither untestable nor open-ended. Full *PMI* examination constitutes the epistemological best that the fact-finder can attain. The fact that this examination was carried out until it was exhausted should, therefore, give the fact-finder the epistemological license to disregard the information that still remains unavailable. A factual proposition that survived comprehensive examination under *PMI* qualifies as adequately evidenced. Fact-finders can rely on this proposition. After completing the appropriate *PMI* procedure, the fact-finder is epistemologically entitled to postulate informational closure. More precisely, the fact-finder is entitled to treat his or her case-specific information as a complete set. This postulation establishes the epistemic stability that fact-generating arguments require. The resulting informational setting becomes fixed. As such, it lets in only a few generalizations, rather than many. Based on these generalizations and the existing rudimentary evidence, the fact-finders can properly determine the relevant probabilities and decide the case.

To continue with my 'disinterested witness' example, assume now that the witness testified as an expert. Further assume that the parties and the judge comprehensively questioned the witness and that this questioning has revealed that two of the witness's academic publications correspond to this testimony. The witness, of course, relies on these publications as a proof of her (or his) credibility. However, the witness also admits that she is 'invested' in the scientific findings that these publications report. She has much to lose—both financially and in terms of reputation—if these findings are falsified. In this scenario, two mutually incompatible generalizations are potentially applicable. The first generalization underscores the fact that the witness testified about findings that she developed independently of the trial and submitted to peer review that could falsify them. This generalization keeps the witness in the 'disinterested witness' category. The second generalization maintains that the witness might be interested in the outcome of the trial. According to this generalization, because the witness is invested in her findings, she might seek their confirmation irrespective of whether they are actually true or false. The fact-finders resolve the clash between these generalizations by analysing case-specific evidence. This analysis determines the intensity of the witness's interest in obtaining confirmation for her findings (it would also employ less contentious generalizations that fact-finders need in order to understand their rudimentary evidence). In the end, the fact-finders compare the probabilities of the clashing fact-generating arguments that invoke the two generalizations. The fact-finders then base their decision on the highest probability. If the two probabilities are equal, the fact-finders decide the issue against the party upon whom the burden of proof lies. In the epistemic domain, fact-finders cannot be expected to go beyond this epistemological best. *PMI*, therefore, seems to successfully remove the problems that attach to fact-generating arguments. Specifically, this principle eradicates the problem of probabilistic deduction (that identifies the unevidenced and, therefore, postulational linking of generalizations to individual cases). Application of *PMI* maximizes case-specificity to the extent feasible. This feature makes the principle particularly attractive for practical reasoning, to which adjudicative fact-finding belongs. It provides epistemological support to the categorization of the case's fact-pattern as falling under the generalization with a similar fact-pattern. So, can the fact-finding problems that this chapter raised be finally put to rest?

Not quite so fast. This solution of the problems is satisfactory only from an epistemological perspective. It is only the epistemological aspect of these problems that can be put to rest. Because these problems arise in adjudicative fact-finding, their solution has a moral and political aspect, too. *PMI* offers no magic formula for eliminating the uncertainty that exists in adjudicative fact-finding. Rather, it recognizes that no such formula can ever be found and offers its methodology for managing the uncertainty. Specifically, this principle offers a methodology for adjudicating legal entitlements and liabilities in conditions of uncertainty. As such, it tells judges and jurors how to handle the possibility of error in fact-finding decisions crucial to the recognition of these entitlements and liabilities and to their subsequent enforcement. Application of this principle allocates the risk of error between the parties to litigation one way or another.

The words 'one way or another' are of crucial significance for litigants. Assuming that all litigants are self-interested, if litigant Xavier prefers one way of allocating the risk of error, his opponent, Yvonne, would then certainly opt for another way. Adjudication of such controversies is an intrinsically moral problem. This problem is political, too, because facts that adjudicators determine are the base for the adjudicators' contemporaneous (or subsequent) decision that either recognizes or refuses to recognize the existence of the litigated liability or entitlement. The problem consequently boils down to whether the State should apply its coercive law-enforcement powers against a particular individual, Xavier or Yvonne. If Xavier happens to be the claimant or the prosecutor, he would promote the idea of applying these powers against Yvonne. Xavier would promote this idea on the basis of the facts that he claims to exist. Yvonne, however, would strongly resist this idea and would possibly ground this resistance on a different set of facts. Correspondingly, Xavier would demand that the risk of error in determining the facts of the case be allocated to Yvonne. Yvonne, in turn, would consider this proposal preposterous: she would claim that the risk of error should go to Xavier.

The risk-apportionment issue does not only relate to the ultimate facts of the case upon which adjudicators allocate liabilities and entitlements. Had this been the case, the controlling standards and burdens of proof would then have settled the issue. The fact-finding problems that this chapter identifies and *PMI* strives to resolve do not attach to the ultimate fact-finding decisions alone. These problems arise in every cluster of the fact-finding inquiries that produce those decisions. Factual propositions that *PMI* disqualifies for being unsusceptible to its scrutiny do not include only the ultimate facts of the case. These propositions include many intermediate allegations (say, 'Witness Xavier is untruthful' or 'Defendant Yvonne drove her car on the M25 on 1 December 2003'). More importantly, these propositions are disqualified together with the rudimentary evidence upon which they rest. *PMI* renders this evidence inadmissible in order to foreclose the entire inquiry that fails to submit itself to the maximal individualized examination. This foreclosure allocates the risk of error to the proponent of the evidence and in favour of its opponent.

To exemplify this strategy, consider the rules regulating the admission of hearsay,[81] character,[82] and opinion[83] evidence. Chapters 6 and 7 demonstrate in relation to criminal and civil trials, respectively, that these mainstays of the Anglo-American evidence systems have one common principle. Under this principle, evidence not susceptible to individualized examination by litigants

[81] See, e.g., Federal Rules of Evidence 801–7.
[82] See, e.g., Federal Rules of Evidence 404, 405, 608, 609.
[83] See, e.g., Federal Rules of Evidence 701–2.

and fact-finders is inadmissible. If the relation of a piece of evidence to the case at hand cannot be individualized, then it is only one of many possible relations. Because the evidence is not open to case-specific scrutiny, its probative impact on the case is indeterminate. Exposing the opponent of this evidence to any adverse consequence that it may produce is unfair. As demonstrated by Chapters 6 and 7, character, hearsay, and opinion are not the only evidential rules that derive from *PMI*. This principle explains and justifies the best evidence rule. Apart from that, it lends support to a number of corroboration requirements and some other evidentiary mechanisms. *PMI* also ought to structure any discretion that judges and juries exercise in fact-finding matters (this argument, of course, is purely normative).

Ultimately, therefore, *PMI* is about the apportionment of the risk of error. Apportionment of the risk of error in adjudication is a moral and political choice. *PMI* therefore needs to have credentials in political morality. What are these credentials? Why follow *PMI*, as opposed to other moral and political principles that apportion the risk of error in fact-finding?

These questions have an adequate answer. *PMI* has a number of virtues that are good for both civil and criminal adjudication. First, *PMI* prevents evidential one-sidedness. Under this principle, evidence that a party adduces in order to promote his or her case would only be admissible if it unfolds itself to individualized scrutiny and the consequent adverse utilization. Evidence not susceptible to this scrutiny would classify as one-sided and inadmissible. This mechanism promotes equality in the apportionment of the risk of error, an attractive feature that makes the mechanism suitable for adoption in civil trials. Arguably, in any such trial, the claimant and the defendant should be treated as equals. Second, by subjecting every fact-generating argument to comprehensive individualized testing, *PMI* uncovers the doubts that attach to the relevant factual allegations. By identifying the doubts that criminal defendants benefit from, *PMI* protects innocent defendants from the risk of wrongful conviction. This principle affords innocent defendants an even more crucial protection from that risk by disqualifying the prosecution's fact-generating arguments that are not susceptible to individualized examination and by rendering their supporting evidence inadmissible. Finally, *PMI* determines the immunities against various impositions of the risk of error that should be vested in litigants in both civil and criminal trials.[84] These virtues and their ramifications are analysed in Chapters 4, 6, and 7.

Despite these virtues, I am far from advocating *PMI* as an all-encompassing fact-finding principle that trumps any utilitarian goal. Utilitarian goals that

---

[84] See Stein, above note 24, at 282–4, 289–96. For subsequent discussion of this issue see Larry Alexander, Are Procedural Rights Derivative Substantive Rights? (1998) 17 Law & Phil. 19.

society may legitimately pursue may dictate—as they often do—an altogether different allocation of the risk of error in adjudicative fact-finding. These goals may permit fact-finders to use any cost-efficient evidence in order to minimize the overall incidence of errors and maximize the aggregate number of correct decisions. This policy promotes deterrence, a substantive utilitarian objective of the law. Minimizing *both types* of erroneous verdicts—those that impose liability on grounds that are factually erroneous ('false positives') and those that erroneously refuse to impose it ('false negatives')—promotes deterrence. False negatives dilute deterrence simply by reducing the expected penalty for potential violators. False positives dilute deterrence less trivially: they do so by eroding the difference between the penalty expected from violating the law and from not violating it.[85]

These and many other issues that pertain to cost-efficiency in fact-finding are taken up in Chapter 5. At this juncture, I wish to emphasize that this book does not promulgate as uniquely correct any particular vision of political morality from which rules and principles that apportion the risk of error in fact-finding can be deduced. I do claim, however, that such rules and principles are necessary. Fact-finding is bound to be driven by political morality.

---

[85] See A. Mitchell Polinsky and Steven Shavell, The Economic Theory of Public Enforcement of Law (2000) 38 *J. Econ. Lit.* 45, 60–2 (drawing on Ivan P. L. Png, Optimal Subsidies and Damages in the Presence of Judicial Error, 6 Int. Rev. L. & Econ. 101). Take a civil servant who faces the prospect of erroneous conviction for taking bribes. The expected disutility associated with this prospect (losses of freedom, money, and reputation brought about by conviction and punishment) is −500. The person can eliminate this prospect by quitting his job. He finds this alternative unattractive because it produces a loss greater than 500. The person therefore considers another course of action: quitting the job after stealing a large amount of money. This prospect promises him the lowest expected disutility: −450. The person calculates this amount in the following way. He multiplies his probability of being apprehended and convicted as a thief by the sanctions (both legal and social) that attach to this prospect. Subsequently, he reduces this negative sum (say, −1,000) by the stolen amount (say, 550). The person therefore steals the money, which he would not do if his initial position were 0, rather than −500.

4

Evidence Law: What is it For?

This chapter examines the conventional evidence doctrine and criticizes it for insufficiently regulating adjudicative fact-finding. This chapter also levels a general opposition to free evaluation of evidence (or free proof).[1] This idea is flawed, but, nonetheless, influential amongst practitioners, law reformers, and legal scholars. The endorsement of this idea by law reformers (both legislative and judicial) is responsible for the ongoing abolition of evidentiary rules and the flowering of discretion in adjudicative fact-finding. This abolitionist trend is especially noticeable in England. There, an elaborate web of rigid rules that, until recently, regulated the admission of hearsay and character evidence was replaced by a broad judicial discretion. This discretion basically allows the trial judge to admit hearsay and character evidence if he or she finds it more probative than prejudicial.[2] Before this development, Parliament did away with most corroboration requirements.[3] Judges, for their part, have intensified their resort to discretion and case-by-case judgments in evidentiary matters.[4] Among other things, they have adopted a rather relaxed 'all-things-considered' standard for admission of expert testimony.[5]

This chapter argues that evidence law should develop in exactly the opposite direction. Legal regulation of adjudicative fact-finding needs to be tightened, rather than scaled down. Specifically, evidence law should regulate the apportionment of the risk of error in adjudicative fact-finding. This regulation should control two categories of decision: (1) allocation of the risk of error between the parties;[6] and (2) the trade-offs between the substantive cost of

---

[1] For a preliminary development of this opposition see Alex Stein, The Refoundation of Evidence Law (1996) 9 Can. J. Law & Jurisp. 279.

[2] See Paul Roberts and Adrian A. S. Zuckerman, *Criminal Evidence* (2004), pp. 519–34, 582–4; Adrian A. S. Zuckerman, *Civil Procedure* (2003), pp. 661–4.

[3] See Criminal Justice and Public Order Act 1994, ss. 32 and 33 (abolishing all traditional corroboration requirements except for perjury); Criminal Justice Act 1988, s. 34 (abolishing the mandatory requirement for a corroboration warning with respect to sworn evidence given by a child of tender years).   [4] See Roberts and Zuckerman, above note 2, at p. 32.

[5] See Roberts and Zuckerman, above note 2, at pp. 305–7; Zuckerman, above note 2, at pp. 617–19.

[6] This category is discussed in Chapters 6 and 7 in relation to criminal and civil trials, respectively.

errors and the cost of fact-finding procedures that aim at avoiding those errors.[7]

A. The Abolitionist Wave

Every system of adjudication that belongs to the Anglo-American legal tradition contains a framework of rules, principles, and doctrines that governs the admission, examination, and evaluation of evidence. Categorized as 'Evidence Law' in scholarly writings and law school curricula, these frameworks appear to have the same status as other specialized branches of the law. This, however, is only seemingly so, because the actual status of evidence law is unclear at best. Few experts, if any, would advocate the idea of repealing contract law, criminal law, or constitutional law. Many would readily join Bentham's notorious claim that rules of evidence should, in principle, be abolished.[8] This abolitionist claim has permeated legal discourse for approximately two centuries.[9]

Evidence law is a peculiarly Anglo-American phenomenon. In the European continent, for example, the legal systems generally do not recognize evidence (as opposed to criminal and civil procedure) as a distinct branch of the law.[10] This non-recognition is not predicated on the absence of civil, criminal, and other trials, in which fact-finders need to process evidence and determine facts. Rather, it originates from the idea that fact-finders generally do not need

---

[7] This category is discussed in Chapter 5.

[8] Jeremy Bentham, *Rationale of Judicial Evidence* Vol. 5 (1827), pp. 477–94.

[9] See Bentham ibid.; Charles F. Chamberlyne, The Modern Law of Evidence and its Purpose (1908) 42 Am. L. Rev. 757 (favouring simplification of evidential rules and a generally unregulated fact-finding system); Learned Hand, The Deficiencies of Trials to Reach the Heart of the Matter, in *Lectures on Legal Topics: 1921–22*, (1926), pp. 89, 96–104 (arguing for the abolition of formal rules of evidence); John H. Wigmore, *A Treatise on the Anglo-American System of Evidence in Trials at Common Law* Vol. 1 (3rd edn., 1940), §8c (endorsing many of Bentham's claims, but still not supporting a wholesale abolition of evidence rules); Kenneth C. Davis, An Approach to Rules of Evidence for Non-Jury Cases (1964) 50 A. B. A. J. 723, 726 (supporting the European model of free proof and diagnosing that 'Our sick body of evidence law will get well sooner if our American doctors will consult with some European evidence doctors'); Kenneth C. Davis, *Administrative Law Treatise* (1980), § 16:2 (arguing for the abolition of evidence rules and in support of discretion in fact-finding); William Twining, *Theories of Evidence: Bentham and Wigmore* (1985), pp. 66–82 (discussing the abolitionist claim, both generally and as related to Bentham); A. D. E. Lewis, The Background to Bentham on Evidence (1990) 2 *Utilitas* 195 (discussing Bentham's abolitionist claim and its intellectual origins); Mirjan R. Damaška, *Evidence Law Adrift* (1997), p. 149 (predicting dissipation of existing evidence rules); Eleanor Swift, One Hundred Years of Evidence Law Reform: Thayer's Triumph (2000) 88 Cal. L. Rev. 2437 (describing, explaining, and criticizing the replacement of evidence rules by trial judges' discretion).

[10] See Mirjan R. Damaška, Evidentiary Barriers to Conviction and Two Models of Criminal Procedure: A Comparative Study (1973) 121 U. Pa. L. Rev. 506; Mirjan R. Damaška, *The Faces of Justice and State Authority* (1986), pp. 29–38, 54–8; Damaška, above note 9, at pp. 8–12, 149–52.

legal rules in order to determine facts. Because many consider this idea fundamental, it had also acquired a trade name. This idea identifies itself as 'free proof' (or 'free evaluation of evidence').[11] By alluding to freedom, this name intimates that liberation of fact-finders from formal legal constraints is a step forward towards a better legal system. This belief is noble, but unfounded. Freedom from legal constraints may actually lead to tyranny (judicial or other) and I examine this possibility in the pages ahead.

Anglo-American laws of evidence have been much richer in the past than they are at present.[12] Unlike other branches of the law that progressed towards enrichment and complexity, evidence laws have been trimmed and simplified. Archaic rules, which once exerted severe constraints upon the admission of potentially probative evidence, have been abrogated. Other evidence-suppressing doctrines—notably, rules excluding hearsay, opinion, and character evidence— were revised. Their revision narrowed down their scope and also introduced into each of them definitional flexibility, exceptions, and discretion.[13] These and other evidential rules, including those that control testimonial competency, judicial notice, and corroboration, have gradually been substituted by discretionary standards and guidelines (in jury systems, these standards and guidelines generally assume the form of jury instructions[14]). Adjudicative fact-finding thus transformed into a virtually uninhibited inquiry into the relevant past events. This system heavily relies upon fact-finders' assessment of the probative value of the evidence. It is common sense, not common law, that functions as its principal guide.

[11] William Twining, *Rethinking Evidence* (1990), pp. 194–7.

[12] This discussion draws on James B. Thayer, *A Preliminary Treatise on Evidence at the Common Law*, (1898), Ch. 12; Wigmore, above note 9, § 8; Ezra R. Thayer, Observations on the Law of Evidence (1915) 13 Mich. L. Rev. 355, 364 ('Ask any able and candid judge of some experience how far he goes by the books in ruling on questions on evidence. His answer will confirm what Mr. Choate once said to me in speaking of my father's Treatise on Evidence, then recently published. He said, "Tell your father it is a good book, but it is a pity he did not publish it while there was still such a thing in existence as the law of evidence" '); Charles McCormick, Tomorrow's Law of Evidence (1938) 24 A. B. A. J. 507; Edmund Morgan and John Maguire, Looking Backward and Forward at Evidence (1937) 50 Harv. L. Rev. 909, 922–3; Edmund Morgan, The Jury and the Exclusionary Rules of Evidence (1937) 4 U. Chi. L. Rev. 247; John Maguire, *Evidence, Common Sense, and Common Law* (1947), p. 10 ff; Edward Cleary, Evidence as a Problem in Communicating (1952) 5 Vand. L. Rev. 277; Jack Weinstein, Some Difficulties in Devising Rules for Determining Truth in Judicial Trials (1966) 66 Colum. L. Rev. 223; Philip McNamara, The Canons of Evidence—Rules of Exclusion or Rules of Use? (1986) 10 Adelaide L. Rev. 341; Thomas M. Mengler, The Theory of Discretion in the Federal Rules of Evidence (1989) 74 Iowa L. Rev. 413; Twining, above note 11, at pp. 178–218; Swift, above note 9. See also David P. Bryden and Roger C. Park, 'Other Crimes' Evidence in Sex Offence Cases (1994) 78 Minn. L. Rev. 529, 561 ('For centuries, the movement has been toward abolition of those evidentiary rules that have as their basis the danger of misleading the fact-finder. Jurists and scholars alike increasingly have agreed with Bentham that technical rules of evidence designed to prevent fact-finders from making mistakes are, at best, more trouble than they are worth').   [13] See sources listed above in note 12.

[14] See McNamara, above note 12; Mengler, above note 12; Twining, above note 11, at pp. 178–218.

Many scholars and practitioners perceive the contemporary evidence rules as disintegrated vessels navigating in the ocean of free proof. The following quotations from the literature represent this widespread view:

The rules of evidence state what matters may be considered in proving facts and, to some extent, what weight they have. They are largely ununified and scattered, existing for disparate and sometimes conflicting reasons: they are [a] mixture of astonishing judicial achievements and sterile, inconvenient disasters. There is a law of contract, and perhaps to some extent a law of tort, but only a group of laws of evidence.[15]

In one of our classics of literature, *Alice in Wonderland*, one of the characters is the Cheshire Cat who keeps appearing and disappearing and fading away, so that sometimes one could see the whole body, sometimes only a head, sometimes only a vague outline and sometimes nothing at all, so that Alice was never sure whether or not he was there or, indeed, whether he existed at all. In practice, our rules of evidence appear to be rather like that.[16]

These quotations are descriptive. Normative theories of evidence law that scholars have produced are not as homogeneous as their descriptive accounts. However, it would still be fair to describe the mainstream normative position as supporting the transition from the legally imposed regulation of admissibility and sufficiency of evidence to a legally uncontrolled, and thus free, evaluation of evidence.[17]

This depiction of the abolitionist wave swaying the Anglo-American laws of evidence requires one reservation. Rules furthering objectives extraneous to fact-finding (identified in Chapter 1 as not really belonging to evidence law) have not been changed by this wave. Anglo-American legal systems continue to protect the confidentiality of certain communications and materials by making them privileged at the expense of accuracy in fact-finding. These systems also maintain rules that suppress probative evidence, such as criminal defendants' confessions, for being obtained unconstitutionally or otherwise unlawfully. These are merely representative, not exhaustive, examples of evidential rules that override accuracy in fact-finding for the sake of other objectives and values. These and similar rules, however, are properly classified as extraneous to fact-finding.[18] They do not belong to the central core of the Anglo-American evidence doctrine, where the demolition of formal legal structures took place.

The effect of this large-scale removal of formal legal structures, unprecedented in other areas of the law, is to make the Anglo-American fact-finding systems

---

[15] J. D. Heydon, *Evidence: Cases and Materials* (2nd edn., 1984), p. 3.

[16] Twining, above note 11, at p. 197.

[17] See sources cited above in notes 9–12. See also Roberts and Zuckerman, above note 2, at pp. 30–2.   [18] Wigmore, above note 9, § 11.

very much like their Continental counterparts.[19] Fulfilment of Bentham's abolitionist prophesy is now closer to a reality. Indeed, some evidence law scholars have even begun questioning the utility of their enterprise.[20] The late Sir Rupert Cross, one of the most prominent evidence law scholars of the twentieth century, even announced 'I am working for the day when my subject is abolished'.[21] Occupational concerns agitated by the abolitionist wave have proved to be premature. The New Evidence Scholarship—an interdisciplinary movement shifting the academic attention from evidential rules to fact-finding reasoning[22]—has established, alongside ongoing controversies, an important uncontroversial insight. That is, dissipation of formal legal structures in evidence law does not entail tenure-threatening repercussions. This movement deserves credit for generating important insights in the fields of probability and induction, as applied to fact-finding in adjudication. Scholarly inquiries into these issues will certainly continue to occupy many minds and journals.[23]

Several factors can possibly explain the abolitionist wave. The most important of these factors is a sweeping endorsement of the empirical method in practical matters. Scientific and technological advances that this method generated have fostered confidence in human cognitive capacities. They have also uncovered the impracticality, if not unwarrantedness, of metaphysical and otherwise postulational knowledge. These advances engender a general theoretical perspective under which the experiential distinction between workable and nonworkable factual hypotheses regulates all practical affairs. The truth-value of factual hypotheses has become identified with their practical value, as determined by the hypotheses' working significance. Often taken as exclusively rational, this empirical methodology has been endorsed overwhelmingly. This empiricist turn characterizes not only natural scientists, but also many social scientists, law reformers, politicians, and people at large. This turn is responsible for instilling epistemic confidence in society at large.[24]

The empiricist turn has also had exclusionary implications. Distrustful of any deductive reasoning from postulated foundations, this turn shattered numerous efforts (ill-motivated and well-motivated alike) at replacing the

---

[19] See, e.g., Karl H. Kunert, Some Observations on the Origin and Structure of Evidence Rules Under the Common Law System and the Civil Law System of 'Free Proof' in the German Code of Criminal Procedure (1966–7) 16 Buffalo L. Rev. 122.

[20] See *Symposium:* Does Evidence Law Matter? (1992) 25 Loyola L.A. L. Rev. 629–1023.

[21] See Twining, above note 9, at p. 1.

[22] Richard Lempert, The New Evidence Scholarship: Analyzing the Process of Proof (1986) 66 B. U. L. Rev. 439; Roger C. Park, Evidence Scholarship, Old and New (1991) 75 Minn. L. Rev. 849, 859–71.   [23] See William Twining and Alex Stein, *Evidence and Proof* (1992), pp. xxi–xxiv.

[24] See L. Jonathan Cohen, Freedom of Proof, in William Twining, ed., Facts in Law (1983) 16 A.R.S.P. 1; Twining, above note 11, at pp. 32–91; Peter Tillers and David Schum, Hearsay Logic (1992) 76 Minn. L. Rev. 813, 815 ('The law of evidence, by its nature, is a type of epistemological theory. The epistemology of the American law of evidence has an empiricist tinge').

fragmented and diversified morality by moral truths. Empiricists denounced such foundationalist efforts for disseminating self-proclaiming 'first principles' that outcast the divergent viewpoints. Some moral truths have also been accused (rightly, in many cases) of contributing to totalitarianism, racism, and poverty. These heinous experiences have further fortified the mood of suspicion in the domain of morality. Fed by the sharp contrast between spectacular achievements in science and technology and no less spectacular failures in the domain of morality and politics, this sceptical mood has grown into an all-encompassing state of alert. This mood submits to distrustful scrutiny any attempt at confining individuals to official moral precepts. As such, it can be characterized as moral scepticism. Moral scepticism is one of the salient features of modern liberalism.[25]

The combined effect of these two social trends—epistemic confidence, on the one side, and moral scepticism, on the other—can explain the abolitionist wave in evidence law:

(i) Epistemic rationality cannot and must not be governed by the law. Indeed, it is the law itself, as far as its reliance upon facts is concerned, that should subordinate itself to epistemic rationality. Fact-finders need no rules that would prescribe to them how to resolve disagreements about empirical facts. By using experiential knowledge that proved creditworthy, they both can and should resolve such disagreements by relying on evidence.

(ii) This observation, however, does not apply to disagreements about values. Such disagreements have no solutions that could rest upon identifiable first principles. Bestowing upon individual judges the authority to mould value-preferences that are subject to coercive enforcement is, therefore, tantamount to licensing judicial dictatorship. Enforceable value-preferences can only be formed by social consensus mechanisms, such as law. After all, law has proved to be the only viable (albeit imperfect) social consensus mechanism.[26]

The abolitionist reform has been driven by the epistemic confidence doctrine alone. For this reason, the reform left intact most evidentiary rules that promote objectives and values extraneous to fact-finding (such as privileges granted to certain confidential communications and the exclusionary rule that suppresses evidence obtained by police through violation of a constitutional entitlement that belongs to the accused). The abolitionist reform targeted

---

[25] See Edward A. Purcell Jr., *The Crisis of Democratic Theory: Scientific Naturalism and the Problem of Value* (1973); James Fishkin, *Beyond Subjective Morality* (1984); James Fishkin, Liberal Theory and the Problem of Justification (1986) XXVIII *NOMOS* 207.

[26] Cf. Joseph Raz, *The Morality of Freedom* (1986), p. 181.

only those rules of evidence that clashed with the epistemic confidence doctrine.[27]

Originally designed for virtually all rules of evidence,[28] Bentham's abolitionist project has, therefore, been implemented only partially. An unqualified utilitarian, Bentham valued accuracy in fact-finding ('rectitude of decision', in his language) as an overarching objective of adjudication.[29] This monistic approach favoured a 'natural system' of 'free proof', imported from 'family tribunals',[30] over a system of fact-finding, imbued with technicalities, that the legal profession ('Judge & Co.') allegedly invented in order to reap profits from its clients.[31] This approach and its family-tribunal model are both too simplistic. The appealing simplicity of the fact-finding procedures that 'family tribunals' apply is predicated upon their acceptability within the family. This acceptability stems from the family's solidarity and the commonality of its members' interests.[32] In this milieu, common interests of the family tend to dominate the selfish interests of individual family members.[33] This altruistic milieu, however, stands far apart from the modern social set-up in which courts, including fact-finders, serve as arbiters of disputes. Unlike family relationships that inspired Bentham, this social set-up does not exhibit commonality of interests. Rather, it exhibits radical individualism that manifests itself in a plurality of purposes, moral sentiments, and forms of life and, correspondingly, in social complexity and alienation. This social set-up, for example, may involve potentially rival groups of people that, interchangeably, need to be protected both *by* and *from* the criminal justice machinery. Some people would require protection against criminals and some from the evils perpetrated by the police and other law-enforcement agencies. The first group of people would thus be interested in enhancing their security, and the second their freedom. Yet another group of people might harbour a self-contradictory desire for freedom and security at once. These people would agree to a monistic system of adjudication, akin to Bentham's 'family tribunal', only if it enforces their value-preferences. Bentham's 'family tribunal' and 'natural fact-finding' ideas could, therefore, only be plausible if adjudicative fact-finding were 'natural' in some unadulterated epistemological sense. But it is not. As demonstrated throughout this book, value-preferences—or, more precisely, preferences with respect to the allocation of the risk of error—permeate adjudicative fact-finding.

[27] Cohen, above note 24, at 12–14.   [28] See Twining, above note 9, at pp. 66–100.

[29] See Bentham Vol. 1, above note 8, at pp. 1–15.

[30] Jeremy Bentham, *A Treatise on Judicial Evidence* (1825), pp. 6–7.

[31] See Twining, above note 9, at pp. 75–9.

[32] Cf. Richard Rorty, Solidarity or Objectivity, in John Rajhman and Cornell West (eds.), *Post-Analytic Philosophy* (1985), p. 3.

[33] See William L. Twining, Hot Air in the Redwoods, A Sequel to the Wind in the Willows (1988) 86 Mich. L. Rev. 1523, 1539–41.

Admittedly, the prevalent evidence doctrine recognizes this phenomenon and the problems it engenders to a more limited extent than I do (and I consider it to be shortsighted). Yet, to the extent that it does recognize this phenomenon, it rejects Bentham's monistic approach to fact-finding as zealously as do I.

Bentham's monistic approach to adjudicative fact-finding is unsustainable. For example, people who believe that criminal law ought to operate with maximal efficiency favour the admission of virtually all probative evidence, so that fact-finders determine the truth both promptly and expediently. Later in this chapter, I challenge this preference on its own terms. Other individuals disagree with this idea because they believe that evidence that the police obtain through violation of the law ought to be suppressed. These individuals, therefore, opt for the integrity-of-justice principle that does not allow the state to enforce criminal law through illegalities. These individuals might also hold the view that the law should constrain the law-enforcement power whenever it poses a disproportionate threat to the well-being of individuals. This view might also justify the suppression of evidence that the police obtained through an egregious misuse of its powers that violated the defendant's well-being. However, people who favour the efficiency of the criminal justice machinery fiercely oppose this idea. These and other conflicting moral outlooks can never be measured against each other, let alone objectively reconciled. To use a technical language, these outlooks are incommensurable.[34] Any claim that they are commensurable is bound to allude to some allegedly superior morality principle, without being able to justify that principle. Moral scepticism reacts to any such allusion with profound suspicion, if not outright rejection. This sceptical ideology is hostile towards all bright-line solutions of moral and political disagreements. As such, it has prevented the Anglo-American evidence doctrine from being transformed into a fixed hierarchy of values, headed by Bentham's 'rectitude of decision'.

The interplay between autonomy and authority invalidates Bentham's 'family tribunal' analogy completely. For a really good reason, a person who values his or her individual autonomy may give it up to the extent justified by that reason. If a person desires to live in a relatively peaceful and orderly society, he or she would then be willing to accept state-sponsored adjudication as a system of resolving disputes between individuals. The person would thereby also accept the system's exclusive authority and coercive power to impose its decisions upon individuals. To the extent that the person accepts these authority and power, he or she gives up his or her autonomy. Authority and autonomy play a zero-sum game: more authority over a person means less autonomy to that person, and vice versa. Thus, if a person decides to behave as a child in a

---

[34] See generally, Ruth Chang (ed.), *Incommensurability, Incomparability, and Practical Reason* (1997).

parentalistic family (a gender-neutral substitute to the family's paternalistic design), he or she may completely give up his or her autonomy by completely subordinating his or her personal reasons for action to reasons and decisions of the 'family tribunal'.[35] Congruently with this major decision, the person would also not care very much about the fact-finding procedures that the 'family tribunal' decides to follow. By putting his or her faith in the tribunal's reasons and decisions, the person accepts them as being good for him or her. This person acts similarly to a medical patient who puts his or her faith in a doctor's prescription of Prozac, without investigating Prozac's chemistry and its impact on human mind and body. The person allows his or her personal reasons for action to be subordinated or pre-empted[36] by reasons and decisions that his or her authoritative decision-maker will devise. A complete pre-emption of the person's reasons for action constitutes a full-length forfeiture of his or her autonomy. On the opposite side, a person's indiscriminate insubordination celebrates his or her autonomy. This celebration would not last for long, though, if the person really needs Prozac but takes aspirin instead; or if he or she happens to be a five-year-old child who decides to live on the street, contrary to the family tribunal's decision. On similar grounds, people unwilling to experience the Hobbesian State of Nature need to accept the court's adjudicative authority as dominating their autonomy and thereby pre-empting their reasons for action. Any person must subordinate his or her autonomy to the appropriate state authorities to the extent necessary for his or her well-being as an individual and as a member of society.[37]

But what extent is necessary for that sacrifice in order to maintain a proper system of adjudication? This is a very difficult question, and I do not believe that anyone can ever answer it properly. Yet, a fundamental distinction between reasons upon which adjudicators should and should not be authorized to decide cases will move the inquiry in the right direction. Adjudicators certainly should not be allowed to base their decisions on any reasons they may have. Outside family tribunal settings, there is no rational reason for people to sacrifice their autonomy to such an unlimited extent. But what is the right extent for that sacrifice? A rational person only needs to allow good adjudicative reasons to pre-empt his or her personal reasons for action. But which reasons qualify as 'good' for that purpose, given the vast number of individuals and perceptions involved? From the individual autonomy perspective, there seems to be only one answer to this question. A reason would be good for individuals if all of

---

[35] Cf. Joseph Raz, *The Authority of Law* (1979), pp. 19–25.

[36] Ibid. See also Joseph Raz, Authority and Justification (1985) 14 *Phil. & Pub. Aff.* 3.

[37] For general philosophical discussions of this issue see Raz, above note 36; Scott J. Shapiro, Authority, in Jules Coleman and Scott J. Shapiro, *The Oxford Handbook of Jurisprudence and Philosophy of Law* (2002), pp. 382, 385–91, 402–8.

them have accepted it or, alternatively, if it was developed by a collective and participatory decision-making mechanism—such as a democratic election of a both accountable and removable legislator—to which all individuals have agreed. To qualify as good and pre-emptive, adjudicative reasons therefore need to acquire some formal validation from society. Adjudicators should not be authorized to develop autonomy-curtailing reasons as they deem fit. They are not parents adjudicating their children in family tribunals, and the society that autonomous individuals form is not one happy family either.

Bentham, of course, had more to say in favour of free proof. According to him, there can be no room for legitimate disagreements about the appropriate fact-finding methodology. This methodology ought to be empiricist. As such, it should favour a system of unregulated fact-finding. According to Bentham, the empiricist rationality is both antecedent to the formulation of legal rules and essential to their accurate implementation. This rationality, therefore, should subordinate the legal domain, rather than allow the legal domain to subordinate it.[38] Adjudicative fact-finding must not be interfered with by legal rules, unless it becomes absolutely necessary for preventing delay and vexation[39] and, in highly exceptional cases, for protecting the sanctity of the Church[40] and (relatedly) the security of the State.[41] For substantive areas of the law, however, Bentham prescribed a system of codified rules that would constrain judges and structure their discretion.[42] Bentham trusted judges as fact-finders, but not as competent creators of substantive legal rules that accommodate value-preferences.[43] For that domain, moral rather than epistemic in nature, Bentham famously prescribed only one value: utilitarianism. He also estimated that a codified system of substantive legal rules would secure better judicial alignment with this preference than would judicial discretion.[44] Similarly to the prevalent evidence doctrine, Bentham professed a sharp analytical separation between the epistemological and the moral.

B. Separating the Epistemological from the Moral

The prevalent evidence doctrine separates the epistemological from the moral by placing free proof in its core and by treating the existing evidential rules as

---

[38] See Twining, above note 9, at pp. 52–66.　　[39] See Twining, above note 9, at pp. 91–4.

[40] See Bentham, above note 30, at p. 237.

[41] See Bentham Vol. 1, above note 8, at pp. 566–8. See also George W. Keeton and O. Roy Marshall, Bentham's Influence on the Law of Evidence, in George W. Keeton and Georg Schwarzenberger (eds.), *Jeremy Bentham and the Law* (1948), pp. 79, 95.

[42] See Gerald J. Postema, *Bentham and the Common Law Tradition* (1986), pp. 442–52.

[43] Ibid, at pp. 345–50.

[44] Ibid, at p. 445 (underscoring the utilitarian reasons that support legal formalities).

both disparate and isolated exceptions to free proof. This marginalization of the rules of evidence and the consequent deregulation of fact-finding originate from the epistemic confidence doctrine that I do not challenge. This epistemological doctrine has many credentials and no practical alternatives.[45] But I do challenge the doctrinal separation between the moral and the epistemological in adjudicative fact-finding.

The prevalent evidence doctrine holds that fact-finders must determine the litigated facts on the basis of common sense, logic, and experience, subject to: (1) a few rules designating particular interests and values to prevail over accuracy in fact-finding; (2) the burdens and standards of proof; (3) some flexible guidelines and instructions; and (4) a few fact-finding rules, such as hearsay, opinion, and character. Free evaluation of evidence lies at the core of this doctrine. For fact-finders, free evaluation of evidence entails freedom from legal constraints in inferring facts from evidence. This fundamental freedom is surrounded, but not interfered with, by legal rules that constitute the law of evidence. These rules promote important adjudicative objectives that relate to, but do not constitute, fact-finding. The prevalent evidence doctrine maintains that fact-finders engage in a purely epistemic activity when they determine the facts of the case under the controlling standard of proof. Fact-determination is a function of the overall weight of the evidence upon which fact-finders proceed. The prevalent evidence doctrine therefore maintains that evaluation of evidential weight by fact-finders is a purely epistemic activity, too. Because law has 'no mandamus to the logical faculty'[46]—and, presumably, to the epistemological faculty as well—it should, arguably, exert no control over this activity. Hence, there is, arguably, no 'general need to write rules of proof into the law, nor to define a corresponding level of intellectual qualification for triers of fact. We need only a reasonable layman, not a logician or statistician, to determine what is beyond reasonable doubt.'[47]

The prevalent evidence doctrine further enhances free proof by consolidating the function of the different exceptions to the rules of evidence. Under this doctrine, exceptions to evidence rules have one general function: reinstatement of free proof. Portraying the existing evidential rules as a series of isolated exceptions to free proof that, in turn, are qualified by their own exceptions— that reinstall free proof—the prevalent doctrine marginalizes the presence of the legal in adjudicative fact-finding. Because legal interference with fact-finding is typically motivated by value preferences, the doctrine marginalizes the impact on fact-finding that moral and political choices exert.

The prevalent evidence doctrine intensifies this marginalization by dividing the already exceptional rules of evidence into two dichotomous categories. One of these categories accommodates rules qualifying as 'probative', 'auxiliary',

---

[45] See Cohen, above note 24.   [46] James B. Thayer, above note 12, at p. 314 n.
[47] Cohen, above note 24, at p. 21.

and 'intrinsic' to fact-finding.[48] Epistemological reasons support these rules. The other category contains rules motivated by preferences altogether extraneous to fact-finding that qualify as 'extra-probative' and 'extrinsic'.[49] These rules set aside accuracy in fact-finding in order to promote moral and political values that are exceptionally important to the legal system. As in Bentham's theory, in this doctrine, the impact of moral and political values upon adjudicative fact-finding is highly exceptional.[50]

By portraying evidential rules as isolated exceptions to free proof, the prevalent evidence doctrine inspires abolitionism. If fact-finders are generally allowed to reason from evidence to conclusions when their epistemic rationality is unfettered, why not expand this license and apply it across the board? This certainly is a fair question to ask. If the traditional portrayal of the law of evidence were normatively sound, answering this question would have been a rather daunting task. But is this portrayal normatively sound? For reasons specified below, I claim that it is not. As explained in Chapter 3, I establish that the doctrinal separation between the moral and the epistemological is analytically wrong. For similar reasons, the doctrinal marginalization of moral choices as affecting adjudicative fact-finding is analytically wrong, too. This critical insight is operationally significant because moral and political choices both do and should exert impact on adjudicative fact-finding. In the pages ahead, I return to this insight and take it a step further. Here, I only point out that allusion to the exception status of evidential rules as a normative platform for free proof is a logical fallacy. Regulation of fact-finding that applies in a both exceptional and sporadic fashion may indeed be unsatisfactory. Yet, such regulation may be unsatisfactory not because it constrains fact-finders where it should not. It may well be unsatisfactory because it does not constrain fact-finders where it should. This chapter and the entire book demonstrate that regulation of adjudicative fact-finding needs to be tightened rather than relaxed.

C. Breaking the Separation: Allocation of the Risk of Error

To be justifiable, the regime of free proof needs to sustain its separation between the moral and the epistemological. This regime also needs to succeed

---

[48] See John H. Wigmore, *Evidence* Vol. 1 (Tillers Rev. 1983), pp. 688–9.   [49] Ibid, at p. 689.

[50] Dale Nance's programmatic article, The Best Evidence Principle (1988) 73 Iowa L. Rev. 227, illustrates this marginalization. There he claims that 'putting aside the rules, such as those governing privileges, which are said to serve extrinsic social policies, the remaining evidentiary rules are more plausibly attributable to the epistemic concerns of a tribunal'; and that 'this operationalized meaning, which can be said to refer to the evidence that is "epistemically best", is the primary focus of our attention'. Ibid, at 229, 240. Any standard treatise on evidence easily verifies this observation. See also Michael S. Pardo, The Field of Evidence and the Field of Knowledge (2005) 24 Law & Phil. (forthcoming) (identifying evidence law concerns as predominately epistemological).

in marginalizing the presence of moral choices in adjudicative fact-finding. Specifically, it needs to maintain a justifiable system of fact-finding in which allocation of the risk of error is a residual, rather than pervasive, function that adjudicators perform. In what follows, however, I demonstrate that the professed separation is unsustainable. This breakdown of the wall of separation renders the regime of free proof normatively indefensible.

The idea of free proof maintains that fact-finders both can and should determine evidential relevancy and weight—the agglomerated probative force of the evidence—without resorting to value-preferences. Fact-finding and value-preferences are thereby maintained in segregation. Moral values, to the extent that the law recognizes and enforces them—and as much as they clash with the ascertainment of empirical truths—may affect the outcomes of adjudicators' decisions. These values, however, do not contain precepts for fact-finding itself. The inner rationality of fact-finding is, and should remain, purely epistemic. This separation between the moral and the epistemological is essential for sustaining freedom of proof. Without this separation, the regime of free proof would rest on a rather dubious theory of political legitimacy that empowers judges and jurors to decide cases by applying their private values. This unattractive theory submits moral and political controversies to individual adjudicators. Those who endorse such a theory are unable to draw any principled distinction between freedom of proof in adjudicative fact-finding and freedom of judgment with respect to, say, contracts, torts, and crimes. Unsurprisingly, the contemporary adherents of free proof have never endorsed such a theory.

Chapters 2 and 3 have developed a number of insights upon which my following discussion draws. To facilitate this, I summarize these insights here.

Fact-finders make their findings under uncertainty by determining the probabilities of the relevant facts. Fact-finders determine these probabilities by invoking experience-based generalizations (such as 'witnesses not interested in the outcome of the trial generally testify truthfully'; 'eyewitness identification of suspects is often inaccurate'; 'experts basing their testimony on peer-review publications are generally trustworthy'; 'out-of-court statements are generally not as credible as in-court testimony'; and so forth). These generalizations are essential for moving the inferential process forward. If these generalizations were unavailable, fact-finders would be unable to draw any conclusion from the evidence that they receive. These generalizations exist in the realm of the general and connecting them to individual cases is far from obvious. Fact-generating arguments that provide this connection are, therefore, deeply problematic. This connection is possible only when there is a real fit between the fact-pattern of the generalization and the case at hand.

This fit, however, is always conditional, rather than unqualified. Evidence that fact-finders need for making accurate decisions is always incomplete. Therefore, any identifiable fit between an individual case and an applicable generalization is conditional on the assumption that the missing evidence could not undo it. More specifically, this assumption holds that, if the missing evidence were to become available, it could not move the case from the coverage that the generalization at hand provides (say, 'disinterested witnesses generally testify truthfully') to a different covering uniformity (say, 'witnesses exhibiting animosity towards a litigant sometimes testify untruthfully against that litigant'). This information-stabilizing assumption replaces epistemic open-endedness with closure. As such, it enables fact-finders to make an inferential progress that otherwise could not be made. By virtue of this assumption, fact-finders can classify the fact-pattern of their case— say, the witness's testimony and the absence of evidence pointing to the witness's personal interest in the outcome of the trial—as similar to the fact-pattern of the generalization ('disinterested witness'). Any such assumption, however, is irreducibly conjectural. The validity of any such assumption therefore thoroughly depends not only on the evidence that fact-finders have, but also—and more critically—on the evidence that they do not have. More precisely, the validity of such assumptions depends on the unrealized potential of the missing evidence to produce a different factual conclusion. Together with the general experience that supports the generalization at hand, the extent to which the relevant stabilizing assumption is cogent determines the evidential weight of the fact-generating argument that invokes that generalization as a covering uniformity for the case. This factor determines the argument's resiliency, that is, the extent to which the argument is evidenced and, more crucially, the extent to which it can withstand changes in its underlying evidential base.

Some fact-generating arguments are weightier, or more resilient, than others. Because these arguments are essential to fact-finding, their relative weight (or resiliency) is crucial to fact-finders' decisions, irrespective of whether it is accounted for explicitly or implicitly. A proposition identified as highly probable does not have much credibility if its high probability derives from a non-weighty fact-generating argument. Such propositions are too risky to rely upon. Verdicts relying on such propositions are epistemologically questionable, if not altogether illegitimate. Adjudicative fact-finding must consequently be perceived as a two-criterial endeavour. Factual findings need to satisfy the appropriate probability standard and the appropriate weight standard at once. Factual propositions that adjudicators adopt as a basis for their decisions need to be sufficiently probable. Fact-generating arguments that attach probabilities to these propositions need to be sufficiently weighty.

As Chapter 3 explains, the weight criterion refers to both *qualitative* and *quantitative* aspects of evidential sufficiency. Ideally, evidence upon which fact-finders make their probability estimates needs to be sufficient both quantitatively and qualitatively. To be quantitatively sufficient, evidence needs to cover every segment of the relevant factual allegations. To satisfy the ideal quantitative sufficiency criterion, evidence needs to provide full information about the case at hand. To be qualitatively sufficient, evidence needs to eliminate any dependency on the information that determines its credibility (the 'second-order evidence'). To satisfy the ideal qualitative sufficiency criterion, a piece of evidence must either be demonstrably true or expose itself to every conceivable examination that could determine its credibility and pass it. In real life, to which adjudicative fact-finding belongs, these criteria can never be met. Fact-finders consequently have to settle for less: their evidential sufficiency criteria, both quantitative and qualitative, need to trade the ideal for the feasible. This trade-off forces fact-finders into making probability estimates upon evidence that suffers from some insufficiency: quantitative, qualitative, or both. Any such estimate therefore inevitably involves risk of error, unaccounted for by the estimate itself. Fact-finders cannot properly account for this risk by letting it affect the probability estimate. The risk of error that originates from evidential insufficiency does not attach peculiarly to a single probability estimate. Rather, it attaches at once to all probability estimates that fact-finders make. Because this risk points to the possible truth of more than one factual scenario, its presence provides no more reasons for reducing the probability of one such scenario than for raising that probability. Thus, if the evidence that fact-finders have points to a high probability of the scenario in which the defendant rapes the victim, the mere fact that this evidence is incomplete does not raise the probability of the competing scenario in which the defendant and the victim have consensual sex. Evidential sufficiency still matters, though, because convicting a person on a slim evidential base (pointing to a sufficiently high probability of his or her guilt) is epistemologically unwarranted. In the absence of a solid moral justification for allocating the risk of error in this particular way, this verdict is also morally indefensible. The relevant estimates of probability and their evidential weights are separate and equally important components of the fact-finding decision.

To handle cases properly, fact-finders need to answer two fundamental questions correctly. First, what are the chances that the factual allegations advanced by the litigants are true? Second, is the evidential base upon which these chances are determined solid enough? The first question is resolved on epistemological grounds. Setting probability thresholds for fact-finding decisions allocates the risk of error—a distinctively moral choice which I discuss in the pages ahead. Here, I assume that the relevant probability threshold is already set by the law. The fact-finders' task is to assess the parties' allegations against this threshold. Fact-finders can make such assessments without leaving

the epistemological terrain. To answer the second question, the epistemological terrain is too narrow. Because evidence available to fact-finders is
always incomplete, treating an evidential base as either sufficient or insufficient
for making a reliable probability estimate allocates the risk of error one way or
another. As discussed throughout this book, on this moral and political issue
epistemology has no say. Fact-finding can consequently be diagnosed as
involving three distinct types of risk-allocating decisions:

    (i)   formulation of the general standards and burdens of proof that set the
        appropriate probability thresholds for factual findings;
   (ii) determination of the quantitative sufficiency of the entire evidential
        base;
  (iii) determination of the qualitative sufficiency (or adequacy) of each
        individual item of evidence that joins the evidential base.

The concept of 'evidential weight' captures both the second and the third type
of risk-allocating decisions.

This analysis raises interesting questions about the existing burdens and
standards of proof. What do the criminal and the civil standards of proof actually require? Does the criminal proof standard, under which the prosecution
needs to prove its case against the accused beyond all reasonable doubt, extend
to evidential weight? Alternatively, is it a standard that only determines the
probability threshold for convictions? If so, what are the criteria for assessing
the weight of fact-generating arguments? And what about the civil standard of
proof? Chapter 3 provides general answers to these questions, and I will say
more about this issue in the pages ahead. At this juncture, I only identify the
domain that holds the key for answering these questions. This domain is political morality, rather than epistemology, as established in Chapter 3.

Two threshold objections to my approach combine a pragmatic response to
the problem of risk-apportionment that fact-generating arguments involve.
According to one of these objections, this problem can be rationally removed
from the agenda once the fact-finders have gathered as much information
needed for their decision as is feasibly available. An informational base that
aligns with this standard can thus be deemed practically complete. This pragmatic approach allows fact-finders to substitute informational open-endedness
with informational closure. Application of the relevant covering uniformities
(generalizations) to the case at hand would consequently acquire determinacy.
This postulation clearly involves risk of error. This risk, however, is unavoidable
because fact-finders can never obtain more information than is feasibly available.
Arguably, the pragmatic approach minimizes this risk to a sufficient degree.

This argument is fallacious. The Benthamite precept 'gather all relevant
information that can practicably be obtained' unwarrantedly postulates the

existence of a linear progression relationship between the amount of information that fact-finders have and the accuracy of their decision. More information arguably produces greater accuracy. The argument begins with the correct premise that completeness of the relevant information guarantees full accuracy in fact-finding. Further, this argument suggests, for settings involving incomplete information, that the degree to which fact-finding is accurate is commensurate with the amount of relevant information fact-finders have. This ostensibly appealing proposition is wrong. There is no *quantitative* parallel between complete and incomplete information. Complete and incomplete information conditions differ from each other not merely quantitatively, but also by their substance. Settings featuring incomplete information bring into play—and, indeed, make pivotal—the information-credibility factor that settings with full information do not require. This factor can be described as 'information about information' or, more technically, as 'second-order information', which once again underscores the intrinsic incompleteness of rudimentary evidence. As in fact-generating arguments, the possible relationship between the existing and the missing information, or, more precisely, the extent to which the credibility of the known is marred by the presence of the unknown, determines this factor. As long as the fact-finders' information remains incomplete, acquisition of further information with uncertain credentials would not improve their epistemic position. The arrival of new information would merely substitute the risk of error that existed before with a new risk of error, associated with the new information's credibility. More importantly, there would be no guarantee that the new risk of error will be smaller than the old one.

Because incomplete information is ubiquitous (adjudicative fact-finding is merely one of its many instances), this point calls for a global epistemic scepticism. Making such a call, however, is not my intention. I believe that the risk of erroneous fact-finding can be effectively controlled in a way that skews it in the chosen direction (but not through sheer augmentation of rudimentary evidence). Far from promulgating such scepticism, my point simply refutes the intuitive (but fallacious) idea that augmentation of information *necessarily* produces more accuracy in fact-finding. This Benthamite idea is plainly wrong. By highlighting the risk-replacement phenomenon as inherent in *any* acquisition of information in conditions of uncertainty, my point entails special implications for adjudicative fact-finding, where some risks of error are acceptable, while others are not. Acquisition of new information should be barred whenever it brings along an unacceptable risk of error. Fact-finding inquiries that are unacceptably risky must not be allowed to get started. This insight justifies introduction of special exclusionary rules that render potentially probative evidence inadmissible. I provide this justification below.

In cases featuring too slim an informational base to justify a verdict, the precept 'gather all relevant information that can feasibly be obtained' is altogether unhelpful. These cases exhibit the problem of weight, identified in Chapter 3. As Chapter 3 explains, there is no way of resolving this problem epistemically, without resorting to risk-allocation. Some risks of error (such as conviction of an innocent defendant) are potentially more harmful than others (such as acquittal of the guilty). Allocation of the risk of error in adjudication therefore cannot be fortuitous. Rather, it should be a product of both an informed and politically legitimate decision. Instead of letting the risk of error to fall upon whom it happens to fall, the legal system needs to assume control over this risk and skew it in the right direction.

The pragmatic opponent of my approach might agree with this observation. Yet, he or she would insist that the legal system would adequately control the risk of error by the standards and burdens of proof. This pragmatic point is describable as a 'slot-machine' approach to the risk of error. As a method of handling factual uncertainties in adjudication, this approach has certain credentials in the conventional evidence doctrine. In a landmark decision that explains the function of the burden of proof at common law, the Lord Chancellor, Earl of Halsbury, had confessed to the following:

> I must admit that . . . the conclusion I have come to is that I cannot say that I can come to a satisfactory conclusion either way; but then the law relieves me from the embarrassment which would otherwise condemn me to the solution of an insoluble problem, because it directs me in my present state of mind to consider upon whom is the burden of proof.[51]

This decision was about William Louis Winans, an American-born Baltimore financier and railway tycoon (and a diamond collector, too). Winans came to England in 1859, where he lived until his death in 1897. Winans left a multi-million estate, mainly in England. His will divided the estate between his successors. Winans came to England for health reasons, following his doctors' advice. He regarded himself as 'entirely American' and frequently expressed his wish to return to Baltimore, which he always referred to as his home. This wish did not come true. The Attorney-General claimed that since Winans domiciled in England, legacy duty ought to be recovered from his estate. Framed by the then controlling definition of domicile, the main issue in the ensuing litigation was: Had Winans formed 'a fixed and settled purpose' to settle in England? Because the stakes were high, it is safe to assume that the parties to this litigation both gathered and adduced all the evidence feasibly available at the time.

---

[51] *Winans v Attorney-General* [1904] AC 287, 289 (HL).

The House of Lords finally resolved this issue in favour of Winans' heirs. As indicated by the above quotation, the Lord Chancellor so concluded because the issue was factually indeterminate and the Attorney-General had to discharge the burden of proof. In this book's taxonomy, the evidential base was *quantitatively insufficient*. Lord Lindley's evaluation of the evidence was different. He held that the Crown met the burden of proof. Lord Lindley explained that, although Winans was a proud American citizen, his illness destroyed any hope of returning to the United States. The hard fact that Winans lived in England for so long was regarded by Lord Lindley as decisive. However, this evaluation of the evidence failed to attract Lord Macnaghten, who joined the Lord Chancellor's decision on separate grounds. Lord Macnaghten estimated that Winans' hope of returning to the United States had never been dashed.

Seemingly, the Lord Chancellor's holding is reasoned better than both Lord Lindley's dissent and Lord Macnaghten's concurring opinion. After certifying his inability to choose between the conflicting evaluations of the evidence, as a last resort, the Lord Chancellor turned to the burden of proof doctrine. This turn had to be justified,[52] though, and the Lord Chancellor's holding altogether exempted itself from this basic requirement. A bald assertion that the claimant's and the defendant's accounts of the events are equally probable does not justifiably establish that they really are. Absence of justifying reasons flavours the Lord Chancellor's holding with arbitrariness.[53] A decision that two conflicting factual scenarios are equally probable is no different from other fact-finding decisions. Any such decision rests upon fact-generating arguments and, therefore, engenders all the problems identified in Chapter 3. Thus, Lord Lindley's dissent rests on the generalization that people usually give up unrealistic hopes. This selection of the covering uniformity for this case contrasts sharply with Lord Macnaghten's selection. According to Lord Macnaghten, individuals with means and character traits comparable to those of Winans adhere to their most ardent desires unconditionally and almost never give them up. This covering uniformity appears as plausible as Lord Lindley's generalization, which explains—but still does not justify—the Lord Chancellor's resort to the burden of proof doctrine. Under this doctrine, the court must dismiss the claimant's allegations as unproven when reasons establish them to be as probable as not. Application of this doctrine requires a reasoned assessment of the competing factual scenarios. Appearances of equal plausibility will not do, because appearances are not reasons. The Lord Chancellor ought to have reasoned against the applicability of both Lord Macnaghten's covering

---

[52] See Albert Ehrenzweig, *Psychoanalytic Jurisprudence* (1971), pp. 278–9 (demanding reasoned justification in matters of *non liquet factum*).

[53] As Ehrenzweig rightly mentioned, 'a judicial power to speak *non liquet factum* would too easily lend itself to abuse'. Albert Ehrenzweig, *Law: A Personal View* (1977), p. 86.

uniformity and Lord Lindley's generalization. The Lord Chancellor estimated that the case at hand was not evidenced enough to fall under either of those two, but why is it so? What evidence was missing? More importantly, were there any grounds for estimating that the missing evidence could *equally* support either of the two scenarios?[54] If not, what made these scenarios equally probable?

A proposition that missing evidence, which is totally unknown, could equally support any of the clashing scenarios is epistemologically problematic. We all say that a coin thrown in the air will fall as either heads or tails. However, if we had full information about the coin, its throw, and the surrounding physical conditions, we would have been able to predict with certainty how it will fall. Information that we do not have could not equally support the 'heads' and the 'tails' scenarios. In reality, William Louis Winans had either decided to settle in England or formed no such decision. Attribution of equal plausibility to these scenarios is therefore both unreal and epistemologically unwarranted. This attribution could only be possible if the case could be moved to the domain of generality that accommodates cases with similar make-ups. Then, if about a half of those cases were to fall under Lord Macnaghten's covering uniformity, with the remaining half falling under Lord Lindley's generalization, the Lord Chancellor's estimation that Winans's case could equally fall under either could be justified. This estimation would then constitute a direct analogy to a series of unrigged coin tosses that produces a roughly equal number of heads and tails. The 'law of large numbers' works.

But the law of small numbers works, too. Why strip the case of its particularities in order to move it to a general 'large number' category when it is possible to keep the case as-is, with all its specifics, and find a uniformity that will explain its fact-pattern one way or another? To allow the fact-finder to find facts, rudimentary evidence that determines the case's specific fact-pattern indeed needs to interact with the relevant generalizations. But why move the specific to the general, as the Lord Chancellor did, instead of moving the general to the specific in either Lord Macnaghten's or Lord Lindley's way?

This question has a seemingly plausible answer. The evidential base of the case was quantitatively insufficient. Because there were two different ways of moving the general to the specific, the general could not be moved to the specific. When anything can be proved, nothing can. For that reason, the specific case of William Louis Winans had to be cleared of its unhelpful particularities and transferred to the general domain. This domain accommodates an unrigged coin in the air along with universally equal distributions of rival

---

[54] The scenario in which Winans remained undecided about his domicile merged with Lord Macnaghten's scenario because in that case, too, Winans would not domicile in England (under the affirmative domicile approach).

hypotheses. The Crown's case against Winans's estate is thus established to be as probable as not.

This proposition may hold true, but the domain in which it holds true is not epistemological. This domain accommodates precepts for making decisions under ignorance, rather than for validating knowledge. The actual distribution of the rival hypotheses occupying this domain is unknown. For that reason, this distribution is deemed unslanted, but unknown and unslanted are not synonymous. Fact-finders are nonetheless allowed to proceed on the assumption that the relevant rival hypotheses are distributed evenly across cases. From an epistemological viewpoint, this assumption is unwarranted, but it does have a certain appeal. By treating all manifestations of ignorance as having equal impact on the fact-finder's decision, it allocates the risk of error in a balanced way. Such allocation of the risk may, however, still be inadequate from both moral and legal points of view. In criminal trials, as long as the legal system is willing to protect defendants from wrongful conviction, this allocation of the risk would be altogether unacceptable. As explained in Chapters 3 and 6, for example, naked statistical evidence must not be regarded as sufficient for conviction even when it points to a very high probability of guilt. In civil litigation, this allocation of the risk should be generally acceptable. By treating errors that harm claimants and defendants as equally harmful, this assumption treats the parties with equal concern and respect. Generally, such a treatment is morally and legally appropriate, but it has nothing to do with epistemology. Epistemology is not about making risk-equalizing decisions; it is about making decisions—balanced and imbalanced alike—on strictly factual grounds.

The fact-finder's diagnosis of evidential insufficiency, quantitative or qualitative, and the subsequent recourse to the domain of equal chances depend on the allocation of the risk of error. Decisions certifying that the evidential base is good enough for making the relevant probability estimate equally depend on the allocation of that risk. In *Winans*, under the principle requiring that the claimant and the defendant should have equal shares in this risk, the case could be deemed balanced. In the absence of reasons preferring the claimant over the defendant, or vice versa, this equality principle has a strong intuitive appeal. The strength of this appeal, however, must not obscure its nature, as it probably did in Winans's case and, presumably, in many other cases as well. This appeal is moral and political, rather than epistemological. By classifying the case as falling under the burden-of-proof doctrine, the Lord Chancellor allocated the risk of error between Winans's estate and the Crown is a balanced way. This allocation of the risk aligns with common sense. Chapter 7 demonstrates that it also aligns with common law. The Lord Chancellor, however, ought to have stated explicitly that his classification of Winans's case as undetermined allocated the risk of error. This clarification would have required him to identify the equality principle by which he allocated that risk. As explained in Chapter 7, this principle is generally applicable in civil litigation, but it is also qualified by some exceptions. Fortunately, none of these exceptions could apply to Winans's case. Therefore, although the Lord Chancellor's application of the burden of proof was unreasoned, his decision was correct in its bottom line.

A remarkable marine insurance litigation, *Rhesa Shipping Co. v Edmunds*,[55] is a more contemporary example of the same point. This case presents a qualitative (rather than quantitative) evidential insufficiency. The claimants' ship, insured with the defendants against 'perils of the seas' and 'negligence of the crew', sank in the Mediterranean. The ship sank along with most of the evidence pertaining to her seaworthiness and to the cause of the accident. The claimants could not activate the seaworthiness presumption, which usually wins a marine insurance lawsuit based on a 'perils of the seas' policy if there is no evidence of scuttling.[56] The defendants had no evidence indicating that the ship was unseaworthy. Evidence presented was scanty. It revealed that something had seriously damaged the ship by creating a large aperture in a shell-plating on her port side. Water had streamed through this aperture into the ship, and the ship sank as a result of severe flooding. The factor responsible for this aperture consequently became the contested issue in the ensuing litigation.

Two theories concerning this factor were ruled out by the trial judge as virtually impossible:

(1) the claimants' theory that the aperture and the consequent loss of the ship resulted from some negligence of the crew;
(2) the defendants' theory that the ship was unseaworthy.

This left the judge with two other theories, namely:

(3) the claimants' theory that the aperture was caused by a submerged submarine;
(4) the defendants' theory that the proximate cause of the aperture was wear and tear.

Evidence supporting these theories could not lift either of them above the conjectural. Both theories were considered by the judge to have low probability.

---

[55] *Edmunds et al (The Popi M) v Rhesa Shipping Co* [1983] 2 Lloyd's Rep. 235 (Commercial Court); *Rhesa Shipping Co v Edmunds et al (The Popi M)* [1984] 2 Lloyd's Rep. 555 (CA); *Rhesa Shipping Co v Edmunds et al (The Popi M)* (1985) 2 All ER 712 (HL) (the House of Lords' decision is subsequently referred to as *Rhesa*).

[56] For analysis of this presumption and its operational significance see G. Brice, Unexplained Losses in Marine Insurance (1991) 16 Tulane Maritime L. J. 105 at 113–14, 120, 122–3, 129.

The judge found theory (3) more probable than theory (4), though. On the basis of this comparative preponderance, he ruled in favour of the claimants.[57] As remarked by the House of Lords,[58] this finding seems to have adhered to Sherlock Holmes' notorious precept, pronounced to Dr. Watson, 'How often have I said to you that when you have eliminated the impossible, whatever remains, however improbable, must be the truth?'[59]

The finding constituted a plain legal error. Under the preponderance-of-the-evidence standard, the claimants' allegations had to be established as being 'more probable *than not*'. In order to succeed, these allegations had to prevail over *any* possible account of the events that could favour the defendants. The defendants flatly denied these allegations and were perfectly entitled to do so. In developing theory (4), they were not endorsing it as their only contention.[60] The trial judge's error passed appellate muster,[61] but ultimately was rectified by the House of Lords, and the claimants were denied recovery.

This could be an unquestionably right decision if the claimants had not put forward another, more promising, argument. They submitted that the fatal aperture had been brought about by some unidentified peril of the seas and that this was the most probable conclusion that could be arrived at on the basis of the evidence. This argument could be translated into formal probabilistic terms as referring to the probability of the disjunctive proposition 'either p_1, or p_2, or p_3, or . . . p_n', in which p_1, p_2, p_3, . . . and p_n represent the full set of perils of the seas, both known and unknown. The argument therefore holds that the probability of event 'p_1 or p_2 or p_3 or . . . p_n' is greater than 0.5. Because the claimants were entitled to win the case upon proof of any member of the p-set, this argument appears sound.[62] The probability of many individual p's in the set was unknown. This probability may have been low, too. Yet, the probability of the all-encompassing proposition holding *one of the p's* responsible for the claimants' loss was high enough to tilt the scales in the claimants' favour. There was also enough evidence to sustain this general probability. Far from implausible in its own right, this argument was also supported by the judgment of the Court of Appeal.[63] However, the House of Lords held that

[57] Cf. Ronald J. Allen, A Reconceptualization of Civil Trials (1986) 66 B. U. L. Rev. 401 (supporting a similar approach on policy grounds).   [58] *Rhesa*, at 718a.

[59] A. Conan Doyle, The Sign of Four, in A. Conan Doyle, *Sherlock Holmes: The Complete Illustrated Novels* (London: Chancellor Press, 1987), p. 138.

[60] This procedural entitlement was recognized in *Theodorou v Chester* [1951] 1 Lloyd's Rep. 204, 238; and, more recently, in *Lamb Head Shipping Co. Ltd. v Jennings* [1994] 1 Lloyd's Rep. 624, 627.

[61] *Rhesa Shipping Co. v Edmunds et al (The Popi M)* [1984] 2 Lloyd's Rep. 555 (CA).

[62] Cf. D. H. Hodgson, The Scales of Justice: Probability and Proof in Legal Fact-finding (1995) 69 Aust. L. J. 731, 750 (supporting the particularity-of-proof requirement laid down by the House of Lords as 'unexceptional', but arguing that 'alternatives on which the plaintiff can succeed can be bracketed').

[63] *Rhesa Shipping Co. v Edmunds et al (The Popi M)* [1984] 2 Lloyd's Rep. 555, 558–9 (Sir John Donaldson, M.R.); 561 (Lord Justice May).

'The shipowners could not ... rely on a ritual incantation of the generic expression "perils of the seas," but were bound, if they were to discharge successfully the burden of proof ... *to condescend to particularity in the matter.*'[64] This holding unequivocally indicates that an abstract probability favourable to the claimant is not sufficient to grant him or her recovery. To enable the claimant to prevail, probability favouring his or her case must represent more than sheer chance. This probability needs to attach to some particular account of events that favours the claimant. To be valid, this attachment must, of course, be sufficiently grounded in the evidence.

The Law Lords' demand for case-specific evidence covering the claimants' account of the events[65] is epistemologically plausible, but is not an epistemological must. Arguably, an abstract probability surpassing the 0.5 threshold should satisfy the preponderance of the evidence standard. Acceptance of this argument, however, is not an epistemological must either. The choice between the two epistemologically valid criteria depends on the status that the law, not epistemology, is willing to afford to naked statistical evidence[66] and, more profoundly, to non-weighty probabilities.[67] Can naked statistical evidence be qualitatively adequate, given its failure to reflect the circumstances of individual cases and the corresponding inability of both parties and fact-finders to examine its applicability to the case at hand? Should fact-finders rely on such evidence? Alternatively, should naked statistical evidence be blocked by the appropriate weight-threshold? More realistically, should fact-finders take a differentiated approach and apply the weight requirement interchangeably, depending on the nature and the implications of their decisions? Epistemological criteria cannot resolve any of these questions. The burden-of-proof doctrine does not contain any criteria for resolving these questions either. As Chapter 3 explains, proper allocation of the risk of error is the key for answering these questions. To answer these questions, fact-finders need to introduce the appropriate risk-allocating criteria, moral and political in character, into the burden-of-proof

---

[64] *Rhesa*, at 716. This holding echoed Judge Devlin's decision in *Waddle v Wallsend Shipping Co. (The Hopestar)* [1952] 2 Lloyd's List L. Rep. 105 at 106 ('in a case where substantially all the facts have been brought to light, it is no doubt legitimate to argue that some cause must be found, and therefore the one that has most to be said for it should be selected. Where it can fairly be said that all possible causes have been canvassed, the strongest must be the winner. But in a case where all direct evidence is missing, there is no ground for saying that the most plausible conjecture must perforce be the true explanation. The answer that may well have to be given is that not enough is known about the circumstances of the loss to enable the inquirer to say how it happened').

[65] By this conditioning of 'large inferences' upon 'small facts', the House of Lords appears to have subscribed to a different precept of Sherlock Holmes. See Conan Doyle, above note 59, at pp. 115–16.

[66] See David Kaye, The Limits of the Preponderance of the Evidence Standard: Justifiably Naked Statistical Evidence and Multiple Causation (1982) Am. Bar Found. Res. J. 487.

[67] See Alex Stein, An Essay on Uncertainty and Fact-Finding in Civil Litigation, with Special Reference to Contract Cases (1998) 48 U. Toronto L.J. 299.

doctrine. Within this doctrine too, morality picks up what the epistemology leaves off. Both *Winans* and *Rhesa* exemplify this point vividly.[68]

Application of the 'slot-machine' approach in criminal cases would be impossible. Under this approach, any epistemic indeterminacy would qualify as a reasonable doubt that erects an insurmountable barrier to conviction. Were this approach carried through to its logical end, then all criminal defendants, perhaps including even those who unequivocally plead guilty, would have to be acquitted. The entire criminal justice system becomes dysfunctional. For obvious reasons, this outcome produces a colossal social disutility.

The 'slot-machine' approach offers no solutions, principled or pragmatic, to the fundamental fact-finding problems that arise in adjudication. This approach does not even begin to resolve the problems concerning the quality of the evidential base to which fact-finders apply the controlling proof standards. These problems arise in connection with decisions that either admit potentially probative evidence or exclude it from the fact-finders' consideration. Exclusion of a potentially probative piece of evidence imposes the risk of error on the proponent of that evidence. Because such evidence may contain credible information which the fact-finders will ignore, the risk of error is transparent. At the same time, since any such evidence may also distort the truth, its admission would mark its opponent as a bearer of the risk of error. The risk of erroneous fact-finding that exists in both cases originates from the absence of information. Exclusion of evidence with a probative potential produces this informational void. For this reason, Bentham and his followers criticized this exclusion. Admission of such evidence also engenders an informational void, albeit differently, which Bentham and other supporters of free proof ignored. As indicated, a newly admitted piece of evidence effects a new set

[68] *Rhesa* was a deeply problematic decision. In that case, as in many others, the judges had four options for allocating the risk of error:

(1) *the equality principle,* demanding that the risk be allocated between the claimant and the defendant in an equal fashion;

(2) *the expectation principle,* allocating the risk in correspondence with the parties' contractual expectations, explicit or implied;

(3) *the penalty-default approach* that allocates the risk in a way the parties cannot mutually accept. which forces them into making an explicit contractual stipulation that allocates this risk differently (which, in turn, would save the litigation costs associated with contract interpretation). See generally, Ian Ayres and Richard Gertner, Filling Gaps in Incomplete Contracts: An Economic Theory of Default Rules (1989) 99 Yale L.J. 87.

(4) *the error-minimizing principle,* prescribing that the risk be allocated in a way that reduces the number of erroneous verdicts to a minimum. This principle is of particular importance in insurance cases, such as *Rhesa,* where it helps to spread the costs of accidents efficiently, thereby implementing one of the key objectives of the law of insurance.

Under each of these principles, if the claimants' allegation that the aperture in their ship resulted from some unidentified peril of the seas was, indeed, more probable than not, the claimants should have been allowed recovery. See Stein, above note 67, at 323–51.

of credibility problems, as long as its probative credentials remain uncertain. Because in adjudication these credentials are never certain, fact-finders need more evidence in order to assess them. This additional evidence engenders credibility problems of its own, which the fact-finders would frequently be unable to resolve. At some point, information that adjudicators need in order to resolve these problems would simply be unavailable. The adjudicators' choice between excluding and admitting evidence with uncertain probative credentials boils down to a decision that prefers one type of informational void over the other. This zero-sum-game situation underscores the risk-allocating character of evidence selection.

Allocation of the risk of error in adjudicative fact-finding is pervasive. Fact-finders allocate this risk by moulding the evidential base upon which they determine the probabilities of the parties' competing allegations. Fact-finders also allocate the risk of error when they determine these probabilities in conditions of uncertainty. The burden-of-proof rules tell fact-finders how to allocate the risk of error on the basis of probabilities already determined. Fact-finders can apply these rules only after determining the probabilities of the relevant factual allegations. These rules, however, do not instruct fact-finders as to how to determine these probabilities. The prevalent evidence doctrine assumes that fact-finders can make such determinations on purely epistemological grounds, but this assumption is incorrect. Some determinations of probability are better evidenced and, consequently, weightier than others, and rational fact-finders ought to take this factor into account.[69] But how exactly should they account for this crucial factor? Any chosen evidential base is potentially distorted and risky to rely upon. Should fact-finders use evidence indiscriminately as a platform for making probability estimates? If not, how should they tell the acceptable risks of error from the unacceptable ones?

As explained, on this critical issue epistemology has no say. Epistemological principles can only help fact-finders to make probability estimates and determine

---

[69] David Schum's observation about hedged inferences advances the understanding of this point Schum writes that:

Inferences can only be probabilistic in nature, and our conclusions have to be hedged in some way. . . . On close examination many apparently simple inferences reveal some remarkably subtle properties that often go unrecognized. Inferences can be decomposed to various levels of 'granularity'. As we make finer decompositions of an inference, we expose additional and often interesting sources of uncertainty. One trouble we face is that there rarely seems to be any final or ultimate decomposition of an inference. Indeed there may be alternative decompositions, none of which we can label as being uniquely 'correct'. We are often forced to simplify an inference task by cutting a few corners here and there. . . . Having acknowledged the necessity for simplifying inferences, . . . it seems advisable to have some awareness and understanding of the evidential subtleties that we may be overlooking or suppressing in the process. In probabilistic inferences what we do *not* consider *can* hurt us, often very badly.

David Schum, *Evidential Foundations of Probabilistic Reasoning* (1994), p. 2.

their relative weights. These principles, however, set no minimal standards with respect to evidential weight (the quantitative and the qualitative sufficiency of the fact-finders' evidential base). Nor do they provide criteria for distinguishing between the acceptable and the unacceptable risk of error in probability determinations. From a purely epistemological perspective, any evidential base—slim and thick alike—is an admissible platform for determining probabilities, as long as the fact-finders take this factor into consideration. From this perspective, it is entirely rational for fact-finders both to certify and to refuse to certify preponderance of the evidence on a slim evidential base. To state it more accurately: it is not a business of epistemology to attach adjudicative consequences to its precepts. Epistemology cannot decide whether fact-finders should base their adjudicative decisions upon probability estimates that do not carry much weight. Any such decision allocates the risk of error one way or another and invokes an important moral and political component. Moral and political choices therefore permeate adjudicative fact-finding at all stages. Adjudicative fact-finding depends upon morality as much as it depends upon epistemology.

D. Allocating the Risk of Error by Evidence Law: Burdens of Proof, Exclusion, Pre-emption, Corroboration, and Cost-Efficiency

Allocation of the risk of error in fact-finding ought to be the principal objective of evidence law. As much as it matters how adjudicators decide cases,[70] it matters how they allocate this risk. While some adjudicators may favour equality in apportioning the risk of fact-finding error, others may opt for economic efficiency. An altogether different group of adjudicators may take a pragmatic approach and let this risk fall upon whom it happens to fall. Adjudicators should not be allowed to choose between these (or other) approaches as they deem fit. To be legitimate, their risk-allocating decisions ought to be justified by moral and political principles classifying as authoritative. These principles ought to reflect societal preferences in the area of risk-allocation. These general preferences need to be both adopted and adapted by the law of evidence. They should translate into a series of specific rules and principles that allocate the risk of fact-finding error. These rules and principles ought to be developed by common law judges or, alternatively, by the legislator. Under the common law model, the legislator of course retains its overriding authority to repeal or modify any judge-made rule.

[70] Ronald Dworkin, *Law's Empire* (1986), p. 1.

Rules and principles allocating the risk of error fall into two general categories. One of these categories accommodates rules and principles that determine probability thresholds for making factual findings in conditions of uncertainty. These rules and principles include burdens and standards of proof that apply in both civil and criminal trials, as well as a number of presumptions. The function of these rules and principles is two-fold. At the general level, they determine the acceptable rate of error in civil and criminal litigation. At the individual level, they identify the bearers of the risk of error in different settings and, as a corollary, allocate the immunity from that risk.

Rules and principles that belong to the second category perform yet another risk-allocating function. They control the weight of the evidential base upon which fact-finders make their estimates of probability. Specifically, these rules and principles set forth different standards for evidential or adequacy, both quantitative and qualitative. By setting these standards, they allocate the risk of error to the party whose evidence fails to satisfy the controlling adequacy standard. As a corollary, they grant the immunity from the risk of error to the opponent of that party. In cases not regulated by these rules and principles, freedom of proof reigns. In such cases, fact-finders are allowed to determine the relevant probabilities upon any evidential base and (subject to the controlling proof standard) to allocate the risk of error as they consider appropriate.

Rules and principles forming the second category follow four basic strategies: exclusionary, pre-emptive, corroborative, and cost-efficient.[71] First, fact-finding inquiries may involve risks of error that are too high and thus altogether unacceptable. An extreme example of such an inquiry features a prosecution witness testifying in a murder trial about an underworld rumour according to which the defendant killed the victim.[72] The risk of error that attaches to inquiries aiming at ascertaining the veracity of such multiple-hearsay testimony would typically be excessive. Such inquiries, therefore, should not be allowed to get started even when they may lead to the truth. Evidence law implements this ban by excluding evidence that opens up an injury considered unacceptably risky. This upfront exclusion places the risk of error on the proponent of the evidence—an outcome that sharply contrasts with the regime of free proof that allows fact-finders to place this risk upon either side.

Second, some fact-finding inquiries, not unacceptably risky per se, are still riskier than other available inquiries that can be directed to the same end.

---

[71] The first three of these strategies derive from PMI, as developed in Chapter 3.

[72] This morbid example is neither unrealistic nor extracted from a totalitarian legal system. In Belgium, a statement made out of court by an unidentified police informer was held to be admissible as evidence incriminating the accused. See Application 8417/78 *X v Belgium* [1979] 16 European Commission of Human Rights—Decisions & Reports 200.

In such cases, the inquiry that keeps the risk of error at its lowest pre-empts other available inquiries. Evidence setting this inquiry in motion should override any piece of evidence that opens up an inferior alternative. Whenever such best evidence is available, any alternative evidence should be excluded. The simplest example of this pre-emptive strategy features an original document and its copy. Generally, if the original document is available, the fact-finders should not admit the copy into evidence. Another simple example involves a witness willing to testify in court correspondingly to a statement that he or she previously made. Here, too, the testimony of this witness should pre-empt the out-of-court statement, and the adjudicators should therefore hold the statement inadmissible. The pre-emptive strategy identifies the initiator of the second-best inquiry as a bearer of the risk of error. This risk still exists because the exclusion of the second-best evidence does not guarantee that the first-best evidence will produce the anticipated accuracy in fact-finding. In some cases, evidence considered second-best may actually facilitate the discovery of the truth.

The first two strategies, exclusion and pre-emption, aim at securing qualitative adequacy of the fact-finders' evidential base. The third regulatory strategy, which I tag corroborative, focuses on the quantitative aspect of the evidential adequacy problem. General experience marks certain types of evidence as generally not safe enough to rely upon. Based on this experience, evidence law may condition the fact-finders' power to base their findings on such evidence upon its verification through an additional inquiry (that would otherwise be optional, rather than compulsory). Accomplice testimony is a paradigmatic example of this regulatory strategy. In several common-law jurisdictions, fact-finders are not permitted to find the accused guilty on his or her accomplice's credible testimony standing alone. To allow the fact-finders to convict the accused, this testimony needs to be corroborated by additional evidence that the fact-finders need to examine and find credible.[73] This rule has an experience-based rationale. Accomplices frequently have a motive to lie. In numerous cases, in order to obtain an exoneration or a relatively lenient punishment, they need to shift the commission of the entire crime or a substantial part thereof to the accused. Accomplices also have the means for successfully obfuscating the truth: they are in possession of insider information that enables them to disguise the falsity of their self-serving testimony. To be sure, not all criminal accomplices give false testimony, but those who do pool with those who do not. Consequently, in the absence of other evidence, fact-finders are generally unable to distinguish between the cheaters and the honest witnesses. Cases featuring accomplice testimony always involve this risk. The regime of

[73] See below at p. 208.

free proof allows fact-finders, if they find the accomplice testimony sufficiently credible, to place the risk of error upon the accused. The corroboration doctrine treats the issue as non-discretionary and places the risk of error on the prosecution.

The fourth regulatory strategy is cost-efficiency. This strategy formulates the trade-off between the cost of errors in fact-finding and the cost of procedures that aim at avoiding those errors. This trade-off originates from the cost-efficiency doctrine that requires fact-finders to minimize the total sum of those costs. As Chapter 5 demonstrates, this doctrine has several manifestations in evidence law. For attaining its economic objective, the cost-efficiency doctrine employs each of the evidence-controlling devices: exclusion, pre-emption, and corroboration. These devices, however, are employed in a strictly instrumental fashion, rather than as immunities from the risk of error to which litigants have an intrinsic entitlement. The utilitarian domain, in which the cost-efficiency doctrine operates, recognizes no utility-trumping entitlements. Under this doctrine, litigants have no vested rights that could force fact-finders to allocate the risk of error in their favour. They benefit from risk-allocation only incidentally, when their private interest happens to align with the social goal that the cost-efficiency doctrine promotes. A general example of this doctrine's exclusionary impact on evidence law is Federal Rule of Evidence 403. Under this rule, any piece of evidence may be excluded 'if its probative value is substantially outweighed by the danger of unfair prejudice, confusion of the issues, or misleading the jury, or by considerations of undue delay, waste of time, or needless presentation of cumulative evidence'. Application of this general rule is bound to differ from case to case, but—if the rule is applied properly—its social outcome would always be the same. This outcome is the maximal reduction of the social loss represented by the sum of two costs: the cost of errors in fact-finding and the cost of fact-finding procedures that reduce those errors.[74] An example of the doctrine's pre-emptive technique can be found in the admissibility arrangement set for public records by Federal Rules of Evidence 803(8), 902(1)–(5), and 1005. Certified copies of such records are generally admissible as evidence to the truth of its contents. There is no need to produce a witness for verifying the record and its truthfulness. This arrangement brushes aside the hearsay rule, the best evidence rule, and the general authentication requirement; and it does so for good reasons. Experience demonstrates that public records and their certified copies are generally trustworthy. Removing such records from files and their subsequent refiling are costly. Society also incurs substantial costs when its public servants routinely are required to

---

[74] See Richard A. Posner, An Economic Approach to the Law of Evidence (1999) 51 Stan. L. Rev. 1477, 1480–7.

appear in courts in order to testify about such records (after a largely artificial refreshment of their individual, as opposed to institutional, memories). If allowed to be spent, these costs could possibly generate a benefit: strict adherence to the traditional evidence rules could possibly eliminate some errors in fact-finding. These errors, however, are rightly expected to be rare and sporadic, given the general trustworthiness of public records and their certified copies. Elimination of these errors does not justify its costs. The replacement of the regular fact-finding procedures, featuring production of original documents and the in-court testimony of qualified witnesses, therefore becomes justified.[75]

Occasionally, the cost-efficiency doctrine may resort to a corroborative strategy as well. In some jurisdictions, for example, a claimant's testimony does not normally win the case even if the court finds it sufficiently credible. To allow the claimant to prevail, his or her testimony needs to be corroborated by additional evidence.[76] This arrangement has an economically sound rationale. The 'word against word' cases—in which fact-finders have no evidence other than the conflicting accounts of the claimant and of the defendant—are notoriously difficult to resolve. In many such cases, the claimant's testimony fails to generate a preponderance of the evidence. To reach this conclusion, however, fact-finders need to go through an expensive trial process and deliberations. The corroboration requirement saves this expenditure by devising a decisional shortcut. If the claimant's testimony is lacking corroboration, the fact-finders dismiss the claimant's allegations as unproven. This shortcut may produce injustice in some individual cases, but its systematic saving of adjudication expenses makes it justifiable. The number of 'word against word' cases in which fact-finders can *justifiably* assess the claimant's testimony as more probable than not is relatively small. Expending adjudication costs on the entire pool of 'word against word' cases in order to identify these outliers is, therefore, economically imprudent.

These and related issues are taken up in Chapter 5. Chapters 6 and 7 examine risk-allocation from a different, non-utilitarian, perspective that centres upon individual rights. They proceed on the assumption that the legal system should be interested in both the number of errors that fact-finders commit and upon whom those errors fall. Unlike Learned Hand, I do not fear litigation as much as sickness and death.[77] Nonetheless, I would not take upon myself the risk of error in fact-finding even in exchange for a sharp augmentation of social welfare. For this reason, I cannot recommend it to other individuals. At the general

---

[75] The opponent of a public-record evidence may still subpoena any relevant witness.

[76] See below at pp. 242–3. This rule merits expansion.

[77] See Learned Hand, above note 9, at 105 ('After now some dozen years of experience I must say that as a litigant I should dread a lawsuit beyond almost anything else short of sickness and death').

level, this rights-based approach holds that distribution of different risks across society matters.[78] As such, it lends support to individuals' demand for immunities from the risk of error in adjudicative fact-finding. These immunities should be allowed to override social utility. Chapters 6 and 7 position this approach against the utilitarian view and identify the immunities against risk of error that apply in criminal and civil litigation, respectively.

The arguments set forth in Chapters 5, 6, and 7 are predominantly normative and only partly descriptive. They analyse the central tenets of the Anglo-American systems of evidence. This analysis demonstrates that evidential rules and principles affiliating to these systems have a single all-important function: allocation of the risk of error. This analysis also moulds the existing rules and principles into four categories, each of which represents a distinct risk-allocating technique. As indicated, these categories are exclusion, pre-emption, corroboration, and the burden of proof. This depiction of the Anglo-American systems of evidence only exemplifies my normative theory and is far from being comprehensive. Chapters 5, 6, and 7 therefore avoid making strong descriptive claims.

This depiction of the Anglo-American systems of evidence is generalized and theorized at once. Far from offering a treatise-like exposition of these legal systems, it singles out their central tenets and perceives them through theoretical lenses developed in this book. This theorized depiction aims at improving the general understanding of evidence law and its foundations, rather than at facilitating the daily application of evidence rules in a given jurisdiction. This objective has obvious merits and also a limitation. I am unable to prove that my theory is uniquely correct, rather than simply valid. If summoned to defend it at the meta-theoretical level, I can only respond that it takes a theory to beat a theory.[79] I should add, though, that my theory does not merely offer yet 'another view of the Cathedral'.[80] Evidence law, as conventionally portrayed, does not make a metaphorical parallel with Monet's Cathedral. Under the conventional wisdom, this branch of the law is conspicuously more reminiscent of Pisa's Leaning Tower. My theory returns the leaning tower of evidence law to its upright position.

As indicated, the discussion in Chapters 5, 6, and 7 is predominantly normative in character. This discussion makes a number of claims as to what evidence law ought to be. The normative ambition of these claims is contextualized,

---

[78] For a recent philosophical discussion of this issue, see Sven Ove Hansson, Ethical Criteria for Risk Acceptance (2003) 59 *Erkenntnis* 291.

[79] See Richard A. Epstein, Common Law, Labor Law and Reality: A Rejoinder to Professors Getman and Kohler (1983) 92 Yale L.J. 1435, 1435.

[80] This metaphor is borrowed from Guido Calabresi and A. Douglas Melamed, Property Rules, Liability Rules, and Inalienability: One View of the Cathedral (1972) 85 Harv. L. Rev. 1089.

rather than abstract. These claims do not attempt to develop the law of evidence from scratch (which, I suspect, would have been a fruitless exercise). Instead, they proceed endogenically, presenting a crucial improvement of this branch of the law. Allocation of the risk of error permeates adjudicative fact-finding. Moral and political in character, this aspect of fact-finding decisions should not depend on the preferences that adjudicators privately endorse. It merits a both principled and comprehensive regulation by the law of evidence. The existing evidential rules and principles fall short of providing such regulation. For this reason, and due to their scattered and ununified appearance, these rules and principles have often been criticized for being redundant. My normative argument goes in the opposite direction. Free proof may or may not be a better regime than an unaccomplished and disorganized regulation of fact-finding; a system that regulates adjudicative fact-finding in a both principled and comprehensive fashion is still better than both. Legal regulation of adjudicative fact-finding therefore needs to be fortified, rather than eliminated. With this goal in mind, I extract from positive law a number of general principles that are yet to receive a formal doctrinal status. These principles reflect the general preferences that the law exhibits with respect to decisions allocating the risk of error in adjudicative fact-finding. These principles include the *equal-best requirement* that applies in criminal trials and both *primary* and *corrective equality* standards that control civil litigation. They also include *PMI*—the maximal individualization principle—that has variable applications in civil and criminal trials, depending on the desired apportionment of the risk of error. My descriptive argument holds that these principles explain many of the existing evidential rules and doctrines. My normative theory holds that evidence law ought to afford formal recognition to these principles and apply them across the board.[81]

This theory does not systematically distinguish between bench trials and trials by jury. Arguably, judges perform better as fact-finders than jurors do because judges are experienced professionals. Lay jurors tend to succumb to popular biases and commit cognitive errors. Empirical support for this popular belief has yet to be provided, and I therefore do not discuss it. My theory assumes that jurors generally follow the trial judge's instructions and that the existing jury-control mechanisms guard sufficiently against biases and cognitive errors. My theory requires trial judges to select evidence for the jury by properly applying the appropriate legal mechanisms, both exclusionary and pre-emptive. This theory also requires trial judges to instruct the jury about the controlling standards and burdens of proof and about the applicable corroboration requirements. To further secure the alignment of jury verdicts with

---

[81] Dworkin's jurisprudence could identify these principles as part of the law. See Ronald Dworkin, above note 70, at pp. 225–75. I refrain from making such an ambitious claim.

the existing evidential mechanisms, trial judges should use their power to deliver judgments as a matter of law (both prior to and after the jury's verdict). Appellate courts should oversee both trial judges' decisions and jury verdicts within the regular framework of appeal. My theory combines its recommendations with the legal mechanisms that already exist.[82]

For bench trials, my theory recommends that trial judges select evidence for themselves by applying the controlling legal mechanisms, exclusionary and pre-emptive alike. Under this theory, rules and principles belonging to these mechanisms do not counter biases or rectify cognitive errors. Rather, they allocate the risk of error in conditions of uncertainty. Based on this understanding, judges, in performing their fact-finding tasks, should not find it difficult to disregard the evidence that they previously excluded. They should also be able to properly apply the appropriate standards of proof and corroboration requirements.[83]

---

[82] Cf. Ronald J. Allen, Structuring Jury Decision-Making in Criminal Cases: A Unified Constitutional Approach to Evidentiary Devices (1980) 94 Harv. L. Rev. 321.

[83] Empirical studies do not offer unequivocal findings as to whether juries and judges avoid being influenced by inadmissible information to which they have previously been exposed. See Gregory Mitchell, Mapping Evidence Law (2003) Mich. St. L. Rev. 1065, 1121 (observing that 'while studies of non-deliberating mock jurors have generally found that such jurors have difficulty disregarding inadmissible evidence heard during a simulated trial when later making decisions, recent studies of deliberating mock jurors have found that these jurors do seem to disregard inadmissible evidence in their decisions made after the deliberations'); Jeffrey J. Rachlinski, Andrew J. Wistrich, and Christopher P. Guthrie, Can Judges Ignore Inadmissible Information? The Difficulty of Deliberately Disregarding (2005) 153 U. Pa. L. Rev. 1251 (subject to special cases, judges are generally unable to disregard inadmissible information of which they are aware). As explained above at pp. 60–3, behavioural studies can only establish flaws in people's cognitive performance, as opposed to competence. Flaws identified by these studies are correctable.

5

Cost-Efficiency

A. The Cost-Efficiency Doctrine: Minimizing the Aggregate Cost of Accuracy and Errors

Adjudicative fact-finding needs to be cost-efficient. To maintain cost-efficiency, fact-finders need to minimize the total cost of errors and error-avoidance. The value of the entitlements that the legal system fails to enforce and the utility of the liabilities that it fails to impose determine the errors' cost. The cost of error-avoidance is comprised of the aggregate cost of trial and pretrial procedures and decisions that enhance accuracy in fact-finding. Fact-finding is efficient whenever it minimizes the sum of the two costs. Fact-finding is inefficient whenever it fails to minimize this sum.

Under this framework, when a procedure that reduces the risk of error by 10 per cent (on the margin) costs £1,000, adjudicators only implement it in cases in which the value of the litigated entitlement or liability exceeds £10,000. When a particular piece of evidence is as likely to engender an error as to be instrumental to the ascertainment of the truth, the adjudicators juxtapose the disutility of the error against the utility of the truth. If the utility of the truth does not exceed the disutility of the error, the adjudicators should rule the evidence inadmissible. Admitting and considering such evidence is wasteful. If the utility of the truth exceeds the disutility of the error by, for example, £1,000, the adjudicators should consider the cost of processing and considering the evidence. Because this evidence offers an expected return in the amount of £500 (50 per cent of £1,000), the adjudicators should only admit it if the cost of processing and considering it falls below £500. To sum up, a procedural or evidential effort should only be made when it generates a positive expected return.[1]

This goal is easy to formulate, but difficult to attain. Attaining this goal requires overcoming two mutually related obstacles. The first obstacle is the

---

[1] See Richard A. Posner, An Economic Approach to the Law of Evidence (1999) 51 Stan. L. Rev. 1477, 1480–7.

divergence between the private and the social benefits that adjudication engenders.[2] This divergence is responsible for the fundamental misalignment between the private incentives that operate in adjudication and the social desiderata.[3] In criminal trials, for example, society is interested in acquitting the innocent and in convicting the guilty. Naturally, guilty defendants have a different motivation. These defendants do not facilitate the discovery of the truth and often attempt to thwart it. Innocent defendants' incentives also do not align with the social interest. These defendants only care about their own acquittals and expenditures. They seek acquittals irrespective of the cost to society. Society's resources are limited. Society's willingness to eliminate erroneous convictions is correspondingly not limitless. Society accepts the conviction of some innocent defendants as unavoidable. Although it may substantially reduce the incidence of erroneous convictions by authorizing adjudicators to convict a person only upon overwhelming and indisputable evidence of guilt, it is unwilling to adopt such a standard. By forcing adjudicators to acquit numerous criminals and by projecting insufficient deterrence to individuals contemplating crimes, such a demanding standard produces substantial harm. Innocent defendants facing the prospect of conviction do not care about this harm, but society still wants to minimize it.

Civil litigation features a similar misalignment between private and social interests. Here, too, society is interested in minimizing the incidence of both false positives (erroneous impositions of liability) and false negatives (erroneous refusals to impose liability). Litigants, however, have an altogether different objective in mind. Both claimants and defendants pursue trial victory and the corresponding private gain irrespective of the truth. They do not care about the social interest (such as deterrence or corrective justice) that civil adjudication promotes. Nor do they care about the magnitude of the subsidy that society channels into civil adjudication. As far as they are concerned, this subsidy can be wasted. Every private litigant does whatever it takes to win the case when his or her investment in the case is less than the expected value of the victory.

The second obstacle of the cost-efficiency doctrine has to do with private information. Virtually any criminal defendant privately knows whether he or she committed the crime of which he or she is accused. Any defendant in a civil lawsuit knows whether he or she committed the misdeed about which the claimant complains. The claimant knows whether he or she suffered any damage related to that misdeed. Causation is a different matter. Opponents of these litigants, as well as fact-finders, are not privy to this knowledge. Any such

---

[2] See Steven Shavell, *Foundations of Economic Analysis of Law* (2004), pp. 415–28.
[3] See Steven Shavell, The Fundamental Divergence Between the Private and the Social Motive to Use the Legal System (1997) 26 J. Leg. Stud. 575.

information remains hidden or private because it is generally unobservable.[4] The private nature of such information (identified as 'the problem of asymmetric information') creates an opportunity for cheating that litigants can exploit.[5] Litigants do not only have the motive to behave opportunistically. More often than not, they have the opportunity and the means. To tackle this problem, the legal system needs to discourage opportunistic behaviour.

The cost-efficiency doctrine accommodates four categories of rules:[6]

(1) *Decision rules* that determine the burdens and standards of proof. These rules minimize the aggregate cost of accuracy and errors by skewing the risk of error in the desirable direction (by preferring false positives over false negatives, or vice versa).

(2) *Process rules* that determine what evidence is admissible and what fact-finding methodologies are allowed. These rules minimize the aggregate cost of accuracy and errors by attaching more accurate and, consequently, more expensive fact-finding methodologies to adjudication in which the cost of error is relatively high and by equipping the adjudication in which the cost of error is relatively low with more rudimentary and inexpensive fact-finding methodologies.

(3) *Credibility rules.* By adjusting and implementing penalties and rewards, these rules elicit credible signalling (information that purports to be true and is verifiable) from litigants with private information. Application of these rules always involves apportionment of the risk of error.

(4) *The evidential damage doctrine.* This doctrine places the risk of error on the litigant best positioned to minimize that risk, the cheapest risk-avoider.

B. Decision Rules

All other things being equal, the party whose allegations are more probable than not must prevail. This allocation of the risk of error is known as the 'P > 0.5 rule'. The P > 0.5 rule minimizes the expected number of adjudicative errors. Any other rule of decision generates more errors and less correct decisions than this rule does. This observation has a straightforward proof. By focusing on the total amount, rather than on the individual consequences of

---

[4] See Ian Molho, *The Economics of Information: Lying and Cheating in Markets and Organizations* (1997). [5] Ibid, at pp. 1–10.

[6] A few rules falling into these categories have already been discussed. See below above, pp. 8–9, 50–6, 136–7.

fact-finding errors, the error-minimizing objective treats every error as a fixed disutility unit (u). Consequently, there is no difference between errors that harm defendants (false positives) and errors that harm claimants or prosecutors (false negatives). Under this assumption, utility demands that a party whose case has probability P prevails whenever $Pu > (1-P)u$, that is, whenever $P > 0.5$. Adjudicators maximize the total number of correct decisions by treating their best chances of arriving at the factually correct result as decisive. This maximization of correct decisions serves an important utilitarian objective, promulgated ever since Bentham. Accuracy of fact-finding ('rectitude of decision', in Bentham's words[7]) is a prerequisite for adequate implementation of the substantive law. With more accurate fact-finding, liability is ascribed more accurately. More wrongdoers and fewer faultless defendants are found liable. The legal system consequently minimizes both under-deterrence and over-deterrence.[8]

The $P > 0.5$ rule predominantly applies in civil, as opposed to criminal, litigation. As such, it has yet another rationale. This rule does not merely maximize the number of correct decisions; it also minimizes the total amount of erroneous and, consequently, inefficient transfers.[9] This rationale assumes that the law allocates substantive entitlements and liabilities by using efficiency criteria. Under that assumption, any deviation from the controlling substantive law would violate efficiency.

Let D denote the value of the litigated good; and let p_1 and p_2 denote, respectively, the probabilities of the claimant's and the defendant's conflicting allegations. As is always the case: $0 < p_1 < 1$; $0 < p_2 < 1$; when 1 stands for certainty and 0 for impossibility. At least one of the parties is, therefore, bound to bear the risk of error, that is, the risk of sustaining damage up to D (trial expenses are ignored, for the sake of simplicity). Under these conditions, adjudicators can deliver the following decisions:

d_1 = the claimant loses (risk of error imposed on the claimant);
d_2 = the defendant loses (risk of error imposed on the defendant);
d_3 = compromise reflecting the expected value of each allegation: the claimant recovers from the defendant p_1D; p_2D goes to the defendant (by not allowing the claimant to recover that amount).

By allowing S_1 and S_2, respectively, to denote the actual states of affairs—that can favour either the claimant or the defendant—policy-makers can calculate

---

[7] See Jeremy Bentham, *Rationale of Judicial Evidence* Vol. 5 (John Stuart Mill ed., 1827), pp. 1–8.
[8] See John Kaplan, Decision Theory and the Factfinding Process (1968) 20 Stan. L. Rev. 1065, 1071–2; David Kaye, Naked Statistical Evidence (1980) 89 Yale L.J. 601, 605 n.19.
[9] See David Kaye, The Limits of the Preponderance of the Evidence Standard: Justifiably Naked Statistical Evidence and Multiple Causation (1982) Am. Bar Found. Res. J. 487.

the average damage and the long-run damage, in terms of wrongful transfers, that each of the above decisions produces. This calculation appears in the table below.

Decision	Damage, if S_1	Damage, if S_2	Total Damage
d_1	p_1D	0	p_1D
d_2	0	p_2D	p_2D
d_3	p_1p_2D	p_2p_1D	$2p_1p_2D$

Decision d_3 produces the greatest damage and must therefore be avoided. Consequently, when the probability of the claimant's case exceeds 0.5, the claimant is granted full recovery. When the probability of the defendant's case is greater than 0.5, the claimant does not recover anything. Preponderance of the evidence becomes the general standard of proof, under which the winner takes all. This standard, however, does not yield a fully accomplished rule of decision. It says nothing about balanced cases where the probabilities of competing factual accounts are equal. For such cases, the law needs to provide a residual decision rule by choosing between d_1, d_2, and d_3. This rule will designate the bearer of the persuasion burden and of the consequent risk of non-persuasion. For reasons specified below, the bearer of that burden and the corresponding risk of error should generally be the claimant (subject to the 'affirmative defence doctrine' that I also discuss in this chapter[10]).

In balanced cases, each available decision (d_1, d_2, or d_3) generates the same amount of inefficient transfers. Yet, in any such case, the defendant normally prevails. This decision rule eliminates the enforcement costs that would be expended if the claimant were to be awarded recovery.[11] Allowing the claimant to recover when $p_1 = p_2 = 0.5$ also intensifies the filing of unmeritorious lawsuits, which increases the overall cost of litigation.[12] Arguably, when $p_1 = p_2 = 0.5$, decision d_1 is optimal because 'taking' is generally more harmful than 'not giving'. The diminishing utility of wealth explains this viewpoint.[13]

---

[10] See below at pp. 151–2.

[11] See Alex Stein, Allocating the Burden of Proof in Sales Litigation: The Law, Its Rationale, A New Theory, And Its Failure (1996) 50 U. Miami L. Rev. 335, 343.

[12] See Ralph K. Winter, The Jury and the Risk of Non-Persuasion (1971) 5 Law & Society Rev. 335, 337.

[13] See Richard A. Posner, *Economic Analysis of Law* (6th edn., 2003), p. 618. Alternatively, this perception may derive from the 'endowment effect' that causes people to put greater value on psychologically vested, as opposed to psychologically unvested, entitlements. See Amos Tversky and Daniel Kahneman, Rational Choice and the Framing of Decisions (1986) 59 *J. Bus.* S251, S260.

This analysis is still incomplete. Based on the assumption that the marginal utility of wealth steadily diminishes, one could arrive at an entirely different policy recommendation. This recommendation would favour decision d_3. For an average person, an addition of £1 to his or her wealth generates less utility than did the previous addition of £1. For such a person, the utility flowing from a £1,000,000 gain falls below £1,000,000. In parallel, the disutility that a £1,000,000 loss brings about to such a person is greater than £1,000,000. This observation favours reduction of *large* errors in adjudicative fact-finding.[14] Consider the previous analysis in which D denotes the litigated amount of money and assume that this amount is very large. Allow D^2 to denote the disutility that an average person would suffer after losing D.

These assumptions would modify the previous analysis as follows:

Decision	Damage, if S_1	Damage, if S_2	Total Damage
d_1	p_1D^2	0	p_1D^2
d_2	0	p_2D^2	p_2D^2
d_3	$p_1(p_2D)^2$	$p_2(p_1D)^2$	$p_1p_2D^2$

Because $p_1p_2D^2$ is less than both p_1D^2 and p_2D^2, decision d_3—under which each party captures the expected value of his or her allegations—becomes optimal.

This analysis, however, is problematic. Its comparison between the relevant rules of decision confines itself to the *immediate* losses that each rule produces. This confinement is unjustified: policy makers need to account for all losses that their rules are expected to engender. As already indicated, the $P > 0.5$ rule maximizes the number of correct decisions. As such, it minimizes the incidence of both false positives and false negatives. Under the expected-value rule (d_3), the number of correctly decided cases is always zero. This rule therefore dilutes people's incentives to obey the law. Two factors, both visible to prospective transgressors, dilute these incentives. The expected-value rule systematically reduces the payments that the law ordinarily exacts from transgressors. This rule also erodes the difference between transgressing and not transgressing.

[14] See Neil Orloff and Jerry Stedinger, A Framework for Evaluating the Preponderance-of-the-Evidence Standard (1983) 131 U. Pa. L. Rev. 1159.

This broader perspective is captured by the following formal model,[15] in which

g = the expected gain from a potentially harmful action that a person contemplates;

p = the probability that the person is detected as a possible violator of the relevant legal standard;

f = a pecuniary sanction (say—a fine that derives from the amount of harm associated with the contemplated action) that the court imposes on the person if found liable;

ϵ_1 = the probability of the type-I error (false positive), that is, the probability that a non-liable defendant is mistakenly found liable;

ϵ_2 = the probability of the type-II error (false negative), that is, the probability that a liable defendant is mistakenly found not liable.

For the sake of simplicity, this model assumes that the person is neutral towards risk (a standard assumption that this book makes in various contexts). The model further assumes that the probability of the person's detection as a possible violator (p) is constant. The latter assumption is made for the sake of simplicity as well. Detection errors are bound to occur. Their actual rate has no impact on the lesson to be learnt from the model. When detection errors are reduced, the incidence of adjudication errors obviously declines as well.

Based on the above assumptions, the person takes the contemplated action whenever

$$g - p(1-\epsilon_2)f > -p\epsilon_1 f.$$

The left side of this inequality represents the difference between the person's gain and expected loss that arise from the harmful action. The person's expected loss equals the fine, multiplied by the person's probability of being detected and found liable. The right side of the inequality is a negative sum that represents the person's initial position. Even if the person does not take the contemplated action, he or she may be erroneously detected as a violator and subsequently found liable. This initial loss is predicated on the existence of errors in the legal system. Its magnitude depends on the size of the fine and on the incidence of both detection and judgmental false positives. The person, therefore, rationally takes the contemplated action when its outcome improves his or her initial position. The action is taken even if the left side of the inequality yields a negative sum, as long as that sum is less than $p\epsilon_1 f$. This

---

[15] This model was developed by A. Mitchell Polinsky and Steven Shavell, The Economic Theory of Public Enforcement of Law (2000) 38 J. Econ. Lit. 45, 60–2; and it draws on Ivan P. L. Png, Optimal Subsidies and Damages in the Presence of Judicial Error (1986) 6 Int'l Rev. L. & Econ. 101.

implies that deterrence is reduced not only by false negatives, but also—albeit less trivially—by false positives.

Formally, the potentially harmful action will be taken if

$$g > p(1-\epsilon_2)f - p\epsilon_1 f,$$

that is, if

$$g > pf(1-\epsilon_2-\epsilon_1).$$

This formula demonstrates that both types of error ought to be reduced in order to optimize deterrence and thereby augment social welfare. False negatives dilute deterrence and thus reduce social welfare by lowering the expected fine for potential violators. False positives dilute deterrence less trivially. They do so by eroding the difference between the penalties expected from acting legally and from acting illegally. To see how this erosion occurs, take a brain surgeon who faces a mistaken liability prospect that brings about −500 (in expected disutility units). To eliminate this prospect, the surgeon may quit her job, but this would bring about an even greater loss. The surgeon considers another alternative: an illegal performance of kidney transplant operations. This alternative promises the surgeon a certain gain of 550 along with the expected loss of 1,000 (originating from the surgeon's probable conviction, punishment, and other repercussions). The value of this alternative is −450. This negative amount is preferable to −500. The surgeon's mistaken liability prospect consequently induces her to commit another crime.

For obvious reasons, false positives also chill socially desirable activities. For example, if courts too often fail to distinguish between the negligent and the careful truck-drivers, some of the drivers who are both rational and careful might decide not to drive their trucks.[16] The lesson to be learnt from this analysis is straightforward: the optimal proof requirement is one that maximizes the total number of correct decisions, an outcome that the $P > 0.5$ rule attains.

As stated at the beginning of this section, the $P > 0.5$ rule should apply in cases in which all other things are equal. That is, this rule should apply when false positives and false negatives are equally harmful, which normally is the case in civil litigation. When one type of error is more harmful than the other, fact-finders should follow a different rule. In criminal adjudication, for example, false positives (wrongful convictions) are generally considered more harmful than false negatives (wrongful acquittals). For such cases, the rule of decision should derive from the disutility differential. Following John

---

[16] See generally Louis Kaplow and Steven Shavell, Accuracy in the Determination of Liability (1994) 37 J. L. & Econ. 1.

Kaplan,[17] this differential can be formalized as I/G, with I and G denoting the harms brought about by erroneously convicting an innocent person (I) and by erroneously acquitting a guilty defendant (G). Under this framework, adjudicators convict the defendant when the probability of his or her guilt is greater than I/(I+G). Thus, when the disutility differential I/G equals 9/1 (convicting an innocent defendant is nine times more harmful than acquitting a guilty criminal), adjudicators should convict the accused if the probability of his or her guilt is greater than 0.9. Otherwise, the accused should be acquitted. And when the differential is set (quite unrealistically) on 900/1 (convicting an innocent defendant is nine hundred times more harmful than acquitting a guilty criminal), adjudicators then only convict the accused on the probability of guilt that exceeds 0.999. The prevalent legal doctrine prefers not to determine the disutility differential with mathematical exactitude. Under this doctrine, the prosecution must prove 'beyond all reasonable doubt' facts constitutive of a criminal defendant's guilt.[18]

The legal system may also adopt a more refined approach. Different cases may require different allocations of the risk of error that translate themselves into different decisional rules. In criminal cases, for example, it makes sense to condition the defendant's ability to benefit from an excusatory defence upon its proof by a preponderance of the evidence.[19] An excusatory defence is a full or partial exculpation originating from the leniency and concession to human

---

[17] See Kaplan, above note 8, at 1071–5.

[18] See generally McCormick, *On Evidence* Vol. 2 (4th edn. 1992), pp. 445–9; Paul Roberts and Adrian Zuckerman, *Criminal Evidence* (2004), pp. 361–73.

[19] See Alex Stein, Criminal Defences and the Burden of Proof (1991) 28 *Coexistence* 133 (laying out this normative claim); Alex Stein, After *HUNT*: The Burden of Proof, Risk of Non-Persuasion and Judicial Pragmatism (1991) 54 M.L.R. 570 (anchoring this claim in positive law); Alex Stein, From Blackstone to *Woolmington*: On the Development of a Legal Doctrine (1993) 14 J. Leg. Hist. 14 (anchoring this claim in the doctrinal history). For a critique of this claim see Timothy H. Jones, Insanity, Automatism, and the Burden of Proof on the Accused (1995) 111 L.Q.R. 475, 495–7. Professor Jones argues that the insanity defence—my 'axiomatic case of an excuse where it is permissible to place a persuasive burden on the accused'—can hardly classify as an excuse. Ibid, at 496. Subject to certain modifications that the insanity defence needs to undergo in order to fit into Professor Jones's scheme, this argument may well be normatively correct. On the descriptive level, however, the argument commits three errors. First, it misidentifies the insanity defence as *my* 'axiomatic' example of an excuse. This example was extracted from the law that Professor Jones both acknowledges and criticizes. See *Woolmington v D.P.P.* [1935] AC 462, 481–2 (HL) (stating the rule requiring the accused to prove insanity on a balance of probabilities); *Leland v Oregon*, 343 U.S. 790 (1952) (affirming as constitutional the Oregon rule requiring the accused to prove insanity beyond all reasonable doubt). Second, it ignores that my theory is invariant in the sense that I can accept Professor Jones's argument and transfer the insanity defence to the domain of the elements of the crime (or even justifications), as opposed to excuses (which I would have done more readily if the prevalent insanity doctrine were not worded as an excuse). Under my theory, it would still be fair and efficient to require that criminal defendants prove by a preponderance of the evidence whatever classifies as an excuse. Finally, because my theory aligns with positive law, branding it as 'eccentric...heterodoxy' (Jones, ibid, at 496) is conceptually wrong.

frailty that liberal systems of criminal justice often exhibit.[20] Excusatory defences derive from the individual circumstances of the perpetrator. These defences include insanity, infancy, duress, diminished responsibility, and several others.[21] They excuse the actor, rather than the act which remains blameworthy. A person invoking such a defence does not disassociate himself or herself from the underlying criminal act. Nor does he or she attempt to justify what he or she did. Rather, such a defendant makes a personalized request for leniency. Adjudication of such special requests may—and, indeed, should— practice a different trade-off between false positives (an excusatory defence erroneously granted) and false negatives (an excusatory defence erroneously denied). Because defendants invoking excusatory defences are not altogether innocent, false negatives would not generate more harm than false positives. The opposite scenario, in which false positives generate more harm than false negatives, is more likely. Acquittal of a guilty criminal endangers—and ultimately harms—society by letting the criminal go free and by diluting the general deterrence for prospective offenders. Society may rationally pay this price in numerous cases in order not to convict an innocent person in a single case. However, paying the same price in order to provide an excusatory defence to a defendant who is otherwise guilty is irrational. Criminal defendants should be required to prove any excusatory defence by a preponderance of the evidence (at the very least). They should only be allowed to benefit from such a defence when its underlying facts are more probable than not.[22] This principle should also extend to excusatory defences available in civil litigation (such as mistake of fact as a ground for avoiding contractual liability).[23]

Positive law commonly requires criminal defendants to prove any 'affirmative defence'[24] or—as in England—any 'exemption, exception, proviso, excuse or qualification' to a statutory offence[25] by a preponderance of the evidence.[26] This requirement is too broad. It encompasses not only excusatory defences, but also justifications, such as self-defence. In the domain of justifications, a false negative (a justificatory defence erroneously denied) is as harmful as a mistaken conviction. Moreover, some justificatory defences extend to activities

---

[20] See H. L. A. Hart, *Punishment and Responsibility* (1968), pp. 13–14.

[21] Stein, above note 19, in (1991) 28 *Coexistence* at 138. These defences do not include automatism—an exoneration that extends to people whose movements cannot plausibly be considered an 'action'.

[22] Stein, above note 19, in (1991) 28 *Coexistence* at 136–40. This scheme is not part of positive law. But in Blackstone's time it was: see Stein, above note 19, in (1993) 14 J. Leg. Hist. 14. For forays of the human rights jurisprudence, see below p. 183, note 33.

[23] See Alex Stein, The Refoundation of Evidence Law (1996) 9 Can. J. Law & Jurisp. 279, 337–8.

[24] See McCormick Vol. 2, above note 18, at pp. 479–94.

[25] See the Magistrates' Courts Act 1980, s. 101; Roberts and Zuckerman, above note 18, at pp. 374–84.   [26] Roberts and Zuckerman, above note 18, at pp. 373–5.

qualifying as socially desirable, rather than just tolerable. Self-defence is the principal example of such activities. Apart from allowing victims of crime to defend themselves against criminals, this defence discourages prospective criminals from committing crimes.[27] By conditioning the availability of self-defence upon its proof by a preponderance of the evidence, the affirmative defence doctrine chills an activity that benefits society.[28]

The same critique holds true with respect to the 'affirmative defence' doctrine that applies in civil litigation. Under this doctrine, the defendant needs to prove any defence that qualifies as affirmative by a preponderance of the evidence.[29] This category is very broad. It extends to any claim that does not simply deny the facts underlying the claimant's cause of action. Affirmative defences include frustration, estoppel, res judicata, waiver and forfeiture, pre-emption, statute of limitations, contributory fault, comparative negligence, and many others.[30] From the efficiency perspective, for reasons given in the next section, defendants only need to bear the burden of adducing evidence (the production burden) in relation to any defence not qualifying as an excuse. Subject to this provision, the ordinary $P > 0.5$ rule should apply. The existing doctrine, however, can be justified on non-economic grounds, set forth in Chapter 7.

The prevalent evidence doctrine often shifts the burden of proof with respect to factual propositions contradicting the ordinary course of events. For example, in the absence of counter-proof, a person missing for seven years or more is generally presumed dead;[31] circumstances exhibiting violence and a dead person are generally presumed not to be a suicide;[32] and (on a more optimistic note) a letter properly addressed, stamped, and mailed is presumed to be duly delivered to the addressee.[33] Such presumptions should be perceived as shifting the production burden alone. If taken (as they sometimes are) as reversing the burden of persuasion, such presumptions would produce anomalous results. Fact-finders are well aware of regularities and, consequently, take them into account in evaluating evidence and in determining the ultimate facts of the case. Shifting the persuasion burden in relation to any such regularity to a party

---

[27] See Shavell, above note 2, at p. 566 (observing in relation to self-defence that 'allowing the use of protective force will enhance deterrence of aggression' and that 'limiting the justified use of such force makes sense under the presumption that courts are better able than threatened parties to decide on sanctions').

[28] Defendants are typically able to lie about self-defence and hide their aggression in the shadows of a 'reasonable doubt'. This ability can be substantially reduced by the appropriate advance pleading requirements and by shifting the production burden to the defendant.

[29] See McCormick, Vol. 2, above note 18, at p. 427.

[30] Ibid. See also Posner, above note 13, at p. 618.

[31] McCormick, Vol. 2, above note 18, at pp. 457–8.   [32] Ibid, at p. 460.

[33] Ibid, at p. 455.

otherwise not carrying that burden would therefore produce double-counting. The same regularity would be counted twice, instead of once.[34]

Only substantive policy grounds can justify a distribution of false positives and false negatives that differs from the distribution achieved under the $P > 0.5$ rule. A good example of this approach is the 'mixed motive' doctrine that applies in the United States in employment discrimination litigation. The 'mixed motive' doctrine holds that presence of a discriminatory motivation in the employer's decision-making process places on the employer the burden of proving by a preponderance of the evidence that an altogether different motivation, non-discriminatory in character, produced the decision about which the employee complains.[35] This doctrine is justified by the need to oust discriminatory motivations from employment decisions even when the motivation does not actually produce the decision. Because these motivations are both inefficient and unjust, the law marks mixed-motive settings as cases in which erroneous findings of discrimination are preferred over erroneous findings of non-discrimination. Another substantive policy example is the 'wedlock presumption'. Under this presumption, a child born to a woman during the period of her marriage is presumed to be the child of the woman's husband.[36] Courts have generally agreed that this presumption places the burden of persuasion on the party contending that the child's father is not the woman's husband.[37] These rulings protected the stability of people's personal status and of the family institution in general. Recognition of these interests as deserving protection favours erroneous decisions upholding the child's legitimacy over erroneous decisions that hold the child illegitimate.

Some claims and contentions adjudicated in civil cases require proof by 'clear and convincing evidence'. This proof threshold is below 'beyond a reasonable doubt', but above 'preponderance of the evidence'. It functions as an exception to the $P > 0.5$ rule.[38] Typically, claims and contentions that require proof by clear and convincing evidence include allegations of

---

[34] See Vaughn C. Ball, The Moment of Truth: Probability Theory and Standards of Proof (1961) 14 Vand. L. Rev. 807, 817–18 ('The risk of non-persuasion is allocated (a great part of the time, at least) upon the basis of the probability of the existence of the fact in the run of cases of the particular kind, absent any specific evidence. Since the evidence and the jury's consideration of it have come to naught, we will make the fewest mistakes if we let the case fall back into the general class, to be decided on those original probabilities. But the jury, unless it lacks the common knowledge we ascribe to it by definition, has begun its own deliberation with those probabilities in mind, and it is the combination of both those and the probabilities drawn from the specific evidence, that the jury says are at balance. If we then use the initial probabilities to remove the balance, we are in some sense counting them twice.').   [35] See *Price Waterhouse v Hopkins*, 490 U.S. 228 (1989).

[36] McCormick, Vol. 2, above note 18, at pp. 458–9, 464.

[37] McCormick, Vol. 2, above note 18, at p. 464.

[38] McCormick, Vol. 2, above note 18, at pp. 441–5.

fraud and deprivations of civil liberties. In the fraud category, a finding that a person committed fraud exposes that person to two sanctions, rather than one. The first sanction is legal. The person assumes liability or loses his or her claim and consequently suffers a reduction in his or her welfare. The second sanction is social. Identified as fraudulent, the person suffers a reputation loss in his or her community, which might bring about further reductions of his or her welfare, such as lost business and social opportunities. For that reason, economic theory may demand that adjudicators deduct the non-legal sanction from the legal sanction in order to avoid excessive deterrence.[39] The legal system, however, may also avoid or substantially reduce excessive deterrence by raising the applicable proof threshold and by thereby reducing a person's ex ante probability of being identified as fraudulent. This is exactly what the 'clear and convincing evidence' standard does. This evidential mechanism reduces a person's expected sanctions, both legal and social (the social sanction is imposed on the basis of the court's decision).[40] This special mechanism does not aim at attaining the socially desirable ratio of false positives versus false negatives. Nor does it aim at driving away frivolous claims by chilling some meritorious claims as well. This mechanism attenuates overenforcement and the consequent overdeterrence that both correct and erroneous liability decisions (as well as both frivolous and meritorious claims) produce on the ground.

Cases falling into the civil liberty category feature risks of error that are manifestly asymmetrical. For example, society views erroneous committal of a person to a mental institution as considerably more harmful (on the average) than a mistaken decision not to commit a person to a mental institution.[41] Similarly, society considers erroneous deportation or de-naturalization decisions as considerably more harmful than the opposite errors.[42] These cases are analogous to criminal litigation (in which the risks of error faced by the parties are unquestionably asymmetrical). Other categories of civil cases that require proof by clear and convincing evidence[43] (in which the criminal litigation analogy is not valid) are problematic. As demonstrated above, the $P > 0.5$ rule is optimal for all cases not qualifying as special. Any deviation from this rule requires unequivocal justification, which is hard to provide in cases not featuring asymmetric risks of error.

---

[39] See Robert Cooter and Ariel Porat, Should Courts Deduct Nonlegal Sanctions from Damages? (2001) 30 J. Leg. Stud. 401.

[40] See Richard A. Bierschbach and Alex Stein, Overenforcement (2005) 93 Georgetown L.J. (forthcoming).   [41] See *Addington v Texas*, 441 U.S. 418 (1979).

[42] See *Schneiderman v United States*, 320 U.S. 118 (1943); *Woodby v INS*, 385 U.S. 276 (1966).

[43] McCormick, Vol. 2, above note 18, at pp. 443–4.

C. Process Rules

Rules falling into this category select fact-finding methodologies for adjudication and determine what evidence is admissible. As stated earlier in this chapter, these rules minimize the aggregate cost of accuracy and errors by attaching more accurate and more expensive fact-finding methodologies to cases in which the cost of error is high and by attaching more rudimentary and, consequently, cheaper fact-finding methodologies to cases in which the cost of error is relatively low.

The most basic rule affiliating to this category is the burden of production doctrine. This doctrine requires the claimant in a civil case and the prosecution in a criminal case to produce evidence upon which a rational fact-finder can find the defendant liable.[44] The rationale of this fundamental doctrine is straightforward. Because trial is an expensive procedure, it should be conducted only on issues that are worthy of trial.[45] This doctrine also assumes that the average claimant has an adequate (that is, not unaffordably expensive) opportunity of obtaining evidence. By enabling litigants to obtain documentary, testimonial, and even physical evidence from their opponents, the existing mechanisms of pretrial discovery make this assumption reasonable.[46]

At the trial stage, the production burden requires the party with the best access to evidence to produce that evidence. Failure to do so leads to adverse inferences and sometimes to adverse rulings.[47] The right to silence conferred upon criminal defendants is the only exception to this general observation (I explain this exception in the pages ahead). The best-access principle makes economic sense, given the parties' self-seeking temptation to withhold unfavourable evidence. By turning adverse inferences and rulings into a standard sanction for withholding evidence, this rule creates an unequivocal incentive against any such conduct. This rule also creates an adversarial incentive for each party to prove evidence-withholding by the party opponent, which contributes to the alignment of the parties' individual interests with the social good.

The best evidence doctrine[48] contains an additional set of general evidential requirements that economic analysis easily explains. This doctrine requires each party to adduce the best evidence available. Failure to do so triggers two sanctions: exclusion of any secondary evidence that the defaulting party may decide to offer and adverse inferences. Both sanctions increase the defaulting

---

[44] McCormick, Vol. 2, above note 18, at pp. 425–6.
[45] See Posner, above note 13, at pp. 617–18.   [46] Ibid, at p. 618.
[47] McCormick, Vol. 2, above note 18, at p. 429.
[48] See generally Dale Nance, The Best Evidence Principle (1988) 73 Iowa L. Rev. 227.

party's probability of losing the case and thus function similarly to the production burden. Truth-lovers do not need this disincentive. This disincentive is set for the self-seeking 'bad man'.[49] To be sure, the latter is still able and willing to avoid disclosure of evidence unfavourable to his or her case. Such disclosure entails a certain loss on the issue, while being exposed to the sanctions that the best evidence doctrine prescribes only involves a probable loss.[50] These sanctions, however, are fully justified as cost-saving shortcuts for generally accurate fact-finding.

As a mechanism countering virtually every suppression of best probative evidence, the best evidence doctrine has numerous manifestations in positive law.[51] For example, Federal Rule of Evidence 613(b) and the common law[52] both limit impeachment of witnesses by prior inconsistent statements in a noteworthy fashion. Generally, such a statement is not admitted into evidence unless the witness undergoing impeachment is afforded an opportunity to explain it and the party opponent is given an opportunity to question the witness about the statement and how it relates to his or her testimony. The threat of the statement's exclusion induces the party entertaining the impeachment to cross-examine the witness in a way that generates the best available evidence for the fact-finders.

Another general rule that falls into the present category is Federal Rule of Evidence 403. This rule requires judges to screen every piece of evidence for admissibility, when contested, by comparing the costs and the benefits that its processing would involve. The rule states,

> although relevant, evidence may be excluded if its probative value is substantially outweighed by the danger of unfair prejudice, confusion of the issues, or misleading the jury, or by considerations of undue delay, waste of time, or needless presentation of cumulative evidence.[53]

This general rule branches into a number of specific provisions. One of those provisions renders inadmissible evidence about a person's general character

---

[49] See Oliver Wendell Holmes, Jr., The Path of the Law (1897) 10 Harv. L. Rev. 457, 459 (defining the 'bad man' as a 'man who cares nothing for an ethical rule which is believed and practised by his neighbors', but 'is likely nevertheless to care a good deal to avoid being made to pay money, and will want to keep out of jail if he can'). See also William Twining, The Bad Man Revisited (1973) 58 Cornell L. Rev. 275.

[50] Ambiguous evidence entails an altogether different scenario. Such evidence will only be produced when it is expected to be more beneficial than harmful to its producer. Neither the production burden nor the best evidence doctrine can affect such calculations. As for hopelessly ambiguous evidence, its extraction is economically unjustified. Cf. Federal Rules of Evidence 102 and 403.

[51] See Nance, above note 48.

[52] See Mason Ladd, Some Observations on Credibility: Impeachment of Witnesses (1967) 52 Cornell L.Q. 239, 247.

[53] For economic analysis of this rule see Posner, above note 1, at 1522–4.

when offered to prove action in conformity with that character.[54] Federal Rule of Evidence 403 also indicates that economic grounds for excluding evidence altogether irrelevant to the facts in issue—as prescribed by Rules 401 and 402—are trivial. The relevancy principle requires no explanation.

On similar grounds, unmitigated hearsay evidence is excluded from consideration by fact-finders. The 'unmitigated hearsay' category includes any statement made out of court in circumstances not exhibiting any special indicia of reliability and subsequently offered into evidence in order to prove the truth of the matters asserted.[55] Such evidence may well have probative value, but the costs of processing it—whenever it is contested—are typically high. Allowing fact-finders to rely on such evidence would trigger ancillary litigation. This litigation would involve a confrontation between the parties' adversarial efforts, with each party attempting to outplay his or her opponent in gathering any indicia of trustworthiness and untrustworthiness that could somehow attach to the contested statement and to the person who made it. Moreover, by making such evidence admissible, the legal system allows a private litigant to force the party opponent into the expense that this ancillary litigation involves. This possibility leaves the doors for opportunistic behaviour wide open. Each party would often have an incentive to adduce unmitigated hearsay evidence in order to increase his or her opponent's trial expenses.[56]

Hearsay evidence should therefore only be admissible when it comes accompanied by indicia of reliability. This is what the American hearsay doctrine actually does (and what the English hearsay doctrine did until recently).[57] Under this doctrine, hearsay evidence is only admissible when it falls into one of the exceptions to the hearsay rule; otherwise, such evidence is inadmissible.[58] To the extent that these exceptions are premised, as they largely claim to be, upon circumstantial guarantees of trustworthiness,[59] the

[54] See Federal Rule of Evidence 404(a).

[55] See Federal Rule of Evidence 801(c). English law had reduced the hearsay rule in civil proceedings 'to an insignificant shadow of its former self'. Adrian A. S. Zuckerman, *Civil Procedure* (2003), p. 669.

[56] Cf. Note, The Theoretical Foundation of the Hearsay Rules (1980) 93 Harv. L. Rev. 1786. This Note offers an economic analysis of the hearsay rules that recommends admission, rather than exclusion, of hearsay evidence. According to this analysis, the risk of overassessment that such evidence brings along would typically be outbalanced by the costs that its exclusion and the consequent loss of information would produce. This analysis, however, fails to account for the costs of ancillary litigation. More crucially, it fails to consider the costs that litigants would impose on each other opportunistically, as described in the text.   [57] See below at pp. 189–96, 228–35.

[58] See Federal Rules of Evidence 801–807.

[59] See, e.g., Federal Rule of Evidence 807 ('A statement not specifically covered by Rule 803 or 804 but having equivalent circumstantial guarantees of trustworthiness, is not excluded by the hearsay rule, if the court determines that (A) the statement is offered as evidence of a material

American hearsay doctrine is economically justified. Economic analysis, however, requires that fact-finders consider any exculpatory hearsay offered by a criminal defendant when it happens to be the best evidence available to him or her. This requirement derives from the utilitarian difference between false positives and false negatives that exists in criminal adjudication.[60]

D. Credibility Rules

Rules falling into this category aim at eliciting credible signalling from parties and witnesses. Parties and witnesses hold unobservable information which remains throughout the trial hidden and private, as opposed to open and public.[61] This information is distributed asymmetrically between the litigants, as well as between each litigant and the fact-finders. Each litigant can perversely exploit this feature. Indeed, asymmetrical information constitutes the means and an ample opportunity for lying and cheating.[62] These means and opportunity are part of the litigant's motive to cheat. The latter originates from the fundamental misalignment between the social good and the private incentives that are at work in civil and criminal litigation.[63] Evidence consequently turns into information that fact-finders must treat as inherently suspicious. The combination of evidence and its surrounding circumstances—that include the underlying motivations of both the party and the witness who provides the evidence—generates signalling upon which the fact-finders determine the facts. Fact-finders therefore need credible signalling, as opposed to signalling that might mislead them. Correspondingly, evidence law needs to elicit credible signalling from both parties and witnesses. It needs to do so cost-efficiently. Evidence law can and should attain this important objective through a system of penalties and rewards. Any such system would differentiate between credible and not credible signalling on the basis of probabilities. There is no other basis for making such differentiations in conditions of uncertainty. Any such system therefore must apportion the risk of error between litigants.

---

fact; (B) the statement is more probative on the point for which it is offered than any other evidence which the proponent can procure through reasonable efforts; and (C) the general purposes of these rules and the interests of justice will best be served by admission of the statement into evidence . . .').

[60] See above, pp. 148–9.   [61] See generally Molho, above note 4.   [62] Ibid.
[63] See generally Shavell, above note 3.

This category of rules may be rather broad. The following rules and doctrines are examples:

(1) The right to silence or the privilege against self-incrimination that the law confers upon criminal defendants and suspects.

(2) The rule effectuating a criminal defendant's waiver of his or her plea negotiations privilege.

(3) The rule generally allowing the prosecution to impeach a testifying criminal defendant by his or her prior convictions.

(4) The falsifiability doctrine that conditions the admissibility of scientific expert testimony under the Federal Rules of Evidence and their state equivalents.

First, I discuss the right to silence. Specifically, I discuss the fierce opposition to this right voiced by Jeremy Bentham and his followers.[64] This discussion invalidates Bentham's claim that the right to silence helps only guilty criminals and for that reason needs to be abolished. This claim holds that, subject to some idiosyncratic exceptions, each person knows whether he or she *did it*. Guilty suspects know that they are guilty, and innocent suspects know that they are innocent. Because criminal conviction and punishment entail harm that a reasonably rational person wants to avoid, guilty suspects are eager to conceal the truth. However, an innocent suspect's 'most ardent wish' is to 'dissipate the cloud which surrounds his conduct and give every explanation which may set it in its true light'.[65] An innocent suspect demands for himself or herself the right to speak out, not the right to silence. Criminals would demand the right to silence exclusively.[66]

This claim appears so compelling that it forced the advocates of the right to silence to abandon the consequentialist terrain. Present-day justifications of the right are deontological in character. They allude to privacy,[67] including the spiritual sanctity of remorse,[68] and to the adversarial notion of 'fairness', allegedly embedded in the Anglo-American criminal justice system[69] and

---

[64] This discussion originates from Daniel J. Seidmann and Alex Stein, The Right to Silence Helps the Innocent: A Game-Theoretic Analysis of the Fifth Amendment Privilege (2000) 114 Harv. L. Rev. 430.

[65] See Jeremy Bentham, *A Treatise on Judicial Evidence* (Etienne Dumont, ed. 1825), p. 241.

[66] Ibid.

[67] See Erwin W. Griswold, The Right to be Let Alone (1960) 55 NW. U. L. Rev. 216; Vincent M. Bonventre, An Alternative to the Constitutional Privilege Against Self-Incrimination (1982) 49 Brooklyn L. Rev. 31; Denis J. Galligan, The Right to Silence Reconsidered [1988] Curr. Leg. Probs. 69; Robert S. Gerstein, Privacy and Self-Incrimination (1970) 80 *Ethics* 87.

[68] See Gerstein, ibid.

[69] For writings discussing the adversarial rationale, see John H. Langbein, The Historical Origins of the Privilege Against Self-Incrimination at Common Law (1994) 92 Mich. L. Rev. 1047. 1066–71; Wigmore On Evidence Vol. 8 (McNaughton Revision, 1961) at p. 317. For the 'fairness'

denounced by Bentham as the 'fox-hunter's reason'.[70] These justifications also point to the cruelty that would result if criminal suspects and defendants were to face 'the trilemma' consisting of confession, contempt, and perjury.[71] Bentham famously criticized this argument, with a flavour of ageism and sexism, as 'the old woman's reason'.[72]

These justifications, not devoid of merit, beg a number of pressing questions. As Bentham pointed out, what is perceived as 'hard' and 'unfair' by his old women and fox-hunters might be perceived rather differently by other beholders.[73] The ultimate subject-matter of the trilemma rationale is a harm associated with criminal punishment, unless, of course, one embraces the dubious claim that choosing between several harmful outcomes is more painful than experiencing the outcomes themselves. But if a criminal punishment is properly imposed, why is it so harmful or cruel? Any effective punishment surely entails hardship, which some may perceive as 'cruelty'. Yet, no legal system can seriously consider doing away with criminal punishment. If so, why draw the lines between permissible and impermissible harshness as does the right to silence?

This question has a number of plausible answers that take us in different directions. Each of those answers, however, is located outside the trilemma rationale. This rationale can only convincingly justify an excuse for silence in the form of the contempt exemption, so that suspects and defendants would be able to remain silent without being punished.[74] This rationale cannot justify the rule against adverse inferences. Excusatory grounds justifying the contempt exemption offer no reason for its supplementation by an evidential immunity against inferences justified or even dictated by the prevalent epistemology.[75]

---

rationale, see Bonventre, above note 67, at 59–63; Ian H. Dennis, Reconstructing the Law of Criminal Evidence [1989] Curr. Leg. Probs. 21, 27; Robert S. Gerstein, The Demise of Boyd: Self-Incrimination and Private Papers in the Burger Court (1979) 27 UCLA L. Rev. 343, 349.

[70] In Bentham's words:

'In the mouth of the lawyer, this reason, were the nature of it to be seen to be what it is, would be consistent and in character. Every villain let loose one term, that he may bring custom the next, is a sort of bag-fox, nursed by the common hunt at Westminster. . . . To different persons, both a fox and a criminal have their use: the use of a fox is to be hunted; the use of a criminal is to be tried.'

Bentham, Vol. 5, above note 7, at p. 239.

[71] See *Schmerber v California*, 384 U.S. 757 (1966).

[72] In the words of Bentham, the trilemma argument is 'the old woman's reason . . . "tis hard upon a man to be obliged to criminate himself"'. See Bentham, above note 65, at pp. 230–8.

[73] See William Twining, *Theories of Evidence: Bentham and Wigmore* (1985), pp. 84–5.

[74] See William J. Stuntz, Self-Incrimination and Excuse (1988) 88 Colum. L. Rev. 1227.

[75] See ss. 34–38 of the Criminal Justice and Public Order Act 1994 (England) that allows such adverse inferences. See also Roberts and Zuckerman, above note 18, at pp. 440–9 (critically examining the switch to adverse inferences from silence in the English law).

Until recently,[76] both sides to the debate about the right to silence have ignored that the basic premise of the entire debate was wrong. Bentham's argument, holding that the right to silence helps only the guilty, is severely flawed in terms of both form and substance. It contains both a logical *non sequitur* and an economic miscalculation. As a matter of logic, innocent suspects can benefit indirectly from the right's existence, even if they do not exercise it themselves. There is nothing that logically excludes this possibility. In terms of substance, Bentham (together with the present-day abolitionists) overlooked a substantial economic problem. He treated the right to silence as if it were a private consumption good: that is, one which only confers benefits on the person who consumes it. This treatment was an offspring of postulation rather than proof. It turns out to be wrong upon examination. In addition, Bentham failed to account for the private nature of the information concerning guilt and innocence, respectively held by guilty and innocent suspects and defendants, and for the corresponding signalling problems.

Finally, Bentham's argument obfuscates the crucial distinction between an *ex ante* and an *ex post* perspective. From an *ex post* point of view, Bentham's claim is irrefutable. Suppose, as he does, that innocent suspects are willing to establish their innocence as promptly as possible, while criminals want to conceal the truth. In this highly plausible scenario, innocents are never silent, while criminals may be. Consequently, when we know that a given suspect has been silent, logic dictates that he or she must be a criminal. Furthermore, given that inference, convicting that suspect cannot affect any innocent suspect. The problem with this argument is that it takes the pattern of behaviour—talkative innocents and silent criminals—as an unmodifiable given. If suspects are more than automata, they may change their behaviour when a right to silence is either introduced or revoked. For example, if criminals alone were silent when exercising a right, then we could assess a right's impact only by considering whether criminals would *otherwise* lie or confess. In short, we need an *ex ante* perspective in order to assess the effects of the right to silence. Bentham's argument totally overlooks that perspective.

The logic of this argument follows the economic principle of 'revealed preference' that explains consumption of private goods, where 'private' (as opposed to 'public') means that the consumer only cares about his or her own act of consumption. Economists have long argued that we can draw valid inferences about a consumer's welfare by observing his or her choices in appropriate situations. Consider a situation in which consumer Yvonne selects one out of two bundles of private goods, A and B. When Yvonne chooses A over B, the revealed preference principle observes that her welfare would remain

---

[76] That is, before the publication of Seidmann and Stein, above note 64.

unchanged if bundle B became unavailable. Yvonne's welfare would be at best unchanged and possibly lessened, if bundle A became unavailable. Now assume that Yvonne always chooses bundle B over some other bundle C. Any consumer who chose A in preference to B could be no worse off if, instead, he or she had to choose between bundles A and C. In any such scenario, the consumer would simply take A. However, a consumer who, unlike Yvonne, chose B from alternatives A and B could be worse off if subsequently forced to choose between bundles A and C.

Analogously to the consumption setting, an innocent suspect chooses between speaking out ('good' A) and remaining silent, when silence may either preclude an adverse inference ('good' B) or allow it ('good' C). Bentham's argument entails that innocents reveal their preference for speaking out ('good' A), absent any right to silence. He deduced that an innocent suspect's welfare would be unaffected by removal of the right to silence, that is, by replacing good B with good C for all suspects. Conversely, criminals who exercise the right (choose B over A) may be harmed by its revocation (when they must choose between A and C). Bentham further deduced that the right to silence is socially undesirable because evidential rules need to reduce the welfare of criminals, rather than do the opposite. According to Bentham, thieves and burglars must not be admitted to a supermarket of legal rights.

The revealed preference principle is inapplicable whenever the good in question is not private: *viz.* if consumer Yvonne's welfare is affected by consumer Xavier's consumption decision, that is, if Xavier's consumption creates an externality for Yvonne, positive or negative. Under these circumstances, Yvonne cares about whether bundles B or C are available to Xavier even when she personally prefers bundle A over both B and C.[77] The revealed preference principle therefore does not apply to Yvonne.

For that reason, this principle is also inapplicable to the right to silence. Suspects and defendants exercising this right are typically guilty, but the good they consume is not private. By exercising the right to silence, a criminal abandons the lying alternative that would have involved pooling with innocents. Any such pooling might impair the credibility of the stories told by innocent suspects not possessing evidence that could corroborate their stories. Fact-finders would rationally deem such stories suspicious and discount their probability, which they will do in relation to all self-exonerating accounts. Some of such accounts come from suspects and defendants who are actually innocent. The probability of the stories told by the innocents would consequently go down. By not pooling with innocents, a criminal minimizes the exposure of an

[77] See Anthony B. Atkinson and Joseph E. Stiglitz, *Lectures on Public Economics* (1980), pp. 482–7.

innocent suspect to the risk of wrongful conviction. Bentham's argument breaks down because it ignored the fact that a criminal's perjured statement imposes negative externalities on an innocent suspect. This negative external-ity is avoided when a criminal exercises the right to silence. By exercising this right, a criminal confers a positive externality on an innocent suspect. An innocent suspect, therefore, would oppose abolition of the right to silence, even though he or she does not exercise this right.

To fully understand this insight,[78] one must examine another problem that Bentham and his followers overlooked. As already indicated, guilty suspects generally know that they are guilty, while innocents usually know that they are innocent; but, not being generally observable, this information is 'hidden' or 'private'. The private nature of the required information—or the asymmetric information problem—creates an opportunity for lying and cheating that criminals exploit.[79] By denouncing the right to silence, together with other evidentiary rules that keep evidence out of fact-finders' sight, Bentham pro-ceeded on the supposition that 'the more information you have, the more likely you are to reach a correct decision'. This assumption is misleading when-ever private information is involved. The key issue in adjudication is not whether the fact-finders have, quantitatively, more or less evidence at their dis-posal. The issue is whether they have, qualitatively, more or less *separation* between false and true signals coming from the evidence. In order to ascribe credibility to any private information, the fact-finder requires a second-order (*separating*) information by which the credibility problem can be resolved. This second-order information must, of course, itself be credible. Mere aug-mentation of private information (that is, of any information with uncertain credentials) does not take the fact-finders closer to accuracy.[80]

In other words, private information can only be relied upon by fact-finders if it is credibly transmitted. That is, its transmission, at worst, should min-imize false signalling. Sellers of used cars, for example, are typically unable to credibly inform potential buyers about the quality of their cars. Consumers cannot discriminate between cars, and would pay no more than the average price for any car that is offered for sale. Owners of the best used cars may therefore decide not to sell them, thereby reducing the average quality and price of second-hand cars. Faced with this situation, owners of the second-best used cars may also decide not to sell their cars, thus dragging the average car quality and price further down. This process will be repeated indefinitely until the market is turned into a 'market for lemons', where only the poorest quality

---

[78] See Seidmann and Stein, above note 64, at 456–8.

[79] See Molho, above note 4, at pp. 1–10.

[80] See Stein, above note 23, at 279, 287–8, *et seq.* (uncovering this fallacy in Bentham's evidence theory and examining its implications).

cars are traded.[81] Sellers who privately know that their cars are high quality cannot back up the true claims which they might make about the value of their product (and thereby convert their private information into public). Consumers would rationally ignore uncorroborated claims because a dishonest car dealer could easily replicate such claims. Conversely, a seller who can certify the quality of his or her car credibly transmits this private information and separates from purveyors of lower quality cars.

This car-seller problem is analogous to that faced by innocent suspects, who decide whether to talk or keep silent. Only an innocent suspect can provide entirely credible evidence (say, an iron-clad alibi) to back up a proclamation of innocence. An innocent suspect who can provide such an alibi can separate from guilty suspects, just as a car seller might separate by certifying the quality of his or her car. An innocent suspect in possession of an iron-clad alibi is also unaffected by the abolition of the right to silence. The suspect's decision to provide the alibi would protect him or her against any negative externalities imposed by guilty suspects. This happy outcome, however, depends on the innocent suspect having an iron-clad alibi. Absent such evidence, an innocent suspect's unsupported proclamation of innocence might not assure acquittal, as criminals could make exactly the same claim. For example, the trier of a rape case rationally discounts an uncorroborated claim of consent because rapists as well as innocents would make this claim if it could signal credibility. Innocent suspects then pool with guilty suspects, just as high-quality car sellers must pool with vendors of worse cars if they cannot certify their claims. If innocents and criminals pool, then, contrary to Bentham's argument, the right to silence might also benefit innocents.

By allowing defendants and suspects to remain silent without suffering any negative consequence—such as adverse inferences—the right to silence offers an attractive course of action to many guilty suspects and defendants. Fearful of being implicated by their lies, these suspects and defendants separate from the pool by exercising the right to silence and thereby improve the innocents' prospect of acquittal. For such suspects and defendants, silence is the best course of action. Silence does not worsen their position, relative to the remaining alternatives: confessions and lies. In the absence of an attractive plea bargain, confession and the consequent conviction and punishment are obviously unattractive. The exception is, of course, when the prosecution's evidence is so overwhelmingly strong that the defendant would be better off not expending his or her money and efforts on trying the case. Lying is not cost-free either.

---

[81] See Molho, above note 4, at pp. 19–31. For the classic statement of the 'market for lemons' problem, see George Akerlof, The Market for Lemons: Quality Uncertainty and the Market Mechanism (1970) 84 *Quart. J. Econ.* 488.

There is always a prospect that the lie will be uncovered and constitute evidence of guilt.[82]

Another mechanism attaining this separation is the rule that generally allows the prosecution to impeach testifying defendants by their prior convictions.[83] To fully understand the workings of this rule, consider a pool accommodating both guilty and innocent defendants all of whom have prior convictions. Innocents in this pool want to separate from the criminals in order to secure their acquittal. Criminals do not help the innocents to fulfill this desire. On the contrary, all of them consider giving a false testimony that imitates and pools with innocents. Note that the defendant's criminal record only has a general—rather than case-specific—evidential capacity. This record does not attach to the defendant's testimony any specific doubt or caveat. It only functions as a residual factor that affects the testimony's general credibility. When there are case-specific reasons for disbelieving this testimony, its probability of being true is further reduced by the defendant's criminal record. When such reasons do not exist, this probability stays unaffected

---

[82] Welcomed by Posner, above note 13, at pp. 715–16, this rationale was criticized by several academic writers. See Gordon Van Kessel, Quieting the Guilty and Acquitting the Innocent: A Close Look at a New Twist on the Right to Silence (2002) 35 Ind. L. Rev. 925; Stephanos Bibas, The Right to Remain Silent Helps Only the Guilty (2003) 88 Iowa L. Rev. 421; Roberts and Zuckerman, above note 18, at pp. 422–5. These critics argue that Seidmann and Stein's model yields unrealistic predictions. Specifically, criminal suspects and defendants are not rational maximizers of their own welfare, and the socio-psychological dynamics of the jury trial do not align with economic reasoning either. Criminals attempt to pool with innocents with and without the right to silence. As a privilege against adverse inferences, this right mainly helps guilty suspects and defendants to choose between silence and pooling.

Because these critics fail to specify the grounds of their predictions, I can only juxtapose them against empirical data that support Seidmann and Stein. See Seidmann and Stein, above note 64, at 498–502 (empirical studies identify a switch from silence to lies following the abolition of the privilege against adverse inferences in England). The critics also ignore the applicability of Seidmann and Stein's model to actors exercising rudimentary rationality (and often acting upon legal advice). The model's focusing on the most basic of economic instincts—that of self-preservation—escapes the critics' attention as well. See Seidmann and Stein, ibid, at 450–1. The model's empirical credentials are substantial, but, admittedly, incomplete. The model's economic logic is unassailable. For many guilty criminals, the right to silence generates probability of acquittal that exceeds the probability of acquittal in the lying scenario. Abolition of the right induces these criminals to lie and pool with innocents. See Seidmann and Stein, ibid, at 467–69. The model also coherently explains the Fifth Amendment jurisprudence (see Seidmann and Stein, ibid, at 474–98)—a feature that the critics do not contest. The combination of these features—economic rationality, empirical support, and the doctrinal fit—aligns the model's predictions with reality. To beat this theory, the critics need to offer a competing theory. See Richard A. Epstein, Common Law, Labor Law, and Reality: A Rejoinder to Professors Getman and Kohler (1983) 92 Yale L.J. 1435, 1435 ('it takes a theory to beat a theory'). Bare intuitions will not do. Cf. Andrew Ashworth, *Human Rights, Serious Crime and Criminal Procedure* (2002), p. 21 ('The anti-pooling rationale differs from the others in that it is not grounded in deep principle but rather in empirically testable assumptions about behaviour, related to one of the primary purposes of criminal justice system (to convict the guilty and acquit the innocent). It should therefore take its place alongside other instrumental rationales').

[83] See Federal Rule of Evidence 609.

by the defendant's prior convictions. Moreover, the defendant's readiness to risk impeachment by prior convictions might signal credibility. By testifying about his or her innocence, the defendant conveys to fact-finders that his or her exculpatory testimony is true and that there are no specific reasons for disbelieving it. Most crucially, the defendant willingly accepts the scenario in which the fact-finders actually find such a reason. In that scenario, the relevant reason combines with the defendant's criminal record and reduces the credibility of the testimony. Because the defendant's signalling is costly, it indicates the defendant's credibility as a witness until the prosecution comes up with specific reasons, backed by evidence, that discredit his or her testimony.[84] On the average, criminals leave behind more incriminating traces than do innocents.[85] Reasons discrediting the defendant's self-exonerating testimony predominantly appear in cases featuring guilty defendants. For criminals, the anticipated (ex ante) probability of being discredited by such reasons is much higher on the average than for innocents. Because the combination of such reasons and the defendant's criminal record is potentially devastating to the defendant's credibility as a witness, many guilty defendants prefer to separate from the pool by not testifying in their defence.[86] This separation increases the probability of exculpatory accounts tendered by innocent defendants.

The two examples discussed have a common denominator. In both, evidence law lays down a legal rule that intensifies credible signalling by inducing a separation of the pool in which guilty and innocent defendants and suspects make self-exonerating statements that mix with each other. My next examples involve a different game-theoretic technique: costly signalling. By making his or her signalling costly, to himself or herself, a person may separate it from cheap talk and make the prospect that fact-finders will find his or her signalling credible more probable. To a certain extent, one of the rules already discussed— the prosecution's licence to impeach a testifying criminal defendant by his or her criminal record—performs the same function. The next set of examples is, however, more compelling than the example that this rule provides.

The first of these examples features a criminal evidence arrangement known in the United States as the *Mezzanatto* rule.[87] Under this rule, a defendant participating in a proffer session or plea negotiations may effectively waive his

[84] For general discussion of costly signalling, see Molho, above note 4, at pp. 63–80, 97–101.

[85] See generally H. Richard Uviller, Evidence of Character to Prove Conduct: Illusion, Illogic, and Injustice in the Courtroom (1982) 130 U. Pa. L. Rev. 845, 847 (distinguishing between trace and predictive evidence).

[86] Provided, of course, that the fact-finders do not draw any adverse inferences from the defendant's silence. See above, notes 74–82 and accompanying text.

[87] See *United States v Mezzanatto*, 513 U.S. 196 (1995).

or her plea negotiations privilege,[88] along with the right to silence, in relation to any self-incriminating statement that he or she may make within that framework.[89] This waiver is controlled by the ordinary principles of contract law that allow defendants to waive these (and some other) protections knowingly and voluntarily.[90]

The *Mezzanatto* rule supports the prosecution's practice of conditioning its negotiations with a defendant upon his or her waiver of the above protections. As such, it may be perceived as promoting the law-and-order objectives at the expense of criminal defendants' civil rights. This perception, however, is incorrect. Some defendants find it in their interest to participate in proffer sessions and negotiate a plea with the prosecution. For any such defendant, effective communication with the prosecution is essential. This communication is not effective so long as the prosecution perceives the defendant's statements as cheap talk that has no credibility. The prosecution sticks to this view so long as the defendant's self-incriminating statement is privileged. So long as the defendant can suppress such a statement, it is nothing but cheap talk. To signal credibility, the defendant needs to convince the prosecution that his or her signalling is costly. To achieve this, the defendant may allow the prosecution to use his or her inculpatory statement as evidence if he or she breaches one of his or her undertakings in the ensuing arrangement or plea bargain. For example, a defendant may make a representation that his or her part in the relevant criminal activity was minor relative to other participants and agree in advance that his or her inculpatory statement will be used against him or her if this representation turns out to be untrue. Based on this representation and the defendant's waiver of the privilege, the prosecution may offer the defendant a plea bargain that otherwise would not be offered. This offer would only be made under the *Mezzanatto* rule that makes the defendant's waiver effective.[91]

My last example is Federal Rule of Evidence 702 as interpreted by the United States Supreme Court. The Supreme Court's famous *Daubert Trilogy—Daubert*,[92] *Joiner*,[93] and *Kumho Tire*[94]—conditions the admissibility

---

[88] These are granted by Federal Rule of Evidence 410, as well as by Federal Rule of Criminal Procedure 11(e)(6).

[89] For a recent example, see *United States v Chan*, 185 F.Supp.2d 305 (S.D.N.Y 2002).

[90] As decided by the Supreme Court in *United States v Mezzanatto*, 513 U.S. 196, 210 (1995), 'We hold that absent some affirmative indication that the agreement was entered into unknowingly or involuntarily, an agreement to waive the exclusionary provisions of the plea-statement Rules is valid and enforceable'.

[91] This explanation belongs to Eric Rasmusen, The Economics of Evidentiary Law: *Mezzanatto* and the Economics of Self-Incrimination (1998) 19 Cardozo L. Rev. 1541.

[92] *Daubert v Merrell Dow Pharmaceuticals, Inc.*, 509 U.S. 579 (1993).

[93] *General Electric Co. v Joiner*, 522 U.S.136 (1997).

[94] *Kumho Tire Co. v Carmichael*, 526 U.S. 137 (1999) (extending *Daubert*'s gatekeeping rules, originally designed for scientific evidence, to all kinds of expert testimony).

of scientific expert evidence on the combined weighing of several criteria.[95] Two of these criteria are important to the present discussion. Under one of them, the theory or the methodology by which the expert generated the evidence needs to be *falsifiable*. Another criterion states that the expert's theory or methodology must preferably (not mandatorily) be published in the academic or professional literature after undergoing peer review.

Satisfaction of the last criterion turns the expert's testimony into costly and, consequently, credible signalling. Because experts testify on matters of opinion rather than fact, an expert's false testimony rarely, if ever, classifies as perjury. Because the risk of prosecution for perjury (let alone conviction) is extremely low for all experts, their testimony may classify as cheap talk. To avoid this inefficiency, evidence law needs to facilitate credible signalling by expert witnesses. The law facilitates this signalling by treating the expert's professional publications, congruent with his or her testimony, as a factor that bolsters his or her credibility as a witness. Finding such publications unrelated to the trial goals of the party calling the expert would support the expert's impartiality.[96] More importantly, by exposing his or her findings to examination at trial, the expert assumes the risk that the entire methodology in which he or she has a vested interest—professional reputation, earnings, or both—will be discredited. Indeed, if the expert were unsure about his or her published methodology, he or she would not assume this risk. The falsifiability standard, with which the expert's testimony needs to comply as well, increases the expert's risk. Under this standard, the expert's findings need to be susceptible to empirical testing by other experts working in the same area.[97] The personal risk that the expert witness assumes qualifies as a costly signalling that bolsters the credibility of his or her testimony.[98]

E. The Evidential Damage Doctrine

The evidential damage doctrine is another mechanism geared towards attaining cost-efficiency.[99] This doctrine is designed for civil litigation.[100] Under this doctrine, a person is responsible for evidential damage when his or her

[95] I discuss these criteria below on pp. 196–7; 235–8.

[96] See Richard A. Posner, The Law and Economics of the Economic Expert Witness (1999) 13 *J. Econ. Persp.* 91.   [97] See *Daubert v Merrell Dow Pharmaceuticals, Inc.*, 509 U.S. 579 (1993).

[98] See Posner, above note 96.

[99] See generally, Ariel Porat and Alex Stein, *Tort Liability under Uncertainty* (2001), pp. 160–206. For critical appraisals of this and related ideas see Jane Stapleton, Book Review (2003) 66 M.L.R. 308; Vern R. Walker, Book Review (2002) 1 Law, Probability & Risk 175.

[100] For its application in criminal cases, see below pp. 199–200.

wrongful actions impair another person's ability—and, consequently, reduce that person's chances—to establish the facts necessary for prevailing in a lawsuit. A paradigmatic example of evidential damage is a medical malpractice case featuring a doctor who breached his or her duty to generate and maintain proper medical records.[101] Consider a case involving a medical patient who died following complications during surgery that the surgeon may or may not have performed with due diligence. Add to this set of facts the surgeon's failure to dictate operative notes or the hospital's failure to keep those records in the patient's file. Any such failure inflicts evidential damage on the patient. The patient may or may not have been treated wrongfully by the defendant, but the defendant (the doctor, the hospital, or both) has definitely wronged the patient by incapacitating him or her evidentially as a tort claimant.[102]

Another paradigmatic example involves an unconcerted infliction of damage by two or more defendants, when the fraction of the damage that each defendant individually inflicted on the claimant cannot be established. To illustrate this category of cases, consider the following set of facts:

(1) Two dogs, each of which belongs to a different wrongdoer, simultaneously attack the claimant.

(2) The ensuing damage is evidentially indivisible because it is impossible to establish which dog did what.[103]

Here, too, the wrongdoers caused the claimant evidential damage. Each wrongdoer inflicted this damage by wrongfully eliminating the claimant's ability to attribute the relevant part of his injury to the actual wrongdoer. This evidential incapacitation deprives the claimant of compensation for his injury.

Finally, consider a factory that emits carcinogenic radiation. In the area affected by the radiation, the incidence of cancer rises by 25 per cent. While prior to the factory's operation, only eighty people contracted cancer each year, one hundred people now become afflicted each year. There is, however, no evidence that could preponderantly identify those people who actually

---

[101] See, e.g., *Smith v United States*, 128 F. Supp. 2d 1227 (2000).

[102] Consider again *Smith v United States*, 128 F. Supp. 2d 1227, 1232 (2000) ('the essential dispute concerns whether Drs. Antakli and Moursi failed to act in accordance with the standard of medical care as accepted for purposes of today's decision, and whether, as a proximate result thereof, Smith suffered injuries which would not otherwise have occurred. Although ordinarily it is plaintiff's burden to establish facts leading to liability, the Court in this case finds that Dr. Moursi, the primary surgeon, failed to follow the appropriate standard of care when he failed to dictate operative notes of the surgical procedure he performed and, thus, the Court infers that Dr. Moursi failed to act in accordance with the degree of skill and learning ordinarily possessed and used by members of his profession ... and that as a proximate result thereof, Smith suffered injuries resulting in his death which would not otherwise have occurred.... That an adverse inference may arise from the fact of missing evidence is a generally accepted principle of law').

[103] For comprehensive analysis of this example see Porat and Stein, above note 99, at 77–83.

contracted cancer as a result of exposure to the radiation, as opposed to those who are simply victims of misfortune. All one hundred people file lawsuits against the factory's owner. The fate of these lawsuits is unclear.[104] Yet, it is clear that the defendant's wrongful activity incapacitated each claimant evidentially by depriving him or her of his or her ability to identify the cause of his or her affliction.[105]

The law can impose liability for evidential damage in two different ways. The evidential damage doctrine can shift the burden of persuasion to the defendant whenever the latter is responsible for inflicting evidential damage on the claimant. If the case is factually indeterminate, in the sense that the accounts of the parties are equally probable, the claimant will prevail. Alternatively, evidentially damaged claimants can recover tort damages—an approach that treats evidential incapacitation as a free-standing tort.

The evidential remedy that shifts the persuasion burden to the defendant is only effective when the claimant's direct and evidential damages are both attributable to the same defendant. When the direct and the evidential wrongdoers are two different persons (as in cases in which a third party wrongfully destroys the claimant's evidence), the evidential remedy is unavailable. Furthermore, in cases in which the claimant's evidential damage is so severe that he or she cannot raise his or her factual scenario up to the 50 per cent probability level, this remedy is ineffective. Because the defendant's case is more probable than not, the burden-of-persuasion doctrine is inapplicable *ab initio*. This doctrine only applies in balanced cases. Hence, the evidential remedy is confined to cases in which the evidence is balanced and in which both direct and evidential damages that the claimant allegedly suffered are attributable to the same defendant. In all other cases involving evidential damage, claimants can only seek the tort remedy. Analysis of this remedy is not part of this book's agenda.[106]

Under the $P > 0.5$ rule, an evidentially balanced case is decided in favour of the defendant. However, this general principle is open to exceptions: on special grounds, the law may justifiably shift the persuasion burden to the defendant. The evidential damage doctrine provides one such ground. Because the defendant wrongfully inflicted the evidential damage on the claimant, it is the defendant—not the claimant—who suffers from the uncertainty of the case.

---

[104] A famous case that illustrates this type of lawsuits and that ended up in a settlement is *In re 'Agent Orange' Product Liability Litigation*, 597 F. Supp. 740 (E.D.N.Y. 1984), *aff'd* 818 F. 2d 145 (2d Cir. 1987). See also Judge Posner's decision in *Adkins v Mid-American Growers Inc.*, 167 F. 3d 355, 359–60 (7th Cir. 1999) (allowing group-based compensation for what was described as 'probabilistic harm'). [105] See Porat and Stein, above note 99, at pp. 193–4.

[106] See Porat and Stein, above note 99, at pp. 165–84.

Chapter 7 justifies this remedy (and sanction) on the grounds of fairness (deriving from the fundamental principle that a person must not be allowed to profit from his or her own wrong).

This remedy also has an economic justification.[107] The evidential remedy promotes social utility. Availability of that remedy deters prospective wrong-doers from inflicting evidential damage. This remedy also induces defendants to shape their trial strategy in a socially desirable way. Instead of hiding in the shadows of uncertainty, for which they might be responsible under the evidential damage doctrine, many such defendants are induced to unfold a straightforward account of the events supported by unambiguous evidence. When factual impasse works against the defendant, he or she attempts to avoid that impasse. Committed to a tidy factual account, the defendant must expose his or her evidence to scrutiny. Subsequently, the defendant's evidence either survives or does not survive the claimant's falsifying attempts. Either way, the evidential deficiency is rectified, partially or even entirely. To sum up, the evidential remedy generates incentives for economically efficient conduct both ex ante and ex post, before and after the infliction of evidential damage.

The evidential damage doctrine has an important branch in the domain of contracts. Civil litigation is heavily subsidized by the state. Any new contract increases the general probability of litigation. Any contract therefore entails the possibility of consuming the state's litigation subsidy. If realized, this possibility would count as a negative externality.

Many contracts are incomplete.[108] Such contracts involve unstated intentions and expectations and other factual uncertainties—gaps that adjudicators subsequently fill. This problem could be attenuated and adjudication could become less expensive if the possibility of uncertainty in a future trial were adverted to and explicitly regulated by contracting parties. Because adjudication is subsidized by public funds, parties to a contract should be encouraged not to leave the uncertainty problem contractually unresolved. They should be encouraged to regulate this problem, whenever it can be reasonably anticipated. By leaving this problem to adjudicators, the parties save in contract negotiation and drafting expenses. At the same time, they increase both the likelihood and the social cost of their future litigation. Contracting parties cast away the prospect of making this saving when it introduces an undesirable element of uncertainty into their relationship. But in some cases, either one of the parties or both will find the uncertainty contractually convenient. By leaving the uncertainty problem unregulated, the contracting parties may

---

107 For comprehensive analysis, see Porat and Stein, above note 99, at pp. 179–206.
108 See Shavell, above note 2, at pp. 299–301.

strike a privately good bargain. This bargain, however, will increase the consumption of the state's litigation subsidy—a free ride at the taxpayers' expense.[109]

A rule that penalizes the party responsible for the contractual gap can reduce this negative externality.[110] Forcing judges and jurors (as opposed to private arbitrators) to adjudicate incomplete bargains, any such gap is tantamount to evidential damage. A party inflicting such damage normally assumes responsibility for its consequences. This responsibility translates into risk-allocation: the risk of error in filling the contractual gap should be placed on the party responsible for the gap (that is, for leaving the uncertainty problem unregulated). This approach is suitable for cases in which at least one of the parties can reasonably anticipate the uncertainty problem before concluding the contract. Under this approach, the gap is filled against the interest of that party, as the *contra proferentem* principle demands.[111]

---

[109] Made originally in Alex Stein, An Essay on Uncertainty and Fact-Finding in Civil Litigation, with Special Reference to Contract Cases (1998) 48 U. Toronto L.J. 299, 341–4, this point was inspired by Ian Ayres and Robert Gertner, Filling Gaps in Incomplete Contracts: An Economic Theory of Default Rules (1989) 99 Yale L.J. 87.

[110] See Stein, ibid. But see Richard A. Posner, The Law and Economics of Contract Interpretation (2005) 83 Texas L. Rev. 1581, 1590–1 (arguing that this tie-breaker approach is the cheapest, but may yield negative benefits by its increase of contractual transaction costs).

[111] Stein, ibid. If both parties are equally responsible for the gap, both of them should pay the costs of the uncertainty problem. This outcome can be achieved by court-imposed cost-payment orders or, more conveniently, by directing the parties to a compulsory arbitration for which they would have to pay.

6

Allocation of the Risk of Error in Criminal Trials

A. The 'Equal Best' Standard

Facts constitutive of criminal defendants' guilt need to be established beyond all reasonable doubt. Any reasonable doubt leads to the defendant's acquittal.[1] This requirement requires elaboration. What precisely does it require? What does 'beyond reasonable doubt' mean? The utility-based determination of the criminal proof standard that the previous chapter provides is a good starting point.

Following John Kaplan,[2] the utility-based criminal proof standard can be formalized as $I/I + G$, where I and G denote, respectively, the social damage inflicted by erroneously convicting an innocent suspect (I) and by erroneously acquitting a criminal (G). For example, by postulating that the disutility ratio I/G equals $9/1$, we set the controlling proof threshold at $9/10$. The probability threshold for convictions can thus be determined by the disutilities deriving from the socially desirable ratio of wrongful acquittals vs. wrongful convictions.[3] The legal system can accordingly reduce the incidence of wrongful acquittals ('false negatives') by increasing the number of wrongful convictions ('false positives'), and vice versa. Each of these outcomes can be attained by bringing the probability threshold for convictions up and down.

The conventional doctrine, however, vigorously resists the explicit introduction of numbers into the $I/I + G$ formula. This resistance signifies the doctrinal unwillingness to reduce the error-related disutilities—false negatives

---

[1] For foundational decisions establishing this principle in the United States and in England, see *In re Winship*, 397 U.S. 358 (1970); *Mullaney v Wilbur*, 421 U.S. 684 (1975); *Woolmington v D.P. P.* [1935] AC 462 (HL).

[2] John Kaplan, Decision Theory and the Fact-Finding Process (1968) 20 Stan. L. Rev. 1065, 1071–5.

[3] See, e.g., Alexander Volokh, n Guilty Men (1997) 146 U. Pa. L. Rev. 173 (examining different probability thresholds for conviction).

and false positives—to a common denominator.[4] This resistance does not make immediate sense because not any doubt, but only 'reasonable', both demands and justifies the defendant's acquittal. By introducing this crucial qualification, the doctrine recognizes the inevitability of convicting innocent people. As Lord Denning observed, criminal law 'would fail to protect the community if it admitted fanciful possibilities to deflect the course of justice'.[5] This reservation makes allowance for utility considerations, which invites all-encompassing balancing. If this balancing were explicit, it would explain the beyond-all-reasonable-doubt standard by openly stating the permissible ratio of wrongful convictions and acquittals.

Any perceptible doubt—that is, any doubt substantiated by the evidence, thus qualifying as 'reasonable'—must work in favour of the accused. Doubts that remain unsubstantiated and, consequently, imperceptible (such doubts can be found in every case) do not pass the threshold of reasonableness. The accused does not benefit from any such doubt. The criminal proof standard immunizes the accused only from the evidentially confirmed risk of erroneous conviction (Risk I). In parallel, this standard exposes the accused to the risk of erroneous conviction when the risk lacks evidential confirmation (Risk II).[6] This doctrinal distinction focuses on the evidential credentials of the risk of error, instead of the harm associated with its possible materialization. Far from intuitive, this distinction requires explanation.

Criminal defendants would rather be exposed to Risk I when charged with assault, than to Risk II in trials for murder. From a social utility perspective, fining a retired tycoon upon his or her conviction of insider dealing, even when the doubts raised by him or her are perceptible and, consequently reasonable, may well be a sound strategy of intensifying deterrence in relation to this almost unprovable crime. More importantly, unbending immunization of criminal defendants from Risk I leaves many dangerous criminals unconvicted and

---

[4] See Glanville Williams, *The Proof of Guilt* (3rd edn., 1963), pp. 183–94; Theodore Waldman, Origins of the Legal Doctrine of Reasonable Doubt (1959) 20 *J. Hist. Ideas* 299; George Fletcher, Two Kinds of Legal Rules: A Comparative Study of Burden-of-Persuasion Practices in Criminal Cases (1968) 77 Yale L.J. 880; Barbara Shapiro, 'To a Moral Certainty': Theories of Knowledge and Anglo-American Juries 1600–1850 (1986) 38 Hast. L. J. 153; Adrian A. S. Zuckerman, *The Principles of Criminal Evidence* (1989), pp. 122–63.

[5] *Miller v Minister of Pensions* [1947] 2 All ER 372, 373–4 (Denning L. J.). An observation similar to this was made by the American Supreme Court in *Herrera v Collins*, 113 S. Ct. 853, 860 (1993) and in *Victor v Nebraska*, 511 U.S. 1, 8 (1994). See, however, *Cage v Louisiana*, 498 U.S. 39 (1990)—a decision invalidating, on due process grounds, a jury instruction describing a reasonable doubt as an actual and substantial doubt that a reasonable man can seriously entertain. According to the United States Supreme Court, such an instruction would allow the jury to base convictions on a relatively low probability of guilt.

[6] Zuckerman, above note 4, at pp. 134–40. Courts, however, are reluctant to articulate this notion. See Henry A. Diamond, Reasonable Doubt: To Define or Not to Define (1990) 90 Colum. L. Rev. 1716; Jon O. Newman, Beyond 'Reasonable Doubt' (1993) 68 N.Y.U.L. Rev. 979.

unpunished. Harm that such exonerations engender often exceeds any damage that erroneous convictions might produce. Indeed, the average rape victim would readily swap her traumatic experience for a year in a civilized jail, but finding a partner for such a bargain would be a rather daunting, if not altogether impossible, task. A rapist's wrongful acquittal and subsequent rapes generate more bare harm than mistaken conviction and punishment of an innocent person.[7] The doctrinal differentiation between Risk I and Risk II runs against social utility and possibly also against justice to the individual victim.[8]

Following the fundamental distinction between injustice and misfortune, this doctrinal approach is best understood as mirroring the moral distinction between accidentally and deliberately erroneous convictions.[9] Accordingly, the criminal proof requirement minimizes a distinct type of moral injustice, rather than bare harm, such as pain, suffering, and frustrated expectations. Bare harm that an erroneous conviction produces is a variable and empirically contingent factor. It can always be balanced against harms generated by acquittals of guilty criminals. Apart from letting criminals go unpunished, such acquittals dilute deterrence and, consequently, expose society and its individual members to more crime. From a utilitarian viewpoint, therefore, any notion of special moral injustice would be unacceptable. The special moral status that this notion ascribes to individual injustice is meant to function as an immunity voucher (a 'trump card'[10]) that allows its owner to exempt his or her private

---

[7] According to Jeremy Bentham, *A Treatise on Judicial Evidence* (1825), pp. 196–7, individuals should be protected from erroneous convictions in order to prevent 'alarm' in the public at large. Bentham estimated that the disutility generated by apprehension of fear and insecurity outweighs the utility of bringing more criminals to justice. This speculation, however, seems to have reflected Bentham's personal 'attitudes and scale of values rather than necessary consequence of a utilitarian analysis'. William L. Twining, *Theories of Evidence: Bentham and Wigmore* (1985), p. 99. Nowadays, most people seem to be more concerned with being protected *by* rather than *from* the criminal law machinery. But see Alan Wertheimer, Punishing the Innocent—Unintentionally (1977) 20 *Inquiry* 45 (arguing that compelling utilitarian reasons necessitate convictions of innocent people).

Another utilitarian attempt at justifying the proof-beyond-all-reasonable-doubt requirement substitutes a rule-utilitarian for act-utilitarian strategy. Arguably, this requirement minimizes bare harm in the aggregate. Not directly contributing to utility, each of its individual applications thus becomes justified as part of the system. This argument has rightly become suspected of *petitio principii*, that is, of 'arguing backward from the fact that our moral intuitions condemn convicting the innocent to the conclusion that such a disability must be in the long-term utilitarian interests of any society'. Ronald Dworkin, *A Matter of Principle* (1986), p. 82. For quite independent reasons, the distinction between rule-utilitarianism and act-utilitarianism can hardly be sustained. See Dworkin, ibid. See also David Lyons, *Forms and Limits of Utilitarianism* (1965), ch. 4, pp. 182ff.

[8] For support of utilitarian balancing as defining the criminal proof standards, see James F. Stephen, *History of the Criminal Law of England* Vol. 1 (1883), p. 438; Edmond H. Cahn, *The Moral Decision* (1955), p. 296. See also R. Erik Lillquist, Recasting Reasonable Doubt: Decision Theory and the Virtues of Variability (2002) 36 U.C. Davis L. Rev. 85 (invoking a behavioural economics approach to justify a flexible 'reasonable doubt' standard for criminal cases).

[9] Dworkin, above note 7, at pp. 82ff.

[10] See Ronald Dworkin, Rights as Trumps, in Jeremy Waldron (ed.), *Theories of Rights* (1984), p. 153.

interest from utilitarian balancing. Because utilitarianism opposes such exemptions, the unbending proof-beyond-all-reasonable-doubt requirement makes no utilitarian sense. But it does have a non-utilitarian rationale.

The anti-utilitarian differentiation between accidentally and deliberately erroneous convictions emphasizes that it is one thing to convict an innocent person accidentally, when there is no evidenced reason for doubting his or her guilt, and quite another to convict an innocent person by knowingly disregarding such a reason. The first case is one of bad luck that may befall any person. The second case involves deliberate singling out of the accused as a risk-absorbing unit, which would violate both equality and fairness. In Ronald Dworkin's terms,[11] such an outcome violates the state's fundamental political obligation to treat its citizens with equal concern and respect.[12] *The legal system may justifiably convict a person only if it did its best in protecting that person from the risk of erroneous conviction and if it does not provide better protection to other individuals.*[13]

This 'equal best' standard appears vague at best and vacuous at worst. Take a hypothetical rule prescribing that 'any person shall be convicted on the probability of the accusations that equals or exceeds 0.9'. Under this rule, adjudicators may convict a person even in the presence of an evidentially substantiated possibility of his or her innocence (Risk I). This rule appears unsatisfactory, but the state convincingly proves that it could not do better, given its limited resources, high crime rates, and other constraints. The state consequently claims that, *as a matter of fact*, it did its 'equal best', which—under appropriate circumstances—could also be the case with probability thresholds below 0.9. The 'equal best' standard turns into an empty shell. Under the appropriate constraints, any allocation of the risk of erroneous conviction is both 'fair' and

---

[11] Dworkin, above note 7, at pp. 72, 79–88.

[12] I assume that the criminal justice system operates under limited resources, so that greater investment could eliminate more judicial errors. This assumption does not undermine the moral harm rationale. Public resources are scarce, and there is no overriding moral imperative which demands their channelling into criminal proceedings, as opposed to health, education, highways, and other amenities. Citizens benefiting from those amenities may occasionally be harmed by the underfunded criminal justice system. Such an outcome, as regrettable as it may be, would be morally indistinguishable from a traffic accident resulting from a poor investment in road safety. If the process of allocating public resources were politically fair, no person could blame the state for being denied equal treatment when the system accidentally works to his or her detriment. See Dworkin, above note 7, at 84–7. This point, however, must not foster complacency, as the (fragile) distinction between injustice and misfortune often does. Victims of accidents should not be left to their own devices just because they have nobody to blame. See Judith Shklar, *The Faces of Injustice* (1988), pp. 51–82. See also Note, The Luck of the Law: Allusions to Fortuity in Legal Discourse (1989) 102 Harv. L. Rev. 1862 (an insightful article demonstrating that luck, both moral and legal, is a value-laden notion).

[13] This criterion differs from both Ronald Dworkin's standard for justified convictions and Judith Shklar's notion of 'injustice' (as opposed to 'misfortune').

'equal', as long as it is general and not directed against particular individuals.[14] This formal and seemingly powerful critique of the 'equal best' standard is, however, misdirected. Chapter 3 demonstrates that naked probability, irrespective of how high it is numerically, can never provide an adequate foundation for criminal convictions. In criminal litigation, probability of guilt does not acquire validity when its evidential base does not cover the specific factual accusations brought against the accused, and, consequently, does not have sufficient weight. As Chapter 3 explains, the best justifiable standard for convictions is dualistic. Probability and its evidential weight ought to work together; probability alone will not do. Chapter 3 also identifies the logical relationship between probability estimates and their weights. As the probability becomes more removed from both factual certainty (probability that equals 1) and impossibility (probability that equals 0), its weight goes down. A 0.9 probability would suffer from the insufficient weight problem. Such probability is not the 'best'. As such it can never satisfy the evidential weight standard that derives from the 'equal best' requirement.

The formal critique of the 'equal best' requirement also fails on its own formal grounds. Under the 'equal best' standard, if a 0.9 probability of guilt works against one person, then *any* probability of guilt should equally work against the individual to whom it attaches. Every person should pay his or her equitable share in the tax that the state decides to exact in order to promote social welfare. Under this requirement, a defendant with a 0.9 probability of guilt only pays ninety per cent of the conviction tax. Moreover, the state would only be justified in imposing this tax if each person with a 0.1 probability of guilt pays ten per cent of the tax. Theoretically, this outcome can be achieved through a lottery mechanism that distributes the appropriate number of conviction tickets (nine tickets for ten defendants with a 0.9 probability of guilt, and only one such ticket for ten defendants with a 0.1 probability of guilt). Such lotteries, however (if they can ever be conducted), would break away with the demand that the state does its best in protecting *the individual* from wrongful conviction. Convicting a person on a 0.1 probability of guilt is assuredly not the best protection that the state can provide. The state, however, cannot exempt such persons from the conviction tax and, in parallel, impose the entire tax on the individuals with a 0.9 probability of guilt. This outcome would violate the principle under which every person counts for one and no person for more or less than one. Under the equality and fairness standard, the state cannot justifiably approach an individual and tell him

---

[14] Cf. Rinat Kitai, Protecting the Guilty (2003) 6 Buff. Crim. L. Rev. 1163, 1172–8 (criticizing the equality-based justification of the criminal proof standard and offering a social contract justification as a replacement).

or her: 'You've got to pay the conviction tax, even though it is not equitably shared by others. If you and similarly situated individuals do not pay it, social welfare would be undermined most severely.' The equality and fairness standards allow any such individual to respond 'I don't really care about social welfare, especially if I have to pay for it more than others.'[15] This response indeed represents the whole essence of the individual's right to fairness and equality, more accurately presented as equal fairness. This right acquires its very meaning by overriding social utility in the event of a conflict between the two.[16]

The ultimate objective of all rules and principles regulating criminal proof is to provide defendants with a both comprehensive and unyielding immunity from Risk I, as opposed to Risk II. The ensuing sections of this chapter substantiate this point by analysing the relevant rules and principles. Before that discussion, I identify the connection between this general immunity and the maximal individualization principle (*PMI*) set forth in Chapter 3. To recall, *PMI* holds that no adverse inference can be drawn against the accused unless the inference, together with its supporting evidence, were exposed to—and survived—the maximal individualized testing. That testing includes every practical possibility of testing the applicability of that inference to the case at hand. The accused, in other words, never assumes the risk of erroneous conviction that accompanies evidence and inferences not open to individualized testing. It is the prosecution that assumes the risk of erroneous acquittal in connection with such evidence. Although *PMI* regulates fact-finding—generally perceivable as an epistemic activity—its adoption by the legal system is not an epistemological move. As Chapter 3 also explains, *PMI*'s ultimate function is to apportion the risk of error. Therefore, it is always possible to argue on non-epistemic grounds in favour of other risk-allocating principles, as I do in Chapter 5 (by invoking the cost-efficiency principle). Under *PMI*, adjudicators are allowed to convict the accused if evidence incriminating him or her both generates probability of guilt that comes close to certainty and survives maximal individualized testing. If these conditions are not fully satisfied, the accused must be acquitted. The standard for convictions set by *PMI* thus

---

[15] Louis Kaplow and Steven Shavell, *Fairness versus Welfare* (2002), pp. 445–9 claim that this notion of equal treatment carries no independent significance. From their perspective, a person complaining about his or her 'unequal treatment' by the legal system must have either been treated unequally due to some error (unrelated to equality) or was actually different from other people in some material respect (see also ibid, at 24–7). More broadly, they claim that to the extent that 'unequal treatment is [believed to be] evil', this 'taste for equality' should be processed within a regular utilitarian calculus that 'would accord weight to it just as to any other taste' (ibid, at 448). This, unfortunately, does not really respond to the individual's claim in my example, who essentially complains about an ad hoc tax. More fundamentally, what exactly are these 'other tastes' that both clash with and deserve to be balanced against the taste for equal treatment!? I suspect these 'other tastes' to represent the utilitarians' taste for social welfare, which would bring the discussion back to square one.   [16] See Dworkin, above note 10.

overlaps the equal-best requirement and the corresponding immunity from Risk I, granted to all criminal defendants. Any criminal conviction that fails to satisfy *PMI* illegitimately exposes the accused to Risk I. Any conviction complying with *PMI* rests on a factual base that underwent and survived maximal individualized testing. The convicted defendant acquires an immunity from Risk I, but still is (legitimately) exposed to Risk II (generated by doubts that are abstract, rather than evidenced).[17]

B. The Burden of Proof

Section A has identified the burden of proof that the prosecution needs to discharge to secure the defendant's conviction. First, the prosecution adduces evidence that verifies its accusations (this is the production burden or the burden of adducing evidence). At the end of the trial, probability of the defendant's guilt, estimated on the trial evidence as a whole, needs to approach certainty. This next-to-certainty standard is qualitative in nature. No cardinal number that symbolizes probability (except for the unrealistic 1) adequately represents this standard. This standard requires elimination of all evidenced and case-specific—as opposed to merely abstract and theoretical—scenarios in which the defendant is innocent. If any such scenario is both evidenced and not fully refuted by the prosecution, the defendant should be acquitted. The prosecution's persuasion burden does not accommodate this standard alone. Evidence and inferences by which the prosecution discharges this burden need to unfold themselves to full adversarial scrutiny. Specifically, the incriminating inferences and their supporting evidence need to undergo and survive their maximal individualized testing by the defendant. If one such inference or evidence is essential for convicting the defendant, but not susceptible to such testing, the defendant ought to be acquitted. If one such inference or evidence is essential for convicting the defendant, but the testing undermines its credibility, the defendant ought to be acquitted as well. This is what proof beyond all reasonable doubt requires.[18]

To see how these requirements work, consider the following case. The prosecution accuses D of bank robbery, an accusation D vehemently denies. Two passers-by independently testify that, shortly after the robbery, they saw D near the bank with a sub-machine gun in his arms. Each of them also identified

---

[17] These legal arrangements are compatible with John Rawls's first principle of justice under which 'each person is to have an equal right to the most extensive basic liberty compatible with a similar liberty for others'. See John Rawls, *A Theory of Justice* (1972), p. 60.

[18] See Alex Stein, The Refoundation of Evidence Law (1996) 9 Can. J. Law & Jurisprudence 279, 323–7.

D at the line-ups conducted by the police shortly after D's arrest. A forensic expert testifies that fingerprints that appeared in several places at the bank are identical to D's fingerprints. Subsequently, D testifies about his alibi and brings witness W to corroborate. In rebuttal, the prosecution introduces a tape that recorded a critical conversation between D and W. In that conversation, W promised D to corroborate his alibi in exchange for £500,000. The adjudicators justifiably find D guilty as charged. They reason that the probability of the accusations being true is very high and that the only evidenced scenario in which D is innocent (the alibi story) was completely refuted (by both the fingerprint evidence and the tape). Because there is no perceptible doubt about D's guilt, his conviction aligns with his immunity from Risk I. D's conviction would violate that immunity if the testimony given by him and W were not refuted.

D's conviction still exposes him to Risk II because he may still be innocent. For example, D may have been framed by corrupt police officers, previously bribed by the actual robber; and it is also possible that his alibi conspiracy with W was, in his mind, his only chance of escaping false conviction. This scenario, however, is completely unevidenced. Such theoretical scenarios do not generate a reasonable doubt.

This set of proof-related requirements—and the corresponding apportionment of the risk of error between the accused and the prosecution—should apply indiscriminately across the board. No trade-off should be allowed between these requirements and the severity of the offence on trial. These requirements ought to apply in trials for theft as they do in trials for murder. The defendant's right against imposition of the risk of error should be equally respected in relation to both categories of crime. If this right is not respected—for example, if a person is convicted of theft despite the existence of an evidenced possibility of his innocence, which the prosecution failed to refute completely—that person's conviction would not satisfy the 'equal best' standard. Failure to satisfy this standard would make the conviction illegitimate, because the convicted person would not be treated with the same concern and respect (the same fact-finding 'best') that other individuals receive from the state. Similarly, if adjudicators in a murder trial immunize the accused from Risk II and, consequently, acquit him or her due to an unevidenced possibility of innocence, then other criminal defendants would rightfully demand from the legal system the same fact-finding 'best'. Reasons justifying a decision only qualify as 'reasons' when the decision-maker is committed to applying them in future cases.[19] Because theoretical doubts are present in every single case, all criminal defendants would be entitled to acquittal.

---

[19] See Frederick Schauer, Giving Reasons (1995) 47 Stan. L. Rev. 633.

The legal system may introduce an exception to this set of requirements. This exception would expose defendants to both Risk I and Risk II in cases involving administrative violations punishable by fines and injunctions alone. In trials for such violations, utilitarian concerns may justify a removal of the Risk I immunity from defendants. These defendants would only be entitled to fact-finding that satisfies the demands of the 'equal', as opposed to 'equal best'. This argument holds that the 'equal best' standard is only appropriate for criminal, but not for administrative, trials. This argument raises important issues in the area of administrative law, far removed from this book's agenda. I therefore leave this argument without discussion.

Another exception differentiates between different categories of fully and partially exonerating arguments that criminal defendants can make. First, the defendant may deny any involvement in the crime. For obvious reasons, in order to obtain conviction, the prosecution has to refute any such denial beyond all reasonable doubt. The general set of proof requirements will apply. Second, the defendant's involvement in a conduct classifying as criminal may only be prima facie criminal, because the defendant may have been *justified* in doing what he or she did. For example, the defendant may have acted in self-defence or under legal authorization. If that happens, the defendant would be no different from an otherwise innocent individual. There is no valid moral distinction between an individual who acted in self-defence when he or she prima facie committed a crime and a person who stayed at home and consequently did not even create a superficial appearance of wrongdoing. An attempt to somehow distinguish between the two can only speak in favour of the person who acted in self-defence. Staying at home is a morally neutral activity—neither blameworthy nor praiseworthy—which is not the case with defending onself against a criminal. Because self-defence does not only protect the prospective victim, but also deters criminals to the benefit of other potential victims, this course of action is praiseworthy rather than neutral.[20] The prosecution, therefore, should be required to disprove beyond all reasonable doubt any justificatory defence that the defendant might raise.[21]

Finally, the defendant's action may only be criminal in the general, as opposed to personalized, liability dimension. The defendant's personalized liability for what generally constitutes a crime may be reduced or altogether removed due to an excuse. An excusatory defence is granted to a defendant, in appropriate circumstances, not as a matter of entitlement—as in the case in

[20] See Paul H. Robinson, Criminal Law Defenses: A Systematic Analysis (1982) 82 Colum. L. Rev. 199, 236 (in most modern codifications, self-defence classifies as a justification).

[21] See Alex Stein, Criminal Defences and the Burden of Proof (1991) 28 *Coexistence* 133, 138–9; Alex Stein, After *HUNT*: The Burden of Proof, Risk of Non-Persuasion and Judicial Pragmatism (1991) 54 M. L. R. 570.

which the defendant's prima facie criminal conduct is justified—but as a matter of leniency and concession to human frailty that a liberal society is prepared to make.[22] This is the case with most criminal law defences which are based upon personal circumstances or characteristics of the perpetrator, such as insanity, infancy, duress, diminished responsibility (including diminished responsibility for infanticide), intoxication, timely withdrawal from a crime, and, possibly, provocation and 'suicide pacts', to the extent that they mitigate liability for intentional homicides.[23] Other examples of excuses include lack of negligence as qualifying strict liability offences, an honest, but still negligent, mistake of fact, and, in rare cases, good motive and mistake of law.[24] Broadly, justifications relate to the general and impersonal characteristics of the act. They remove blameworthiness from actions that otherwise classify as blameworthy and, consequently, criminal. Excuses, in contrast, focus on the personal traits and circumstances of the actor. An excusatory defence removes criminal liability from the actor (partly or entirely) without removing the blameworthiness from the act.[25]

Because excuses are special—actor-related, but act-irrelevant—defences, defendants invoking them do not disassociate themselves from the underlying criminal activity. Nor do they attempt to justify what they did. Such defendants make special personalized requests for leniency. For this reason, their entitlement to the 'equal best' standard in fact-finding is not as obvious as that of other criminal defendants. Why allow their demand for that standard to override social utility? The 'equal best' standard should only apply to equals, while a criminal defendant whose only defence is an excuse—rather than a justification or an outright denial of any involvement in the crime—makes a plea that sets him or her apart. Indeed, a number of considerations support shifting the persuasion burden to criminal defendants with regard to any excusatory defence they may rely upon. Specifically, any such defendant should be required to establish his or her excuse by a preponderance of the evidence.[26]

First, as shown in Chapter 5, this requirement minimizes the incidence of errors in fact-finding and produces the greatest possible number of correct

---

[22] See H. L. A. Hart, *Punishment and Responsibility* (1968), pp. 13–14.

[23] Criminal Defences and the Burden of Proof, above note 21, at 138. In England, provocation and self-defence are common law defences not requiring proof by a preponderance of the evidence. To benefit from any such defence, the defendant only needs to raise a reasonable doubt. See *Woolmington v DPP* [1935] AC 462 (HL). See also note 33 below.

[24] Criminal Defences and the Burden of Proof, above note 21, at 138–9.

[25] See George Fletcher, *Rethinking Criminal Law* (1978), pp. 576–9.

[26] This argument was criticized by Timothy H. Jones, Insanity, Automatism, and the Burden of Proof on the Accused (1995) 111 L.Q.R. 475, 495–7. For my response to this critique, see above at p. 149, note 19.

decisions. This socially beneficial outcome may justifiably be trumped by an individual's right not to be convicted if innocent, but this proviso has a substantive, rather than merely technical, meaning. Innocent means either uninvolved or justified. A person who committed a crime does not become substantively innocent by virtue of an excuse, even when the latter leads to a verdict of not guilty. Any such person is 'not guilty because excused' rather than 'not guilty because innocent'. Therefore, leniency reasons that make such a person eligible to an excuse do not ipso facto provide him or her with a utility-trumping right. Society unwilling to punish such a person may be equally unwilling to punish itself.[27]

Second, verdicts exonerating the perpetrators of criminal, but excusable, acts must avoid sending general normative messages to society at large. Such verdicts must not crystallize into norms upon which individuals can rely and plan their actions. If the benefit of doubt were granted to every criminal defendant invoking an excuse, the excuse would then rapidly transform into a norm, which would dilute deterrence to the detriment of society. Once again, a lenient liberal society need not be also self-destructive. Excuse-recognizing verdicts therefore need to be individualized in order not to develop precedents. There should also be as few as possible false positives among these verdicts.[28]

Relatedly, to avoid transformation of excuses into general conduct-guiding standards, adjudicators need to have excusatory discretion (rather than duty) and exercise it on a case-by-case basis. In that form, excuses would function as decision rules for adjudicators, but not as conduct rules for society at large. To maintain a separation between the two sets of rules,[29] adjudicators need discretion. If any reasonable doubt with respect to an excusatory fact were automatically to work in favour of the defendant, this discretion—and the adjudicators' corresponding ability to individualize their recognitions of excuses—would be diluted. Under the preponderance of the evidence standard, this discretion is more likely to be individualized.[30]

These proposals are not far removed from positive law, but have yet to be adopted.[31] In England and the United States, legislators and judges routinely require criminal defendants to preponderantly establish any 'affirmative defence',[32] including insanity, diminished responsibility, provocation, and self-defence, as well as any 'exception, exemption, proviso, excuse or qualification'

[27] Criminal Defences and the Burden of Proof, above note 21, at 139.   [28] Ibid.

[29] See Meir Dan-Cohen, Decision-Rules and Conduct Rules: On Acoustic Separation in Criminal Law (1984) 97 Harv. L. Rev. 625.

[30] Criminal Defences and the Burden of Proof, above note 21, at 140.

[31] Their underlying ideology influenced the criminal proof doctrine since old times: see Alex Stein, From Blackstone to *Woolmington*: On the Development of a Legal Doctrine (1993) 14 J. Leg. Hist. 14.   [32] McCormick, *On Evidence* Vol. 2 (4th edn., 1992), pp. 481–5.

to a statutory offence.[33] These rules and rulings are predominantly pragmatic, rather than principled, in their underlying motivation.

C. Exclusion

Under the 'equal best' standard, proof beyond all reasonable doubt is not synonymous with a high probability of guilt. This probability also needs to rest on an evidential base strong enough to rely upon. According to the terminology developed in Chapter 3, this probability needs to have sufficient weight. In order to have this, it needs to have evidential support that covers the factual grounds of the accusations and, as *PMI* demands, is open to maximal individualized testing. When any of these conditions is not satisfied, the state fails to provide the defendant the best equal protection from erroneous conviction. Convicting the defendant becomes illegitimate.

This criterion identifies as illegitimate and inadmissible any evidence undermining the 'equal best' standard. Evidence failing to satisfy *PMI* undermines this standard. Evidence incriminating the defendant without being susceptible to maximal individualized testing exposes the defendant to an illegitimate risk of erroneous conviction. Such evidence should be excluded.

Under this framework, an attempt to use character evidence, such as prior convictions, in order to establish a causal connection between the defendant's personality and his or her actions almost invariably fails.[34] Arguments establishing such a connection are applicable to some cases, but not to others,

---

[33] This is the English definition that applies both at common law and under s. 101 of the Magistrates' Courts Act 1980. See Paul Roberts and Adrian A. S. Zuckerman, *Criminal Evidence* (2004), pp. 374–84. In England, a criminal defendant also needs to preponderantly establish insanity, as well as any other defence in relation to which the persuasion burden was explicitly placed upon him by statute. See Roberts and Zuckerman, ibid, at pp. 373–4. The evolving human rights jurisprudence emphasizes the judicial authority under s. 3 of the Human Rights Act 1998 to read down any such provision to the extent needed for its alignment with the presumption of innocence. This has the practical effect of reinterpreting the provision as imposing on the accused an evidential burden, as opposed to the burden of persuasion. In order to be acquitted, the accused would thus only need to raise a reasonable doubt with respect to the relevant defence. See *R v Lambert* [2002] AC 545 (HL) (observing that statutory provisions requiring the accused to prove lack of mens rea ought to be read down in this way); *Sheldrake v DPP* [2005] 1 AC 264 (HL) (holding that a statute placing the persuasion burden on the accused can survive scrutiny only when it constitutes a proportionate and justifiable response to an important social concern; and that a rule that allows a conviction for a serious crime to be based on a conduct not in any way blameworthy will generally be read down). See also Paul Roberts, Drug-Dealing and the Presumption of Innocence: The Human Rights Act (Almost) Bites (2002) 6 Int. J. Evidence & Proof 17 (identifying and critically examining the emerging 'ad-hoc scrutiny' approach to deviations from the proof-beyond-all-reasonable-doubt requirement).

[34] See Federal Rule of Evidence 404(a). As Dworkin wrote, 'it is unjust to put someone in jail on the basis of a judgment about a class, however accurate, because that denies his claim to equal respect as an individual'. Ronald Dworkin, *Taking Rights Seriously* (1978), p. 13.

because sometimes people act in conformity with their characters and sometimes do not.[35] Any such argument therefore hopelessly hangs in the air. Bringing it down to the ground is impossible because there is no way of examining the proposition that the defendant acted in conformity with his or her character in the event on trial. A generalization suggesting that he or she acted in this way is available, but this covering uniformity is one of many. More crucially, it is not susceptible to individualized testing by the defendant. There is no *testable* way of relating this uniformity to the defendant's individual case.

Fingerprint evidence, for example, also rests on a generalization. This generalization holds that two separate fingerprints are virtually never identical; therefore, each fingerprint is practically unique. This generalization is as statistical as evidence about the defendant's character, but the defendant can test and meaningfully oppose its applicability to his or her case. Fingerprints at the scene of the crime integrate with other evidence that tells how the perpetrator committed the crime. Fingerprints on the gun with which the perpetrator killed the victim integrate with the gun and, ultimately, with the wound on the victim's body. Fingerprints on the door of the victim's house integrate with other evidence pointing to the defendant's presence (or nonpresence) in that house. These and other case-specific interactions make fingerprint evidence susceptible to individualized testing. For example, a defendant against whom fingerprint evidence is adduced can testify about his or her alibi. The fingerprint evidence affects the credibility of this testimony by reducing its probability. This testimony, however, stands unfalsified until the prosecution comes up with a case-specific refutation of the defendant's alibi. Case-specific evidence that disproves this alibi joins forces with the fingerprint statistic that links the defendant with the scene of the crime. The defendant will likely be found guilty.

Character evidence forms no such interactions. This deindividualizing feature makes character evidence defective. The generalization underlying character evidence—'bad people are prone to commit crimes'—is exceedingly

---

[35] As explained by A. E. Acorn, Similar Fact Evidence and the Principle of Inductive Reasoning: *Makin* Sense (1991) 11 OJLS 63, 68–70, 'There is a leap of faith involved in accepting the premise that, because things have happened in a certain way, or have been observed to be a certain way in the past, they will continue to be observed in the same way in the present and the future. . . . The assumption of constancy or uniformity . . . cannot be proved true. It is clear . . . that it is upon the basis of the fundamental belief in the individual's power to alter past conduct and to make radical choice about present action that the assumption of constancy or uniformity is judged by the common law to be wrong in relation to human action.' See, however, Mike Redmayne, The Relevance of Bad Character (2002) 61 CLJ 684 (favouring admission of prior crimes as evidence against the accused on the basis of empirical data concerning recidivism); Roger C. Park, Character at the Crossroads (1998) 49 Hast. L.J. 717, 756–79 (expressing scepticism about recidivism data as supporting admission of prior crimes as evidence against the accused).

general. It purports to prove too much and, therefore, proves nothing. Assume from now on that the defendant in my last example has a criminal record that makes him or her 'a person of bad character generally disposed to commit crimes'. This record also evidences the defendant's dishonesty and affects the credibility of his or her testimony by reducing its probability. This testimony, however, stands unfalsified until the prosecution disproves it with case-specific evidence. To the extent that it increases the defendant's probability of being a perjurious witness, his or her criminal record joins forces with that evidence. There is, however, no integration whatsoever between the defendant's general disposition to commit crimes and other case-specific evidence in the case. The defendant's disposition, for example, does not integrate with his or her alibi testimony. Nor does it integrate with the fingerprint evidence that tends to incriminate the defendant. Mental and emotional forces, into which such dispositions generally transform, do not remove the defendant's alibi or make his or her fingerprints on the victim's door more vivid than before. These forces belong to a different level of generality, where they never confront and are never confronted by case-specific proof. Character evidence, therefore, does not integrate with case-specific proof in any testable way. Character evidence can only override or be overridden by case-specific proof, and the law generally prefers the latter over the former.[36] This fundamental preference is a manifestation of *PMI*.

On similar grounds, the law differentiates between character evidence and evidence establishing the defendant's motive or opportunity to commit the crime on trial. The law also differentiates between character evidence and evidence pointing to the defendant's 'intent, preparation, plan, knowledge, identity, absence of mistake or accident', and the like.[37] Any such evidence identifies a concrete event that involves the defendant. More crucially, such evidence always integrates with case-specific proof, a feature that makes it susceptible to individualized testing.[38] Such evidence consequently becomes admissible.[39]

---

[36] But see Federal Rules of Evidence 413, 414, and 415 that generally allow the prosecution to use similar crime evidence in proving allegations of sexual assault and child molestation. These rules run against my approach. For a powerful feminist critique of these rules, see Katherine K. Baker, Once a Rapist? Motivational Evidence and Relevancy in Rape Law (1997) 110 Harv. L. Rev. 563 (arguing that application of Federal Rules of Evidence 413, 414, and 415 might engender rapist stereotyping that would both undermine the integrity of the criminal justice system and deepen the vulnerability of non-standardized victims).   [37] See Federal Rule of Evidence 404(b).

[38] This feature parallels the distinction, famously laid down by Lord Hailsham in *DPP v Boardman* [1975] AC 421 (HL), between the fact-based and, therefore, permissible reasoning from the defendant's past acts and the morality-based and, therefore, impermissible reasoning from the defendant's portrayal as a 'bad person'.

[39] In Acorn's terminology, such evidence should be admissible because it 'suggests a much more specific form of generalization which includes the elements of the accused, the specific crime and an identifying feature of the crime'. See Acorn, above note 35, at 73. To repeat, there is no analytical

A paradigmatic example of such evidence is modus operandi. This concept refers to the peculiar way in which the defendant acted on more than one criminal occasion, so that his or her actions can be described metaphorically (as they often are) as a signature at the scene of the crime. In such cases, what constitutes evidence is the factual similarity between the actions taken by the defendant on different occasions. This case-specific evidence qualitatively differs from the defendant's statistical affiliation to the socially constructed category that features uniformly ill-motivated people. Three English causes celebre, *Makin*,[40] *Smith*,[41] and *Straffen*,[42] illustrate this point.

In *Makin*, children in the defendants' care were discovered buried in the defendants' garden. In *Smith*, three of the defendant's successive wives died by drowning in bath tubs. Each death conferred on the defendant a substantial financial benefit (inheritance or life insurance payment). In *Straffen*, in order to prove that the accused strangled a young girl, left her body unconcealed, and did not sexually assault her, the judge allowed the prosecution to adduce evidence of two other occurrences in which the accused had strangled two young girls, did not assault them sexually and left their naked bodies at the scene of the crime. In each of these cases, the fact-finders had to invoke an assumption of uniformity of conduct and thereby allude to generalizations. These generalizations, however, did not attempt to establish the defendants' actions by their respective personalities and dispositions. Rather, actions taken by each defendant were proven by their factual (and thus morally neutral) comparison to the *traces* that he or she had left on previous occasions.[43] The defendant was able to subject this comparison to a case-specific examination. This crucial factor aligns the defendant's conviction with *PMI*.[44]

difference between the *inferences* that fact-finders draw from this type of evidence and from evidence pointing to the defendant's general character. Any such inference alludes to statistics. What separates the two types of evidence is their susceptibility to case-specific testing by the defendant.

[40] *Makin v Attorney General of New South Wales* [1894] AC 57 (HL).

[41] *R v Smith* (1915) 11 Crim. App. 229.   [42] *R v Straffen* [1952] 2 All ER 657 (CA).

[43] The concept of 'trace evidence' originates from H. Richard Uviller, Evidence of Character to Prove Conduct: Illusion, Illogic, and Injustice in the Courtroom (1982) 130 U. Pa. L. Rev. 845, 847 (distinguishing trace and predictive evidence).

[44] Chris William Sanchirico, Character Evidence and the Object of Trial (2001) 101 Colum. L. Rev. 1227, also distinguishes between trace and general character (or predictive) evidence, but with an altogether different purpose in mind. According to him, the rule against character evidence is instrumental to regulating behaviour outside the courtroom (the 'primary activity'). Because character evidence simply exists out there—and so a criminal defendant cannot undo it—its admission as evidence of guilt would have no impact on people's primary activities. Such evidence, therefore, should be generally inadmissible. In contrast, trace evidence changes with conduct. Depending on how he or she decides to act, an individual may or may not generate such evidence. Trace evidence, therefore, should be generally admissible. In Sanchirico's words, 'keying penalties and rewards to the production of trace evidence is the only way to make penalties and rewards change with conduct. And making penalties and rewards change with conduct is the only way to create incentives.' Ibid,

Character evidence engenders more complex problems when adduced to impeach a witness. For reasons stated, a person's group-based association with 'bad people' does not appear to support the inference that he or she is a perjurious witness. Yet, a legal regime not permitting criminal defendants to impeach prosecution witnesses by their bad characters is problematic. Under this regime, criminal defendants are not able to raise all reasonable doubts that pertain to the accusations. Take a prosecution witness whose bad character is evidenced by serious crimes that he or she had committed in the past. There is a rational basis for considering such a witness *possibly* untrustworthy, which is exactly the claim that the defendant wants to make in order to raise a reasonable doubt about his or her guilt. Silencing this claim is deeply problematic. If the defendant is found guilty, his or her conviction would not align with the 'equal best' standard. Because this legal regime would apply across the board, the defendant would receive a treatment no different from the treatment of other criminal defendants. The defendant's treatment by the criminal justice machinery would satisfy the equality standard. Yet, this treatment would fail to provide the defendant the best protection from erroneous conviction that is reasonably available.

These observations support an asymmetric doctrine under which prosecution witnesses are exposed to character-based impeachment, while defence witnesses, and defendants in particular, are immune from character-based attacks. Alternatively, all witnesses, except criminal defendants, testify subject to character-based impeachment. This special immunity is given to a testifying defendant until he or she decides to forfeit the immunity by turning character into an issue (either by adducing evidence that portrays him or her as a good person or by launching a character-based attack on another defendant or upon one of the prosecution's witnesses).[45]

These observations, however, do not necessarily hold true. Consider prior-conviction evidence as representing bad character and imagine a pool that accommodates both guilty and innocent defendants with prior convictions.

at 1235. For further explanation see Sanchirico, ibid, at 1259–63. This argument tracks Sanchirico's more general claim that primary activities should be regulated by directly conditioning legal sanctions upon production of particular types of evidence. See Chris Sanchirico, Games, Information and Evidence Production: With Application to English Legal History (2000) 2 Am. L. & Econ. Rev. 342; Chris Sanchirico, Relying on the Information of Interested—and Potentially Dishonest—Parties (2001) 3 Am. L. & Econ. Rev. 320. As explained in Chapter 1, such direct-incentive mechanisms (similarly to other uses of evidence for purposes unrelated to fact-finding) do not belong to evidence law. Rather, they belong to the relevant branches of substantive law, such as torts, contracts, or criminal law. For this reason, I only acknowledge the importance of Sanchirico's theory and do not discuss its virtues and vices.

[45] An insightful discussion of this issue can be found in Richard Friedman, Character Impeachment Evidence: Psycho-Bayesian [!?] Analysis and a Proposed Overhaul (1991) 38 UCLA L. Rev. 637.

In this pool, innocents obviously want to separate from the criminals to secure their acquittal. This desire, however, is not honoured by the criminals, many of whom give false testimony that attempts to imitate the innocent. Crucially to this and similar settings, criminal record has a limited evidential capacity. The defendant's prior convictions can only function as a residual factor that affects the credibility of his or her testimony. When there are case-specific reasons for disbelieving this testimony, its probability of being true must be further reduced by the defendant's criminal record. When such reasons do not exist, this probability is unaffected by the defendant's prior convictions. Moreover, the defendant's readiness to risk impeachment by prior convictions signals credibility. By testifying about his or her innocence, the defendant sends fact-finders the following message: 'My testimony is true. There are no case-specific reasons for disbelieving it, and you won't find any. Therefore, I am prepared to accept the scenario in which such a reason combines with my criminal record and ruins my credibility.' Because this signalling is potentially costly, it provides a strong indication of the defendant's credibility as a witness until the prosecution comes up with specific reasons that discredit his or her testimony.[46]

For obvious reasons, criminals leave behind more incriminating traces than innocents do. On the average, reasons discrediting the defendant's self-exonerating testimony would predominantly appear in cases featuring guilty defendants. For criminals, the anticipated *ex ante* probability of being discredited by such reasons is much higher than for innocent defendants. Because the combination of such reasons and the defendant's criminal record is potentially devastating to the defendant's credibility as a witness, many guilty criminals would separate from the pool by not testifying in their defence.[47] This separation increases the probability of self-exonerating accounts tendered by the innocents. Note that costly signalling activating this self-selection mechanism is only possible in a legal regime that allows the prosecution to impeach defendants by their prior convictions. In a regime that immunizes criminal defendants from such impeachment, more innocents would find themselves unable to credibly signal their innocence to fact-finders.[48] More criminals would also estimate that reasons for disbelieving their innocent-imitating stories would not be strong enough by themselves to remove every reasonable doubt about their guilt. More criminals would pool with innocent defendants

---

[46] For more details, see above at pp. 164–6. For general discussion of costly signalling as indicating the signaller's credibility, see Ian Molho, *The Economics of Information: Lying and Cheating in Markets and Organizations* (1997), pp. 63–80, 97–101.

[47] Provided, of course, that the fact-finders do not draw any adverse inferences from the defendant's silence. See above, at pp. 158–64, and below, at pp. 200–4.

[48] Fact-finders would categorize their self-exonerating accounts as 'cheap talk'. See Molho, above note 46, at pp. 97–8.

and thereby increase the incidence of erroneous convictions. Under the immunity regime, therefore, a greater number of unfortunate innocents, who cannot corroborate their self-exonerating testimony by objective evidence, would be found guilty.[49]

Under the hearsay rule, as applied in the United States[50] and, until recently, in England,[51] an out-of-court statement (or other intentionally assertive conduct) cannot be admitted as evidence of the truth of its contents. Such statements are generally excluded for lack of cross-examination. Because the person who made such a statement (the declarant) cannot be cross-examined, the statement's credibility cannot be properly tested.[52] To the extent that the hearsay rule prescribes that untestable assertions do not make evidence of guilt, the rule squarely aligns with *PMI*. Under *PMI*, fact-finders do not use an out-of-court statement incriminating the defendant as evidence to the truth of its contents if there is no way of examining its individual (non-generalized) probative credentials. The defendant ought to be able to subject any such statement to maximal individualized testing, usually by cross-examining the declarant. To the extent that it operates in favour of the accused, this rule is fully justified under *PMI* as a criminal defendant's immunity from the risk of error.[53]

Hearsay statements, however, may also be offered into evidence in various mitigated versions. These versions generally align with the existing exceptions to the hearsay rule. Under *PMI*, when the prosecution uses a hearsay statement as evidence against the accused, only two routes of admissibility are available. A hearsay statement is admitted into evidence implicating the accused if the accused can properly cross-examine the declarant (at the trial itself or in a prior proceeding).[54] Alternatively, such a statement is admitted as evidence against the accused if he or she obtains a functionally equivalent substitute to cross-examination of the declarant. The foundation-fact evidence

---

[49] As Chapter 5 explains, this rationalization also supports the underlying rule on the grounds of cost-efficiency.　　[50] See, e.g., Federal Rules of Evidence 801–807.

[51] See Zuckerman, above note 4, at 179–83.

[52] See Federal Rule of Evidence 801. For a broader definition, see *Wright v Doe d. Tatham* (1837) 7 A & E 313; *R v Kearley* [1992] 2 All ER 345 (HL).

[53] As observed by Roger C. Park, A Subject Matter Approach to Hearsay Reform (1987) 86 Mich. L. Rev. 51, 102, 'The hearsay rule contributes to ... individualization of the determination of guilt ... The goal of individualization is achieved when the trier's decision is not a vote of confidence for or against the government, but a unique determination about the guilt of the particular defendant.'

[54] See *Crawford v Washington*, 541 U.S. 36 (2004) (interpreting the Sixth Amendment Confrontation Clause as setting a similar pre-condition for admitting testimonial hearsay statements against the defendant); *California v Green*, 399 U.S. 149 (1970) (holding that the Confrontation Clause permits the prosecution to introduce against a defendant a prior statement made by a witness inconsistently with his or her testimony, since the defendant can cross-examine the witness and exploit the contradiction between the testimony and the statement).

highlighting the declarant's testimonial parameters—perception, memory, narration, and sincerity, as related to the event on trial[55]—forms the basis for this substitute. Because witnesses testify about these parameters from their personal knowledge (otherwise, the testimony classifies as a double-hearsay and becomes inadmissible) and can be adequately cross-examined by the defendant,[56] such evidence always satisfies the demands of *PMI*.

These admissibility routes lead to a fundamental distinction between *event-statements* and *proceeding-statements*. The first non-testimonial category of hearsay statements includes any statement that the declarant makes, explicitly or implicitly, during any event outside of legal proceedings. The second testimonial category accommodates statements made in legal proceedings, such as trial, grand jury hearing, or police interrogation.[57] An event-statement can evidence its truth if a witness testifies from his or her first-hand knowledge about both the statement's contents and the circumstances in which it was made. The statement becomes admissible when these circumstances contain basic information about the declarant's perception, memory, narration, and sincerity. Two or more separate witnesses may also provide this information. By using this information, fact-finders are able to consider how the statement and the event interacted with each other. Because witnesses bringing this information along can also be cross-examined about this interaction, the court's admission of the statement does not violate *PMI* even when the declarant is not available for cross-examination. The defendant's ability to cross-examine first-hand witnesses about the unmediated interaction between the declarant and the event provides an adequate substitute for the declarant's cross-examination.

A proceeding-statement interacts with the declarant's questioning in the proceeding, rather than with the event itself. For any such statement to be admissible as hearsay evidence against a criminal defendant, the defendant needs to be given an opportunity to cross-examine the declarant. The defendant must be afforded this opportunity at the proceeding itself. Alternatively, the declarant should be available for cross-examination at the defendant's trial. There is no other way of satisfying *PMI* in relation to a proceeding-statement. Such a statement never comes along with the information about the *unmediated* interaction between the declarant and the event on trial.

---

[55] See Eleanor Swift, A Foundation Fact Approach to Hearsay (1987) 75 Calif. L. Rev. 1339.

[56] Ibid, at 1356–61.

[57] This discussion draws on a persuasive constitutional argument developed by Richard D. Friedman, Confrontation: The Search for Basic Principles (1998) 86 Geo. L.J. 1011 (criminal defendants should have a robust right to cross-examine each and every provider of potentially incriminating information that would extend not only to in-court testimony and sworn statements, but also to any other statement accompanied by testimonial intent).

Moreover, as the United States Supreme Court recently emphasized, admission of a proceeding-statement as evidence incriminating the defendant disrupts the balance of power between the defendant and the state. This disruption results from the state's unilateral control over the provision of the statement and the consequent ability to manipulate it.[58]

To see how the distinction between event-statements and proceeding-statements works, consider the res gestae exceptions to the hearsay rule.[59] Under these exceptions, a hearsay statement becomes admissible when it explains or describes the relevant event (or sensation) contemporaneously with its perception (or experience) by the declarant. The traditional view justifies these exceptions on the theory that emphasizes the declarant's spontaneity. Arguably, this factor rules out deliberate or conscious (as opposed to subconscious) misrepresentation.[60] This justification, however, is flawed because it fails to account for errors that an out-of-court witness makes in good faith. To repeat: the hearsay dangers include not only insincerity, but also misleading, although sincere, narration of the event, as well as memory failures and perception errors.[61] If so, what can possibly justify the admissibility of res gestae statements as evidence against criminal defendants?

PMI provides the required justification. Statements falling under the res gestae exceptions to the hearsay rule are event-statements that satisfy *PMI*. To make such a statement admissible, its proponent needs to produce a witness testifying from his or her personal knowledge about the interaction between the statement and the event on trial. Any such witness has to testify about the statement's background conditions. Specifically, he or she has to provide the information indicating that the declarant made the statement spontaneously. The statement's opponent must be able to cross-examine the witness about this and other information pertaining to the statement's credibility. This

---

[58] See *Crawford v Washington*, 541 U.S. 36 (2004). The *Crawford* doctrine has been further developed by American courts. See *Snowden v State*, 846 A.2d 36 (2004) (statements by child victims to a social worker, whose purpose was to develop the victims' testimony for trial were held 'testimonial' and consequently inadmissible under the Sixth Amendment confrontation clause); *People v Sisavath*, 118 Cal.App.4th 1396, 1402 (2004) (a crime victim's statement to an investigating police officer classified as 'testimonial' and inadmissible under the Sixth Amendment); *In re T.T.*, 815 N.E.2d 789 (2004) (statements made by a child victim at her home to an investigator from the Department of Children and Family Services that subsequently accused a juvenile of assaulting the child, were held 'testimonial', which barred their introduction at delinquency proceedings against the juvenile). Cf. *People v Moscat*, 777 N.Y.S.2d 875, 880 (2004) (an emergency 911 call of a domestic violence victim classified as a 'non-testimonial' cry for help, which rendered it admissible).   [59] See Federal Rules of Evidence 803(1)–(3).

[60] See, e.g., Edmund Morgan, *Basic Problems of Evidence* (1962), pp. 340–1.

[61] Edmund Morgan, Hearsay Dangers and the Application of the Hearsay Concept (1948) 62 Harv. L. Rev. 177.

cross-examination aligns with *PMI*. In a typical case, it is almost as effective as direct cross-examination of the declarant.[62]

This justification equally extends to virtually all documentary evidence made admissible by the existing exceptions to the hearsay rule. Business and public records[63] are event-statements that exemplify the alignment of these exceptions with *PMI* most vividly.[64] These records are admissible as evidence documenting the events taking place in the regular run of a business or public service. Also, the documentation itself needs to qualify as a regularly conducted activity and a person with knowledge must compile it more or less contemporaneously with the event.[65] Any such record both interacts with the documented event and constitutes an event itself (data recording). A witness with personal knowledge must provide evidence about the above. This witness, an organizational or business insider, has to identify the record as belonging to the organization's regular documentation. The witness can be effectively cross-examined about the record, about its functional significance within the organization, and about the interaction between the record and the documented event. This cross-examination satisfies the demands of *PMI*.

A final judgment adjudicating the accused guilty of a crime classifies as a proceeding-statement. For this reason, the admissibility of such verdicts as evidencing their truth is generally limited to civil, as opposed to criminal, trials. In criminal trials, apart from being admissible, when relevant, for impeachment purposes, a guilty verdict is only admitted as evidence against the defendant when it convicts that defendant.[66] This provision makes sense under *PMI*'s admissibility standard—the declarant's cross-examination by the defendant—that applies to all proceeding-statements. Because the defendant had an opportunity to cross-examine the witnesses at his or her prior trial, the verdict's admissibility does not violate *PMI*.

All of these rules are subject to the general principle of forfeiture. The defendant may forfeit his or her rights under these rules by not objecting to the hearsay evidence that the prosecution adduces.[67] Alternatively, the

---

[62] The defendant should also be permitted to cross-examine the witness about matters beyond the scope of the witness's examination-in-chief. This special permission is often required under the American law: see Federal Rule of Evidence 611(b). The court would normally grant it if the additional questioning of the testifying witness pertains to the credibility of the declarant's statement (see Federal Rule of Evidence 806).

[63] See Federal Rules of Evidence 803(6)–(12), (14), and (17).

[64] Other exceptions to the hearsay rule that turn documents into admissible evidence (Federal Rules of Evidence 803(13), (15), and (16)) are generally not required in criminal trials. Admission of hearsay documents covered by these exceptions as evidence against the accused would not always align with *PMI* and the 'equal best' standard.   [65] See Federal Rule of Evidence 803(6).

[66] See Federal Rule of Evidence 803(22).

[67] For an insightful discussion of this and related issues, see John W. Strong, Consensual Modifications of the Rules of Evidence: The Limits of Party Autonomy in an Adversary System (2001) 80 Neb. L. Rev. 159.

defendant's wrongdoing may effect forfeiture. The declarant's statement would be admitted as evidence against the defendant if the defendant wrongfully prevented the declarant from testifying as a witness at his or her trial.[68] To make the statement admissible under the forfeiture provision, this preliminary fact (the defendant's wrongdoing against the declarant) has to be proven by a preponderance of the evidence.[69]

Under *PMI* and the 'equal best' standard, the hearsay rule operates in a one-sided fashion by imposing its constraints on the prosecution, but not on the accused. *PMI* opposes the exclusion of hearsay evidence offered by the accused when it is the best evidence that he or she can produce. Suppression of the defendant's best available evidence violates both *PMI* and the 'equal best' standard. This asymmetrical hearsay doctrine is yet to become part of the law. In England, prior to the virtual abolition of the hearsay rule by the Criminal Justice Act 2003,[70] the rule's admissibility barrier was erected for both the prosecution and the accused.[71] In the United States, the defendant's constitutional entitlements to 'due process of law' and to 'compulsory process for obtaining witnesses in his favour'[72] lend support to a different approach. Arguably, these entitlements do not allow the court to suppress exonerating evidence the defendant offers, especially when he or she cannot reasonably be expected to produce better evidence. The United States Supreme Court's decision in *Chambers v Mississippi*[73] supports this argument. In that case, the defendant brought witnesses to testify that another person confessed to the crime for which the defendant stood trial. The trial judge refused to admit this third-party admission evidence. The Supreme Court held that this suppression of defence evidence was unconstitutional. Formally, the defendant offered this evidence for impeachment purposes. But *Chambers* may be construed more broadly, as opening the gates for defence hearsay on constitutional grounds.[74]

By focusing on the allocation of the risk of error, the 'equal best' standard and *PMI* also resolve the problem of hearsay definition. The traditional definitions of hearsay are either statement-based or declarant-oriented. The statement-based definition is too narrow, while the declarant-oriented definition

---

[68] See Federal Rule of Evidence 804(b)(6).

[69] See *United States v Gray*, 405 F. 3d 227, 241 (4th Cir. 2005).

[70] See Criminal Justice Act 2003, s. 114(1)(d); Roberts and Zuckerman, above note 33, at p. 632 (describing Criminal Justice Act 2003, s. 114(1)(d) as 'an overriding "safety-valve" inclusionary discretion to admit hearsay evidence in the interests of justice').

[71] See *R v Blastland* [1985] 2 All ER 1095 (HL) (an out-of-court admission of guilt by a third party held inadmissible).   [72] See United States Constitution, Amendments V, VI, and XIV.

[73] *Chambers v Mississippi*, 410 U.S. 284 (1973).

[74] See McCormick, *On Evidence* Vol. 2 (4th edn, 1992), p. 129; Edward J. Imwinkelried, The Constitutionalization of Hearsay: The Extent to Which the Fifth and Sixth Amendments Permit or Require the Liberalization of the Hearsay Rules (1992) 76 Minn. L. Rev. 521, 542–8.

is too broad. The statement-based definition defines hearsay as an out-of-court statement offered to establish the truth of its explicit assertive content. The declarant-oriented definition focuses on whether the declarant's testimonial mechanism—observation, memory, narration, and sincerity—is instrumental to establish the facts that his or her statement or conduct evidences. This definition focuses on whether the declarant's testimonial properties attach to the inferences that fact-finders draw from his or her assertion, verbal or non-verbal, explicit or implied. More generally, this definition examines whether the declarant functioned as a witness in relation to any fact that his or her statement or non-verbal conduct aims to prove. An affirmative answer to this question classifies the declarant's statement or conduct as hearsay. The statement-oriented definition is too narrow because it does not extend to any communication or assertive conduct apart from express assertions. The declarant-oriented definition is too broad because it extends to and potentially renders inadmissible all forms of out-of-court communications (such as those made by victims who communicate fear by escaping from their assailants without making a single utterance).[75] The Federal Rules of Evidence and their state equivalents strike a balance. Under these rules, the definition of hearsay only covers *intentional* communications that aim to prove the truth of the matter that the declarant intended to communicate. The form of the declarant's communication—verbal, non-verbal, express or implicit—is immaterial. What matters is the declarant's intention to communicate the facts that his or her assertion or conduct aims to prove.[76]

Although workable, this pragmatic definition replaces one problem with another. Ascertainment of the declarant's communicative intent is a substitute problem.[77] For example, if several unidentified people call the defendant and express their desire to buy drugs, should their requests be admitted as evidencing drug-dealing on the part of the defendant? In England, the House of Lords classified such evidence as inadmissible hearsay under the declarant-oriented definition.[78] In the United States, a federal court categorized similar utterances as non-hearsay in a prosecution for illegal bookmaking activities.[79]

[75] For analysis of the two definitions of hearsay see Stephen Guest, Hearsay Revisited (1988) Curr. Leg. Probs. 33.   [76] See Federal Rule of Evidence 801(a).

[77] See Eustace Seligman, An Exception to the Hearsay Rule (1912) 26 Harv. L. Rev. 146; Edmund Morgan, Hearsay Dangers and the Application of the Hearsay Concept (1948) 62 Harv. L. Rev. 177; Ted Finman, Implied Assertions as Hearsay: Some Criticisms of the Uniform Rules of Evidence (1962) 14 Stan. L. Rev. 682; Laurence Tribe, Triangulating Hearsay (1974) 87 Harv. L. Rev. 957; Michael Graham, Stickperson Hearsay: A Simplified Approach to Understanding the Rule Against Hearsay (1982) U. Ill. L. Rev. 887; Olin Guy Wellborn III, The Definition of Hearsay in the Federal Rules of Evidence (1982) 61 Tex. L. Rev. 49; Guest, above note 75; C. R. Williams, Issues at the Penumbra of Hearsay (1987) 11 Adelaide L. Rev. 113; Craig R. Callen, Hearsay and Informal Reasoning (1994) 47 Vand. L. Rev. 43.   [78] *R v Kearley* [1992] 2 All ER 345 (HL).

[79] *United States v Zenni*, 492 F. Supp. 464 (E.D. Ky. 1980).

The prosecution attempted to prove its case with utterances made by unidentified callers who called the premises of one of the defendants and gave instructions for the placing of bets on various sporting events. In deciding the case, the court emphasized the difference between the English and the American definitions of hearsay. The declarants' statements in my example would not, therefore, classify as hearsay under the Federal Rules of Evidence because the declarants only intended to communicate their desire to buy drugs, rather than the defendant's drug-dealer status. The following question, however, was left open: Did the declarants' intention to communicate their desire to buy drugs also include their intention to communicate to their designated listener on the other side of the line—the defendant—that he, as a drug-dealer, is expected to sell them the drugs that they asked for? Does the intent accompanying the declarant's statement only refer to his or her mental or conscious experience, or does it also include the statement's anticipated effect on the listener? The American approach to hearsay has yet to provide unequivocal answers to these questions.

The 'equal best' standard and *PMI* altogether avoid this and all other definitional problems. Under this regime, criminal defendants are entitled to the maximal individualized testing of any evidence, hearsay and non-hearsay. A defendant is also entitled to adduce in his or her defence any evidence—hearsay and non-hearsay—if that evidence is the best evidence available. Any proceeding-statement—hearsay and non-hearsay—should only be admitted as evidence proving the defendant's guilt when he or she can cross-examine the declarant at the trial or, alternatively, was able adequately to cross-examine the declarant at a prior proceeding. For event-statements, a functionally equivalent substitute to cross-examination is also acceptable. To provide a substitute that makes the declarant's statement admissible, the prosecution has to produce evidence highlighting the declarant's testimonial traits. The traits that the prosecution's evidence has to cover are those that are instrumental to the allegations that the prosecution levels against the defendant. Adequacy of the substitute for the declarant's cross-examination depends on the declarant's testimonial traits classifying as instrumental for making out the prosecution's case. The more traits are instrumental, the more demanding the adequacy requirement. In certain cases, the declarant's cross-examination by the defendant is the only means for satisfying *PMI*. The declarant's event-statement would then be excluded[80] when he or she does not testify at the defendant's

<hr/>

[80] *R v Kearley* [1992] 2 All ER 345 (HL) exemplifies one such statement. In that case, the House of Lords categorized as inadmissible hearsay a testimony about numerous orders for drugs that different callers—who did not testify in court—placed in the defendant's apartment. The prosecution offered this testimony to prove that the defendant was a drug dealer. The Law Lords' decision was absolutely correct. The defendant, Alan Kearley, might have attracted the drug-seekers who called

trial. This standard makes a straightforward point: failure to satisfy *PMI* by any evidence—hearsay and non-hearsay alike—violates the 'equal best' requirement. Any such evidence exposes the defendant to an illegitimate risk of error. To avoid this illegitimate outcome, courts must exclude such evidence systematically.

Admissibility of expert evidence is another important area for applying *PMI* and the 'equal best' standard. To be admissible in federal and several state courts across the United States, expert evidence needs to satisfy the criteria set by Federal Rule of Evidence 702 and the Supreme Court's *Daubert Trilogy—Daubert*,[81] *Joiner*,[82] and *Kumho Tire*.[83] These criteria replaced *Frye v United States*,[84] an influential precedent that conditioned the admissibility of scientific evidence upon 'standing and scientific recognition' of its underlying theory or methodology.[85] Much criticized and not always followed by judges,[86] the *Frye* rigid standard was abolished when it was approximately seventy years old. The new admissibility criteria set by the *Daubert Trilogy* require that scientific evidence be susceptible to empirical testing and falsifiability.[87] Under these criteria, standing and scientific recognition is a factor that only affects the probative value, rather than admissibility, of scientific findings. In England, courts take an extremely liberal approach to the admissibility of expert evidence. These courts disassociate themselves not only from *Frye's* threshold for admissibility, but also from *Daubert's* criteria for admitting expert evidence.[88] This approach has supporters in

---

to his apartment not because he was actually selling drugs. Drug-selling might have been attributed to him by an underworld rumour. Cross-examination of the drug-seekers was therefore necessary for testing the applicability of the evidence to the case at hand. Without such cross-examination, there is no way of individualizing the generalization 'Drug-seekers do not recurrently request drugs from a person who does not sell them.' See Alex Stein, The Form and Substance of the Hearsay Doctrine (1995) 16 Miss. C. L. Rev. 55, 57. In rare instances, a proceeding-statement can classify as an event-statement. This would be the case when a person's testimony in Trial I is adduced as evidence in Trial II to prove that the person was not mute on that occasion. In this example, the person's non-muteness would classify as an event. Words spoken in Trial I would consequently constitute evidence in and by themselves. Their affiliation to a formal legal proceeding would be coincidental.

[81] *Daubert v Merrell Dow Pharmaceuticals, Inc.*, 509 U.S. 579 (1993).
[82] *General Electric Co. v Joiner*, 522 U.S.136 (1997).
[83] *Kumho Tire Co. v Carmichael*, 526 U.S. 137 (1999).
[84] *Frye v United States*, 293 F. 1013 (D.C. Cir. 1923).
[85] For analysis of *Frye* and its influence see Paul C. Giannelli, The Admissibility of Novel Scientific Evidence. Frye v. United States: A Half-Century Later (1980) 80 Colum. L. Rev. 1197.
[86] Giannelli, ibid.   [87] Chapter 7 offers a more comprehensive discussion of these criteria.
[88] See *R v Robb* 93 Cr. App. R. 161, 164–6 (1991); *R v Dallagher* [2002] Crim. L. Rev. 821 (CA). See, in particular, *R v Luttrell* [2004] 2 Cr. App. R. 31 ('the appellants argued that [expert] evidence should not be admitted unless it passes a further test, that the evidence can be seen to be reliable because the methods used are sufficiently explained to be tested in cross-examination and

the United States, who criticize *Frye* and *Daubert* for silencing potentially good experts.[89]

Much of this controversy could be eliminated by properly defining its stakes. As must already be apparent, adjudicative fact-finding ultimately allocates the risk of error. Allocation of this risk—the risk of erroneous conviction or, alternatively, the risk of erroneous acquittal in a criminal case—can only be guided by moral and political criteria that the law decides to adopt. Science has no say on these criteria. More specifically, it has no say on how many criminals should be allowed to go free in order not to convict a single innocent person. Nor does it have any say on how many innocents can be convicted in order not to acquit too many criminals. Allocation of the risk of error in criminal (and also in civil[90]) trials cannot derive from judicial forecasting of the success or failure of the ongoing scientific evolution or revolution. Scientific findings failing to satisfy the *Frye* standard should therefore always be excluded when offered against the defendant in a criminal case. Such findings should be excluded for two mutually related reasons. First, there is no *individualized* way of relating such a finding—as opposed to its opposite—to the case at hand. Because such findings are not susceptible to full individualized testing, their admission as evidence against the defendant would violate *PMI*. Second, the risk of error that would attach to any such finding is evidenced, rather than abstract. Using such findings as evidence against criminal defendants would therefore directly violate the 'equal best' standard.[91]

As with hearsay evidence, here, too, the admissibility barrier should only apply to evidence the prosecution presents. Criminal defendants should be allowed to put forward any expert evidence, which the fact-finders will evaluate in terms of its case-specific probative value. Any other approach is at odds with the 'equal best' standard.

---

so to be verifiable or falsifiable. Where, as here, the Crown is seeking to adduce the evidence in a criminal trial, this could properly be considered by the court when deciding whether to refuse to allow the evidence, under s.78 of the Police and Criminal Evidence Act 1984 or otherwise, in order to ensure a fair trial. We cannot accept that this is a requirement of admissibility. In established fields of science, the court may take the view that expert evidence would fall beyond the recognised limits of the field or that methods are too unconventional to be regarded as subject to the scientific discipline. But a skill or expertise can be recognised and respected, and thus satisfy the conditions for admissible expert evidence, although the discipline is not susceptible to this sort of scientific discipline').

[89] See, e.g., McCormick, *On Evidence* Vol. 1 (4th edn., 1992), pp. 871–6.

[90] But the admissibility standards set by the *Daubert Trilogy* are still right for civil cases. See Chapter 7 below.

[91] For another sceptical view regarding *Daubert*'s applicability to inculpatory evidence see Margaret A. Berger, Procedural Paradigms for Applying the *Daubert* Test (1994) 78 Minn. L. Rev. 1345, 1352–63. Berger, however, does not favour reinstatement of *Frye*.

D. Pre-emption

The 'equal best' standard and *PMI* install hierarchy between different fact-generating arguments. Some of such arguments are more compatible than others with maximally individualized fact-finding. *PMI* accords preference to these arguments and their supporting evidence. At its broadest, this *pre-emptive strategy* transforms into the best evidence principle. The most straightforward manifestation of this principle is the best evidence rule that generally prefers original documents over their duplicates.[92] A duplicate, however, is still admitted into evidence when the original document is unavailable, provided that the duplicate's proponent did not remove or destroy the original in bad faith.[93] This proviso rests on forfeiture grounds: evidence spoliators are not allowed to profit from their own wrongs. Apart from that, on purely epistemic grounds, intentional destruction or removal of evidence give rise to factual findings against the spoliator. Exclusion of the spoliator's evidence and the appropriate adverse inferences are, consequently, in order. Also, for reasons that are self-explanatory, a duplicate is admissible when no genuine controversy over the contents of the original document exists.[94]

On similar grounds, witness testimony generally is preferable to an out-of-court statement of the same witness.[95] The hearsay rule renders many such statements inadmissible. However, some such statements classify as non-hearsay and some fall under the exceptions to the hearsay rule. Note that under the theory advocated in this chapter, such an exception would be justified when the statement tends to exonerate the accused or when it supports the prosecution's case, but the accused receives a functionally adequate substitute to his or her right to cross-examine the declarant. Under the best evidence principle, an out-of-court statement that the hearsay doctrine holds admissible would still be excluded if the declarant is available as a witness and his or her testimony can help the fact-finders to determine the relevant facts. In any such case, the declarant must testify at trial in order to be cross-examined by the statement's opponent. The proponent of the evidence—the accused or the prosecution—must make every diligent effort to secure the declarant's testimony at the trial.[96]

---

[92] See Federal Rule of Evidence 1004.   [93] Federal Rule of Evidence 1004(1).
[94] Federal Rule of Evidence 1003.
[95] See Dale Nance, The Best Evidence Principle (1998) 73 Iowa L. Rev. 227; cf. Michael L. Seigel, Rationalizing Hearsay: A Proposal for a Best Evidence Hearsay Rule (1992) 72 B. U. L. Rev. 893 (a more radical proposal to replace the hearsay doctrine by a broad best evidence principle).
[96] For obvious reasons, the diligence standard should be far more demanding in the prosecution's case. See, e.g., *Barber v Page*, 390 U.S. 719 (1968).

As indicated above, when a prosecution's witness does not testify at the defendant's trial as a result of violence, intimidation, or other improper means originating from the defendant, the prosecution should be allowed to adduce against the defendant any statement that this witness had previously made. This rule represents admissibility by forfeiture. The defendant's objection to the statement's admission, ordinarily sustainable under both the hearsay rule and the Confrontation Clause, is silenced.[97] The pre-emption mechanism, however, does more than certifying the statement's admissibility. The defendant's attempt at silencing the witness also constitutes evidence supporting the defendant's conviction.[98] Fact-generating arguments pointing to the defendant's likely guilt pre-empt the defendant's fact-generating arguments. Criminal defendants should only be allowed to derive benefits from *PMI* if they do not maliciously frustrate the administration of this principle.

Under *PMI*, both the defendant and the prosecution assume the fact-finding consequences originating from the absence of evidence. Under the 'equal best' standard, these consequences generally benefit the defendant, given that any reasonable doubt normally leads to his or her acquittal.[99] Thus, if a potentially important piece of evidence is unavailable and its contents are unknown, the defendant's conviction on whatever evidence is available would never satisfy the demands of *PMI* and the 'equal best' standard. For that reason alone, the defendant is entitled to an acquittal.

Consider another example. A prosecution witness testifies in-chief and incriminates the defendant. Subsequently, the witness refuses to answer the defendant's questions at cross-examination. For reasons already apparent, such testimony should not be used as evidence against the defendant. Whatever the prosecution's witness said during his or her examination in-chief must be offset—that is, pre-empted—by *PMI*. Because the witness did not expose his or her testimony to the defendant's individualized examination, the fact-finders should not be allowed to use it.[100]

These entitlements of criminal defendants should have only one exception. This exception derives from the forfeiture principle. If the missing evidence became unavailable due to the defendant's intentional conduct, such as witness intimidation, then, instead of acquitting the defendant, the fact-finders

---

[97] See above, notes 68–9 and accompanying text.

[98] The defendant's illegal attempt at silencing the witness needs to be proven beyond all reasonable doubt, as demanded by the English law in a not so distant past. See *R v Acton Justices, ex parte McMullen and others; R v Tower Bridge Magistrates' Court, ex parte Lawlor* (1991) 92 Cr. App. Rep. 98, 104. In the United States, forfeiture needs to be established by a mere preponderance of the evidence. See above, note 69.

[99] See *In re Winship*, 397 U.S. 358 (1970); *Mullaney v Wilbur*, 421 U.S. 684 (1975); *Woolmington v DPP* [1935] AC 462 (HL).   [100] See, e.g., *Douglas v Alabama*, 380 U.S. 415 (1965).

should treat his or her evidence-tampering conduct as evidence of guilt. This adverse inference should always pre-empt the defendant's reliance on a reasonable doubt.

Apart from that, any destruction or suppression of *material exculpatory evidence* by the police or prosecution—even when it is faultless—should lead to the defendant's automatic acquittal. Such an action would violate *PMI*, so that the defendant's conviction could never align with the 'equal best' standard. The defendant's entitlement to every favourable inference would pre-empt any scenario in which the accusations levelled against him or her are true. In the United States, this entitlement of criminal defendants is recognized on the constitutional due process grounds.[101] Furthermore, if any evidence *potentially useful* to the defendant is destroyed or suppressed in bad faith by the police or the prosecution, the defendant should then be acquitted without showing that the evidence actually had exculpatory potential.[102] In any such case, adverse inferences that fact-finders should draw against the enforcers of criminal law should pre-empt any factual scenario in which the defendant is guilty as charged.

Seemingly, the best evidence theory also supports the idea of drawing adverse inferences from the defendant's silence at trial or interrogation and from his or her withholding of other evidence. The English law (after its amendment about a decade ago) generally allows fact-finders to draw such inferences.[103] Careful analysis of this issue, however, would support a more refined approach.

I first examine the possibility of drawing adverse inferences from the defendant's silence at trial or during police interrogation. In the United States, the Fifth Amendment to the constitution bans this possibility. Fact-finders are not allowed to draw adverse inferences from the silence of a criminal suspect[104] or defendant.[105] Yet, in practically every criminal case, the best evidence one can think of is the defendant's information about the truth of the accusations. The defendant's silence obstructs *PMI*. The constitution, nonetheless, does not allow adverse inferences as a response to this obstruction.

The rationale for that special privilege points out the special way in which the privilege allocates the risk of error. The Fifth Amendment privilege

---

[101] *Illinois v Fisher*, 124 S. Ct. 1200 (2004).   [102] *Arizona v Youngblood*, 488 U.S. 51 (1988).

[103] See Criminal Justice and Public Order Act 1994, ss. 34–37 (allowing fact-finders to draw adverse inferences from the defendant's silence at trial or during police interrogation).

[104] See *Doyle v Ohio*, 426 U.S. 610 (1976) (adverse inferences not allowed to be drawn from the fact that the defendant stood mute or took the Fifth Amendment privilege during his or her custodial interrogation). See also *Miranda v Arizona*, 384 U.S. 436 (1966) (laying down the first principles of the right-to-silence doctrine under the Fifth Amendment, including the ban on adverse inferences from silence).

[105] See *Griffin v California*, 380 U.S. 609 (1965) (adverse inferences not allowed to be drawn from the defendant's failure to testify in his or her defence).

affords special protection to innocent suspects and defendants, who often find themselves unable to corroborate their self-exonerating accounts by objective evidence. Absent the privilege, guilty criminals would pool with innocents by making false exculpatory statements (to the extent they believe that their lies are unlikely to be exposed). Aware of these criminals' incentives, fact-finders would rationally discount the probative value of *all* uncorroborated exculpatory statements, at the expense of the unfortunate innocents who cannot corroborate their true exculpatory stories. The Fifth Amendment privilege minimizes this pooling effect and correspondingly reduces the rate of wrongful convictions. Under this regime, rational innocents still tell the truth, whereas rational criminals—fearful of being implicated by their lies—separate from the pool by exercising the right to silence.[106] For many rational criminals, silence is the best course of action because it does not worsen their position. Lies, in contrast, are not cost-free. There is always a prospect that a defendant's lie will be uncovered and provide evidence of his or her guilt. False self-exonerating testimony therefore increases the defendant's probability of conviction and punishment. The remaining option of a guilty criminal is confessing to the crime. Absent a favourable plea bargain, this option is altogether unattractive because it makes the defendant's conviction and punishment virtually certain. For this reason, as already mentioned, the right to silence should remain on the criminal defendants' menu: for guilty criminals, confessions are generally less attractive than self-exonerating lies. Removal of the right to silence would lead to more lies, not to more confessions, and to a more intensive pooling of the guilty and the innocent.[107] This intensified pooling would obviously violate the 'equal best' standard. The increased difficulty in separating between innocent and guilty defendants would also obstruct *PMI*.

This rationale for the self-incrimination privilege also distinguishes between two fundamentally different categories of evidence that suspects and defendants can be expected to produce. The first category includes evidence by which a guilty defendant can externalize the risk of erroneous conviction upon innocent defendants and suspects. This category includes, first and foremost, self-exonerating testimony by which criminals can imitate and pool with innocents. Self-exonerating stories that come from guilty suspects and defendants reduce the probability of uncorroborated self-exonerating

---

[106] See Daniel J. Seidmann and Alex Stein, The Right to Silence Helps the Innocent: A Game-Theoretic Analysis of the Fifth Amendment Privilege (2000) 114 Harv. L. Rev. 430.

[107] Ibid. Empirical evidence to this effect had emerged in England following the Criminal Justice and Public Order Act 1994, ss. 34–37, that allowed fact-finders to draw adverse inferences from the defendant's failure to testify at trial and from the suspect's silence (including failure to explain away incriminating evidence) at interrogation. For summary and analysis of this evidence see Seidmann and Stein, ibid, at 501–2.

accounts that innocent defendants and suspects provide. Another example of externality-laden evidence is handwriting samples. Because a criminal might be able to replicate an innocent's handwriting, such evidence must be distinguished from past samples of the suspect's handwriting, over which he or she exercises no control.[108] The Fifth Amendment's protection against a compelled assembly and production of documents extends to externality-laden evidence alone. Here, too, the pooling-through-lying alternative is available to a guilty suspect, who can choose between the documents that he or she will produce. Under the 'act of production' doctrine that became part of the Fifth Amendment privilege, documents that already exist do not qualify as 'testimonial' and, consequently, privileged. Yet, the compelled production of documents is 'testimonial' and privileged when entailing the person's admission 'that the papers existed' and 'were in his possession or control and were authentic'.[109]

The Supreme Court classified the 'act of production' as testimonial evidence that requires 'use immunity'.[110] Its landmark decision in *United States v Hubbell*[111] illustrates this immunity. Hubbell was subpoenaed by the Government to produce a large number of unspecified documents relating to a criminal investigation (the 'Whitewater affair') before a grand jury. Hubbell invoked the privilege against self-incrimination in response to the subpoena. Unable to describe the subpoenaed documents with reasonable particularity, the Government nevertheless obtained an order[112] forcing Hubbell to produce them subject to 'use immunity'. The Government used these documents in an investigation that led to tax and fraud charges against Hubbell. Hubbell contended that the charges—based on the immunized testimonial aspects of his production of the documents—should be dismissed. The Government agreed with this contention and accepted that its indictment would have to be dismissed were the privilege indeed violated. However, the Government disputed the alleged violation of the privilege, on the grounds that Hubbell's act of production was insufficiently testimonial. In support, the Government enlisted *Fisher v United States*,[113] a decision in which the Supreme Court held that an act of producing ordinary business records was insufficiently

---

[108] This argument runs against *Gilbert v California*, 388 U.S. 263, 266 (1967), a case in which the Supreme Court decided that handwriting samples are not protected by the privilege against self-incrimination on the theory that they are not 'testimonial'.

[109] *United States v Doe*, 465 U.S. 605, 613 (1984).

[110] *United States v Doe*, 465 U.S. 605 (1984). The Court also decided that this immunity can be granted only on a statutory request and cannot be imposed judicially. Under the 'use immunity', 18 U.S.C. § 6002, although the Government would be entitled to use the subpoenaed documents, it may not use in any criminal proceeding against the person (except a prosecution for perjury, for giving a false statement, or for failing to comply with the document production order) any information directly or indirectly deriving from the act of their production.

[111] *United States v Hubbell*, 120 S.Ct. 2037 (2000).   [112] Issued under 18 U.S.C. § 6003(a).

[113] *Fisher v United States*, 425 U.S. 391, 411 (1976).

testimonial to sustain a claim of privilege. The existence and possession of such records by any business person were a 'foregone conclusion'.[114]

The *Hubbell* Justices rejected this comparison:

The assembly of literally hundreds of pages of material in response to a request for 'any and all documents reflecting, referring, or relating to any direct or indirect sources of money or other things of value received by or provided to' an individual or members of his family during a 3-year period... is the functional equivalent of the preparation of an answer to either a detailed written interrogatory or a series of oral questions at a discovery deposition... It was only through respondent's *truthful reply* to the subpoena that the Government received the incriminating documents... The assembly of those documents was like telling an inquisitor the combination to a wall safe, not like being forced to surrender the key to a strongbox.... While in *Fisher* the Government already knew that the documents were in the attorneys' possession and could independently confirm their existence and authenticity through the accountants who created them, here the Government has not shown that it had any prior knowledge of either the existence or the whereabouts of the 13,120 pages of documents ultimately produced by the respondent.[115]

The Supreme Court therefore held that the indictment against Hubbell should be dismissed.

The distinction that the Supreme Court drew between *Hubbell* and *Fisher* substantiates the anti-pooling rationale. By what criterion should courts distinguish between a trivially testimonial act of producing documents, as in *Fisher*, and a non-trivially testimonial document-production that took place in *Hubbell*? The *Hubbell* Justices have supplied the required criterion. In *Fisher*, the Government did not rely on the *truthtelling* of the person forced to produce the documents; in *Hubbell*, it did rely upon it.[116] In other words, the person's ability to choose between truth and falsehood distinguishes the two cases and delineates the boundaries between the protected and the unprotected acts of document-production. This criterion is identical to the anti-pooling rationale for the privilege. Under this rationale, a suspect's ability to tell uncontradicted lies can impose externalities, as guilty suspects might harm innocents by pooling with them through fabrications, lies, or omissions. Thus, guilty suspects situated similarly to Hubbell are in a position to fabricate the assembly of subpoenaed documents, which would inevitably reduce the credibility of document assembly by their innocent counterparts. In *Fisher*, this ability was held not to exist. Consequently, there was no reason to immunize the act of production.[117]

---

[114] See Seidman and Stein, above note 106, at 477–81.

[115] *United States v Hubbell*, 120 S.Ct. 2037, 2046–8 (2000).   [116] Ibid, at 2047.

[117] In *Fisher*, the subpoenaed documents could not practically be forged prior to their production, and their producer was not required to confirm their authenticity.

Under the anti-pooling rationale, evidence already existing at the time of its compelled production classifies as unprivileged. The self-incrimination privilege does not extend to a suspect's refusal to provide incriminating evidence by participating in a line-up, by giving away bodily samples, or otherwise. The privilege also affords no protection to suspects in breathalyser and similar cases. If a guilty suspect agrees to undergo a breathalyser examination, then he or she would be separated from innocents due to the breathalyser evidence (which cannot lie). If guilty suspects have no fabrication alternative that harms innocents, they should not be exempted from potential self-incrimination. In any such case, fact-finders should normally draw adverse inferences against the defendant if he or she had refused to provide evidence situated under his or her control.[118]

Under *PMI* and the 'equal best' standard, naked statistical evidence *alone* never warrants the defendant's conviction, regardless of how probable the accusations are. Inferences of guilt based upon naked statistical evidence alone are pre-empted. The general reasons for this pre-emption are set forth in Chapter 3. These reasons are basically similar to those that justify the exclusion of character evidence.[119] There is nothing intrinsically wrong with naked statistical evidence. As Chapter 3 explains, any factual inference is nakedly statistical. Fact-finders can rely on such evidence whenever they can bring it down to the ground. This fact-finders only can do when a naked statistical proof integrates with individualized evidence that relates the naked statistics to the specifics of the case at hand. This individualizing component is necessary not because there is something special about it from the epistemological point of view. This component is essential to fact-finding in criminal trials because it enables the accused to subject the evidence incriminating him or her to individualized testing. Without this testing, exposing the accused to the risk of erroneous conviction is unfair for reasons stated at the beginning of this chapter (Chapter 5 demonstrates that this form of risk-allocation might also be economically inefficient, even when the naked statistical proof points to a high probability of the defendant's guilt). The next paragraphs exemplify these observations. Examples provided in these paragraphs add to my discussion of *State v Skipper*[120] in Chapter 3.

---

[118] The qualifier 'normally' was introduced for special cases in which circumstances unrelated to guilt (say, health or a religious belief) explain the defendant's refusal to provide the requested evidence (say, a blood sample).   [119] See above, notes 34–7 and accompanying text.

[120] *State v Skipper*, 637 A.2d 1101 (1994). This case and its discussion in Chapter 3 demonstrate that DNA evidence alone is never sufficient for convicting the accused. Even when the match probability is in the billions, it needs to refute the accused's self-exonerating account or other evidence pointing to his innocence. The DNA match probability turns into individualized evidence when it practically eliminates all suspects other than the accused. The accused can then be convicted on the DNA evidence alone. The same holds true in relation to fingerprint evidence.

R v Abadom, an English case decided in 1982, involved accusations of robbery.[121] A credible expert testified that it was highly probable (96 per cent) that glass fragments that the police had recovered from the defendant's shoes came from the window which was broken during the robbery. The expert relied on the Home Office's statistics deriving from the refractive index of glass fragments. Such evidence alone is not sufficient for convicting the accused. In the absence of case-specific evidence implicating the accused, the factual grounds of the accusations are not sufficiently covered.[122] The 96 per cent match does not carry much weight. It refers to glass samples in general, not to the glass found on the accused's shoes. Because this datum fails to satisfy *PMI*, it is pre-empted by the scenario in which the glass fragments belong to a window unrelated to the robbery victims. If the prosecution does not produce evidence singling out the accused as a likely perpetrator of the crime, this scenario should be given the benefit of the doubt. The police probably did not pick the accused at random, but this proposition is not evidence.

United States v Veysey,[123] a recent American case, features a series of egregious crimes of which the defendant was found guilty. These crimes included four instances of arson: allegedly, at four different points in time, the defendant set fire to four residential houses—each of which he had previously insured—in order to recover money from the insurers. To prove these accusations, the prosecution produced an actuary whose testimony conservatively estimated that the probability of four residential fires occurring by chance during the relevant period was only one in 1.773 trillion. In his appeal against conviction, the defendant complained that 'the actuary usurped the jury's function by testifying in effect that [the defendant] was guilty of the crimes with which he was charged *way* beyond a reasonable doubt, as the probability of his innocence was not 1 or 2 or 5 per cent or whatever might be thought the implicit probability of innocence sufficient to prevent a finding of guilt beyond a reasonable doubt, but, if the actuary was believed, a mere .0000000000564 per cent'.[124] The Court of Appeal (Judge Richard Posner) found this complaint unfounded. Judge Posner reiterated his observation, 'All evidence is probabilistic—statistical evidence merely explicitly so',[125] originally made in a civil case involving allegations of sex discrimination in employment.[126] He explained that because adjudicative fact-finding is

---

[121] *R v Abadom* [1983] 1 All ER 364.

[122] The reported decision of the Court of Appeal provides no information as to whether such evidence actually existed.

[123] *United States v Veysey*, 334 F.3d 600 (7th Cir. 2003), cert. den. 540 U.S. 1129 (2004).

[124] Ibid, at 604.   [125] Ibid, at 605.

[126] *Riordan v Kempiners*, 831 F.2d 690, 698 (7th Cir.1987).

intrinsically uncertain, it is bound to rest upon probability. All evidence that fact-finders consider is probabilistic in character: 'Statistical evidence is merely probabilistic evidence coded in numbers rather than words.'[127]

This observation is inaccurate. From a purely epistemological perspective, statistical evidence is no different from other evidence. The two categories of evidence differ only in the language that describes their probative significance. The probative significance of statistical evidence is coded in cardinal numbers, ranging somewhere between 0 (factual impossibility) and 1 (factual certainty). The probative significance of non-statistical evidence is stated in words, which obviously involves a greater degree of imprecision. There is, however, a meaningful distinction between naked statistical and particularized (or individualized) *proof*. As explained in Chapter 3, the statistical proof system is aleatory. It calculates chances instead of focusing upon evidential substantiation for individual events. From a purely epistemological perspective, each system is good for pursuing its chosen objectives. There is no epistemological reason that accords preference to the Pascalian calculus of chances over the Baconian measurement of case-specific evidential support. The two systems, however, also allocate the risk of error in distinctly different ways. The choice between these systems is moral and political, rather than epistemological. In this domain of political morality, the 'equal best' standard favours an unbending application of *PMI* in order to make criminal convictions legitimate. For reasons articulated in the next paragraph, the 'equal best' standard and *PMI* pre-empt nakedly statistical proof of guilt.

Naked statistical evidence affiliates to the predictive, as opposed to the trace-based, mode of fact-finding.[128] The predictive mode of fact-finding is invariably generalized. Fact-finders endorsing this mode of reasoning assume that regularities observed in the past will reproduce themselves in future cases with roughly the same frequency as in the past. The trace-based mode—under which 'proving that a nail was struck by a hammer is to examine the head of the nail and there discover the trace of a hammer blow'[129]—is case-specific and individualized in character (because each trace is unique). Trace evidence, therefore, can always be tested for its connection to the individual defendant,

---

[127] *United States v Veysey*, 334 F.3d 600, 606 (7th Cir. 2003).

[128] As stated in notes 43–4 above, the distinction between 'predictive' and 'trace' evidence was originally formulated by H. Richard Uviller, Evidence of Character to Prove Conduct: Illusion, Illogic, and Injustice in the Courtroom (1982) 130 U. Pa. L. Rev. 845, 847. Uviller, however, argued that this distinction is operationally insignificant because both types of evidence have probative value.

[129] Uviller, ibid.

which is not the case with predictive evidence. The applicability of predictive evidence to a discrete event is an untestable issue. The statistical inference, to which predictive evidence gives rise, is simply imposed (or superimposed) on the case by the general statistical theory. If, as in *Veysey*, a person's four houses were destroyed by fire within a relatively short period of time, then—as in virtually all such cases—the fire must have been set intentionally in order to fraudulently collect money from the insurers. The person in my example becomes guilty of arson and insurance fraud without being able to resist the incriminating implications of the evidence by testing its applicability to his individual case. Under the purely statistical mode of fact-finding, this defendant would not avail himself by responding to the four accusations of arson and insurance fraud with four separate alibis (one for each accusation). This response would not necessarily be farfetched. For example, the defendant may have an unknown enemy determined to burn his property. The fact-finders would nonetheless use the same statistical evidence as a reason for disbelieving each of the defendant's alibis, which might produce double-counting grossly unfair to the defendant.[130] Because the defendant is deprived of an opportunity to disassociate his individual case from the statistically dominant category, his conviction violates both *PMI* and the 'equal best' standard.[131] Under *PMI* and the 'equal best' standard, the defendant is only convicted if each of his or her alibis (or any other exculpatory explanation for the fires) are disproved beyond all reasonable doubt by case-specific evidence. In any such case, as in *Skipper*,[132] the prosecution satisfies both the probability and the weight aspects of the criminal proof standard. The probability standard is satisfied by the high probability of guilt generated by the prosecution's statistical (or predictive) evidence. The weight standard is satisfied by the case-specific evidence that covers the factual ground of the accusations (by refuting the defendant's alibis or other innocent explanations for the fires). This combined body of case-specific and statistical evidence gives rise to fact-generating arguments that unfold themselves to full individualized examination by the defendant. The defendant's ability to examine these arguments—or, more precisely, their applicability to his or her individual case—satisfies the demands of *PMI*. Finally, the combination of these factors unequivocally establishes that the state did its 'equal best' to protect the defendant against erroneous conviction.

---

[130] Cf. Vaughn C. Ball, The Moment of Truth: Probability Theory and Standards of Proof (1961) 14 Vand. L. Rev. 807, 817–18 (making a substantially similar point).

[131] Cf. *United States v Shonubi*, 103 F.3d 1085 (2nd Cir.1997) (requiring case-specific evidence for proving sentencing facts and disapproving the use of naked statistics).

[132] See *State v Skipper*, 637 A.2d 1101 (1994), and its analysis in Chapter 3 of this book.

E. Corroboration

Apart from pursuing its exclusionary and pre-emptive strategies, *PMI* insists on the individualized removal of doubts and suspicions that experience-based generalizations cast upon particular categories of evidence. First and foremost, these categories include a suspect's confession at interrogation,[133] accomplice testimony,[134] and pretrial identification.[135] Under this regime, fact-finders are only allowed to base their findings upon such suspicious evidence if one crucial condition is satisfied. A credible piece of case-specific evidence has to corroborate the generally suspicious evidence in a way that removes the suspicion-throwing generalization from the case at hand. This fact-finding strategy identifies itself as *corroborative*.

Together with other specific requirements that derive from *PMI*—and in conjunction with the criminal standard of proof—this strategy protects criminal defendants from erroneous convictions. The resulting immunity from the risk of error aligns with the 'equal best' standard.

F. Discretion

The 'equal best' standard and *PMI* also structure all discretionary decisions that affect fact-finding in criminal trials. Any such decision allocates the risk of error. The accused is entitled to demand reasons for a decision to place the risk of erroneous conviction upon him or her. These reasons may differ from

---

[133] See, e.g., *Opper v United States*, 348 U.S. 84, 89 (1954) (confession made by the accused needs corroborating evidence to serve as basis for conviction); *State v Polly*, 657 N.W.2d 462, 466 (Iowa 2003) ('the general rule is that a confession standing alone will not warrant a criminal conviction unless other proof shows the defendant committed the crime'); McKinney's C.P.L. (New York) § 60.50 ('A person may not be convicted of any offense solely upon evidence of a confession or admission made by him without additional proof that the offense charged has been committed').

[134] See, e.g., Minnesota Statutes Ann. § 634.04 ('A conviction cannot be had upon the testimony of an accomplice, unless it is corroborated by such other evidence as tends to convict the defendant of the commission of the offense, and the corroboration is not sufficient if it merely shows the commission of the offense or the circumstances thereof'); West's Ann. Cal. Penal Code § 1111 (same); Vernon's Ann. Texas C.C.P. Art. 38.14 (same); McKinney's C.P.L. (New York) § 60.22(1) ('A defendant may not be convicted of any offense upon the testimony of an accomplice unsupported by corroborative evidence tending to connect the defendant with the commission of such offense').

[135] *In the Matter of the Welfare of M.E.M., Jr.*, 674 N.W.2d 208, 215 (2004) ('Absent corroboration, eyewitness identification based on "fleeting or limited observation" should not be the basis for conviction'); *People v Cuevas*, 906 P.2d 1290 (CA 1995) (substituting corroboration requirement for out-of-court identifications by the 'substantial evidence' standard); *R v Turnbull* (1976) 63 Cr. App. R. 132, 138–9 (corroboration or at least some supporting evidence is required in cases involving a poor quality identification).

one legal system to another. Any legal system, however, must provide these reasons. These reasons must also be justifiable. Otherwise, the legal system would act arbitrarily against individuals accused of crimes. More specifically, failure to align with the 'equal best' standard and *PMI* makes any decision— discretionary and non-discretionary—morally and politically questionable. This chapter developed a system of risk-allocation that rests upon individual rights. Under this system—as opposed to its utilitarian alternative, set forth in Chapter 5—any decision that fails to comply with *PMI* and the 'equal best' standard is unjustifiable.

This point is of special importance to the English law of criminal evidence that shifted from rules to discretion in three important aspects. First, under the Criminal Justice Act 2003, admission of all hearsay evidence—including evidence implicating the accused—is a matter of discretion that trial judges are called upon to exercise under the guidelines set by the Act.[136] The same Act had also liberalized the admission of bad character evidence against the accused. Such evidence is now admissible when the trial judge estimates that its probative value outweighs its prejudicial potential.[137] Almost a decade before this legislation, the Criminal Justice and Public Order Act 1994[138] did away with all traditional corroboration requirements except for perjury.[139] This development was predated by section 34 of the Criminal Justice Act 1988 that repealed the mandatory requirement for a corroboration warning with respect to sworn evidence given by a child of tender years. This reform did not abolish the discretionary corroboration warning doctrine, set in *R v Beck*.[140] Trial judges still retain their general discretion to warn the jury, in relation to any suspect evidence, that convicting the accused on that evidence, when uncorroborated, involves the risk of erroneous conviction. The judge may instruct the jury to exercise special caution in relation to a piece of evidence that is both suspicious and uncorroborated.[141] Are these discretionary powers as broad as they appear to be?

---

[136] See Criminal Justice Act 2003, ss. 114(1)(d) and 114(2).

[137] See Criminal Justice Act 2003, ss. 101(1)(c) and (d); 102, 103.

[138] See Criminal Justice and Public Order Act 1994, ss. 32 and 33.

[139] See Perjury Act 1911, s. 13 and its discussion above at pp. 20–5. Another corroboration require-ment that has not been abolished is s. 89(2) of the Road Traffic Regulation Act 1984. Under this requirement, uncorroborated testimony of a single witness (as opposed to electro-mechanical speed detectors) is not sufficient for establishing a vehicle's speed. See Roberts and Zuckerman, above note 33, at p. 144.   [140] *R v Beck* [1982] 1 All ER 807. See also *R v Spencer* [1987] AC 128.

[141] For a current statement of the law see *R v Makanjuola* [1995] 3 All ER 730 (stating, by way of illustration, that 'Whether, as a matter of discretion, a judge should give any warning and if so its strength and terms must depend on the content and manner of the witness's evidence, the circum-stances of the case and the issues raised . . . Where . . . the witness has been shown to be unreliable, he or she may consider it necessary to urge caution. In a more extreme case, if the witness is shown to have lied, to have made previous false complaints, or to bear the defendant some grudge, a stronger

Not necessarily so. Under the hearsay provisions of the Criminal Justice Act 2003, in deciding whether it is 'in the interests of justice' for a hearsay statement to be admitted into evidence,[142] the court considers—apart from the statement's probative significance[143] and whether it constitutes the best evidence available[144]—every factor that affects its reliability.[145] Specifically, the court considers the 'difficulty involved in challenging the statement'[146] and the extent to which 'that difficulty would be likely to prejudice the party facing it'.[147] These specific provisions evidently refer to the allocation of the risk of error by the court.

A hearsay statement also becomes admissible when the declarant is unavailable as a witness and the court considers that the statement should be admitted into evidence 'in the interests of justice, having regard', specifically, 'to any risk that its admission or exclusion will result in unfairness to any party to the proceedings (and in particular to how difficult it will be to challenge the statement if the relevant person does not give oral evidence)'.[148]

These and several other (less important) discretionary powers to admit hearsay evidence[149] need to be exercised in a way that makes the resulting allocation of the risk of error justified. Courts have to differentiate between exculpatory and inculpatory hearsay evidence. Evidence falling into the exculpatory category is usually tendered by the accused. Courts should admit such evidence whenever it is shown to be the best evidence available to the accused. Evidence falling into the inculpatory category is normally adduced by the prosecution. Such evidence splits into two sub-categories: proceeding-statements and event-statements, as explained above. Courts should not admit an inculpatory proceeding-statement into evidence unless the accused is or was afforded a meaningful opportunity to cross-examine the declarant.

---

warning may be thought appropriate and the judge may suggest it would be wise to look for some supporting material before acting on the impugned witness's evidence'). See also *Regina v R* [2004] EWCA Crim. 1964 (CA) (absence of special features such as those listed in *Makanjuola* identifies the case as not requiring a special warning). Similarly, under *R v Turnbull* (1976) 63 Cr. App. R. 132, 138–9, corroboration or some supporting evidence is required for suspicious identification evidence adduced against the accused. For full analysis of the discretionary corroboration doctrine see Roberts and Zuckerman, above note 33, at pp. 484–7; Diane Birch, Corroboration: Good-bye To All That [1995] Crim. L. Rev. 524; Peter Mirfield, Corroboration After the 1994 Act [1995] Crim. L. Rev. 448.

[142] Criminal Justice Act 2003, s. 114(1)(d).

[143] That needs to be considered under Criminal Justice Act 2003, s. 114(2)(a)–(c).

[144] Under Criminal Justice Act 2003, s. 114(2)(g), the court needs to consider 'whether oral evidence of the matter stated can be given and, if not, why it cannot'.

[145] Criminal Justice Act 2003, s. 114(2)(d)–(f).

[146] Criminal Justice Act 2003, s. 114(2)(h).   [147] Criminal Justice Act 2003, s. 114(2)(i).

[148] Criminal Justice Act 2003, s. 116.

[149] For a comprehensive discussion of these powers, see Roberts and Zuckerman, above note 33, at pp. 623–42.

Courts should only admit an inculpatory event-statement when there is a functionally adequate substitute for the declarant's cross-examination by the accused. Otherwise, the statement's admission violates *PMI* and the 'equal best' standard.

Under section 101(c) and (d) of the Criminal Justice Act 2003, evidence of the defendant's bad character is admissible when it constitutes 'important explanatory evidence' or when it is 'relevant to an important matter in issue between the defendant and the prosecution'. Under sections 102 and 103, respectively, the trial judge decides whether the contested piece of bad character evidence qualifies as 'important explanatory evidence' and can contribute to a resolution of material issues between the defendant and the prosecution.[150] As two authoritative evidence scholars explain, the court essentially has to balance the probative value of the evidence against its prejudicial potential. If the probative value of the bad character evidence outweighs its prejudicial potential, then the court should admit it. Otherwise, the evidence should be excluded.[151] This statutory arrangement codified *DPP v P*,[152] a House of Lords' decision that substituted the discretionary balancing of probative value versus prejudice for the 'categories approach' to character evidence, previously promulgated by *Makin*[153] and relaxed in *Boardman*.[154] This discretionary power allows judges to allocate the risk of error.[155]

The ways in which judges exercise this power also need to align with *PMI* and the 'equal best' standard. As explained, evidence of the defendant's bad character in general should only be admitted in order to discredit him or her as a witness (because this rule actually helps innocent defendants with prior convictions to exonerate themselves). Otherwise, such evidence should be excluded as long as it remains in the general-character, as opposed to

---

[150] Here, the court has an even greater discretion, modelled on s. 78 of the Police and Criminal Evidence Act 1984, which allows it not to admit the bad character evidence if its admission 'would have such an adverse effect on the fairness of the proceedings that the court ought not to admit it'. See Criminal Justice Act 2003, s. 101(3).

[151] See Roberts and Zuckerman, above note 33, at pp. 511–38. This discretion is identical to that bestowed upon trial judges across the United States under Federal Rule of Evidence 403 and its state equivalents.   [152] *DPP v P* [1991] 2 AC 447 (HL).

[153] *Makin v Attorney-General for New South Wales* [1894] AC 57 (PC).

[154] *DPP v Boardman* [1975] AC 421 (HL).

[155] Other instances in which evidence of the defendant's bad character becomes admissible involve defendants who turn character into an issue one way or another. See Criminal Justice Act 2003, ss. 101(1)(a) (character evidence made admissible by the parties' stipulation); 101(1)(b) (character evidence adduced by the defendant himself or herself or elicited by his or her cross-examination of a witness); 101(1)(f) and 105 (character evidence adduced by the prosecution to rebut a misleading or false impression that the defendant previously made to the court or the jury); 101(1)(g) and 106 (character evidence adduced by the prosecution to counter the defendant's attack on another person's character). In each of those instances, admission of character evidence against the accused would generally be legitimate.

case-specific, category. Admission of general bad-character evidence against the accused would violate *PMI* and the 'equal best' standard.

The same applies to discretionary corroboration warnings that trial judges may administer in relation to any evidence that general experience identifies as suspicious. Under *PMI* and the 'equal best' standard, the judge has to instruct the jury about this experience. Specifically, he or she has to tell the jury that in order to remove the generalization that throws suspicion on such evidence in general, the prosecution needs to produce case-specific proof that supports the credibility of its particular piece of evidence. Abolition of formal corroboration requirements did not eradicate the reliability problems that attach to generally suspicious evidence such as accomplice testimony, suspect identification, and confessions. To the extent that the legal system is willing to protect defendants from the risk of erroneous conviction, it is bound to develop evidentiary substitutes to corroboration requirements. These substitutes would not be tagged 'corroboration', nor would they exhibit the same degree of legal formality. Their gist, however, would not much differ from what traditionally passed for corroboration.

The exclusionary, pre-emptive, and corroborative mechanisms that *PMI* and the 'equal best' standard set in motion may either be mandatory or discretionary. Because discretionary is not synonymous with arbitrary or tyrannical, any discretion that may exist in fact-finding matters should be exercised within a framework of justifying reasons. Any chosen framework would regulate allocation of the risk of error. As such, it would generate broad standards and principles (and sometimes even hard-and-fast rules) that would structure the fact-finders' discretion in that area. This book has identified two sets of such standards, principles and rules. As Chapter 5 explains in relation to both civil and criminal evidence, one of these sets derives from the cost-efficiency ideal. The other set of reasons, articulated in the present chapter, rests upon *PMI* and the foundational 'equal best' standard. These sets of standards, principles, and rules formulate the only defensible reasons for allocating the risk of error under the Anglo-American systems of litigation.

The present-day shift towards broad discretion in fact-finding matters runs against such ideas. This shift is meant to install the regime of free proof, in which politically unaccountable adjudicators allocate the risk of error upon whom they deem fit for reasons they consider attractive. Eagerness to remove all unbending immunities from the risk of erroneous conviction (aka 'technical rules') that criminal defendants (a.k.a. 'criminals') still have motivates this shift. Manifested most saliently by the radical reshaping of the English system of criminal evidence, this shift may and probably will be understood as establishing prevalence of the pragmatic over the principled. This prevalence cannot be established by argument, but it can—and probably will—be established by populist fiat. In criminal adjudication and in many other legal domains, 'pragmatic' alludes to an 'all-things-considered' judgement (that is, to an intellectual process too complex to be articulated, let alone defended). This allusion, however, is tendered on a 'believe us' basis. To me, the notion of 'pragmatic' appears to be a euphemism obfuscating the power to convict the accused whenever it feels right. This notion convolutes the adjudicators' unwillingness or inability to articulate reasons for resolving fact-finding issues. Understandably, pragmatic adjudicators are willing to remain uncommitted to reasons that they decide to employ in deciding individual cases.[156] Criminal defendants, however, are equally unwilling to be committed to prison for reasons that their judges are unwilling (or unable) to articulate. All adjudicative decisions, discretionary and non-discretionary alike, should be accompanied by justifying reasons. Unarticulated allusions to pragmatic 'all-things-considered' decisions (or simply to intuition) will not do. For these reasons (fully articulated in Chapter 4), fact-finding decisions that are not open to scrutiny are both morally and politically objectionable.

---

[156] As explained by Frederick Schauer, above note 19, giving reasons involves the reasoner's *commitment* to act upon those reasons in similar cases. That is why giving reasons may not always be appropriate, and so unreasoned decisions should not be considered irrational.

7

Allocation of the Risk of Error in Civil Litigation

A. Fairness vs. Efficiency

Allocation of the risk of error accompanying fact-finding decisions in civil litigation can be fair, efficient, both, or neither. 'Neither' means arbitrary and, therefore, is not a defensible option. Adjudicators need to allocate the risk of error fairly and efficiently. When it becomes necessary, they also need to choose between fairness and efficiency. The efficiency criterion allocates the risk of error in a way that minimizes the magnitude of the harm that materialization of the risk produces. This harm needs to be minimized cost-efficiently. Time and effort that adjudicators and litigants expend on enhancing accuracy in fact-finding are costly. Their marginal cost needs to be offset by the ensuing marginal reduction of the harm. Fact-finding is consequently conducted in a way that minimizes the sum of two costs: the cost of the harm that fact-finding errors produce and the cost of procedures that reduce the incidence of those errors and the resulting harm.[1]

The fairness perspective rejects the utilitarian postulation that treats the two costs as commensurable. From this non-economic perspective, trial expenditures and the cost of injustice qualitatively differ from each other. There is no common denominator. An arithmetic comparison does not make an adequate trade-off between these costs. A more nuanced social picture provides a viable alternative to an exclusively economic one. In that picture, victims of the substantive injustice that fact-finding errors produce do not appear as faceless economic units. They appear as individuals that demand reasons for decisions that place upon them the risk of error and the consequent injustice. Under this framework, any rule or decision that places the risk of error on Yvonne in her lawsuit against Xavier *entitles* Yvonne to demand an individualized justification from the entire legal system. Yvonne is morally entitled to ask 'Why I?', and the legal system needs to provide a morally

---

[1] These issues are discussed in Chapter 5.

compelling answer. A proposition that this particular allocation of the risk is cost-efficient and, as such, increases social welfare does not provide such an answer. To this proposition Yvonne will respond that she is unwilling to contribute to social welfare above and beyond her taxes, and these she already paid. Some utilitarians (and Marxist-Leninists) would insist that Yvonne pays more to make society better off. From their perspective, this end justifies the means. Against this Yvonne (and I) have very little to say because the proffered justification imposes an anti-argumentative closure on the debate. Because this justification constitutes postulation, rather than proof, Yvonne (and I) can only probe its viability, not validity, through the axes of 'voice', 'exit', and 'loyalty'.[2] If the legal system taxes Yvonne inequitably (in the present case, by shifting to her the risk of error in fact-finding), Yvonne may attempt to change the system democratically by using her 'voice' as a citizen. After losing her voice vs. vice battle,[3] Yvonne may do well by taking the 'exit'. She may move herself, her family, and her business to a different jurisdiction that promises a more favourable treatment to her and similarly situated individuals. The 'exit' threat may induce the legal system—that is, the community that wants to keep Yvonne in—to treat Yvonne more favourably in the first place, which would make the present scenario hypothetical.[4] But if this does not happen, and if Yvonne's treatment by the legal system is too harsh for her to bear, she would take the 'exit'.

Yvonne's 'Why I?' question must be taken seriously. Its direct utilitarian dismissal is unwarranted. An adequate response begins with demonstrating that the cost-efficiency of the legal system also benefits Yvonne. However imperfect, this system facilitates people's consumption of justice by making it accessible, affordable, and expedient. As a citizen, Yvonne systematically benefits from these virtues of the justice machinery. She should, therefore, take the sweet with the bitter by occasionally suffering from some of the machinery's vices. On a broader scale, because resources are limited, savings on the legal system add to the funds that support other socially beneficial amenities, such as health, education, and highways. As a citizen, Yvonne systematically benefits from these amenities, too. If so, the occasional injustice that she and other citizens would suffer can be perceived as yet another justifiable tax.[5]

---

[2] See Albert O. Hirschman, *Exit, Voice, and Loyalty: Responses to Decline in Firms, Organizations, and States* (1970) (developing the 'voice', 'exit', and 'loyalty' mechanism).

[3] The actual practice of Marxism-Leninism proved (by clear and convincing evidence!) that collective vices silence individual voices. About unqualified utilitarianism I have no empirical evidence, but anticipate the same result.

[4] The practice of Marxism-Leninism tackled this threat by prohibiting the exit, an option not available to a non-totalitarian regime that commits itself to uninhibited augmentation of social welfare.   [5] See Ronald Dworkin, *A Matter of Principle* (1986), pp. 72, 82–9.

The validity of this response to Yvonne's question still depends on one crucial condition: the unbiased distribution of costs and benefits to all citizens. There should be nothing in the system that *predetermines* Yvonne's participation in the social costs and benefits to be greater (or smaller) than that of other citizens. As utilitarians put it, every person counts for one and no person for more than one. Under this criterion, no one's share in the social costs and benefits can be singled out in advance as being larger or smaller than the regular share.

This response answers Yvonne's question only partially. It only helps her to come to terms with the *general* idea that citizens need to expose themselves to the risk of error in adjudicative fact-finding in order to have social conditions that are both agreeable and equitable.[6] Because general propositions do not decide concrete cases,[7] Yvonne may legitimately ask 'Why place the risk of error on me, instead of placing it on defendant Xavier?' This question is legitimate because litigation is a zero-sum game, which means that allocation of the risk of error in litigation is a zero-sum game, too. To the extent that risk of error constitutes a problem, this problem can be resolved in three possible ways: by placing the risk on the claimant, on the defendant, or by making the claimant and the defendant share the risk. The last two possibilities underscore the legitimacy of Yvonne's question, which cannot be answered by 'Well, somebody's got to take the risk of error'. An obvious retort to this answer insists on using the alphabetical order and places the risk of error upon Xavier, instead of Yvonne. To be fair, allocation of the risk of error does not only need to be unbiased. It needs to be unbiased in some principled way, rather than adventitiously.

To be fair to Yvonne and Xavier, allocation of the risk of error needs to affect them equally. This alignment with the equality standard is fundamental. The state acts through its courts as an arbiter of civil disputes. It forces its dispute-resolving decisions upon citizens. To be fair in applying this power, the state must treat the claimant (Yvonne) and the defendant (Xavier) with equal concern and respect.[8] In the domain of adjudicative fact-finding that involves allocation of the risk of error, this general standard branches into two separate,

[6] Cf. Sven Ove Hansson, Ethical Criteria for Risk Acceptance (2003) 59 *Erkenntnis* 291, 305 (arguing about risk generally that 'exposure of a person to a risk is acceptable if and only if this exposure is part of an equitable social system of risk-taking that works to her advantage').

[7] *Lochner v New York*, 198 U.S. 45, 76 (1905) (Holmes, J., dissenting) ('General propositions do not decide concrete cases').

[8] See Ronald Dworkin, *Taking Rights Seriously* (1977), pp. 46–130; Ronald Dworkin, *Law's Empire* (1986), pp. 176–238. See also Robert G. Bone, Agreeing to Fair Process: the Problem with Contractarian Theories of Procedural Fairness (2003) 83 B. U. L. Rev. 485, 495–542 (associating fairness of adjudicative procedures with equality); Lawrence B. Solum, Procedural Justice (2004) 78 So. Ca. L. Rev. 181, 306 (identifying equitable distribution of the risk of error with the 'Accuracy Principle').

but mutually related, requirements. The first of these requirements aims at attaining *primary equality* in risk-allocation and extends to every decision that relates to fact-finding. This requirement demands that in making such decisions adjudicators do not expose the claimant to a greater risk of error than the defendant, or vice versa. The objective of the second requirement is *corrective equality*. This requirement focuses on the claimant's and the defendant's forensic conduct. Adversarial litigation gives each litigant an ample opportunity to present his or her evidence and demonstrate its credibility, as well as to discredit the evidence of his or her opponent. Each party may consequently use this opportunity in a way that imposes the risk of fact-finding error upon his or her adversary. This adversarial warfare is acceptable up to a certain point: the parties' mutual impositions of the risk of error must take place within the bounds of the reciprocal. Here, the term 'reciprocal' stands for the exact opposite of the unilateral and one-sided. For example, if a particular piece of evidence generates risk of error for one party only, adjudicators should not admit it. Adjudicators ought to prevent the proponent of such evidence from imposing a non-reciprocal risk of error upon his or her opponent. They should do so because violation of the reciprocity requirement generates inequality in the allocation of the risk of error.[9]

What follows is a discussion of the evidential rules and doctrines that achieve both primary and corrective equality in the apportionment of the risk of error between claimants and defendants. This understanding of civil evidence is an antidote to its economic understanding, developed in Chapter 5. As discussed below, the equality principle explains some of the evidential rules and doctrines that apply in civil litigation better than the cost-efficiency doctrine does. Chapter 5, however, demonstrates that a number of other evidential rules and doctrines that apply in civil trials are explained more convincingly by their cost-efficiency. Together with Chapter 5, the present chapter also reveals that most evidential rules and doctrines that apply in civil litigation are open to the cost-efficiency and the equality-based explanations at once (as are many evidential rules and doctrines that apply in criminal trials—a point made by Chapters 5 and 6).[10] This moral dualism is not surprising. Every

---

[9] Cf. George P. Fletcher, Fairness and Utility in Tort Theory (1972) 85 Harv. L. Rev. 537 (arguing, on corrective justice grounds, that the doctrine of non-reciprocal risk should govern the doer–sufferer relationship in torts; specifically, an individual ought to be liable for tort damages resulting from his or her imposition of a non-reciprocal risk on another person).

[10] Richard Posner's article, An Economic Approach to the Law of Evidence (1999) 51 Stan. L. Rev. 1477, has been criticized (inter alia) for being a simple restatement of common sense dressed up in a fancy economic jargon. See Richard Lempert, The Economic Analysis of Evidence Law: Common Sense on Stilts (2001) 87 Va. L. Rev. 1619. This critique is misdirected, and not just because finding an alignment between common sense and economics is far from trivial. As demonstrated in Chapters 5, 6, and 7, many evidential rules and doctrines can equally be explained by both

branch of the law deals with the tension between fairness and efficiency. Evidence law is no exception. Like many other branches of the law, it is not committed to a single value or objective. In areas of convergence, in which efficiency and fairness beget similar rules and doctrines of evidence, this lack of exclusivity is unproblematic, even desirable. Bypassing clashes between values is commendable in any legal system. This strategy promotes political tolerance and neutrality and reduces the legal system's justification burden. Fairness and efficiency, however, do not produce identical systems of apportioning the risk of error. Some evidential rules and doctrines align with fairness, others with efficiency. For a pluralistic legal system that manages to avoid clashes between its rules and doctrines, this divergence is unproblematic. In such a system, every rule and doctrine occupies its own space. Different ideologies that transform into legal arrangements exercise control over different domains. In some domains, efficiency overrides fairness, in others fairness prevails in its contest against efficiency.

The conflicting presence of fairness and efficiency principles in evidence law constitutes a problem for cases featuring no specific rules that determine the apportionment of the risk of error. In such cases, adjudicators exercise an unfettered discretion that allows them to choose between efficiency and fairness or even to opt for solutions that are neither fair nor efficient. Chapter 4 argues against this discretion that provides adjudicators with a licence to allocate the risk of error as they deem fit. This discussion underscores the drawbacks of free proof and the need to set up a comprehensive regulatory framework for adjudicative fact-finding. At the end of this chapter, I propose to structure the adjudicators' fact-finding discretion by the principle of equality.

The discussion proceeds as follows. First, I offer the equality-based rationale to the burden-of-proof rules that generally apply in civil litigation. Next, I deploy the same rationale, along with its primary and corrective equality ramifications, in order to explain and justify other evidential mechanisms,

---

fairness and efficiency. Yet, because fairness and efficiency are incompatible, a theory demonstrating that one of the two systems—say, efficiency—offers a convincing rationale to an important branch of the law cannot be dismissed for obviousness. Together with the present chapter, Chapter 6 demonstrates that an economic account of evidence law (such as Posner's theory or the account provided above in Chapter 5) is only partially convincing. Accepting it, at the expense of fairness, as an overarching theory of evidence law would, therefore, be too simplistic. Louis Kaplow and Steven Shavell, *Fairness Versus Welfare* (2002), claim that economic efficiency (that transforms into social welfare) is preferable to fairness. Specifically, they argue that people's tastes for fairness should be processed through an ordinary utilitarian calculus, which would always prove that both society and individuals are better off with efficiency. I do not believe that such sweeping claims can ever be sustained (What if some individuals have a taste for fairness that overrides social welfare? And why is social welfare not a 'taste'?). My book has no ambition to adjudicate the contest between Bentham's and Kant's ideologies. Instead, it allows these conflicting ideologies to function together under the same theoretical roof, pluralistic, rather than monistic in character.

divided, as previously, into exclusion, pre-emption, and corroboration. Finally, I identify the impact of this rationale upon discretionary apportionment of the risk of error.

B. Burden of Proof and Equality

The equality principle demands that risk of error be allocated equally between the claimant and the defendant. When this risk materializes, the party upon whom it was initially allocated suffers an undeserved loss. Under the equality principle, losses that the claimant and the defendant might undeservedly suffer are equally regrettable. The state has no moral licence to prefer one such loss over the other. The risk of error in civil litigation is consequently apportioned between the parties in a way that does not favour one party over the other.[11]

The ideal version of the equality principle requires that each party be awarded the relative value of his or her allegations. This value equals the value of the litigated entitlement multiplied by the probability of the party's allegations (in economic terms, the expected value of the case). The risk of error apportioned to each party thus equals the probability of his or her opponent's case. When fact-finders are unable to determine the relevant probabilities, they treat them as equal (as prescribed by the indifference principle, also known as the 'principle of insufficient reason'). A claimant recovers from the defendant a sum of money equalling PD, when P represents the probability of the claimant's allegations and D represents the value of the litigated good. Accordingly, the sum amounting to $(1-P)D$ goes to the defendant.

Under this approach, pursuit of equality in the allocation of the risk of error in fact-finding acquires its own significance, independent of the substantive law. Equality in the apportionment of the risk of error is pursued for its own sake. This approach breaks away from the notion of adjectivity that lies at the heart of the burden of proof doctrine and subordinates the doctrine, together with other procedural and evidentiary mechanisms, to the substantive law and

---

[11] See *Grogan v Garner*, 498 U.S. 279, 286 (1991) ('Because the preponderance-of-the-evidence standard results in a roughly equal allocation of the risk of error between litigants, we presume that this standard is applicable in civil actions between private litigants unless particularly important individual interests or rights are at stake'). For analysis of this rationale and its theoretical underpinnings see Alex Stein, The Refoundation of Evidence Law (1996) 9 Can. J. Law & Jurisp. 279, 333–42. For other writings grounding the burden-of-proof rules on equality-based rationales see James Brook, Inevitable Errors: The Preponderance of the Evidence Standard in Civil Litigation (1982) 18 Tulsa L. J. 79, 85; Ronald J. Allen, Burdens of Proof, Uncertainty and Ambiguity in Modern Legal Discourse (1994) 17 Harv. J. L. & Pub. Pol'y 627, 634; David Hamer, The Civil Standard of Proof Uncertainty: Probability, Belief and Justice (1994) 16 Sydney L. Rev. 506.

its underlying objectives. This approach frustrates the principal objective of the law of evidence and procedure: accurate implementation of the substantive law.[12] Substantive law structures adjudicative decisions by setting a framework of dichotomous legal categories, such as 'contract/no-contract', 'tort/no-tort', 'will/no-will'; and so forth.[13] Under this framework, cases are adjudicated in an all-or-nothing fashion. In a typical tort action, for example, adjudicators need to determine whether or not the defendant owed the claimant a duty to take precautions against damage; whether or not the defendant acted negligently by exposing the claimant to a risk of sustaining the litigated damage; whether or not the claimant actually sustained that damage; and, finally, whether or not the damage is a consequence of the defendant's negligent action. Each of the four elements of the action—duty, negligence, damage, and causation—need to be established as either proven or not proven. There is no third possibility. More nuanced doctrines—such as those that apportion liability for damage by accounting for the parties' comparative fault—operate in a similar way. For example, in applying the comparative fault doctrine, adjudicators need to determine whether or not the claimant was at fault, i.e., whether or not the claimant negligently contributed to the occurrence of the litigated damage or negligently failed to mitigate it. Although this and affiliated doctrines apportion liability for damages, the fault activating those doctrines always has to be determined in an all-or-nothing fashion. Adjudicators, for instance, are not allowed to hold a claimant responsible for 30 per cent of the litigated damage upon finding a 0.3 probability that the damage was self-inflicted. When the scenario in which the damage is caused by the defendant has a 0.7 probability, they must hold the defendant liable for the entire damage.

Substantive justice is indivisible. This vision of justice under the law cannot be disturbed by the presence of uncertainty in adjudicative fact-finding. If there are preponderantly persuasive reasons for finding that the defendant wrongfully inflicted damage on the claimant, these reasons ought to be considered good enough for affording the claimant full justice under the law. The defendant should then be forced to make good the whole damage, rather than its probabilistic fraction. Conversely, the fact-finders' estimation that these reasons are not preponderantly strong would entail that there are

[12] This instrumentalist conception is, of course, closely associated with Bentham. See Gerald Postema, The Principle of Utility and the Law of Procedure: Bentham's Theory of Adjudication (1977) 11 Georgia L. Rev. 1393. But see Robert Summers, Evaluating and Improving Legal Process—A Plea for 'Process Values' (1974) 60 Cornell L. Rev. 1; Michael D. Bayles, Principles for Legal Procedure (1986) 5 Law & Phil. 33 (ascribing intrinsic value to certain procedural arrangements).

[13] Dworkin, above note 5, at 119–22, termed such categories 'dispositive concepts' because the law requires judges to dispose cases only through these categories.

preponderantly persuasive reasons for finding that the defendant did not wrongfully damage the claimant (an estimation that the claimant's allegations are unproven would also qualify as such a reason). In any such case, adjudicators should grant the defendant full, rather than fractional, justice.

This dichotomous approach protects the stability of legal entitlements. If legal entitlements were to become fractional, so that each entitlement would be defined by the probability of its underlying facts, the justice mechanism—representing its underlying social vision of right and wrong—would then be eroded beyond repair. The concept of wrongfulness, along with the very notion of right, would disappear altogether.[14] The resulting indeterminacy would create a chaotic legal world with no rights and no wrongs and with virtually nothing that individuals indisputably can or cannot do under the law. Inasmuch as morally defensible social order in place of anarchy is its aim, the law needs to embody a set of unwavering rights and wrongs. The law has to reject the relativist approach that does away with rights and wrongs by conditioning their social meaning and operational significance on the probabilities of their underlying facts.[15]

Under this framework, risk of error attendant upon the determination of factual issues that pertain to a single legal category—tort, breach of contract, and so forth—cannot be equitably divided between the parties. If the equality principle were independent and autonomous in its application—that is, if it were unrelated to the substantive law—it could then prescribe equitable sharing of the risk of error by allowing a claimant to recover from the defendant in proportion to the probability of the claimant's case. This principle, however, belongs to the law of evidence and procedure—a mechanism that executes the substantive law. The equality principle cannot acquire independence and autonomy and needs to be applied differently. Not allowed to divide the risk of error with regard to an indivisible legal category (such as tort or breach of contract), this principle is bound to place the entire risk upon one of the parties. Under this constraint, the claimant and the defendant are treated as equals in the sense that neither is accorded preference over the other in factual findings unless his or her case is supported by better reasons. A party whose factual allegations (true or false) are supported by weaker reasons consequently bears the risk of error. A party prevails in the entire case when his or her allegations are more probable than not.

This allocation of the risk of error still does not provide a tie-breaking rule for balanced cases, in which the probabilities of the claimant's and the defendant's conflicting allegations are equal (formally presentable as $P = 0.5$ cases).

---

[14] Cf. George P. Fletcher, The Right and the Reasonable (1985) 98 Harv. L. Rev. 949.

[15] For the law's function as generating the social meaning of rights and wrongs see Dan M. Kahan, Social Influence, Social Meaning, and Deterrence (1997) 83 Va. L. Rev. 349.

A possible rule for such cases is a strict $P > 0.5$ rule that requires a claimant to prove *the entire case* by a preponderance of the evidence. If the claimant fails to discharge this burden, he or she would not be allowed to recover from the defendant. As demonstrated in Chapter 5, this rule certainly is desirable from the utilitarian cost-efficiency perspective. The equality principle, however, cannot justify this rule as a rule of decision for *all* balanced cases. Although this principle is indifferent as to which party—the claimant or the defendant— bears the risk of error in a single $P = 0.5$ case, it opposes the global $P > 0.5$ rule that systematically favours defendants over claimants. Unwilling to accommodate this rule, the equality principle allocates the risk of error through *apportionment of discrete legal categories*— that constitute the objects of proof in the underlying litigation—between the claimant and the defendant. Under this apportionment, the claimant establishes as more probable than not facts relevant to a legal category that benefits him or her. The defendant establishes as more probable than not facts pertaining to a category that benefits him or her (the 'affirmative defence' category). Each litigant is exposed to the risk of error that attaches to *his or her own allegations*, that is, to the risk of error that relates to the facts making out his or her case under the controlling substantive law. In a typical tort lawsuit, the claimant needs to establish, on a balance of probabilities, that the defendant wrongfully inflicted his or her damage. The defendant, in turn, has to preponderantly establish contributory fault, when he or she raises this defence to defeat the lawsuit. The risk of fact-finding error is thus allocated between the parties in a roughly equal fashion.[16]

---

[16] Dale Nance justifies the prevalent burden-of-proof doctrine by another principle originating from fairness. Specifically, he justifies this doctrine by the principle of civility that presumes general compliance with the standards laid down by the law. A person who attributes non-compliance to his or her fellow has, therefore, to prove this allegation by a preponderance of the evidence. See Dale A. Nance, Civility and the Burden of Proof (1994) 17 Harv. J. L. & Pub. Pol'y 647. This justification is attractive. As Nance rightly points out (ibid, at 661–72), the doctrine's alternative rationales (other than equality) that allude to the structure of pleadings in civil procedure, to unarticulated 'policy considerations' and to the fact that affirmative defences are generally disfavoured are question-begging. Equality in the apportionment of the risk of error between the claimant and the defendant is, therefore, the only competitor of the civility principle.

Nance's analysis does not explicitly accommodate excusatory defences that function in civil litigation. Consider, for example, a case in which the defendant raises unilateral mistake as a ground for escaping contractual liability. By raising this defence the defendant does not invoke any civility-related imputation against the claimant. At the same time, the defendant cannot seriously claim that entering into a contract upon unilateral mistake and subsequently disavowing any contractual responsibility is a conduct that squarely aligns with civility. This conduct falls below the general contractual norm, and yet, as a matter of concession to human frailty, a person responsible for it can, nevertheless, be excused. Any such defence therefore needs to be preponderantly established by its proponent. See Stein, above note 11, at 337. The civility principle both can and should accommodate this requirement by removing its presumption from litigants relying upon excuses.

This form of equality classifies as primary, which suggests that it might require protective measures. Otherwise, equality in the ultimate apportionment of the risk of error cannot be guaranteed. Evidence law therefore needs to develop the appropriate corrective equality mechanism.[17] This mechanism reallocates the burden of proof in order to maintain equality in the apportionment of the risk of error between the claimant and the defendant. This reallocation of the burden takes place when a party upon whom the burden lies is unable to discharge it due to his or her opponent's fault. Consider a case in which hospital patient P required urgent surgery that promised a 60 per cent chance of recovery. The doctors negligently delayed the surgery. The delayed surgery was performed impeccably, but it promised P only a 40 per cent chance of recovery. Ultimately, P does not recover. His lawsuit against the doctors attributes his terminal illness to the doctors' malpractice.[18] P is unable to prove the existence of causation between the doctors' malpractice and his affliction. A simple statistical analysis reveals that the probability of P's causative allegation against the doctors equals 1/3.[19] Because the controlling negligence doctrine identifies this allegation as belonging to P's cause of action, the general burden-of-proof doctrine dooms P's lawsuit to dismissal.

Application of this principle is still problematic because strength of presumptions admits different degrees. See Edna Ullmann-Margalit, On Presumption (1983) 80 J. Phil. 143. Why make the civility presumption as strong as Nance wants it to be? The civility principle provides a plausible reason for placing the production burden (or the burden of adducing evidence) on the party portraying his or her opponent as a transgressor. There is, however, no compelling reason for applying this presumption when the probability of transgression equals 0.5 (which is the only case in which the burden of persuasion comes into play). The civility principle does not justify allocation of the *risk of non-persuasion* in balanced cases.

[17] Civil litigation may accommodate different conceptions of corrective equality. For one such conception (not adopted by the present book) see Alan Wertheimer, The Equalization of Legal Resources (1988) 17 Phil. & Pub. Affairs 303 (proposing to downsize litigation opportunities in order to make them more equal).

[18] These facts are adapted from the landmark House of Lords' decision, *Hotson v East Berkshire Area Health Authority* [1987] 1 A.C. 750 (holding that a patient's lost chances to recover from his or her illness do not constitute damage actionable in torts). The Canadian Supreme Court delivered a similar holding in *Lawson v Laferriere*, 78 D.L.R. 4th 609 (1991). For an American example, see *Herskovits v Group Health Cooperative of Puget Sound*, 664 P.2d 474 (1983) (holding that when medical malpractice reduces the patient's chances to recover, his or her lost chances constitute actionable damage). For comprehensive discussions of this issue, see Ariel Porat and Alex Stein, *Tort Liability Under Uncertainty* (2001), pp. 116–29; Ariel Porat and Alex Stein, Indeterminate Causation and Apportionment of Damages: An Essay on *Holtby*, *Allen* and *Fairchild* (2003) 23 OJLS 667.

[19] According to this analysis, the doctors' malpractice had transferred P from one group of similarly situated patients (group A) to another (group B). In group A, 60 out of 100 similarly situated patients recover from their illness. In group B, only 40 patients recover, while 60 do not. Because P did not recover, he belongs to the sub-group of 60 patients in group B. Amongst these 60 patients, 40 were initially doomed not to recover, while the remaining 20 were prevented from recovering by their doctors' malpractice. The probability of P's contention that he was one of the 20 wronged patients consequently equals 20/60, that is, 1/3.

Note, however, that P's doctors should be blamed not only for their negligent activities that increased P's risk of becoming terminally ill by 20 per cent—a risk that may or may have not actually materialized into the litigated damage. They should also be blamed for the causal indeterminacy of the case. More specifically, they should be blamed for the *evidential damage* that they negligently inflicted upon P. Due to their negligence, P became unable to identify the cause of his affliction and prove it in court. The defendants, in other words, evidentially incapacitated the claimant. Therefore, if the claimant's lawsuit were to be dismissed for being causally unproven, the defendants would profit from their own wrong. In such a scenario, in addition to the risk of error that civil litigants generally assume, the claimant would bear the risk of fact-finding error that the defendants unilaterally created. By placing this risk on the claimant, the defendants have immunized themselves from the very same risk. This outcome violates the equality principle that, under the present theory, determines the apportionment of the risk of error. The equality principle is violated because the risk of error placed on the claimant does not merely amount to 1/3. The 1/3 figure fails to capture the claimant's *individualized* prospect[20] of recovery in the absence of malpractice. The defendants' malpractice made this probability unascertainable, which constitutes a non-reciprocal risk of error.

This risk is non-reciprocal because of the presence of fault on the defendants' side. The defendants' fault directed the risk of error against the claimant. Faultless creation of the risk of fact-finding error does not necessarily direct that risk against the adversary of the risk-creator. A faultless person not externalizing any risk of harm upon others may inadvertently inflict evidential damage upon himself or herself. Evidential damage originating from a person's wrongful conduct that exposed another individual to a risk of sustaining harm is, in contrast, invariably one-sided.[21] The corrective equality doctrine should, therefore, enter the scene and rectify the imbalance by reallocating the burden of proof.

This somewhat complex example affiliates to a group of straightforward cases featuring evidential damage inflicted by defendants. These examples, known as spoliation cases,[22] involve withholding and destruction of evidence, both negligent and intentional. They also involve tampering with evidence

---

[20] See above at pp. 72–3, 100–2. If this prospect is not recognized, shifting the persuasion burden to the defendant would not change the outcome of the case. The claimant's lawsuit would still be doomed to dismissal.　　　　　[21] See *Tort Liability Under Uncertainty*, above note 18, at pp. 160–9.

[22] See generally Lawrence B. Solum and Stephen J. Marzen, Truth and Uncertainty: Legal Control of the Destruction of Evidence (1987) 36 Emory L. J. 1085; Jamie S. Gorelick, Stephen J. Marzen, and Lawrence B. Solum, *Destruction of Evidence* (1989); Dale A. Nance, Missing Evidence (1991) 13 Cardozo L. Rev. 831.

and intimidation of witnesses. For such cases, too, the corrective equality doctrine prescribes reallocation of the burden of proof—and, correspondingly, of the risk of fact-finding error—from the faultless claimant to the faulty defendant. The evidential damage doctrine[23] and the corrective equality doctrine are functionally identical.

C. Exclusion of Evidence as Corrective Equality

The equality principle generally favours admission of all evidence relevant to the trial. By excluding a piece of relevant evidence categorized as inadmissible, evidence law places the risk of error associated with this evidence upon its proponent. The opponent of the evidence consequently acquires an immunity from that risk. This one-sided outcome is generally inferior to a system of free proof. Arguably, a free-proof system apportions the risk of error more equitably by allowing fact-finders to consider all relevant evidence and determine its probative value on a case-by-case basis. This system avoids any systematic skewing of the risk of error. Under this system, fact-finders consider every factual scenario and make every practicable effort to avoid errors. Fact-finding errors are thus entirely accidental in their occurrence. Their distribution between claimants and defendants is unslanted, perhaps even as randomized as a lottery. This system exposes claimants and defendants to a roughly equal risk of error in fact-finding. It also equally protects them from that risk. Free proof thus seems to possess an important egalitarian feature.[24]

Free proof, however, only guarantees rudimentary equality in risk-allocation and is still far from guaranteeing equality in the final apportionment of the risk of error. Application of this system in civil litigation only installs primary equality. To be properly maintained, this set-up constantly requires corrective equality mechanisms. *These mechanisms render inadmissible any evidence that creates inequality between the litigating parties by imposing a non-reciprocal—and, therefore, inequitable—risk of error upon its opponent.*

[23] See *Tort Liability Under Uncertainty*, above note 18, at pp. 160–206. For critical appraisals of this idea see Jane Stapleton, Book Review (2003) 66 M.L.R. 308; Vern R. Walker, Book Review (2002) 1 Law, Probability & Risk 175; Richard Friedman, Dealing with Evidentiary Deficiency (1997) 18 Cardozo L. Rev. 1961. These and other critics of the evidential damage doctrine criticize it predominantly for conferring a free-standing entitlement in torts. They are largely content with its burden-shifting mechanism.

[24] This feature may possibly explain Hermann Kantorowitz's poetic remark 'From the ruins of torture arose triumphantly, to the horror of all the despondent, free proof-assessment, the pride of the present', cited by James E. Herget and Stephen Wallace, The German Free Law Movement as the Source of American Legal Realism (1987) 73 Va. L. Rev. 399, 415. As explained in Chapter 4, this egalitarian appearance of free proof is merely superficial.

As Chapters 3 and 4 explain, an adjudicator's decision to consider *any* piece of evidence with uncertain probative impact and credentials involves risk of error. This risk classifies as non-reciprocal when the evidence that the fact-finder considers is both one-sided—in that it predominantly favours its proponent's case—and untestable (unfalsifiable and unverifiable at once). Such evidence only benefits its proponent and entails no utilization prospects for its opponent. Because the opponent of such evidence cannot properly examine its probative impact and credentials, the risk of error that the evidence brings about falls exclusively upon him or her. More crucially, such evidence exposes its proponent to no risk whatsoever, a factor that creates inequality between the parties. The corrective equality requirement renders such evidence inadmissible.

By excluding such evidence, corrective equality joins forces with the maximal individualization principle (*PMI*), set forth in Chapter 3. As Chapter 3 explains, *PMI* offers an epistemologically sound precept for fact-finding. As such, it can legitimately operate in the epistemic domain of adjudicative fact-finding. The maximal individualization principle does not operate alone. This principle often clashes with the cost-efficiency doctrine (proven equally sound in Chapter 5). Under the cost-efficiency doctrine, fact-finders generally process evidence and proof in a way that reduces the aggregate cost of fact-findings errors and error-avoidance.[25] This utilitarian principle may support a non-individualized fact-finding system. Epistemological reasons are incapable of resolving this clash. The maximal individualization principle may nonetheless be found to be attractive enough to trump cost-efficiency. This principle is attractive not only epistemologically, but also as an instrument for installing equality in the allocation of the risk of error. By insisting upon individualized proof—a fact-finding requirement that all admissible evidence be susceptible to case-specific testing and adverse utilization—this principle prevents evidential one-sidedness and thus contributes to equality. Equality in the risk-apportionment that *PMI* helps to install is a moral and political virtue that epistemological reasons can neither commend nor reproach. Epistemological reasons also cannot support or reject the adoption of the cost-efficiency doctrine. The choice between the two principles is a matter of political morality. Epistemological concerns do not dictate that the maximal

---

[25] Sometimes, the legal system needs to employ heightened evidential and procedural requirements to attenuate the overdeterrence generated by overbroad liability rules and excessive penalties (both legal and extralegal). These special requirements reduce the frequency of liability impositions. As a result, the ex ante probability for prospective transgressors shrinks and brings the transgressors' expected penalty down. Necessary in cases involving unavoidable overenforcement of the law, these evidential and procedural mechanisms are briefly discussed above at pp. 20–5, 153. For comprehensive discussion see Richard A. Bierschbach and Alex Stein, Overenforcement (2005) 93 Georgetown L. J. (forthcoming).

individualization principle prevails. Moral and political reasons that favour equal, rather than robustly utilitarian, apportionment of the risk of error accord preference to this principle. *PMI* consequently affiliates to the principle of equality, rudimentary and corrective. My following discussion—including the analysis of pre-emption, corroboration, and discretion—therefore treats *PMI* as an equality principle.

My discussion of the exclusionary mechanisms that promote corrective equality focuses on the rules regulating the admission of hearsay,[26] character,[27] and opinion[28] evidence. These mainstays of the Anglo-American evidence system have one common principle: *evidence not susceptible to individualized examination by litigants and fact-finders or, alternatively, to adverse utilization by the party opponent is inadmissible.* When the relation of a piece of evidence to the case at hand cannot be individualized, then this relation is just one of many possible relations. When a piece of evidence is not susceptible to scrutiny by which its opponent could utilize it or individualize its impact, exposing him or her to any adverse consequence that the piece of evidence brings about is inequitable. For these reasons, an attempt to use character evidence to establish a causal connection between personality and action almost invariably fails.[29] Arguments establishing such a connection are applicable to some cases, but not to others. Sometimes people act in conformity with their characters and sometimes not. More crucially, any such argument hangs in the air. Bringing it down to the ground is impossible because there is no way of examining the proposition that the relevant individual acted in conformity with his or her character in the event on trial. A generalization suggesting that he or she acted in this way is available, but this covering uniformity is one of many and it is not susceptible to individualized testing. Exposing the opponent of this generalization to the risk of error associated with its possible adoption by the fact-finders becomes inequitable. Fact-finders, of course, may or may not adopt such a generalization, but the risk of error associated with the possibility of adopting it is one-sided. This risk is slanted against the opponent of the evidence, who can neither subject it to individualized testing nor utilize it in promoting his or her trial objectives. The proponent of such evidence, in contrast, risks nothing. For him or her, the worst scenario is the fact-finders' refusal to base their findings on the 'action in conformity' generalization.

This, however, is not the case with case-specific—that is, individualized—evidence that, apart from *incidentally* spotlighting a person's character, tends to case-specifically prove his or her 'motive, opportunity, intent, preparation, plan,

---

[26] See, e.g., Federal Rules of Evidence 801–807.
[27] See, e.g., Federal Rules of Evidence 404, 405, 608, 609.
[28] See, e.g., Federal Rules of Evidence 701–702.   [29] See Federal Rule of Evidence 404(a).

knowledge, identity, absence of mistake or accident' and the like.[30] The same holds true for evidence that provides a factual, as opposed to moralized, description of some habit or routine practice of a person or an organization.[31] Such evidence is susceptible to individualized testing and is consequently admissible.

The hearsay doctrine is yet another exclusionary mechanism aimed at attaining corrective equality. This doctrine differentiates between two categories of hearsay statements, broadly defined as out-of-court communications, explicit or implicit, that purport to establish the truth of their contents.[32] The first category includes unmitigated hearsay evidence, one-sided in its content and not susceptible to adversarial scrutiny by in-court cross-examination and other appropriate means. The second category includes hearsay evidence either open to adversarial scrutiny or utilizable by its opponent as evidence supporting his or her case. Statements falling into the first category are generally inadmissible under the rule against hearsay. Statements belonging to the second category are generally admissible under the exceptions to the hearsay rule.

Before demonstrating that this categorization corresponds to positive law in the United States,[33] I need to make another general observation. Hearsay statements falling under either of the two categories have probative value. Any such statement mobilizes fact-generating arguments upon which (subject to the ever-present risk of error) fact-finders can rationally rely. The probative value of any such statement always depends on the specifics of each individual case. Both categories of hearsay evidence also generate risk of error. Similar to the statement's probative value, this risk varies from one case to another. Yet, one feature characterizing the apportionment of this risk always remains constant: admission of an untestable and one-sided hearsay statement would impose a non-reciprocal risk of error upon the statement's opponent. Fact-generating arguments that derive from any such statement favour its proponent almost invariably (otherwise, the proponent would not offer the statement into evidence). Because the statement is untestable, its opponent is unable to examine the validity of these arguments and their applicability to the case at hand. The statement's opponent also is unable to utilize the statement or its examination in court by educing additional information that would further his or her trial objectives. Consequently, the statement's proponent risks virtually nothing while its opponent faces the prospect of an erroneous finding against his or her interest. The worst possible prospect for the statement's proponent (and,

---

[30] See Federal Rule of Evidence 404(b).   [31] See Federal Rule of Evidence 406.

[32] See Federal Rule of Evidence 801(a–c); *Wright v Doe d. Tatham* (1837) 7 A & E 313; *R v Kearley* [1992] 2 All ER 345 (HL).

[33] The discretionary regime that applies in England is discussed below in Section F.

correspondingly, the opponent's best prospect) is the fact-finders' refusal to treat the statement as credibly evidencing the proponent's allegations. The worst prospect for the opponent—and, inversely, the proponent's best prospect—is a positive finding that the statement is true. Any such statement, if admitted, would therefore expose its opponent to a non-reciprocal and, consequently, inequitable risk of error.

Take a witness who testifies in a breach-of-contract lawsuit that his friend Heather related to him that the defendant confided to her that he intends not to perform his contract with the claimant. This is the only pertinent information that the witness is aware of and testifies about. As for Heather's statement, this statement may or may not be true: the fact-finders would have to determine its credibility if the witness's testimony is admitted. Under these circumstances, the defendant is unable to advance his case by cross-examining the witness instead of Heather. If admitted as evidence to the truth of its contents, Heather's statement would expose its proponent, the claimant, to no risk whatsoever. The worst scenario for the claimant is the fact-finders' refusal to treat this statement as proving the alleged breach. The best scenario for the claimant is, of course, the fact-finders' decision to treat the statement as sufficiently probative of the alleged breach. This scenario is also the worst scenario for the defendant. Because Heather's statement is untestable, its admission imposes on the defendant a non-reciprocal risk of error. Under the corrective equality principle, implemented in the present example by the rule against hearsay, this statement should therefore classify as inadmissible.

Against this conclusion, the claimant may argue that equality could also be maintained by admitting Heather's statement into evidence and by allowing the defendant to adduce as much hearsay evidence as he pleases. This argument alludes to the parties' equal opportunity for conducting adversarial warfare. Arguably, this opportunity is equal for both parties because it is open-ended. As already explained, this argument, superficially appealing, is ultimately unpersuasive. This argument is doomed to failure not merely because it alludes to an altogether formal and hollow[34] concept of 'equality under the law', one that ignores the disparities in the individuals' social conditions and actual opportunities and, consequently, forbids 'rich and poor alike to sleep under the bridges, to beg in the streets, and to steal their bread'.[35] This argument is doomed to failure for a more prosaic reason, divorced from grand socio-economic politics. A litigant's actual opportunity for conducting adversarial warfare against his or her opponent always depends on the contingencies of the individual case. Because this opportunity depends on the evidence

---

[34] See Peter Westen, The Empty Idea of Equality (1982) 95 Harv. L. Rev. 537.

[35] Anatole France, Le Lys Rouge, in *Five Works of Anatole France* (W. Stephens trans. 1924) (1896), p. 91.

available to each litigant, it is inherently fortuitous: some litigants have more evidence than others, and some have less. Fact-finding can never be completely insulated from such fortuities. Under any legal regime, some evidence will always be missing and some will not. However, making trial outcomes depend on the sheer amount of evidence—both testable and untestable—that one litigant obtains and the other does not would produce a grossly unequal allocation of the risk of error in many cases.

To satisfy the equality demand, evidence law ought to lay down an affirmative requirement that the fact-finders' evidential base be always open to a two-sided adversarial contest. For that purpose, evidence law needs to exercise control over evidence that litigants adduce. Specifically, it needs to make sure that every segment of the fact-finders' evidential base allows each party to advance his or her fact-generating arguments or—at the very least—to falsify the fact-generating arguments of the party opponent. Adjudicators should consequently exclude any evidence failing to meet this standard. Hearsay statements that are neither falsifiable nor utilizable by their opponents form a distinct category of such inadmissible evidence.

Note that the ever-present possibility that fact-finders will decline to base their decision on a particular piece of evidence does not categorize the evidence as falsifiable. For a proponent of a factual allegation, the prospect that fact-finders reject the allegation as unproven is better than the scenario in which the allegation is falsified. Correspondingly, falsification of the proponent's allegation constitutes a better scenario for the party opponent. The case that each litigant strives to make out usually consists of numerous factual allegations. A positive finding that one of those allegations is false (rather than just unproven) may project untrustworthiness upon the proponent's entire case. The opponent, therefore, may utilize the proponent's evidence not only directly—when the evidence or its examination in court produces information that advances the opponent's case—but also indirectly, when the evidence is falsified and when its falsification projects untrustworthiness upon the proponent's case. Evidence accompanied with this *adverse utilization prospect* satisfies the reciprocal risk standard. By joining the fact-finders' evidential base, such evidence does not disrupt the equality in the apportionment of the risk of error. Evidence unaccompanied by an adverse utilization prospect violates the equality requirement. The prospect that the fact-finders will not ultimately count such evidence as establishing the relevant factual proposition (the 'unproven' scenario) is not beneficial enough to its opponent to offset the proponent's positive proof prospect.

Statements that the existing exceptions to the hearsay rule render admissible are generally susceptible to adverse utilization by the party opponent. Any such statement consequently satisfies the equality demand in the apportionment of the risk of error. As such, it should be admissible as evidence to the truth of its contents. This justification supplements the rationale for the hearsay exceptions offered in the previous chapter in connection with criminal trials. The traditional view rationalizes the existing exceptions to the hearsay rule by alluding to their social necessity and to the circumstantial guarantees of trustworthiness that attach to hearsay statements that the exceptions render admissible.[36] As demonstrated in Chapter 6, this rationalization fails to point to a justifiable allocation of the risk of error in criminal trials (in the United States, the constitutional improvement of the hearsay doctrine largely rectifies this problem). This rationalization is equally unsuitable for civil litigation in which the risk of error falls either on the claimant or on the defendant. The 'social necessity' rationale cannot justify skewing the risk of error in one such direction. As for the circumstantial guarantees of trustworthiness, this feature is contingent on the individual characteristics of each case. It can hardly attach to general categories of evidence. The proposed rationale to the hearsay exceptions is, therefore, more convincing than their traditional justification.

Consider spontaneous statements made admissible by the res gestae exceptions to the hearsay rule.[37] Under these exceptions, a hearsay statement would become admissible if it explains or describes an event or a sensation contemporaneously with its perception or experience by the declarant. The traditional view justifies these exceptions on the theory that the declarant's spontaneity usually rules out deliberate or conscious (as opposed to subconscious) misrepresentation.[38] This justification fails to account for errors that an out-of-court witness makes in good faith. The hearsay dangers include not just insincerity on the part of the declarant, but also misleading, although sincere, narration of the event, as well as memory failures and perception errors.[39] Arguably, a well-articulated hearsay statement not suffering from the insincerity prospect should be admissible; in the same vein, courts should generally admit any hearsay statement coming from a declarant whose ability to perceive and memorize the event was established to fall within or above the average.[40] The traditional approach thus appears to favour the admission of hearsay statements when the number of hearsay dangers is two rather than four.[41] However sound it may be from a descriptive point of view, this

---

[36] See John H. Wigmore, *A Treatise on the Anglo-American System of Evidence in Trials at Common Law* Vol. 2 (3rd edn., 1940), §§ 1420–2.

[37] See Federal Rules of Evidence 803(1)–(3); McCormick *On Evidence* Vol. 2 (4th edn., 1992), pp. 206–45.   [38] See, e.g., Edmund Morgan, *Basic Problems of Evidence* (1962), pp. 340–1.

[39] Edmund Morgan, Hearsay Dangers and the Application of the Hearsay Concept (1948) 62 Harv. L. Rev. 177.

[40] See Laurence Tribe, Triangulating Hearsay (1974) 87 Harv. L. Rev. 957.   [41] Ibid.

explanation does not properly justify the res gestae (and other[42]) exceptions to the hearsay rule.

The adverse utilization criterion, favoured by the equality principle, offers the required justification. To make a hearsay statement admissible as res gestae, its proponent has to produce a witness with the first-hand knowledge of the statement's background conditions. This witness has to provide the information indicating that the declarant made the statement spontaneously. The statement's opponent consequently becomes able to cross-examine the witness about this and other information pertaining to the statement's credibility. Considering what any such witness—an insider to the relevant event—needs to know directly to qualify as a witness for a res gestae statement, this cross-examination becomes meaningful. First, it may falsify the declarant's statement. Second, it may elicit from the witness additional information favourable to the opponent's case, especially when the opponent is permitted to cross-examine the witness about matters beyond the scope of the witness's questioning by the proponent.[43] The statement, therefore, may produce an advantage and a disadvantage to its proponent and opponent, respectively. Each of these outcomes may or may not correspond to the true facts (these are generally unknowable). The risk of error, therefore, falls equally on both parties—an apportionment that unmitigated hearsay statements fail to achieve.

On similar grounds, courts should admit into evidence any statement made for purposes of medical diagnosis or treatment to the extent that it describes the declarant's medical history, sensations, symptoms, and their causes.[44] Admission of such a statement would typically require, as a supporting witness, a doctor, a nurse, or another member of medical personnel. At cross-examination, such witnesses would generally be able to provide full information about the declarant's diagnosis and treatment and about any additional statement that he or she may have made. This factor makes the declarant's statement utilizable by its opponent.

Hearsay exceptions premised upon the opponent's ability or opportunity to cross-examine the declarant directly also maintain equality in the apportionment of the risk of error. These exceptions also extend to records documenting a witness's past—as opposed to present—recollection of the event;[45] to a prior

---

[42] Tribe (ibid) offered this explanation as a unifying descriptive theory of exceptions to the hearsay rule.

[43] See Federal Rule of Evidence 611(b). The court normally grants this permission when the additional questioning of the testifying witness pertains to the credibility of the declarant's statement. See Federal Rule of Evidence 806; McCormick *On Evidence* Vol. 1 (4th edn., 1992), pp. 85–90; McCormick, Vol. 2 above note 37, at pp. 370–1.   [44] Federal Rule of Evidence 803(4).

[45] Federal Rule of Evidence 803(5). To make such a record admissible as evidence to the truth of its contents, the witness would normally have to authenticate it and also to testify about his or her insufficient recollection of the events and the consequent inability to testify fully and accurately. See McCormick Vol. 2 above note 37, at 254.

statement inconsistent with the witness's present testimony;[46] to a prior statement consistent with the witness's present testimony when the opponent of the testimony claims it to be a recent fabrication or a product of an improper influence or motive;[47] and to an out-of-court identification of a person that the witness previously made.[48] These exceptions also extend to a declarant's testimony in another legal proceeding or deposition, if the opponent of that evidence or his or her predecessor in interest had both an opportunity and a similar motive to question the declarant,[49] as well as to any facts essential for sustaining a judgment that adjudged the opponent of those facts guilty of a crime.[50] Finally, any statement made by an academic or other reputable publication is admissible to the extent that an expert witness was questioned about it and acknowledged its truth in court.[51] In such settings, the existing prospect or the past opportunity for adverse utilization of the evidence secures equitable apportionment of the risk of error.

Another group of hearsay exceptions accommodates records documenting activities carried out in the course and for the furtherance of any business (including public and religious enterprises, such as registration of ownerships and personal status).[52] This group of exceptions also includes family history statements[53] and records.[54] Examination in court cannot usually falsify evidence belonging to this group of exceptions. The adverse utilization prospect that such evidence entails is, consequently, limited. However, because information offered by such evidence is not generated selectively with a particular trial in mind, it can potentially benefit both parties to a civil litigation. More importantly, to the extent that such evidence engenders the risk of erroneous fact-finding, the way in which the evidence is generated over time guarantees equitable distribution of that risk between claimants and defendants. Errors that occur throughout the process of generating such evidence are entirely accidental. They may fall in either direction and are not systematically slanted.

A number of hearsay exceptions extend to statements practically involving none of the hearsay dangers. This category includes party-opponent statements, typically, out-of-court admissions, both personal and by an agent.[55] The

---

[46] See Federal Rule of Evidence 801(d)(A).

[47] See Federal Rule of Evidence 801(d)(1)(B); *Tome v United States*, 513 U.S. 150 (1995).

[48] Federal Rule of Evidence 801(d)(1)(C).   [49] Federal Rule of Evidence 804(b)(1).

[50] Federal Rule of Evidence 803(22). This rule is too broad, though. Under this rule, the convicted person does not have to be a party to the subsequent civil proceeding. In criminal prosecutions, judgments against persons other than the accused are only admissible for impeachment purposes.   [51] Federal Rule of Evidence 803(18).

[52] Federal Rules of Evidence 803(6)–(12); (14)–(17) and (23).

[53] Federal Rule of Evidence 804(b)(4).   [54] Federal Rule of Evidence 803(13).

[55] Federal Rule of Evidence 801(d)(2)(A)–(D). Co-conspirator statements, made admissible by Rule 801(d)(2)(E), pertain mostly to criminal litigation.

opponent of any such statement can always controvert it by his or her own testimony and can raise no valid complaint about his or her inability to cross-examine the declarant. Such evidence does not classify as one-sided or untestable. Hearsay exceptions forming this category also include knowledge about land boundaries, customs, history, character, and marriage that exists in a particular community.[56] Technically, such evidence could function as circumstantial proof, rather than hearsay, as its very existence has probative value. Community knowledge that these exceptions turn into admissible evidence requires attestation by a witness with personal knowledge, who can be adequately cross-examined by the opponent of the evidence. Admission of such evidence therefore does not produce inequitable apportionment of the risk of error.

The dying-declaration exception to the hearsay rule[57] does not easily fit into this scheme. This exception renders admissible any statement made by a person while believing that his or her death was imminent 'concerning the cause or circumstances of what [he or she] believed to be impending death'. Underlying this exception is a time-honoured, but psychologically questionable, rationale: 'no man wants to die with a lie on his lips.'[58] For obvious reasons, only the first half of this proposition can be claimed to be predominantly correct. Hearsay statements that fall under the dying-declaration exception are not always accompanied by an adverse utilization prospect. This exception, however, occupies a relatively narrow informational space. Under this exception, only statements purporting to explain the cause or the circumstances of the declarant's subjectively anticipated death are admissible. More importantly, this exception only applies when the declarant is unavailable as a witness.[59] In such circumstances, the declarant's statement is typically the only evidence shedding light on the cause and the circumstances of his or her death.[60] If this evidence is refused an admissibility ticket, the risk of error that the declarant's successor would assume would, arguably, be imbalanced. Arguably, a more equitable apportionment of that risk can be achieved by admitting the declarant's dying declaration and by allowing the fact-finders to evaluate its probative value. This apportionment of the risk of error and the corresponding justification of the dying-declaration exception are both plausible, but, admittedly, still problematic.

---

[56] Federal Rules of Evidence 803(19), (20), and (21).

[57] Federal Rule of Evidence 804(b)(2).

[58] See *Idaho v Wright*, 497 U.S. 805, 820 (1990), quoting from *Queen v Osman*, 15 Cox Crim.Cas. 1, 3 (Eng.N.Wales Cir.1881) (Lush L. J.) ('no person, who is immediately going into the presence of his Maker, will do so with a lie upon his lips').

[59] This unavailability condition applies to all hearsay exceptions listed by Federal Rule of Evidence 804 (but Rule 804(a) contains a rather broad definition of 'unavailability as a witness').

[60] See McCormick Vol. 2, above note 37, at pp. 329–30.

The forfeiture exception to the hearsay rule allows an out-of-court statement to be adduced against a party who kept the declarant out of the way as a potential witness in the trial.[61] This exception squarely aligns with my general theory, but not with the mechanism presently discussed. As explained below, the evidential damage doctrine—that also derives from the equality principle—fully justifies the adoption of this exception. Another exception to the hearsay rule that I discuss later in this chapter is the discretionary catchall.[62] In the United States, this exception is residual. In England, the Civil Evidence Act 1995 had abolished the hearsay rule, but judges still retain a broad discretion that allows them to refuse to base their judgments upon hearsay evidence.[63] The American catchall and England's shift to free proof are discussed below in the section that deals with discretion.

Another important exclusionary mechanism that attains corrective equality is in the rules controlling the admissibility of scientific and other expert testimony (that constitute an important exception to the rule against opinion evidence[64]). The American legal system and the new English civil procedure reveal that different rules can be geared toward the same end. In the United States, Federal Rule of Evidence 702 and the Supreme Court's *Daubert Trilogy*—*Daubert*,[65] *Joiner*,[66] and *Kumho Tire*[67]—condition the admissibility of any expert evidence on the fulfilment of six criteria.[68] First, the trial court makes sure that the theory or the methodology by which the expert generated the evidence is *falsifiable* in principle; and the court should, of course, also consider the tests to which the theory or the methodology was actually put. Second, it is desirable, although not mandatory, that the expert's theory or methodology is published in the academic or professional literature after undergoing peer examination for possible flaws. Third, the expert must

---

[61] Federal Rule of Evidence 804(b)(6).   [62] Federal Rule of Evidence 807.

[63] See Adrian A. S. Zuckerman, *Civil Procedure* (2003), pp. 669–70. In England, virtually all civil cases are tried by judge alone (Zuckerman, ibid, at p. 642 n.1).

[64] Non-expert opinions are inadmissible when tendered as bald assertions, unsubstantiated by case-specific facts to which the witness can attest from his or her personal knowledge. See McCormick Vol. 1, above note 43, at pp. 41–7; Zuckerman, above note 63, at pp. 617–18. Such assertions are practically meaningless. They are neither susceptible to individualized testing nor open to adverse utilization. The corrective equality principle consequently favours their exclusion.

[65] *Daubert v Merrell Dow Pharmaceuticals, Inc.*, 509 U.S. 579 (1993).

[66] *General Electric Co. v Joiner*, 522 U.S. 136 (1997).

[67] *Kumho Tire Co. v Carmichael*, 526 U.S. 137 (1999) (extending *Daubert*'s gatekeeping rules, originally designed for scientific evidence, to all kinds of expert testimony).

[68] In England, the admissibility criteria are not well-specified. There, expert evidence is admissible when it falls within 'an acknowledged body of expertise, in the sense of a field governed by established principles and rules, and only if the court considers that expert evidence would assist the determination of the issues'. Zuckerman, above note 63, at 617–18. Recently, this principle underwent liberalization in the area of criminal evidence. See *R v Robb* (1991) 93 Cr. App. R. 161, 164–6; *R v Dallagher* [2002] Crim. L. Rev. 821 (CA); and, in particular, *R v Luttrell* [2004] 2 Cr. App. R. 31.

indicate the error rate, actual or potential, that attaches to his or her theory or methodology. The court normally considers a high error rate as a reason for excluding the testimony. Fourth, it is desirable, but still not mandatory, that the expert's theory or methodology attains general acceptance in the relevant scientific community. Fifth, the court examines the expert's inferences from theory (or methodology) to conclusions in order to detect analytical gaps: a serious analytical gap would constitute a compelling reason for excluding the expert's testimony.[69] Finally, the court measures the potential probativity of the expert's testimony against any prejudicial or misleading potential that it may have. This balancing is mandated by Federal Rule of Evidence 403.

These new admissibility standards replaced *Frye v United States*,[70] a highly influential precedent that conditioned the admissibility of scientific evidence upon 'standing and scientific recognition' of its underlying theory or method-ology.[71] Although it is entirely possible to interpret these standards as reflecting the Supreme Court's view of scientific rationality[72] and, correspondingly, to criticize them for either excluding good science[73] or (inversely) for allowing courts to reconsider bad science as a potential source of probative evidence,[74] I suggest a different interpretation. As explained throughout this book, adjudicative fact-finding is ultimately about the apportionment of the risk of error. This apportionment needs to reflect the parties' legal entitlements. Specifically, it should reflect the parties' rights or immunities against different impositions of the risk of error. In the present context, to the extent that the controlling apportionment standard requires that the claimant and the defendant have equal shares in the risk of error, rules setting the conditions for admitting scientific and other expert findings into evidence ought to align with this standard. Mechanisms for screening expert evidence for quality should aim at promoting good verdicts, not good science.

From this point of view, the replacement of *Frye* by the *Daubert Trilogy* introduced a profound improvement into the civil, as opposed to

---

69 This condition was added in *General Electric Co. v Joiner*, 522 U.S. 136 (1997).

70 *Frye v United States*, 293 F. 1013 (D.C. Cir. 1923).

71 For analysis of *Frye* and its influence see Paul C. Giannelli, The Admissibility of Novel Scientific Evidence. Frye v. United States: A Half-Century Later (1980) 80 Colum. L. Rev. 1197.

72 The Supreme Court had seemingly adjudicated the notorious Popper–Kuhn controversy in the philosophy of science (compare Karl Popper, *Conjectures and Refutations* (5th edn., 1989) with Thomas Kuhn, *The Structure of Scientific Revolutions* (2nd edn., 1970)) favourably to Karl Popper. See *Daubert*, above note 65, at p. 593 (adopting Popper's falsifiability criterion for science).

73 See David L. Faigman, Is Science Different for Lawyers? (2002) 297 *Science* 339; Ronald J. Allen, Expertise and the *Daubert* Decision (1994) 84 J. Crim. L. & Criminology 1157; Margaret G. Farrell, *Daubert v. Merrell Dow Pharmaceuticals Inc.*: Epistemology and Legal Process (1994) 15 Cardozo L. Rev. 2183.

74 See David L. Faigman et al., *Modern Scientific Evidence: The Law and Science of Expert Testimony* (2nd edn., 2002), pp. 10–13.

criminal,[75] justice systems across the United States.[76] Under *Frye*, lasting recognition by an appropriate scientific community could legitimize scientific evidence that lacked empirical credentials and could not be submitted to any testing.[77] Admission of such evidence violates the maximal individualization principle. Correspondingly, because the evidence is one-sided, it forces an unequal—and thus illegitimate—apportionment of the risk of error upon its opponent. *Frye* also rendered inadmissible scientific evidence that is yet to become recognized by the relevant scientific community even when the evidence was falsifiable.[78] Exclusion of such evidence exposes its proponent to an unequal apportionment of the risk of error. Because falsifiable evidence satisfies the demands of *PMI* and, consequently, cannot classify as one-sided, there is no good reason to exclude it.

Under the equality principle, when the parties' experts disagree in their evaluations, adjudicators appoint and normally accord preference to a court-appointed expert. By pre-empting the potentially partial accounts of adversarial experts, testimony given by such an expert functions as best evidence as a matter of law.[79] Federal Rule of Evidence 706 allows such appointments not only in response to a litigant's request, but also on the court's own motion. Courts may implement the equality principle also by appointing special masters under Federal Rule of Civil Procedure 53.[80] In England, the same

---

[75] For criminal litigation, the *Frye* standard is more appropriate than the *Trilogy*. See above, Chapter 6.

[76] Most states, however, are yet to adopt the *Trilogy*. See David E. Bernstein and Jeffrey D. Jackson, The *Daubert* Trilogy in the States (2004) 44 Jurimetrics J. 351. For an insightful comparison between the *Frye* and the *Daubert* standards see Edward K. Cheng and Albert H. Yoon, Does Frye or Daubert Matter? A Study of Scientific Admissibility Standards (2005) 91 Virginia L. Rev. 471 (under a jurisdiction-removal criterion for ascertaining tort defendants' revealed preference, the shift from *Frye* to *Daubert* is operationally insignificant).

[77] See Michael J. Saks, The Aftermath of *Daubert*: An Evolving Jurisprudence of Expert Evidence (2000) 40 Jurimetrics J. 229, 230.   [78] Ibid.

[79] See McCormick Vol. 1, above note 43, at pp. 70–2; Margaret G. Farrell, Coping with Scientific Evidence: The Use of Special Masters (1994) 43 Emory L. J. 927.

[80] Federal Rule of Civil Procedure 53 holds that 'The court in which any action is pending may appoint a special master therein ... [T]he word "master" includes a referee, an auditor, an examiner, and an assessor ... The order of reference to the master may specify or limit the master's powers and may direct the master to report only upon particular issues or to do or perform particular acts or to receive and report evidence only and may fix the time and place for beginning and closing the hearings and for the filing of the master's report. Subject to the specifications and limitations stated in the order, the master has and shall exercise the power to regulate all proceedings in every hearing before the master and to do all acts and take all measures necessary or proper for the efficient performance of the master's duties under the order. The master may require the production before the master of evidence upon all matters embraced in the reference, including the production of all books, papers, vouchers, documents, and writings applicable thereto. The master may rule upon the admissibility of evidence unless otherwise directed by the order of reference and has the authority to put witnesses on oath and may examine them and may call the parties to the action and examine them upon oath.'

objective is attainable by appointing a joint expert,[81] an appointment that 'can make a substantial contribution to the quality of the fact-finding process by instilling a level of detachment and objectivity into expert testimony which is hard to obtain in adversarial expertise'.[82] This point identifies pre-emption as yet another evidential mechanism that corrective equality employs.

D. Equality and Pre-emption

As an instrument for maintaining equality in the apportionment of the risk of error, *PMI* introduces preferential hierarchy between different evidential items. Some evidential items are more open than others to adversarial testing and potential adverse utilization. Such items are also more compatible than others with the maximal individualization mechanism and, correspondingly, with equality. Such evidential items should consequently be accorded preference. This principle applies not only to adjudicative choices between conflicting evidential items, but also to the choices between competing factual inferences. Inferences more compatible with equality in risk-allocation should trump any competing inference.

The most straightforward and, perhaps, trivial instantiation of this *preemptive strategy* is the best evidence rule. Under this rule, to prove the disputed contents of a document, its proponent needs to produce the original.[83] Copies and other duplicates become admissible only when the proponent shows good faith and establishes the unavailability of the original document.[84] This rule facilitates the examination of documentary evidence by both parties and the opportunity for adverse utilization of such evidence. If duplicates were to be freely admitted into evidence, the adverse utilization opportunity would be systematically diluted. Adversarial examination of documentary evidence as a tool for equalizing the risk of error would also lose much of its effectiveness.

Another example of pre-emption is in the law's general preference of case-specific proof over naked statistical evidence.[85] *Smith v Rapid Transit*[86] is

---

[81] Civil Procedure Rule 35.7 allows the court to appoint a joint expert on its own initiative.

[82] Zuckerman, above note 63, at pp. 623–4.

[83] Under Rule 1002, 'To prove the content of a writing, recording, or photograph, the original writing, recording, or photograph is required, except as otherwise provided in these rules or by Act of Congress'. In turn, Rule 1003 holds that 'A duplicate is admissible to the same extent as an original unless (1) a genuine question is raised as to the authenticity of the original or (2) in the circumstances it would be unfair to admit the duplicate in lieu of the original'.

[84] Federal Rule of Evidence 1004.

[85] The qualifier 'general' leaves room for exceptions. See below, at pp. 239–40.

[86] *Smith v Rapid Transit*, 58 N.E. 2d 754 (1945). For critical examination of this decision (technically, obiter), see Daniel Shaviro, Statistical-Probability Evidence and the Appearance of Justice (1988) 103 Harv. L. Rev. 530.

a traditional American authority for this doctrinal preference.[87] The factual setting of this case involves two transportation companies, say Blue Bus and Red Bus, with unequal fleets of vehicles in the relevant location. Blue Bus, for example, may have 80 per cent of the buses in town, with the remaining 20 per cent being Red buses. Injured by a bus which she cannot identify as either blue or red, a colour-blind claimant attempts to recover money damages from the Blue Bus company. She claims her case against Blue Bus to be 80 per cent probable. Here, the claimant's action should be dismissed because it relies on a non-individualized generalization that the doctrine of chances provides. Under this generalization, the most likely factual scenario in a case affiliating to a broad category of cases (Blue and Red buses endanger and, ultimately, injure pedestrians) is one that belongs to the largest sub-category (Blue Bus). By linking the defendant, Blue Bus, with an accident rate hypothesized to parallel the relative size of its fleet, this generalization deems the defendant responsible for the unevidenced accident. This postulation apportions the risk of error between the parties in a starkly unequal fashion. Thus, why not invoke a different generalization, namely, that people situated similarly to the claimant would tend to attribute liability to the largest bus company regardless of the facts of the case? Indeed, what makes the former generalization preferable to this one? This question is unanswerable. Under the equality principle, case-specific evidence is required to enable the factfinders to make the right choice between the clashing generalizations. When such evidence is not present, choosing an applicable generalization always skews the risk of error in one direction. The equality principle forestalls such one-sided decisions.

Fact-finders, however, can rely upon naked statistical evidence when it yields a resilient probability datum (strictly speaking, such evidence would not then be 'naked statistical'[88]). A landmark marine insurance case litigated in England[89] (and analysed in Chapter 4[90]) exemplifies this point. This case had produced a definitive ruling outcasting naked statistical proof. Shipowners, whose vessel sank in the Mediterranean, sought to recover insurance money from their underwriters. Under the insurance policy, the shipowners' entitlement to this money depended on whether the vessel was lost due to a 'peril of

---

[87] For references to additional cases, see Mary Dant, Gambling on the Truth: The Use of Purely Statistical Evidence as a Basis for Civil Liability (1988) 22 Colum. J. Law & Social Probs. 31 at 31n.1. See also *United States v Shonubi*, 103 F.3d 1085 (2nd Cir. 1997) (requiring case-specific evidence for proving sentencing facts and disapproving the use of naked statistics). But see Judge Posner's recent decision in *United States v Veysey*, 334 F.3d 600 (7th Cir. 2003) (holding that verdicts, both civil and criminal, can rest upon naked statistical evidence). [88] See above at pp. 88–91.

[89] See *Edmunds et al. (The Popi M) v Rhesa Shipping Co.* [1983] 2 Lloyd's Rep. 235 (Commercial Court); *Rhesa Shipping Co. v Edmunds et al. (The Popi M)* [1984] 2 Lloyd's Rep. 555 (CA); *Rhesa Shipping Co. v Edmunds et al. (The Popi M)* [1985] 2 All ER 712 (HL). [90] See above at pp. 128–31.

the seas'. The shipowners contended (inter alia) that one such peril, which they could not identify, was the cause of the loss underwritten by the defendants. The House of Lords' decision in favour of the defendants ended this litigation. The Law Lords held that a nameless peril of the seas will not do, and that only case-specific evidence identifying the relevant peril could allow the claimants to discharge the burden of proof.[91] As already explained, this decision is deeply problematic. The shipowners' argument referred to the probability of the disjunctive proposition 'either p_1, or p_2, or p_3, or ... p_n', in which p_1, p_2, p_3, ... and p_n represent the full set of perils of the seas, both known and unknown. The argument therefore holds that the probability of event 'p_1 or p_2 or p_3 or ... p_n' is greater than 0.5. The Law Lords dismissed this argument for not being capable of promoting the shipowners' case. This threshold dismissal was wrong. Because the shipowners were entitled to win the case upon proof of any member of the p-set, their argument appears sound.[92] The probability upon which the shipowners relied was both high enough and resilient enough to justify recovery.[93]

Rules applicable in cases in which crucial evidence is missing exemplify the pre-emptive mechanism in a more significant way. Under one such rule, failure to produce a witness for trial, who is available and whom a party would naturally be expected to call, warrants an adverse inference against the party who would be expected to call that witness.[94] Under another rule, the judge may give the jury the 'missing witness' instruction that focuses on the party who failed to produce a key witness in circumstances in which it is natural to expect the party to have called the witness. This instruction urges the jury to infer that the missing witness would have testified against that party.[95] Another missing-evidence rule is widely known as spoliation inference. Similar to the 'missing witness' instruction, this inference applies in cases featuring withholding and destruction of evidence, both negligent and intentional;[96]

---

[91] Specifically, the Law Lords decided that 'The shipowners could not ... rely on a ritual incantation of the generic expression "perils of the seas", but were bound, if they were to discharge successfully the burden of proof ... to condescend to particularity in the matter'. *Rhesa Shipping Co. v Edmunds et al. (The Popi M)* [1985] 2 All ER 712, 716.

[92] Cf. D. H. Hodgson, The Scales of Justice: Probability and Proof in Legal Fact-finding (1995) 69 Aust. L.J. 731, 750 (supporting the particularity-of-proof requirement laid down by the House of Lords as 'unexceptionable', but arguing that 'alternatives on which the plaintiff can succeed can be bracketed').   [93] For further discussion of the *Rhesa* decision, see above at pp. 128–31.

[94] See, e.g., *State v Young*, 779 A.2d 112 (2001); *Kersey v Rush Trucking, Inc.*, 800 N.E.2d 847 (2003).   [95] See, e.g., *McPherson-Corder v Chinkhota*, 835 A.2d 1081 (2003).

[96] See *Destruction of Evidence*, above note 22, at pp. 5–7 and 2002 *Cumulative Supplement* 6–11 (summarizing case law that predominantly limits the spoliation inference rule to cases involving intentional, rather than merely negligent, destruction of evidence); *Battocchi v Wash. Hosp. Ctr.*, 581 A.2d 759, 765–6 (D.C. 1990) (both intentional and reckless spoliation of evidence justifies adverse inferences). From the normative perspective advanced here, negligent destruction of evidence by the defendant is good enough a reason for drawing the spoliation inference against the defendant.

violation of a duty to generate and maintain records and other documentation;[97] and tampering with evidence and intimidation of witnesses.[98] Adverse inferences are also due when a party abstains from cross-examining an adverse witness about his or her prior inconsistent statement and subsequently uses that statement, which the witness is no longer able to explain, to discredit the witness's testimony. To make such inferences effective, the court rules the witness's prior statement inadmissible.[99]

These rules derive from the general 'evidential damage' doctrine that shifts the persuasion burden to the defendant whenever he or she has wrongfully contributed to the uncertainty of the case.[100] A paradigmatic evidential damage case was stated earlier in this chapter. There, the defendant-doctor committed malpractice against the claimant, but the claimant was unable to causally attribute his or her affliction to this malpractice because the affliction may well have resulted from the claimant's pre-existing medical condition. The evidential damage doctrine still allows such claimants to succeed. Under this doctrine, it is the defendant who needs to disassociate himself or herself from the claimant's damage. The entire burden of proof shifts to the defendant because it is his or her malpractice that created the uncertainty in the case and evidentially incapacitated the claimant.[101] This doctrine pre-empts any factual inference benefiting the defendant that the informational void, for which the defendant is responsible, could otherwise allow. By not allowing the defendant to benefit from the uncertainty that he or she wrongfully created or intensified, this apportionment of the risk of error implements corrective equality.[102]

---

[97] See, e.g., *Smith v United States*, 128 F.Supp.2d 1227 (2000) (strongest possible adverse inferences drawn against the claimant's primary surgeon in a medical malpractice lawsuit for the surgeon's failure to dictate operative notes of the surgical procedure).

[98] See, e.g., *Wong v Swier*, 267 F.2d 749, 761 (9th Cir. 1959) ('A proper instruction would, therefore, necessarily, have to tell the jury that an inference of alteration or tampering could be drawn if the jury first found that there was an alteration, and if it found that the appellees did it'). See also Federal Rule of Evidence 804(6), titled 'Forfeiture by wrongdoing' and prescribing that a hearsay statement would be admissible when 'offered against a party that has engaged or acquiesced in wrongdoing that was intended to, and did, procure the unavailability of the declarant as a witness'.

[99] See Federal Rule of Evidence 613(b) ('Extrinsic evidence of a prior inconsistent statement by a witness is not admissible unless the witness is afforded an opportunity to explain or deny the same and the opposite party is afforded an opportunity to interrogate the witness thereon, or the interests of justice otherwise require').

[100] See *Tort Liability Under Uncertainty*, above note 18, at pp. 160–7.   [101] Ibid.

[102] Old cases underscore the fairness of this approach. In *Armory v Delamirie*, 93 Eng. Rep. 664 (K.B. 1722), the defendant goldsmith converted a jewel from the claimant's ring, a wrongful action that disabled the claimant from proving the true value of the ring. On fairness grounds, the jury were consequently told to 'presume the strongest' against the goldsmith by appraising the missing jewel as having the conceivably highest value. In *Pomeroy v Benton*, 77 Mo. 64, 86 (1882), the Supreme Court of Missouri followed the same intuition in a more elaborate fashion by holding that 'We see no reason

E. Corroboration as Corrective Equality

Corrective equality may also demand an individualized removal of doubts and suspicions that experience-based generalizations project upon particular categories of evidence. This strategy identifies categories of evidence that experience-based generalizations mark out as potentially untrustworthy. Evidence falling under any such category becomes statistically unreliable. Any such evidence would then be deemed untrustworthy unless there are individualized case-specific reasons that identify it as special and remove the suspicion-throwing generalization. These reasons must, of course, derive from case-specific evidence. Evidence generating these reasons classifies as corroboration.

This strategy is suitable for cases featuring self-serving testimony of a claimant (or a defendant, if his or her testimony constitutes an effort at discharging the burden of persuasion in relation to an affirmative defence).[103] In a 'claimant's word against the defendant's word' case, allowing the claimant to recover from the defendant on a preponderance of the evidence alone involves a problematic apportionment of the risk of error. Any such decision has to choose between two generalizations. One of these generalizations holds that 'testimony (such as that of the claimant) exhibiting the comparatively

now to change, but every reason to support and confirm the conclusion then reached, that defendant destroyed that book after suit brought, for the deliberate and sole purpose of cutting off investigation into the magnitude of his operations in whisky. As, then, the defendant has done these things, as he has endeavored by all these means to baffle inquiry and shut out investigation; as in consequence thereof, it has become impossible to ascertain the amount out of which he has defrauded his partner, to whom, as he says in one of his letters, he was bound by the ties of gratitude, for giving him his start in life, nothing remains to us but to apply to the defendant, the stern rule recognized alike in equity and at law embodied in the maxim _omnia praesumuntur in odium spoliatoris_ . . . It is because of the very fact that the evidence of the plaintiff, the proofs of his claim or the muniments of his title, have been destroyed, that the law, in hatred of the spoiler, baffles the destroyer, and thwarts his iniquitous purpose, by indulging a presumption which supplies the lost proof, and thus defeats the wrong-doer by the very means he had so confidently employed to perpetrate the wrong.'

[103] See, e.g., Louisiana Civil Code, Art. 1846 ('When a writing is not required by law, a contract not reduced to writing, for a price or, in the absence of a price, for a value not in excess of five hundred dollars may be proved by competent evidence. If the price or value is in excess of five hundred dollars, the contract must be proved by at least one witness and other corroborating circumstances'); _Finnigan Corp. v Int. Trade Comm._, 180 F.3d 1354, 1367–69 (1999) (testimony of single witness requires corroboration to invalidate a patent); _American Ambassador Casualty Comp. v Cash_, 445 S.E.2nd 364 (Ga., 1994) (in actions for uninsured motorist benefits, recoverable in connection with accidents caused by phantom vehicles, the claimant's testimony needs to be accompanied by proof of physical contact between the unknown vehicle and the claimant's person or property; in the absence of physical contact, the claimant's testimony needs to be corroborated by an eyewitness to the occurrence other than the claimant); _Moore v Davidson_, 145 S.W.3d 833 (Ark. App., 2004) (allegations of matrimonial misconduct supporting a divorce action require corroborating evidence in addition to the claimant's testimony).

greatest number of features that general experience associates with truthfulness is most likely to be true'. The other generalization holds that 'in the absence of objective evidence favouring the claimant's or the defendant's account of the events, each party, regardless of the truth, attempts to display in his or her testimony as many truthfulness features as possible'. The maximal individualization principle insists on the introduction of case-specific evidence that would bring one of these generalizations down to the ground. When such evidence is not present, preferring the claimant's testimony over that of the defendant allocates the risk of error unequally. Corroboration, therefore, is in order.

The corroborative strategy is also appropriate in lawsuits that ascribe liability to deceased persons in order to recover from their estates. Because in any such lawsuit, 'the survivor could testify though the adverse party's lips would be sealed in death,'[104] allowing the claimant to recover on a preponderance of the evidence alone would engender inequality in the apportionment of the risk of error. Imposition of an appropriate corroboration requirement removes this inequality. This rationale both explains and justifies a number of statutory provisions.[105]

F. Equality and Discretion

Adjudicative fact-finding involves many discretionary decisions. Such decisions should promote fairness and equality in the apportionment of the risk of error. Alternatively, they should follow the cost-efficiency doctrine, laid out in Chapter 5. Such decisions cannot discard both fairness and efficiency concerns, for if they do it, they would be unjustified. Here, I briefly discuss how the principle of corrective equality should structure discretionary decisions pertaining to adjudicative fact-finding.

In England, the rule against hearsay is no longer applicable in civil trials.[106] Adjudicators, however, retain a general discretion to exclude any hearsay evidence and may refuse to base their findings upon hearsay, if the interests of justice so require and, in particular, if the opponent of such evidence cannot

---

[104] See McCormick Vol. 1, above note 43, at p. 250.

[105] See (1952) 21 A.L.R. 2d 1013–43. See, in particular, Va. Code Ann. § 8.01-397 ('In an action by or against a person who, from any cause, is incapable of testifying, or by or against the committee, trustee, executor, administrator, heir, or other representative of the person so incapable of testifying, no judgment or decree shall be rendered in favor of an adverse or interested party founded on his uncorroborated testimony'); and *Williams v Condit*, 265 Va. 249 (2003) (interpreting the Virginia statute as 'designed to prevent a litigant from having the benefit of his own testimony when, because of death or incapacity, the personal representative of another litigant has been deprived of the testimony of the decedent or incapacitated person'). I am grateful to Professor James Duane for making me aware of the Virginia statute and its authoritative rationale.

[106] See Zuckerman, above note 63, at pp. 669–70.

controvert it.[107] Following the terminology developed in this chapter, if a hearsay statement is not susceptible to individualized testing and does not hold an adverse utilization opportunity, the adjudicators ought to exclude it. The same argument applies to the residual exception to the hearsay rule, codified in the United States in Federal Rule of Evidence 807 and its state equivalents. Under this exception, hearsay statements not rendered admissible by any specific exception to the hearsay rule may still be admitted into evidence when they have 'equivalent circumstantial guarantees of trustworthiness' and when the interests of justice favour their admission. This exception should only extend to evidence satisfying the individualized testing standard or, alternatively, the adverse utilization opportunity requirement. Evidence not satisfying any of these requirements cannot classify as having the appropriate guarantees of trustworthiness. The interests of justice, manifested by the corrective equality demands, favour the exclusion, rather than admission, of such evidence.

Another important discretionary setting features a witness who testifies in a deposition or in a direct examination at trial and subsequently refuses to answer questions at his or her cross-examination. For obvious reasons, any such testimony fails to conform with the demands of both individualized testing and adverse-utilization opportunity. Any such testimony is manifestly one-sided. The prevalent doctrine holds that if such a testimony covers an important issue in the trial, the judge must strike it out completely. However, if the testimony relates to a collateral issue, then the judge may use his or her discretion and leave the testimony with the evidence; in appropriate cases, striking out a fragment of the testimony may qualify as an appropriate discretionary remedy.[108] The corrective equality principle denounces *any* evidential one-sidedness, including one-sidedness in apportioning the risk of error with respect to collateral issues. Consequently, any deposition and testimony should be stricken out completely if the witness refused to answer questions at his or her cross-examination.[109]

Finally, Federal Rule of Evidence 611(c) and its state equivalents provide that when a party calls a hostile or an adverse witness to testify, 'interrogation may be by leading questions', so that the hostile or adverse witness will be effectively cross-examined at his or her examination in chief. To the extent that such cross-examination offsets an unfair advantage of the party associated with the witness, the judge should permit it. The corrective equality principle requires the judge to give this permission in virtually every case.

---

[107] Zuckerman, above note 63, at pp. 671–2.

[108] For a comprehensive statement of this doctrine and a summary of the relevant authorities, see *Burke v Harman*, 574 N.W.2d 156 (1998).

[109] Subject to the forfeiture rule: see above note 98 and accompanying text.

Index

Lightning Source UK Ltd.
Milton Keynes UK
16 April 2010

152911UK00001B/61/P